THE COUNTRY	THE ARTS	
Whiskey Insurrection, Pennsylvania, 1794	Royal Taylor, *The Contrast*, first comedy, 1787	Washington," 1799
First railroad, the Boston Tramway, 1795	Noah Webster, *Dissertation on the English Language*, 1789	"The Gay Negro Boy," from *Oroonoko*, early example of minstrelsy, 1799
XYZ Affair, 1797	Susanna Rowson, *Charlotte Temple*, novel, 1791	Raynor Taylor and Alexander Reinagle, *Pizzaro; or, The Spaniards in Peru*, opera, Philadelphia, 1800
Alien and Sedition Acts, 1798	Gilbert Stuart, *George Washington*, painting, 1793	
Undeclared naval war with France, 1798–1800		

1801 TO 1850

THE COUNTRY	THE ARTS	
Louisiana Purchase, 1803	American Academy of Fine Arts, New York, 1808	Shape notes introduced, 1802
Lewis and Clark Expedition, 1804–06	"Star Spangled Banner," lyrics by Francis Scott Key (to the tune "Anacreon in Heaven"), 1814	James Nelson Barker, *The Indian Princess*, 1808
Embargo Act, 1807	William Rush carves full-sized figure of Washington in wood, 1814	Benjamin Carr, *The Lady of the Lake*, song cycle, 1810
Slave importation prohibited, 1808		"Hail to the Chief," anonymous, 1812
Battle of Tippecanoe, defeat of Tecumseh, 1811	William Cullen Bryant, "To a Waterfowl," poem, 1818	Raynor Taylor, *The Aethiop; or, The Child of the Desert*, Philadelphia, 1814
War of 1812, 1812–14	Washington Irving, *The Sketch Book*, stories, 1819	Anthony Philip Heinrich moves to Kentucky, 1818
Temperance League founded, Massachusetts, 1813	James Fenimore Cooper, *The Last of the Mohicans*, novel, 1826	Lowell Mason, *Collection of Church Music*, 1822
Steamboat service on the Great Lakes, 1816	John James Audubon, *Birds of America, aquatint plates*, 1827–38	Mary Browne, "The Messenger Bird," 1828
Missouri Compromise, 1820	*Encyclopedia Americana*, 1829	Samuel Francis Smith, "America," 1831
First abolitionist paper in the South, *The Emancipator*, 1820	Edward Hicks, *Peaceable Kingdom* (one of 18 paintings), 1830	Lowell Mason, *Manual of the Boston Academy*, 1834
Monroe Doctrine, 1823	Alexis de Toqueville, *Democracy in America*, 1835	Music taught in Boston public schools, 1837
First strike of women workers, Rhode Island, 1824	McGuffey's Readers, schoolbooks— sold 122 million copies, 1836–57	St. Louis Symphony founded, 1838
Erie Canal opened, 1825	Samuel F. B. Morse imports photographic techniques from France, 1839	Anthony Philip Heinrich, *The Ornithological Combat of Kings*, 1838
First lead pencils, Salem, Massachusetts, 1827	Richard Henry Dana Jr., *Two Years Before the Mast*, novel, 1840	Francis Johnson's band plays at Queen Victoria's coronation celebration, 1838
First steam locomotive, "Tom Thumb," 1830	Statue of Washington in Capitol Rotunda, 1842	Louis Gottschalk arrives in Paris, 1842
First covered wagons head west, 1830	Edgar Allan Poe, *The Raven, And Other Poems*, 1845	New York Philharmonic founded, 1842
Nat Turner's slave rebellion, 1831	First autobiography of Frederick Douglass, 1845	Hutchinson Family's first concert in New York, 1843
South Carolina Ordinance of Nullification, 1832	Thomas Cole, *Oxbow*, painting (Hudson River School), 1846	Daniel Emmett, "Ethiopian concert," first minstrel show in New York, 1843
Siege of the Alamo, 1836	Nathaniel Hawthorne, *The Scarlet Letter*, novel, 1850	Stephen Foster, "Susanna," 1849
Oregon Trail "great migration," 1842–43		
Annexation of Texas, 1845		
War with Mexico, 1846–48		
First chewing gum, Bangor, Maine, 1848		
California Gold Rush, 1849		
First woman physician, Elizabeth Blackwell, 1849		

	THE COUNTRY	THE ARTS	MUSIC
1851 TO 1900	First elevator (Otis), 1852	Herman Melville, *Moby Dick*, novel, 1851	"The Arkansas Traveler," anonymous, 1851
	Gadsen Purchase, 1853	Uncle Sam first portrayed, in cartoon, 1852	Stephen Foster, "Old Folks at Home," 1851
	Admiral Perry opens Japan to the West, 1854	Harriet Beecher Stowe, *Uncle Tom's Cabin*, novel, 1852	Richard Milburn, "Listen to the Mocking Bird," 1855
	Bessemer steel process patented, 1856	Henry David Thoreau, "Walden," essay, 1854	James Pierpont, "Jingle Bells," 1857
	Dred Scott Decision, 1857	Walt Whitman, *Leaves of Grass*, poetry, 1855	"John Brown's Body," anonymous, 1858
	Lincoln-Douglas debates, 1858	Henry Wadsworth Longfellow, *The Song of Hiawatha*, poem, 1855	Daniel Butterfield, "Taps," 1862
	John Brown's raid, 1859	Matthew Brady establishes photography studio, New York, 1858	John Paine, *Mass in D*, 1866
	A&P Grocery founded, 1859	Ralph Waldo Emerson, "The Conduct of Life," essay, 1860	*The Black Crook*, gala production, New York, 1866
	Pony Express, 1860	Emily Dickinson, *Poems*, 1862	New England Conservatory founded, Boston, 1867
	Civil War, 1861–65	John Greenleaf Whittier, *In War Time, And Other Poems*, 1864	American piano (Steinway) wins prize at Paris Exposition, 1867
	Homestead Act, 1862	Louisa May Alcott, *Little Women*, novel, 1868	Spirituals published by Jubilee Singers, 1872
	Gettysburg Address, 1863	Bret Harte, *The Luck of Roaring Camp*, novel, 1870	World Peace Jubilee features the Gilmore Band, 1872
	Emancipation Proclamation, 1863	P. T. Barnum circus, Brooklyn, 1871	Daniel E. Kelly, "Home on the Range," 1873
	Pullman sleeping car invented, 1864	James A. McNeill Whistler, *Study in Grey and Black* ("Whistler's Mother"), painting, 1872	First American professor of music, John Paine (Harvard), 1875
	Assassination of President Lincoln, 1865	Chatauqua Assembly formed, 1874	James Bland, "Carry Me Back to Old Virginny," 1878
	Formation of the Ku Klux Klan, 1866	Joel Chandler Harris, *Uncle Remus*, stories, 1880	James Bland, "Oh Dem Golden Slippers," 1879
	Purchase of Alaska, 1867	Lew Wallace, *Ben-Hur*, novel, 1880	Boston Symphony Orchestra founded, 1881
	First salaried baseball team (Cincinnati Redstockings), 1869	Metropolitan Opera opens, New York, 1883	American Conservatory founded, Chicago, 1883
	East-West railroad system completed, 1869	James Whitcomb Riley, *The Old Swimmin'-Hole and 'leven More Poems*, 1883	George Chadwick, *Symphony #2*, 1886
	First state board of health established, Massachusetts, 1869	John Singer Sargent, *Madame X*, painting, 1884	Gramophone invented, 1888
	Great Chicago Fire, 1871	Mark Twain, *Huckleberry Finn*, novel, 1885	John Philip Sousa, "Semper Fidelis," 1888
	Celluloid commercially produced, 1872	William Dean Howells, *The Rise of Silas Lapham*, novel, 1885	First vaudeville theater, 1890
	Women's Christian Temperance Union founded, 1874	Edward Bellamy, *Looking Backward*, novel, 1888	Chicago Symphony Orchestra founded, 1891
	Alexander Graham Bell patents telephone, 1876	Wainwright Building, Chicago, 1890	First mass productions of music records, 1892
	Battle of Little Big Horn, 1876	Winslow Homer, *Rowing Home*, painting, 1890	Mildred Hill, "Good Morning to All" ("Happy Birthday"), 1892
	Nez Perce Chief Joseph speech, "I will fight no more forever," 1877		Horatio Parker made professor at Yale, 1894
	Edison Electric Light Company founded, 1878		
	Statue of Liberty, 1886		
	Haymarket Massacre, 1886		
	American Federation of Labor organized, 1886		
	Interstate Commerce Act, 1887		
	First Kodak camera, 1888		
	Sherman Antitrust Act, 1890		

(continued at the back of the book)

MUSIC
MELTING
ROUND

MUSIC MELTING ROUND

A HISTORY OF MUSIC IN THE UNITED STATES

Edith Borroff

BINGHAMTON UNIVERSITY

ARDSLEY HOUSE, PUBLISHERS, INC.   NEW YORK

Address orders and editorial
correspondence to:
Ardsley House, Publishers, Inc.
320 Central Park West
New York, NY 10025

ISBN: 1-880157-17-9

Printed in the United States of America

10 9 8 7 6 5 4 3 2 1

To Marie

Oh! I would die with music melting round,
And float to bliss upon a sea of sound!

Francis Hopkinson
Description of a Church
1762

Other Titles by the Author

Elisabeth Jacquet de La Guerre. Institute of Mediaeval Music, 1966.

The Music of the Baroque. Da Capo Press, 1978.

Music in Europe and the United States: A History. Second edition. Ardsley House Publishers, Inc., 1990.

Notations and Editions (A Book in Honor of Louise Cuyler). Da Capo Press, 1977.

Music in Perspective, with Marjory Irvin. Harcourt Brace Jovanovich, 1976.

Three American Composers. University Press of America, 1986.

The Violin Works of J. J. C. de Mondonville (preface and facsimile). Johnson Reprint Corp., 1982.

The Violin Works of Michel Corrette (preface and facsimile). Johnson Reprint Corp., 1982.

American Opera: A Checklist. Detroit Studies in Music Bibliography, No. 69. Harmonie Park Press, 1992.

CONTENTS

3 A Nation Struggling for Maturity (1840 to 1880)   55

4 A Nation Coming of Age (1880 to 1923) 89

5 Other Venues (1880 to 1923) 119

6 The Business and Dissemination of Music   155

7 Boom, Depression, and War (1923 to 1961)   179

8 Other Venues (1923 to 1961)   211

11 Other Venues (1961 to 1993) 303

12 A Musical Nation

Appendix: Basic Musical Concepts

PREFACE

Contemplating a book about music in the United States is daunting indeed. The scope of musical expression is wide; probably no one person can perceive the entire gamut of musical types, styles, and performance agencies that have blessed our nation.

The writer who loves the gamut for its own sake and much of the music within it can organize the spread and bring relevance to the whole. I am fortunate enough to love it all and to feel genuine affection and admiration for it all.

The basic decisions to be made concerning the book were the important decisions of size: how long should the book be and how much information should be included in it? There is much too much material for everything to be put in; that concept leads to vacuous listings—all nouns and no verbs. The book should not *include* everything, even though it must leave out a great deal of interesting material: it should *explain* everything, in the sense that whatever music the student encounters after studying the book can be placed and absorbed. No two people would agree on what to put in and what to leave out, but primary to this concept is the question of balance. This means that I left out many of my own personal favorites (as a young person growing up in the swing era, for example, my favorite band leader was Guy Mitchell, but he is not in the book!); the price that authors pay for going with what they know the most about or enjoy the most is imbalance.

Readers have related problems: readers too have music that they love the most and know the most about—and they will inevitably see those sections of the book, whichever they may be, as short-changed. But the subject is huge and the space is small, and the answer to problems of desiring more about certain areas of American musical adventure is to find a book that narrows focus to those areas.

Teachers have less of a problem. An individual classroom can lack balance—in fact, *should* lack balance; for the region of the country in which the book is used, the backgrounds of the students, and the predilections of the teacher all come into play here. Perhaps even more important is the fact that the playing of one recording in class rather than another will automatically lead to a focus for that particular class that no other class can have (or should have).

The organization of the book is horizontal, vertical, and diagonal. The horizontal is the scope of musical styles and venues; it cannot include separate histories of southern, western, or northeastern music, as much as that is desirable. This must be done in deeper, regional studies. The vertical is the sweep of time; similar chapter titles and subtitles alert the reader to continuing strands of musical importance. The diagonal is the suggestion of other cultural activities, from novels and poetry to painting and dancing; any sort of thoroughness here is out of the question—one or two aspects of the other arts is suggested in each time period, and expansion of any category in time or detail is the province of the individual teacher. This is not a history of the arts in the United States, and, within the concept of balance upon which the book is based, only a flimsy outline of a culture can be attempted. Nonetheless, in any period certain cultural expressions are more vital than others.

The time cut-off years were selected on the basis of musical developments; many decisions have been made in this regard by many authors. My decisions were based upon the hope of putting musical expressions into one chapter when they have goals in common and when they involve techniques that parallel interests of the culture as a whole. The cut-off year 1961, for example, stems from the cultural interest in the computer (and related technical machinery), which has been of vital importance to the culture in virtually every way, and which has been of importance within the field of music in ways unique to this discipline.

The book contains a number of features that should aid in an understanding of this wealth of material.

- Most chapters begin with a **historical introduction** to the period discussed. Along with a chronology of major developments there generally is a discussion of works other than music. And the period is brought to life with copy from popular sheet music and other illustrations.

- In addition, a **time line** is presented for reference in the front and back of the book. National events are juxtaposed with developments in the arts and music of each era.

- **Recommended Recordings and Video Cassettes** are presented throughout the book together with a brief discussion of the artist or genre considered, as well as specific works. Addresses for recordings and videos not readily available in regular commercial outlets are given at the end of this preface.

- Because many musical concepts will be unfamiliar to the reader, **marginal definitions** are presented when a term is first given. A **glossary** at the back of the book collects all these definitions for easy reference.

- **Basic Musical Concepts** of time, sound, and fabric are briefly explained in an appendix.

- Each chapter contains its own **bibliography**. Students interested in delving further into specific types or styles of music may peruse some of these references. Then, too, they are useful in working on more extended projects, such as term papers.

- **Two indexes** are given. In addition to the usual index of names, events, and concepts, there is an index of musical works—both short and long—as well as works mentioned from other fields.

- Finally, an **Instructors Manual** is available, with suggestions on presentation of the material, on items not included in the text that are suitable for class presentation, and on possible assignments, discussion points, papers, and quizzes.

In working on such a vast canvas, an author is humbled by the amount of material; one telescopes the vast work of many other people, being grateful for the musicians and the scholars that have gone before. And in producing a manuscript, one depends upon the kind help of many people; it would be impossible to thank them all. Of special importance, however, have been my sister, Marie Borroff, a poet and teacher whose knowledge of music is deep, whose cultural overview is splendid, and to whom the book is dedicated; Janet Regier, whose subtle wisdom on musical and cultural matters has added immensely to my work and who gave me the gift of a marvelously helpful reading of the first version of the manuscript; Stephen Zank, whose encouragement has come to me in many guises, personal and professional; Seymour Fink, whose musical and cultural enthusiasm have meant a great deal in the preparation of the text; and Mary Ruth Miller, who vetted the entire manuscript. I have sought help from several libraries for both textual and illustrative material: I want to thank particularly Diana Haskell of the Newberry Library in Chicago and Lois Schultz of the Duke University Library, whose personal attention to my needs went far beyond the call of duty. Special thanks are due the reviewers for their many helpful suggestions: James Albert of Eastern Washington University and Barbara Reeder Lundquist of the University of Washington. Many friends have been patient and supportive throughout the long period of preparation. The project has blessed me, and, I hope, will prove a positive force for the music that I love so much.

Addresses for Not Readily Available Recordings and Videos

American Express Special Offer Center, PO Box 520, Great Neck, NY
Cambria Records, PO Box 374, Lomita, GA 90717
cro2, Dan Gilvary, 605 Riverview Drive, Raleigh, NC 27601
Educational Audio Visual, Inc., 17 Marble Ave., Pleasantville, NY 10570
Glendale Legend Records, PO Box 1841, Glendale, CA 91209
Jabberwocky, PO Box 6727, San Francisco, CA 94101
Jamey Aebersold Jazz Aids, PO Box 1244C, New Albany, IN 47151-1244
Kultur International Films Ltd., 121 Highway 36, West Long Branch, NJ 07764
Mark 56 Records, PO Box 1, Anaheim, CA 92805
Sony Video Software, 9 West 57 Street, New York, NY 10019
Viewfinders, Inc., PO Box 1665, Evanston, IL 60204

Chapter-Opening Pictures

Chapter 1. The cover of *That Banner A Hundred Years Old,* music by Eddie Fox, 1876. The Newberry Library.

Chapter 2. The cover of *The Flag of the Free,* by Harrison Millard, 1845. The Newberry Library.

Chapter 3. The cover of *The American Flag,* by Rev. J. B. Dickson, c. 1862. The Newberry Library.

Chapter 4. The cover of the "Boating" Valse, arranged by Archibald Joyce, 1909. The Newberry Library.

Chapter 5. The cover of the *Picnic Polka,* by Theo. La Hache, 1883. The Newberry Library.

Chapter 6. An 1887 ad for Sohmer Pianos. Picture Collection, The Branch Libraries, The New York Public Library.

Chapter 7. Social Dancing, c. 1925. Picture Collection, The Branch Libraries, The New York Public Library.

Chapter 8. *Anchors Aweigh.* Picture Collection, The Branch Libraries, The New York Public Library.)

Chapter 9. Optical checkout scanner at a supermarket. Giant Food.

Chapter 10. A space exhibit at the Smithsonian. Josh Siegel.

Chapter 11. *Guess Who's Coming to Dinner.* Picture Collection, The Branch Libraries, The New York Public Library.

Chapter 12. Lincoln Center for the Performing Arts. Dena Wallenstein.

MUSIC
MELTING
ROUND

THAT BANNER A HUNDRED YEARS OLD.

WORDS BY B. DEVERE.

MUSIC BY EDDIE FOX.

1

Early Music in America
(to 1783)

dance: aesthetic body movement

scale: an orderly listing of musical pitches

romanticism: a nineteenth-century intensification of classical musical goals

impressionism: a late-romantic development featuring responses to places and people

raga: in India, a melodic entity subject to variation and elaboration

tala: a repeated rhythmic figure in India

sansa: a box fitted with reeds activated by the thumbs of the player

ethnomusicology: the study of the music of other cultures

zydeco: a style of black Cajun music

country-and-western: country music of western (cowboy) type

jazz: a twentieth-century popular development from ragtime, combining African, American, and western European influences

gospel: popular, rhythmic religious music

melody: the horizontal element in music—a meaningful succession of pitches

rhythm: the impetus that makes music move forward in time

flute: the highest woodwind instrument

I t is fascinating to envision the Western Hemisphere before human habitation, dominated (millions of years ago) by the dinosaur, then, later, by mammoth and buffalo. And, very late in this long, long history, gradually adding *Homo sapiens*, trickling down in group after group from the north, via the land bridge from Asia. This infiltration took place as recently as thirty thousand years ago. It is fascinating also to envision these early inhabitants, perhaps hunter/gatherers, slowly working their way southward as the centuries passed. Since musical instruments dating from before the time of their immigration have been found (in Europe and Africa as well as Asia), we must envision these first groups as arriving with their musical art already confirmed in their lives. Vocal and instrumental music were associated in virtually all early cultures with religious ceremony, including prayer, poetry, drama, and the dance, so it can be assumed that this was the case with these people.

Estimates of the number of Native American groups range from one to three thousand, roughly divided half and half between the two continents.[1] Estimates of languages are in the same numbers,[2] but something like three hundred language families spoken by these peoples incorporate the linguistic array, an array so splendid that linguists are still working to encompass knowledge of them all.[3] It is thus logical to believe that an array of musical styles and types paralleled the linguistic array, since music is, in fact, a language, with its own vocabulary and its own grammar.

Musical *scales* and systems are very different throughout the world; in our own day, we recognize the individuality of Spanish *dances*, of German *romanticism*, of French *impressionism* in foreign music; of the *ragas* and *talas* of India and the *sansa* music of Africa in *ethnomusicological* studies; of *zydeco, country-and-western, jazz,* and *gospel* styles in our own country. The bases of our styles came to us from other nations, but we have made them our own in very American ways.

In days before the arrival of Europeans, the Americans were surprisingly diverse. Musically, they were diverse as well, but their musical worlds shared important elements. They were all a heady mix of *melody* and *rhythm*, with *flutes* and *drums, vocal music* and dance, *rattles* and body sounds—clapping, stomping, and vocal effects other than singing, such as *yodeling*, singing to syllables that are not part of the language and so convey no meaning other than their sound (*scat* is a modern form of singing to syllables), and singing a text (story or welcome or praise). Communication with the Godhead was universally in the form of music, song, or dance.

The musical art of the Native American centered in these concerns, along with simultaneous variation, sometimes direct and simple, sometimes developed and intricate. Such music is called *heterophony*, meaning "other sound" or the same musical idea done by others at the same time but in another way. One person might play a tune on a flute, while another might sing it in an ornamental fashion, while *percussionists* might present the main *beat* with drums and varied rhythms with rattles (or vice versa).

In addition, music contained a vital utilization of space. No two elements would come from the same place, but music would derive in appositions and oppositions, *stereophonic* effects from across compounds or mobile effects from dancing percussionists or *choral* singers moving around the audience in sweeping circles. Unity of sound or effect was no ideal; it was frowned upon, in fact, as lacking imagination and authority. Only story songs would derive from a single spot in space, and, of course, story songs were literature embellished with music, rather than music with words, very much like *background music* for dramatic films today. Musical sounds and effects of energized contrast were sought worldwide in early days, and the Europeans enjoyed them up until (and including) the medieval era—that is, through the fourteenth century and into the fifteenth—and we still enjoy them in *popular music*.

Unlike many cultures in which the art of music remained the same for many centuries, Europe had a vested interest in the change of musical style, and by the time of the arrival of Columbus in 1492, Europeans valued a very different style from the forceful, dynamic medieval. It was called *polyphony*, which means "many sounds," but really meant the combination of *pitches* (melodic tones) simultaneously (we call it "*harmony*") and that style was very different. In the Europe of Columbus's day, the old spatially energized, melodic/rhythmic art was considered hopelessly old-fashioned: the latest thing was a group of people playing at the same time, with the same basic rhythmic beat, in a group that emphasized sameness, not difference, and which prided itself in being one sound made of a number of similar parts, or "voices," delicate in sound, and intricately interrelated.

SPANISH CONQUESTS

So the Spaniards coming to the Western Hemisphere at the very end of the fifteenth century and the start of the sixteenth found the music of the Americans (whom they named "Indians" in the mistaken belief that they

drum: a hollow instrument played by percussive means

vocal music: music of the human voice

rattle: a hollow percussion instrument with seeds or stones inside, played by shaking it

yodeling: alternating regular and falsetto notes

scat: singing to sounds rather than to texts

heterophony: the simultaneous performance of a melody with variation

percussion: instruments, often unpitched, generally struck

beat: the basic rhythmic unit; pulse

stereophonic sound: sound from two or more speakers placed apart to obtain a richer effect

choral: pertaining to a choir

background music: music behind dramatic action

popular music: music loved by many people rather than by a few—so, often commercialized

polyphony: an interplay of elements—in particular, the simultaneous combination of melodies

pitch: the particular melodic tone achieved in a musical sound; intonation

harmony: the vertical element in music—that is, the relationship of tones sounded simultaneously

trumpet: a soprano brass instrument

çarabanda: an Aztec dance

saraband: a slow dance, derived from the Aztec çarabanda

had landed in India) exactly that: hopelessly old fashioned. It is interesting that the invasion of the Europeans coincided with this view of music; had it taken place two hundred years before, the Europeans would have shared the musical ideals of the Native Americans and perhaps been more inclined to admire their resplendent civilizations.

But in Italy, the Renaissance, as its proponents called it, prized wealth and business aggressiveness, while Spain was still also under the influence of religious campaigns of intolerance. The attitude of the Spaniards toward the Americans was lordly and, under the guise of religious fervor, gold crazy.

The splendid empires of the Incas and the Aztecs were doomed by Renaissance thinking, and the splendid music of these people was regarded as less than quaint. The Aztec empire, relatively young (beginning in the twelfth century as the Toltec civilization fell), was typical. King Nezahualcóyotl ("hungry coyote"—who reigned from 1428 to 1472) had been admired as a singer, and some sixty of his songs remain.[4] A school of music was an important institution in Texcoco, a city of 300,000 (when London had 120,000), known for its educational institutes, including medical, religious, and astronomical (the Aztec calendar was more accurate than any other at the time).

Flutes and drums were perhaps the most popular instruments, but many others were known, including *trumpets* (both marine shell and metal, generally copper). Aztec dances were both religious and social, and the Europeans took the *çarabanda* back to their own culture as the *saraband*.

The highly rhythmic nature of the music was considered uncivilized, and the loud sounds of metal trumpets and conch shells frightening, "a terrible din" according to one Spaniard.[5] The rhythms were so complex

🔊 Recommended Recordings and Video Cassettes

Folkways has issued many disks of authentic folk music of South America. Most of the old music is lost, but much can be done with current folk music, particularly recordings of traditional instruments, such as the panpipes.

A religious choral work, the motet *Dixit Dominus*, by Juan de Araujo (1646–1714), a composer of Inca and black lineage who directed music at the cathedral in Lima, Peru, at the end of the seventeenth century, is included in Compact Discs to Accompany *Music in Europe and the United States: A History*, 2nd ed., by Edith Borroff, Ardsley House, Publishers, 1990.*

Musical Heritage Society MHS 4077. *Music in The New World* (LP). Works by Spanish-American composers, including Hernando Franco (1532–1585), Fabian Ximeno (c. 1595–1654), and Araujo; also William Billings and four early spirituals.

*Henceforth, this will be referred to as "Borroff, Compact Discs."

An illustration from an early account of the arrival of the Spaniards in the New World. The Indians are dancing with ceremonial staff rattles, called chicahuatl, to the music of Spanish bagpipes. (Arents Collection, The New York Public Library, Astor, Lenox, and Tilden Foundations.)

that they were thought meaningless, but were interwoven in patterns, over seven hundred of which have been identified.[6]

The Incas were much the same, but their art also included the *panpipes*, a lineup of tubes (three to fifteen) most often of clay (but the Cuna people made their panpipes of bamboo). They were held up to the mouth and moved right and left to enable the player to sound the various pipes at will.

panpipes: a South American instrument made of small tubes of different sizes, played by blowing across the tops

BRITISH CONQUESTS

In the northern continent, the Indians were less settled, but there were several hundreds of tribes (nobody knows the exact number). They included the Big Game Hunters (as they were called) in the Southwest, such as the Apache, Hopi, and Anasazi; and Eastern Woodlands

Panpipes.

Bull dance of the Mandan Indians, by George Catlin (c. 1832). (National Collection of Fine Arts, The Smithsonian Institution.)

groups—such as the one that built the Cahokia Mounds, which are 1000 by 600 feet in area, 50 feet high in the south, and 100 feet high in the north—along with the Iroquois and Algonquin groups; the Plains Indians, including Comanche, Sioux and Blackfoot; the Indians of the Great Basin, including Paiute and Shoshoni; those of the Plateau, including the Nez Perce and Cayuse; and the Northwest Coast tribes, including the Chinook and the Tlingit. Faced with a changeable climate, the more northern Indians were basically nomadic, following the food supply but with semipermanent hunting grounds and, from about 7,000 BC, agricultural areas. Many lived in temporary dwellings, tepees or hogans, a few in permanent settlements (pueblos, in the Southwest). They were more difficult for the Europeans to deal with because they did not remain in one place, and the conquest of the land took considerably longer for the English and other immigrants to achieve than did the Spanish conquest of the Aztecs and Incas in lands further south.

North American Indians were cultured, with a rich artistic life of the visual arts, music, and the dance, often mixed with their necessary activities; the Hopi, for example, sang and danced at ceremonies at harvest time, "so the corn will be glad that we are bringing it in."[7]

There was considerable interaction (and intermating) of European and Indian individuals, considerable socializing between groups of Europeans and Native Americans—our celebration of Thanksgiving is one heritage of interaction. At a mutual celebration, one of the Englishmen wrote that "there was likewise a merry song made, which, to make their Revells more fashionable, was sung with a Corus, every man bearing his part; which they performed in a daunce, hand in hand."[8]

The British came to the New World in the seventeenth and early eighteenth centuries during a period of musical style known as the *baroque*, very different in its ideals from those of the Renaissance—as different as the Renaissance had been from the medieval. In general baroque musicians again welcomed and respected a diversity of musical ideal, and specifically they embraced robust sounds and spatial musical effects. So British writers were more generous in their assessment of Indian music than the Spanish had been a century earlier; one writer spoke of Native American singing, saying that "to hear one of these Indian's unseene, a good Eare might easily mistake their untaught Voyce for the warbling of a well tuned Instrument."[9] No such tolerance had come out of the Renaissance view. The Algonquins held dance contests, called *canticos*, and one contemporary wrote that "many a time Indians and settlers cut a cantico together."[10]

cantico: an Algonquin dance contest

▶ Recommended Recordings and Video Cassettes

Native American music is suddenly becoming available. But it must be cautioned that that music is never abstract, that is, never separated from the religious or social occasion with which it is one part of an entire experience. Therefore, video cassettes featuring Native American music are ideal, for they capture the entire experience. But some good discs have been issued through the Library of Congress:

Rykodisc 10199. *Honor the Earth Powwow*. Recorded at an actual powwow in northern Wisconsin in 1990, including Ojibway, Menominee, and Winnebago singing, with helpful commentary on each item.

Heritage Center MHC-1 (cassette). *Where the Ravens Roost: Cherokee Traditional Songs*. Singing and recollections by Walker Calhoun, a member of the North Carolina Cherokee group.

New World Records 80246-2. *Songs of Earth, Water, Fire, and Sky: Music of the American Indian*. A good record, particularly if only one is to be heard.

THE SETTLERS

fiddle: another name for the violin, especially in folk music

harpsichord: a keyboard instrument with strings plucked by the key mechanism

spinet: a small harpsichord; later, a small piano

consort: a small group of singers or instrumentalists

choir: a group of singers

ballad opera: (in the United States) a play with songs interspersed

musical: a popular twentieth-century form of musical theater; also, a film in which the action stops occasionally for formal musical numbers

The music of the early settlers in what is now the United States was in many ways close to the Native American ideal. Most of the early settlers sang and danced, and many played home-made instruments, from flutes to *fiddles*. They too had their story songs, telling of "Sally in Our Alley" and of "The Girl I Left Behind Me," or, later, singing "Yankee Doodle Dandy" and "The Vicar of Bray."

City Music

The more citified settlers, particularly in the early and middle eighteenth century, had imported small *harpsichords* and *spinets*, particularly the British style known (for its shape) as "leg o' mutton," and they had brought with them the art of Renaissance group singing, called the *consort*, as well. A *choir* director at Boston's Old South Church, early in the eighteenth century, wrote of his Harvard days, "we were Fellows together at College and have sung many a tune in Consort."[11] The urbanites also enjoyed performances of public concerts and *ballad operas* (similar to Broadway *musicals* in their mix of speech and song), beginning in the 1730s, in Charleston, New York, and Boston. But amateur *concerts*,

Dutch patroons and ladies of New Amsterdam, about 1640. (The Newberry Library.)

English spinet in the leg-o'-mutton shape, by John Crang (c. 1759). (The Victoria and Albert Museum.)

in churches, halls, and homes, were common throughout the colonies. Music in private homes was a vital part of life in our country from earliest times until well into the twentieth century, when such activities were preempted by records, radio, and television.

Country Music

In the countryside, settlers had as rich a musical life, but it centered in the kinds of music we still associate with country *folk music*. Lonely people on the trail or in a covered wagon played the *Jew's harp* (also

concert: a musical performance

folk music: music, usually simple in nature, often of anonymous authorship, handed down by oral tradition

Jew's harp: a simple iron frame with one vibrating strip; the instrument is held between the teeth

Colonial Costumes. (The Newberry Library.)

▶◯ Recommended Recordings and Video Cassettes

The heritage of eighteenth-century pioneers is strong in bluegrass and much other folk music today. The banjo has a history in the United States, and is still used in folk music .

Bear Family Records 15636. *Folk Songs of the Hills*, with Merle Travis (recorded from 1945 to 1963).

Columbia-Legacy 48956. *The Essential Roy Acuff* (recorded from 1936 to 1949).

Bear Family Records BCD 15652 (2 CDs). *King of Country Music*, with Roy Acuff (recorded from 1953 to 1958).

New World Records 80278-2. *Georgia Sea Island Songs*. A recording of a culture that was isolated for a long time and hence retains much of its early nature.

jaw's harp, juice harp: other names for the Jew's harp

kazoo: a mirliton instrument

barn dance: a dance featuring country music, originally held in a barn

musicologist: a scholar who studies music from a technical point of view

called the *jaw's harp* and *juice harp*) or *fife* or *kazoo*, or even a fiddle. But the building of a house or barn was the cause of parties, calling people from as far as word could carry, to attend the barn or roof raising. Putting up a roof involved many people, and after the initial planning and preparations were accomplished, the whole community rallied round to help: the men came to raise the roof and the women to prepare food. This was the origin of the *barn dance*: after the roof was up, a dance would be held on the barn floor, before the stall partitions, lofts, and other fittings were added. Thus, having such a party also became known as "raising the roof."

There were country singers who sang British songs, sometimes with new American words, and new American songs too. People sang and made music and dance everywhere, and the musical lives of even isolated settlers were rich indeed.

We have little of this music now, except in the country fiddling of the Appalachias and the folk songs collected and published, first by singers who sang them as a form of popular music, and then by musicologists.

The years of the Revolutionary War (1775–83), like most war years, showed little change or cultural growth, but the state of the musical art at the end of the period of initial colonization was exciting enough. In addition to the country and city styles of music, there was the establishment of musical training in the colonies, roughly equivalent to the training in England at the time, but already significantly influenced by American ideals.

Music Education

Music was taught in three basic educational venues or types: the music of tutorial education, the music of university education, and the music of apprenticeship. All three of these types exist today, though the places

Jew's harp.

Kazoo.

Arithmetic and Boethius; Pythagorus and Music. Arithmetic and music were two of the *quadrivium* **of the liberal arts. From an illuminated manuscript, Bavaria, 1240.**

where they are offered have changed. Tutorial education took place in the homes of affluent families, whose children were taught by schoolmasters hired as servants by one family, or perhaps two, to live with the family or to board nearby. This education was basically that of the liberal arts *trivium*. University education began and continues in the colleges and universities of this country; in the eighteenth century (and well into the nineteenth), music in the university was confined to the *quadrivium* of the liberal arts. And apprenticeship learning, that is, training to enter the profession of music, is alive and well in the popular musical scene, though absorbed into the university system in its other aspects.

The seven liberal arts had been defined about a thousand years earlier; they were basic to ideas about education in the days of colonization. The essential, basic, or elementary group of three was called the *trivium*;

harp: an open frame strung with strings to be plucked

piano: a large instrument whose strings are struck by hammers controlled from a keyboard

cornet: a brass instrument similar to a trumpet

piano four hands: a piano played by two people

clarinet: a reed instrument with finger holes and keys

violin: the standard soprano string instrument

it consisted of grammar, rhetoric, and logic—how to reason and how to write in good sound prose, that is, the basic, defining concerns of the educated human animal. The secondary, advanced group of four was called the *quadrivium*; it consisted of number (arithmetic), geometry, astronomy, and music—all conceived as scientific in method and meaning. Music was actually a part of both *trivium* and *quadrivium*, since singers were considered rhetoricians (and were so called well into the eighteenth century).

As the liberal arts were considered philosophical or abstract elements of learning, apprenticeship was the practical and professional meat. Every professional, from cobbler, physician, and druggist, butcher, and baker, and candlestick maker, to writer, painter, and dancer was the product of apprenticeship. Anyone else was an amateur.

Most city amateurs, at least those with an average amount of money, were musically trained in tutorials. Throughout the first 335 years of our history, that is, from the arrival of the British settlers to World War II, the amateur, performing at home, was the mainstay of musical life. The amateurs of the mid-eighteenth century concentrated upon singing and on playing the *harp* and the harpsichord (soon to be replaced by the *piano*, which would be the mainstay of the rest of that period), to be joined early in the nineteenth century by the *cornet*.

Music in the Home

A home performance might be simply the family entertainment of an evening, before the advent of mechanical pleasures such as television. Music was published for piano solo, but also for piano played by two people; this is called *piano four hands* to distinguish it from either solo piano or from two people playing two pianos—which required a substantial piano training plus enough money to have two pianos and a parlor big enough to put them in! A great deal of music was published for four hands, and it was played by sisters and brothers, mothers (or fathers) and daughters (or sons), and by courting couples—they found the proximity exciting, but they also could enjoy the wordless communication that music provides.

Dances were held in homes; of course, the bigger the house, the more guests that could be invited. And the bigger the house, the larger the group that could play. Combinations of instruments were largely *ad hoc*, but piano, *clarinet*, and *violin* or flute made a popular combination.

Professional Musicians

Professional dance musicians were rare, but they did exist. The most famous in the Colonies was Sy Gilliat, a black fiddler who played as the official dance master at Williamsburg, Virginia; both slaves and free

THE SETTLERS • 13

blacks were famous as dance musicians—Gilliat was a free black. At midcentury, the fiddle was the most sought-after dance instrument, but soon that place of honor would be usurped by the newly improved clarinet, first used as a *chamber instrument* in France, but soon imported to the Colonies.

For the most part no clear line can be drawn between amateur and professional musicianship. It was not a matter of skill or excellence or popularity, but of technicality: it depended upon whether or not the musician was paid. But that is complicated by a pattern of necessity: many dance musicians were paid (some nominally), but most of them made their living in other employment. Many city musicians were full-time professionals in other careers who played for dances as part-time employment or as a hobby.

In any case, something like professional concerts were begun in several cities by the 1760s. This included New York's subscription concerts in 1760; Charleston's St. Cecelia Society, founded in 1762; Boston's concert hall program in 1763; New York's outdoor park concerts in 1765; and Philadelphia's concert series in 1767. Charleston's concerts were typical, as described by a visitor in their tenth season:

> The music was good—the two base [*sic*] viols and French horns were grand [these were instruments played only in professional engagements]. One Abercrombie, a Frenchman just arrived, played the first violin, and a solo incomparably better than anyone I ever heard. He cannot speak a word of English, and has a salary of five hundred guineas a year from the St. Cecelia Society. There were upwards of two hundred and fifty ladies present, and it was called no great number.[12]

chamber instrument: an instrument suited for chamber music

viol: a delicate, six-string predecessor of the violin

French horn: a middle-range brass instrument

▶◯ Recommended Recordings and Video Cassettes

Perhaps European concert music of the colonial period can be sampled. Johann Christian Bach, trained in Italy and a British citizen living in London, was popular in the Colonies. His symphonies were a mainstay of these concerts, but care should be taken to procure a recording that uses only a few instruments, in order to duplicate the original forces and to capture that delicate, lively sound.

Hungaroton HCD 31448. *Concerto Armonico.* A small group playing period instruments.

Philips 422498-2. *Six Sinfonias* (as J. C. Bach called them). A small group conducted by Neville Marriner.

Johann Christian Bach's piano sonatas were also most likely played in the Colonies.

Arabesque Z-6549. *The London Piano School, Vol. 1.* Contains several early works that were probably played in America through the first third of the nineteenth century.

orchestra: a large ensemble of varied instruments

overture: a short orchestral piece played at the beginning of a musical show or opera

opera: a play performed in music

symphony: a long orchestral work, generally of four movements

mandolin: a small lute

voice: the human voice used as a musical instrument

chamber music: music designed to be played in a room or hall

trio: a group of three performers

quartet: four people playing or singing together

minuet: a stately popular dance of the seventeenth and eighteenth centuries

gavotte: a dance popular in the seventeenth and eighteenth centuries

waltz: the most popular dance of the nineteenth century, in which the dancing couples revolve in perpetual circles

reel: a fast dance in which partners face each other in two lines

jig: an old sailor's dance, known for its speed

square dance: a folk dance for four couples forming a square

quadrille: a nineteenth-century dance for four or more couples

keyboard: a row of keys

The Charleston St. Cecelia Society maintained an *orchestra* (the usual orchestra of that period was of fifteen-or-so musicians) and was host to a number of soloists. A typical program began with what was called an *overture*, which could be a real overture (no doubt from a popular *opera*), but could also be the first movement of a *symphony*, most likely one by a British composer. The concert proceeded with solos of violin, flute, clarinet, harpsichord (or piano), *mandolin*, and, of course, the *voice*, accompanied by piano or harp. *Chamber music*, generally *trios* or *quartets*, would also be featured. All in all, these were varied and interesting concerts.

Philadelphia, Boston, and New York were particularly active cities musically. The Colonial gentleman and his lady would have considered themselves lacking if they were not musically literate, that is, if they did not know how to play an instrument, sing, read music "from the notes," and dance the *minuet* and *gavotte* (the European favorites, soon to be displaced by the *waltz*), and the American favorites as well: the *reel*, *jig*, and *square dance* (also known as the *quadrille*).

The replacement of the harpsichord, the baroque *keyboard* instrument, with the piano took place in the late 1760s. The process was very swift: by 1775, Philadelphia had two busy piano manufacturers.

Military Music

Especially as the war approached, military music became more and more important. *Fife-and-drum corps* were part of every army unit, and military *bands* were established as part of the civilian as well as the military life of the communities in which they served. The difference between a *march* and a dance was not very great, in fact. The verb "to walk" also meant "to dance," as in the song, "Oh Madame, Will You Take a Walk with Me?" The word "step" (in dance step) also comes from the idea of walking, as does the name for a dance party, "promenade," which means "a leisurely walk, especially one taken in a public place as a social activity." (It can also mean a "formal ball"; the modern high school "prom" is a shortened form of it.) Bands were hugely popular, and have been a prominent feature of American life ever since; the bands were excellent, by all accounts, and would prove to be a vital—and vitalizing—element of American music to this day.

THE SINGING SCHOOLS

Perhaps the most particularly American of musical institutions was the *singing school*. In the largest cities singing schools were permanently established; elsewhere, they were run for two or three months a year by itinerant music masters traveling from city to city. (The Colonies were

A singing school.
(Picture Collection, The Branch Libraries, The New York Public Library.)

full of itinerant preachers, painters, tinkers, and even grammar school teachers.) By the 1760s, such schools were functioning as an accepted part of life in the Colonies, in towns and rural areas alike. The purpose of the schools was ostensibly the preparation of the young to sing in church choirs, but approved social events for young people were rare, and the singing-school meetings must have been cherished as courting places and occasions of social enjoyment. They were held in churches or schools or other business buildings. One contemporary description tells it all:

fife-and-drum corps: a small group, most often military, limited to fifers and drummers

band: a performing group made of wind and percussion instruments

march: a piece of music designed to be marched to

singing school: late eighteenth- and early nineteenth-century courses in singing and music fundamentals

▶○ Recommended Recordings and Video Cassettes

The New England singing schools are fairly well represented on discs. But many of the performances are "modern," that is, with a large choir singing with trained romantic voices.

Folkways Records FA 2377. *New England Harmony.* This recording not only has good sound, but it also has an excellent booklet (by Alan C. Buechner) with illustrative materials

The most authentic sound is captured in recordings of current sacred harp meetings, several of which have been issued.

New World 80205. *White Spirituals from the Sacred Harp.* Recorded at the Alabama Sacred Harp Convention.

Nonesuch H-71360. *Rivers of Delight: American Folk Hymns of the Sacred Harp Tradition,* c. 1780–1935. Suitable also for later chapters.

tune: melody

note: a single musical
sound

A singing school was got up about two miles from my father's house. In
much fear and trembling I went with the rest of the boys in our town.
Quite a number of young ladies and gentlemen had come to the school.
We were soon paraded all around the room, standing up to boards
supported by old fashioned kitchen chairs. The master took his place
inside the circle, took out of his pocket a paper manuscript, with rules and
tunes all written with pen and ink, read to us the rules, and then said we
must attend to the rising and falling of the notes. . . . The good master
began, "Come boys, you must rise and fall the notes first and then the gals
must try." . . . Then the gals had their turn to rise and fall the notes. "Come
gals, now see if you can't beat the boys." . . . A good number of tunes were
learned in this school, and were sung very well as we thought. . . . I
attended some kind of singing school every winter but two until I was
twenty-one years old.[13]

The first book of tunes suited to the singing school was published in
the Colonies in 1761; in the next half-century almost three hundred such
books, containing over four thousand *tunes*, would be published. Some
of these made use of a teaching aid of "shape notes," that is, round,

The cover of the
first of Billing's six
tune books, *The
New England
Psalm Singer*,
1770. The cover
was engraved
by Paul Revere.
(Music Division, The
Library of Congress.)

Read's "Sherburne" was one of the most popular tunes of the day. It was published in shape notes in a collection called *The Easy Instructor.* (Music Division, The Library of Congress.)

square, triangular, and diamond-shaped to represent different syllables of the musical scale. These tune books are still used by groups that hold to the singing-school tradition, particularly in the South.

Early Composers

The most famous of the composers of these tunes was William Billings (1746–1800), who was representative of part-time musicians in being professionally a tanner; a Bostonian, he was choirmaster at the Brattle Street Church before and during the Revolutionary War. He published six volumes that included over two hundred *hymn* tunes and fifty *anthems*, plus miscellaneous pieces. His tune "Chester" (tunes were given names separate from the titles of their poems) was a rallying song during the war.

Daniel Read (1757–1836) was even more diversified: he settled in New Haven, Connecticut, and became involved with the manufacture of combs and with a publishing company, but also ran a singing school (from 1782), published a magazine, and, of course, composed for the singing school (two books of tunes). In all he produced over 400 compositions.

hymn: a religious poem

anthem: a choral setting of a religious text for use in a church service

The composers for the singing schools, of which Billings and Read are representative, are considered the first group of truly American composers of "formal" music. (Since the singers of folk songs and the fiddlers are undocumented, and did not write music down, they must, unhappily, be left out of consideration.) Their music was strong and powerful, with a mix of Renaissance, baroque, and modern characteristics that in itself is American in its breadth of viewpoint.

THE SLAVES

Music of the Slaves

Many of the Colonists were aware of a vital enrichment of the American musical art: that was the music of the slaves. The first black slaves in the Western Hemisphere had been brought to the Caribbean by the Spanish; the founding of tobacco plantations in Virginia shortly after 1600 led the owners to turn to slave labor, and by 1620, the first slaves were being imported to the Colonies directly from the West African lands. By 1700, about fifty thousand blacks were in the plantation colonies in the South;

Slaves on a South Carolina plantation dancing to African music, about 1800.
(Abby Aldrich Rockefeller Folk Art Collection, The Williamsburg Museum.)

by 1750, about one hundred twenty thousand were in the Colonies, including several thousand freemen.

psalmody: the singing of hymns or psalms

It was clear from the beginning that the Africans were possessed of a remarkable gift for musical invention. Early comments on the music of the slaves were in the baroque tradition, reflecting an interest in the culture and instruments of other people. Later comments grew comparative, judging everything in relation to the current European musical style. African music was much more intricate rhythmically than the European, highly skilled in heterophony, which European music no longer was, and not at all interested in harmony (which was becoming more and more important in the European tradition). As harmony grew in importance to the Europeans, melody suffered in their music, while melody remained a primary focus of the music of the slaves.

The baroque observer was happy to comment on the singing skill displayed by the blacks. In the middle of the eighteenth century, a minister devoted his work to the slaves, and he wrote of the response of about three hundred of them whom he had taught to read, write, and sing. He introduced them to the American singing-school hymns, with which he said they were "exceedingly delighted."

> They have a kind of ecstatic delight in *psalmody* [the singing of hymns]; nor are there any books they so soon learn, or take so much pleasure in, as those used in that heavenly part of divine worship. . . . All the books were very acceptable, but none more so, than the Psalms and Hymns, which enabled them to gratify their particular taste for psalmody. Sundry of them lodged all night in my kitchen; and sometime when I have awaked at two or three in the morning a torrent of sacred psalmody has poured into my chamber. In this exercise some of them spend the whole night.[14]

It is erroneous to picture the slaves as living without cultural interaction with the whites, particularly in regard to music. The informal music of the slaves, the popular and folk music of the whites, and to a much lesser extent the music of the Native Americans, maintained an interaction, while the formal music of the concert hall and the living room remained aloof from any but European influences.

◗🔊 Recommended Recordings and Video Cassettes

Black gospel singing is, of course, directly developed from early slave culture. Some attempt has been made to preserve it, but little has been recorded.

Campbell Folk School CFS001 (issued through the Library of Congress—cassette). *Mountain Valley Music: Grassroots Music from Western North Carolina and North Georgia.* This includes both Anglo-American and Afro-American gospel as well as fiddling. A booklet contains additional historical background.

Franklin and Jefferson

glass harmonica: an instrument, invented by Benjamin Franklin, in which sound is produced by rubbing the fingers on the rims of glass discs, revolving on a spindle

musical glasses: drinking glasses filled with differing amounts of water and played by rubbing the rims with wet fingers

pedal: a foot mechanism on pianos and organs

banjo: a plucked string instrument with circular frame

banjar: banjo

Benjamin Franklin (1706–90) and Thomas Jefferson (1743–1826) represent the baroque and classical attitudes toward the music of the blacks quite wonderfully. Franklin, ever the apprenticeship man, was a born tinker: in addition to the Franklin stove and bifocal eyeglasses, he invented the *glass harmonica* (in 1761), a mechanism for the *musical glasses*, a popular form of music making, accomplished by filling glasses with differing amounts of water to have them give different pitches when the rims were rubbed with wet fingers. He put discs of glass on a spindle, arranging them horizontally within a trough of water, and engaged the spindle with a foot *pedal* to spin the discs and keep them wet. When these revolving discs were touched, they sounded a lovely pearly tone. He was a robust companionable singer as well. Franklin was the baroque observer who rejoiced in seeing the musical art of the blacks.

Jefferson was the university man, a philosopher of music, who invented less practical musical items, such as a four-way music stand for four people to use when playing quartets (but this is impracticable, for the stand must come to the musician, not the musician to the stand), and he made notes on the musical accomplishments of his slaves. These included the first reference to the *banjo*, an instrument constructed by his slaves in their compounds, of which he wrote: "The instrument proper to them is the Banjar, which they brought hither from Africa."[15] Jefferson was also the classicist, who noted the musical activities of the slaves

The glass harmonica, an invention of Benjamin Franklin. (Photo Lauros, Paris.)

🔊 Recommended Recordings and Video Cassettes

Music, mostly European, was played on musical glasses. The glass harmonica, a mechanism for the musical glasses, was invented by Benjamin Franklin. Franklin spent 1776–84 in France (as Ambassador to the Court of Louis XVI) and was a popular figure there; several European composers wrote music for Franklin's new instrument.

Syrinx CSR 91101. *Music for the Glass Harmonica.*

almost as a scientific observer, comparing them with European ideals of music.

Jefferson acknowledged the innate musical gift of the blacks, but was impelled to note that it lacked harmony: "In music they are more generally gifted than the whites with accurate ears for tune and time, . . . [but] whether they will be equal to the composition of a more extensive run of melody, or of complicated harmony, is yet to be proved."[16] The attitude is essentially condescending; it simply never occurred to Jefferson that if "rhythm" were substituted for "harmony," the reverse would be true and that blacks could have serious doubts about him.

ndamutsu: a Congolese drum-music type played at the appearance of the king

ncabagome: a Congolese drum-music type played at the announcement of a guilty verdict by a court

African Culture

African culture was complex and lively. There were over seven hundred groups, each with its own art, and they all had had sophisticated and knowledgeable artistic and musical lives long before the Europeans invaded Africa's coasts and forests.

No summary of African cultures can suggest the variety of that continent in the eighteenth century. The African heritage was a rich one, but a few generalizations can be made about it. Music was honored to an unusual degree, and virtually all the African cultures were rich in poetry, song, sculpture, ritual, and dance. In general, Africans saw the arts as means of being in harmony with God, earth, animals, plants, and other people; certain instruments and certain songs were connected with particular facets of life. For example, in Rwanda, just east of the Congo, the *ndamutsu* and *nchabagome* were two types of drum music among many. The first was played only at the appearance of the king, and the latter only at an announcement in a court of a verdict of guilty.

The quality of sound, rhythm, and the relationships among musical elements were (and still are) the basic focuses of African music, and from these many of the other elements can be seen to have derived. The cultures have a long, long tradition, and this tradition predates any history of the area. Some cultures did combine elements, though not in the manner of Europeans. A description of a landing in Africa by Vasco da Gama in 1497, by one of the crew, was, of course, influenced by Renaissance ears:

drumhead: the top of a
drum, often of hide; the
part of the drum that is
struck

The Saterday next after came to the number of two hundreth blacke men.
. . . and as our men went on shore, they began to play upon foure Flutes
accordingly with foure sundry voyces, the Musicke whereof sounded very
well, which the Generall [da Gama] hearing commaunded the trumpets to
sound, and so they daunced with our men.[17]

Like the Native American cultures, the African cultures had much in
common with European medieval techniques and concerns. The vocal
art was poetic and often religious, and the instrumental art was highly
rhythmic and full of percussion. The rhythmic language was complex
and centered in a steady beat. In addition, the Africans tended toward
more universal participation. Some groups assumed that all members
would compose music, so individual people sang only their own songs.
Special instruments were made for the children, who, in general, were
given more attention than those in Europe. And the Africans had
developed an amazingly rich vocabulary of vocal techniques, including
yodeling, used as embellishments before and after *beats*; a variety of tone
qualities; and clear, penetrating nasal voices, typical of cultures throughout the world where outdoor performance has predominated.

African Instruments

Most of the slavers in the American trade took blacks from the western
coastal areas now defined by the crescent extending from Zaire to Ghana
and including Gabon, Cameroon, Nigeria, and Benin. That area of
Africa, large as it is, shared a generally homogeneous musical esthetic
and used many of the same instruments, even though the individual
musical arts were rich in variation. The practices of the peoples from
that area, notably those of the Ashanti, Bantu, Benin, Yoruba, and Bini
groups, were of the greatest importance in shaping the music of the
blacks in the New World.

The West African groups used most of the musical instruments
known in Africa, the number and variety of which rival those of any
other culture. It would be impossible to list even the main types; the
percussion contingent is well known, but even that is underestimated.

In our culture, where drum types are limited, the drums of Africa are
difficult to conceive. They could be classified physically by shape, by
the particularities of construction, and by the manner of playing.
Shapes included the cylinder, cone, barrel, goblet, kettle, frame, mush-
room, beehive, and hourglass. The body could be made of wood,
carved tree trunk, metal, clay, bone, ivory, or gourd; and the head (the
area to be struck) could be made of antelope or other hide, parchment,
lizard skin, elephant ear, or resin. The *drumhead* could be glued, nailed,
or laced to the body. There might be one or two heads—one on each

African drum from Zaire. (The American Museum of Natural History.)

end of the drum. If two, they could be the same or different in size or material or both; if there was only one head, the other end could be open or stopped.

Each drum was played in a specific way. Some were held vertically—on the ground, on a stand, or strung on the body of the player. Others were held horizontally—on the ground, in the lap, or on a stand. Some were played by one person, others by two or more persons, according to the length of the drum. Some were played by the hand, which could produce several effects through the use of the fingers, fists, flat palm, or heel of the hand. Most often, the effects were mixed in quick, imaginative patterns. Others were struck with beaters, and the beaters might have rubber, hide, sinew, resin, or wooden ends, and they might be flexible or sturdy, single or compound, straight or fan-shaped. In addition, the size and proportion of the drums could alter their tone. They varied, from those made of gourd or clay, which were smaller than the hand, to tree-trunk drums that have been measured as large as thirty feet. A cylinder or cone could be tall and narrow or short and squat. Further refinements included slits, tongues, sound holes, membranes, variable thickness of the body, or enclosure of some rattling object, such as a pebble (which made a buzzing sound—such an added buzzer is called a *mirliton*).

With their variety of quality and quick responsiveness, drums could be made to imitate speech so exactly that court decisions were often rendered by the chief with a *talking drum*. This was, of course, facilitated by the fact that West African languages were most often labial, rhythmic, and inflected in from two to four high and low pitch areas (called *tones*). In tonal languages, the pitch of a syllable is as much a part of its

mirliton: a buzzing device added to a musical instrument

talking drum: a drum with such a variety of tones that it could imitate speech

tone: a musical sound

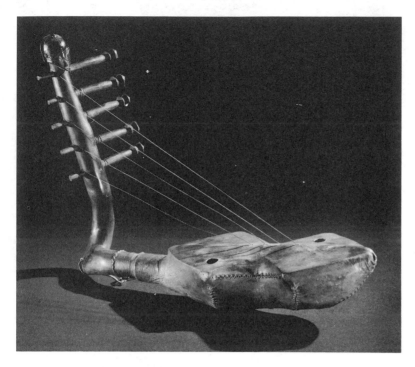

Harp, native to Mangbetu, Congo. (The American Museum of Natural History.)

An eleven-tongued sansa. The instrument is held between the hands and played with the thumbs. A tongue is made to speak by pressing down on it and then releasing it sharply; the release causes the tongue to vibrate. Tongues can be tuned by pulling them out or pushing them in to change their sounding length. (The American Museum of Natural History.)

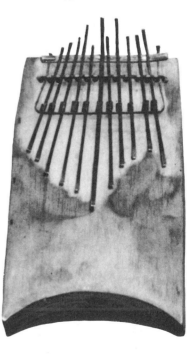

Musical bow from the Wa'husha tribe. The strings are split from sections of the cane from which the instrument is made. (The American Museum of Natural History.)

definition as its vowel-consonant aspects, and the same syllable has three different, and often unrelated, meanings in three different inflections. The talking drums were often considered to be the heightened speech of God or of an ancestor speaking through the chief.

Other African instruments included the sansa or *thumb piano*, a hand instrument with tongues made of cane or metal that sounded when they were depressed and then quickly released; the *marimba*, a *xylophone* or instrument of wooden slabs variously tuned and played with sticks; the *musical bow* (thought by many to be the first musical instrument), a hunting bow played by tapping the string with a stick; the *pluriarc* or multiple bow; and the banjar or banjo, a plucked string instrument with a circular frame (the instrument built by Jefferson's slaves).

thumb piano: a sansa

marimba: a large xylophone

xylophone: an instrument made of wooden bars, played with soft mallets

musical bow: a hunting bow played by tapping the string with a stick

pluriarc: a multiple musical bow

African Song

In addition, the West Africans had developed song to a rich art in itself. Singing to syllables was one aspect of their vocal music; the many sounds of the drums were paralleled by many sounds of the voice: yodels, clicks, and combined sounds, as well as singing on pitches. Subject matter of the songs with texts was broad; music was necessary in virtually all of the symbolic acknowledgments that the people made in life—the birth of a baby, the decision to hunt, or to battle, or to marry; the arrival of a guest; the sorrow of death or loss; or the joy of success, in a project of construction perhaps, or in a successful battle.

Many of the songs were story songs—some telling of events that had occurred and were of importance to the group, some simply interesting or perhaps humorous tales. One song told of a young man who had to choose a wife from among three candidates from three different villages. The song depicts his journey to the three villages, interspersed with comments on the girls: the first is a good fisherwoman and fills her basket, but cannot cook; the second is a terrible fisherwoman but she cooks fish wonderfully well; the third can neither fish nor cook but is marvelous at making love. The young man carefully weighs the girls' relative merits and after considerable suspense, finally decides which one to marry. (The young man selects the third girl.)[18]

▶◯ Recommended Recordings and Video Cassettes

Several albums of African music contain songs of venerable age. But age is difficult to ascertain, and many albums of African folk music illustrate the early ideals. Music in Europe and the United States *by Edith Borroff (2nd ed., Ardsley House, Publishers, 1990), pages 448–49, contain analyses of two Bakwesi songs and one Basuku song from:*

Ethnic Folkways FE4427. *Folk Music of the Western Congo.* A helpful booklet comes with it. These songs are also contained in Borroff, Compact Discs.

MUSIC DURING THE REVOLUTIONARY WAR

oboe: a soprano reed instrument using two reeds vibrating together

contrafactum: a process in which new words for a tune have been substituted for the original ones

The Revolutionary War, spurred by such events as the Boston Massacre (1770) and the Boston Tea Party (1773), took its toll on the arts of the new settlements. Music reduced itself in large part to rousing folk protest items such as "The Liberty Song" and "Hearts of Oak" (1759—by the British composer William Boyce), published in the *Boston Gazette* in 1765. The British taunted the Bostonians in 1770 by calling them Yankees, and they enjoyed disrupting the Colonists' church services by singing "Yankee Doodle" at the top of their lungs while the congregation was trying to sing hymns. Later, in 1775, the Americans returned the favor by racing after the British, singing "Yankee Doodle" just as lustily at them. This heckling endowed the song with enduring popularity.

Philadelphia turned almost entirely to military music. A military band, of *oboes* and fifes, had been established there in 1756, but the war caused the band to change to a fife-and-drum corps (oboes used reeds, which could not be kept playable under difficult conditions). The fife-and-drum corps became the chief musical group during the war; new tunes were composed, and new words were put to old tunes that the soldiers loved (a venerable practice called *contrafactum*). "God Save the King" was changed in 1775 to "God Save America"—we now know it through still another contrafactum as "My Country, 'Tis of Thee." And, of course, Billings's "Chester" became even more popular. What was so quintessentially American about these groups was that they served social as well as military needs, and they continued, in the ensuing peacetime, to be as popular as they had been during the war. There was not a great difference between marches and dances, for example, and many march tunes were extremely popular in the dance hall.

There were, of course, Americans who could not fight in the war and who maintained musical establishments in the cities that had developed them. Billings, for example, had a crippled leg and was blind in one eye. Francis Hopkinson (1737–91) was too short; he was a lawyer and writer who composed what is probably the first song in the European tradition published in Colonial territory: "My Days Have Been So Wondrous Free," published in Philadelphia in 1760. Hopkinson continued working (musically and otherwise) during the war; and published a book of songs in 1788, *Seven Songs for the Harpsichord* (that is, to be sung with a harpsichord accompaniment). Hopkinson, who never was able to fight, was a great admirer of George Washington and dedicated the songs to

Continental colors, 1776.

▶◖ Recommended Recordings and Video Cassettes

The Goldman Band specialized in early American marches.

New World 80266. *The Goldman Band.*

him. Actually, the volume contains eight songs—he composed the eighth after the title page had been engraved!

Other cities continued with prewar ensembles, some using young people not yet accepted for military service. Charleston, for example, had a concert ensemble of twenty players in 1776: eleven *bowed string* players, two flutists, two clarinetists (who also played oboes), two *bassoonists*, two horn players, and a harpsichordist. But dance halls more often used fiddlers—one writer in 1783 spoke of one in Rhode Island that employed "two negro violins."[19]

But the war years were a time of cultural *status quo*: few cultural matters were given serious consideration; no ships were docking with

bowed string instrument: an instrument with strings, played with a bow

bassoon: the bass member of the woodwind instruments

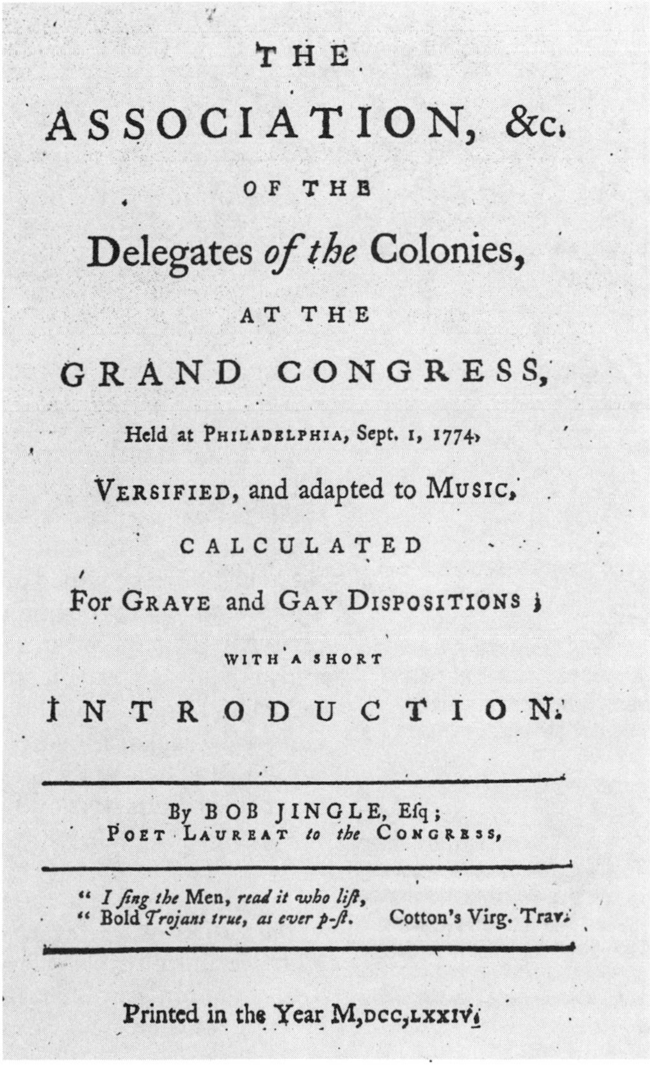

THE.

ASSOCIATION, &c.

OF THE

Delegates *of the* Colonies,

AT THE

GRAND CONGRESS,

Held at PHILADELPHIA, Sept. 1, 1774,

VERSIFIED, and adapted to MUSIC,

CALCULATED

For GRAVE and GAY DISPOSITIONS ;

WITH A SHORT

INTRODUCTION.

By BOB JINGLE, Esq;
POET LAUREAT *to the* CONGRESS,

" *I sing the* Men, *read it who list,*
" Bold *Trojans true, as ever p-st.*   Cotton's Virg. Trav.

Printed in the Year M,DCC,LXXIV.

The title page of this anti-Congress lampoon lists "Bob Jingle," a pseudonym for Francis Hopkinson, as its author, although it seems unlikely that Hopkinson, a patriot, would have written this. (Rare Books Division, The New York Public Library.)

The original of "The Toast to Washington" (1778) was written in Hopkinson's own hand. (The New York Public Library, Special Collections.)

Two versions of the flag of 1777.

the latest clothes, books, and music, or with visiting musicians; and life was so devoted to the war that little else was given houseroom. And the war must have provided an intensification of song sharing, for singing is a traditional form of socializing around a campfire. Moreover, wherever people have gathered in song, they have singled out the beautiful voice and outstanding singer, regardless of race—and the white, black, and red men were all involved in fighting the war. About five thousand Colonial blacks, plus about seven hundred Haitians, fought in the Continental Army. Even the fife-and-drum corps had its contingent of free blacks. Thus, it is probable that the blacks did more than their share of singing. At home, too, women, old men, and children must have sung together. Unfortunately, however, the songs that were sung around the army campfires and in the homes the soldiers had left are unknown.

Nevertheless, the war would be over, the battles won, and the soldiers would return to their homes, to begin the arduous task of building a new nation. And in creating that nation, those early citizens would create a new culture. Music would be a salient part of that culture.

NOTES

1. *Encyclopedia Americana* (Danbury, CT: Grolier Incorporated, 1992).

2. Ibid.

3. David Crystal, *The Cambridge Encyclopedia of Language* (Cambridge University Press, 1987).

4. Robert Stevenson, *Music in Aztec & Inca Territories* (Berkeley and Los Angeles: University of California Press, 1968), pp. 49–53.

5. Ibid, p. 75.

6. Ibid, pp. 49–53.

7. Alvin M. Josephy, Jr., ed., *The American Heritage Book of Indians* (New York: American Heritage Publishing Co., Inc., 1961), p. 117.

8. Thomas Morton, about 1640, in Gilbert Chase, *America's Music* (New York: McGraw-Hill, 1955), p. 11.

9. Josephy, *Indians*, p. 26.

10. Ibid, p. 163.

11. Samuel Sewall (1652–1730), in Chase, *America's Music* , p. 9.

12. Josiah Quincy, in Chase, *America's Music* , p. 108.

13. Moses Cheney, 1788, in Alan C. Buechner, "New England Harmony" (New York: Folkways Records and Service Corporation, 1964), p. 3f.

14. Chase, *America's Music* , p. 80.

15. Ibid, p. 67.

16. Ibid, p. 80.

17. C. M. Bowra, *Primitive Song* (New York: Mentor Books, New American Library of World Literature, Inc., 1963), p. 198.

18. Ibid, pp. 179–80.

19. William Lichtenwanger, ed., *Oscar Sonneck and American Music* (Urbana, IL: University of Illinois Press, 1983), p. 96f.

BIBLIOGRAPHY

Bowra, C. M., *Primitive Song*. New York: Mentor Books, New American Library of World Literature, Inc., 1963.

Brian, Robert. *The Last Primitive Peoples*. New York: Crown Publishers, 1976.

Buechner, Alan C. "New England Harmony." Folkways Records and Service Corp., 1964.

Caso, Alfonso. *The Aztecs: People of the Sun*. Translated by Lowell Dunham. Norman: University of Oklahoma Press, 1970.

Chase, Gilbert. *America's Music: From the Pilgrims to the Present*. rev. ed. Urbana: University of Illinois Press, 1992.

Howard, John Tasker. *The Music of George Washington's Time*. Washington D. C.: United States George Washington Bicentennial Commission, 1931.

Josephy, Alvin M. Jr., ed. *The American Heritage Book of Indians*. New York: American Heritage Publishing Co., Inc., 1961.

———. *The Horizon History of Africa*. New York: American Heritage Publishing Co., Inc., 1971.

La Rue, Jan, ed. *Aspects of Medieval & Renaissance Music*. New York: W. W. Norton & Co., 1966.

Lichtenwanger, William, ed., *Oscar Sonneck and American Music*. Urbana: University of Illinois Press, 1983.

Loesser, Arthur. *Men, Women, and Pianos*. New York: Simon & Schuster, 1954.

Nathan, Hans, ed. *The Continental Harmony of William Billings*. Cambridge, MA: Harvard University Press, The Belknap Press, 1961.

Nettl, Bruno. *Folk and Traditional Music of the Western Continents*. Englewood Cliffs, NJ: Prentice-Hall, 1965.

Pinney, Roy. *Vanishing Tribes*. New York: Crowell, 1968.

Silverberg, Robert. *Mound Builders of Ancient America*. Greenwich, CT: New York Graphic Society Books, 1968.

Stevenson, Robert. "The Afro-American Musical Legacy to 1800." *Musical Quarterly* 54 (October 1968).

———. *Music in Aztec & Inca Territories*. Berkeley and Los Angeles: University of California Press, 1968.

Tufts, John. *A Very Plain and Easy Introduction to the Whole Art of Singing Psalm Tunes*. Boston: Samuel Garrish, 1720.

Weir, Christopher. *Village and Town Bands*. Shire, 1981.

NATIONAL ODE.

The Flag of the Free

Written and Composed by

Harrison Millard.

AUTHOR OF: THOU ART FAR AWAY, VOCALISTS TEXT BOOK &C

Plain Colored

NEW YORK,
Published by S.T. GORDON & SON 13 East 14th St.

2

An Energetic New Nation
(1783 to 1840)

E arly citizens of the United States of America were eager to give their country the form—cultural as well as geographical—that they had dreamed of. In its way, the American Revolution was as idealistic and as well-conceived as any such upheaval could hope to be; the years after the war were the same. The years from, roughly, 1783 to 1840 were years of definition: the energy of democracy, after all, was not known in essence, and in other countries the adventures of new governmental forms did not succeed. But the leaders of the American movement for independence from Great Britain were classicists at heart—George Washington refused the crown and became the first president in a search not for personal glory, but for national balance, and he was followed during that first period by other presidents who had been part of that marvelous search, through Andrew Jackson (president 1829–37), forty-six years later. (Jackson, born in 1767, had joined the army at thirteen, was captured by the British, imprisoned at Charleston, and liberated at sixteen.)

The early citizens got to work, having virtually to create a nation and formulate a government. They faced an initial depression, which lasted about four years (1783–87), and this was both hindered and helped by the fact that they were building a new type of country just at the time of the Industrial Revolution.

They had many jobs to do. The first was that of pulling the country strongly together. The separate states had their own governments as colonies, and they changed their governments to fit into the new national system. But they also had to work hard as a group: ratifying the Constitution, setting up the three-pronged system (legislative, executive, judicial—itself a classical balance) once the Constitution was ratified, issuing money, electing a president, and so forth. The progress was steady and good, yet it was ten years before the government was fully operative—they even built a new city to house the new government! The activation of the new government was amazingly peaceful: the first House of Representatives quorum convened on April 1, 1789; the Senate, a few days later. The Congress had first to decide how oaths should be taken; George Washington was inaugurated in New York City on April 30 as the first president. On September 26, John Jay was appointed Chief Justice of the Supreme Court. In 1791, the Bill of Rights became effective, with its ratification at last by Virginia. That same year, primogeniture was rendered illegal; Colonists were leery of family inheritance of power and nullified it, an act that had effect in all the arts, since it divided fortunes and thus made patronage a matter of many small donations, rather than one

American costumes, 1790–1800. (The Newberry Library.)

big one. In 1792, the Mint Act provided a currency based on the decimal system and the unit of the dollar. In 1793, Washington held the first cabinet meeting with five members: secretary of state, secretary of the treasury, secretary of war, postmaster general, and attorney general—but the idea of the cabinet would become official only in Teddy Roosevelt's administration, in 1907.

John Adams became president in 1797; the following year, the Alien and Sedition Acts were enacted and the United States Navy was created. In 1800, Congress met in Washington for the first time (John and Abigail Adams were the first occupants of the White House).

Thomas Jefferson was the first nineteenth-century president, from 1801 to 1809. His term was concerned with international matters, and included the purchase from France of the Louisiana Territory (827,987 square miles containing what would become nine states and parts of several others—basically the land between the Mississippi River and the Rocky Mountains). The slave trade was abolished in 1808 (though it would not be rooted out for some time—in 1820, the importation of slaves was declared a piracy and its practitioners punishable by death). James Madison (1809–17) was also less national than international, involved primarily in the War of 1812, a war with Great Britain that would determine much of the international policy of the United States. Madison's successor, James Monroe (1817–25), was equally international, propounding the Monroe Doctrine (1823), which, in its concern with stopping all settlement by foreign powers in the area west of what was then the United States, turned the nation's attention back home, to future western expansion, and to unity of purpose.

Meanwhile, other forces were at work. Population was rising quickly, as much by immigration as by native births, and each group brought with it its own music. The population of the Colonies has been estimated at 2,781,000 in 1780; the first census took place in 1790 and the figure had risen to 3,929,214 (including about 900,000 slaves and 100,000 free blacks), and it rose briskly thereafter: 5,308,483 in 1800, 7,239,881 in 1810, 9,638,453 in 1820, 12,866,020 in 1830, and 17,069,453 in 1840. The rural population far outnumbered the urban, and this too had implications for the music of the country as a whole.

Part of the establishment of the new nation, which was, of course, primary, was the assurance of safe borders. The thirteen original states were:

Connecticut	New Hampshire	Rhode Island
Delaware	New Jersey	South Carolina
Georgia	New York	Virginia
Maryland	North Carolina	
Massachusetts	Pennsylvania	

These made a sweep of the eastern seacoast from Maine, which was then part of Massachusetts, to the Carolinas and Georgia, plus a modest amount of west-reaching land. The first fifty years pushed the southern half of the nation westward, to assure the borders, and completed the New England group. This continental nucleus expanded by the gradual incorporation of additional states:

1791 Vermont	1818 Illinois
1792 Kentucky	1819 Alabama
1796 Tennessee	1820 Maine
1803 Ohio	1821 Missouri
1812 Louisiana	1836 Arkansas
1816 Indiana	1837 Michigan
1817 Mississippi	

Thus, by 1840, the number of states had doubled to 26 and the United States flag had officially (by Act of Congress in 1818) been

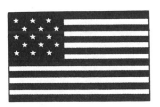

The American flag, 1795–1818.

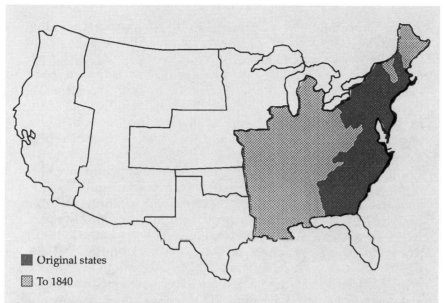

Original states

To 1840

The United States in 1840.

set with the thirteen stripes to represent the original colonies and with the number of stars variable, to represent the number of states as that number changed. This eastern view of the country was accepted in 1840, and the borders were expressive of that view. But already the nation was thinking in westward terms: Father Junipero Serra had founded missions in California—in San Diego in 1769 (the first settlement in what would be that state), and in Los Angeles (called the *Pueblo de los Angeles*) in 1781. In 1792, the Columbia River territory was explored; in 1822, the Santa Fe Trail opened and ten years later the Oregon Trail. The West would be the area of focus for the next generation.

The Industrial Revolution took powerful hold in the United States because here industry did not have to be retooled, but was being built anew. Inventiveness was strongly within the American character, typified by Franklin and his experiments with electricity (published in 1751) and his invention of bifocal glasses (1784), not to mention the many pioneers who furnished their simple log dwellings with surprising conveniences (one cabin had a cradle-rocking device worked by someone at a stove, across the room). New adventures in manufacture include the cotton gin (Eli Whitney, 1793), cook stove (1819), fish-canning equipment (1819), an iron plow with interchangeable parts (1819), a copying lathe (1820), a mechanical typesetter (1822), lead pencils (invented in

mouth organ: a small reed instrument sounded by blowing and sucking

harmonica: a mouth organ

Salem, Massachusetts, manufactured from 1827), paper made from straw (1829), the T-rail (1830), wool-manufacturing equipment (1830), power-knitting machinery (1832), shoe pegging (1833), the horse-drawn reaper (Cyrus McCormick, 1834), the electric motor (1834), the telegraph (Samuel F. B. Morse, 1835), type-casting machinery (1836), the revolver ("six-shooter," Samuel Colt, 1836), the steel-faced plow (John Deere, 1837), the corn planter (1839), the power loom for carpets (1839), and the vulcanization of rubber (Charles Goodyear, also 1839).

John Quincy Adams (1825–29) believed in opening up the entire country to trade, and encouraged the building of ships (Robert Fulton's *Clermont* was the first steamboat, inaugurated with a journey from New York City to Albany in thirty-two hours in 1807), canals, and riverboat systems. Andrew Jackson (1829–37) saw steamboat service established in routes from the Buffalo-Chicago lake/river/canal ferries to luxury Mississippi River boats, originally from Pittsburgh to New Orleans in 1811. Jackson saw the national debt paid off (in 1835) and turned his attention more and more to the matter of slavery, as did his successor, Martin Van Buren (1837–41). Slavery was closely associated with the production of cotton, and, spurred by Whitney's gin, which lessened the cost of refining, that production skyrocketed from 73,000 bales in 1800 to 1,248,000 bales in 1840.

MUSIC ON THE FRONTIER

Frontier Instruments

Every place in the United States was part of the frontier at one time or another. And each frontier was different. But they all had certain characteristics in common. Each single frontiersman carried only what could be put into a backpack, and each family or group carried only what could be put into a wagon. This means they were limited to small artifacts on the one hand and encouraged to be inventive on the other. The fiddle was fairly large, and, as popular as fiddling was, few violins were brought into the country; fiddlers made their own instruments. The Jew's harp was the handiest of instruments to carry, demanding only a pocket, but the *mouth organ* or *harmonica*, a variation on an oriental instrument, was manufactured early in the nineteenth century and became extremely popular beginning with the 1830s. It is easy

Mouth organ.

View of the Rocky Mountains on the Platte, 50 miles from their base, from Stephen H. Lang, *Account of an Expedition from Pittsburgh to the Rocky Mountains Performed in the Years 1819 and '20.* (The Newberry Library.)

enough to play roughly, but can also be played with great skill, and, like the fiddle, it was played both ways at country barn-raisings. It could be both melodic and harmonic (very simply so, but harmonies were in fact simple in country music), it had a considerable and subtle dynamic range, and it provided a very personal expression.

Recommended Recordings and Video Cassettes

Many of the folk-music recordings mentioned in Chapter 1 reach through the early years of the New Nation. In addition, some recordings specialize in a slightly later sound.

cro2* *Shepherd's Wife's Waltz.* Old music. Features the dulcimer, but also includes fiddle, flute, and banjo, as well as vocals. (cassette) The same company offers *How Great Thou Art,* "Old-time hymns." (cassette)

*For addresses for recordings and videos not readily available in regular commercial outlets, see p. xxiv.

accordion: a hand-held reed organ in which the melody is presented by a keyboard held vertically at the player's chest while the player opens and closes the wind chest with sideways pumping motions

keyboard: a row of keys

A much larger version of the same instrument was the *accordion*, in which the melody was presented by a keyboard held vertically at the player's chest while the player opened and closed the wind chest with a sideways pumping motion (which caused it to be called a "squeeze-box").

Vocal Music

And, of course, vocal music was always popular. Songs told stories, exploited moods or even established them, and brought people together. Music could also sustain the single pioneer, singing or playing the

Rochester, New York in 1812, shown on a sheet-music cover. (The Newberry Library.)

William Sidney Mount, *Rustic Dance after a Sleigh Ride*, c. 1830. (The Karolik Collection, The Museum of Fine Arts, Boston.)

harmonica as he walked through the woods alone. Most of the music was improvised on the spot or was of familiar material: the songs of Colonial days, such as "Yankee Doodle," or songs published in London, such as "The Irish Washerwoman" (1794), "The Minstrel Boy" (1813), "The Old Oaken Bucket" (1817), or "Home! Sweet Home!" (1821), all of unknown musical origin, or "Annie Laurie" (1838) by Scotswoman Alicia Ann Spottiswoode, Lady John Scott. But the most popular of all was one of the many reels, the fiddle tune "Turkey in the Straw," of anonymous, but American, composition, first published about 1830, but soon with words as the "comic song, as sung by all the celebrated comic singers,"[1] published about 1834 as "Old Zip Coon."

Europe had changed its musical stance from classical to romantic, but Americans never embraced that philosophy; only the Americans who

▶ Recommended Recordings and Video Cassettes

British eighteenth-century pop music, frequently heard in America, is rare but is available. Very little is available on recordings of the music of early American composers, though it is excellent music.

Saydisc CD-SDL 382. *The City Waits.* Features materials from early in the eighteenth century, but popular well into the nineteenth century.

cotillion: a town dance featuring many different types of steps

hoedown: a musical celebration at the end of a day's farm work

musicale: a private musical performance at a party or social gathering

studied abroad (and they were few—most musicians were trained in American apprenticeship) became romantics, and they were seldom whole-hearted. The kind of fresh, pungent energy in American music, with its high texture and natural (and *ex tempore*) embellishment, was classical in the best sense, and remained so.

The Romantic Tradition

In contrast, writers about music, historians and critics, were trained in the European-dominated tradition strongest on the Eastern Seaboard. They were dyed-in-the-wool romantics; they began, and they continued, a denigration of American music that stemmed largely from this basic difference. The romantics liked BIG music—the orchestra had begun as a dozen or eighteen players, and ended up as eighty players, or even more—and LOUD music, SMOOTH music, SLOW music, and music dominated by HARMONY. The Americans preferred agility to size, clarity to loudness, high texture to smoothness, liveliness to slowness, rhythm and melody to harmony.

Two problems stem from the anti-American prejudice of these romantically committed writers. One is that most of the music is lost; only a few American works remain, since the writers didn't believe they were worth saving. The other is that the songs that do remain (and they are mostly later, such as Stephen Foster's "Old Folks at Home," 1851, the most honored song in the United States in its day and now the state song of Florida) are performed in highly-charged romantic arrangements by singers (or even orchestras!) playing in the loud, slow, smooth romantic tradition, and thus drearily misrepresented.

MUSIC IN TOWN

Perhaps it was at home that Americans made their own music come most alive. In the country log cabin, yes, but also in the towns, where most everybody had training at a singing school and thus was part of a lively, musically intelligent audience. The rude apprenticeship of country people had its own strengths, and the more decorous apprenticeship of the village and town, and even of the city, had its own strengths too. The square dances of the country folk were no less wonderful than the town *cotillions*, and the fiddling of a skilled dance player was no less energetic than the fiddler's tunes at a *hoedown*.

Five kinds of formal music were common in the villages and towns of early nineteenth-century America: the *musicale* (private performance, formal or informal, in the home), the *social dance* (of any size, from a small group at home to the whole town at a public building), the *church*

Living-room music, 1837. (The Newberry Library.)

service (with lusty singing by people who had attended the singing school), the *concert* (again of any size, from home to public hall), and *musical theater* (opera).

musical theater: plays with music

Musicales

The *musicale* could include a wide scope of activities, from recitations (called *elocution*) and dramatic songs to piano, harp, mandolin, clarinet, flute, or cornet solos (among others); chamber groups of many types; pieces just for listening, and pieces to be danced to—and no clear distinction between them (some dances might be listened to without dancing; and some pieces not called dances might be danced to). It could feature the children of the host (or guests), skillful amateurs known for their excellence and widely admired, and professionals (paid or unpaid), if they happened to be there; most probably, a musicale included a cross section of types of music, types of performance, and types of performers with variable degrees of skill.

They screw'd up their pegs, and they shoulder'd their fiddles,
They finger'd the notes of their heigh diddle diddles—
Spectators looked on—they were many a million
To see the performers in this Great Cotillion.

"Presidential Cotillion," Anonymous, New York Statesman, September 24, 1824. (The Library of Congress.)

Social Dances

organ: a wind instrument whose sounding elements are controlled from a console

The *social dance* included occasions of all kinds: private celebrations of birthdays and wedding anniversaries; more public events, such as weddings or holidays; or professionally run promenades or balls, generally kept rather formal, with dance cards for the young ladies (the young gentlemen would sign up for dances) and a set social procedure—rather like a high school prom in the middle of the twentieth century. A concert item or two might be included, but most usually the occasion centered in the dance.

Church Services

The church services varied, of course, by denomination. The Episcopal churches and many other Protestant denominations had a full and extremely satisfying musical component, from anthems for the small group to hymns sung by everybody, and, where the congregation desired it, instruments such as *organ* or piano, or groups of instruments, to augment the choral sound. People associated the churches with the beloved singing schools and their social elements, and they associated music with the whole idea of harmony—the harmony of God and humankind, and the harmony of life in general. There were exceptions (the Quakers, for example, disallowed music at their services), but they were few.

Concerts

The *concert*, too, came in many types and sizes. The touring of virtuoso musicians was akin to the touring of tinkers and limners (portrait painters), and musicians still tour today. The typical concert might have a small orchestra (still the classical orchestra of twelve to eighteen players) playing symphonies or parts of symphonies, a singer with a group of songs, perhaps a *string quartet*, a piano playing a solo (perhaps a set of variations on a popular song), and, if possible, a famous soloist, perhaps a clarinetist or a cornetist, thrilling everyone with a virtuoso *concerto*. A few concert halls charged admission and were set up fairly much like halls presenting a concert series today; other concerts might be held in the larger salons of wealthy homes. (Such concerts were held in private homes well into the twentieth century.)

Musical Theater

Musical theater was thriving. All theater productions (plays, other entertainments) included musical components, and few musical offerings

string quartet: two violins, a viola, and a cello as a group

concerto: a work combining a soloist with an orchestra

The first theater in St. Louis (from a painting in the Missouri Historical Society).
(Picture Collection, The Branch Libraries, The New York Public Library.)

grand opera: an opera in which everything is sung and nothing is spoken

English opera: British ballad opera, a stage work in which speech and song, action and dance, were mixed

comprised all-sung drama, but included a component of the spoken word. In Europe, rigid definitions of *opera* and *grand opera* curtailed performances and clouded criticism, but the United States was free of that hairsplitting. Opera was a play in which the thrust was achieved or heightened by means of music. National aspirations can be shared in the listening to an opera, and opera was extremely popular in the larger cities of the United States, chiefly Charleston (where the earliest known performance of an opera took place in 1735), New Orleans, Baltimore, Philadelphia, Boston, Hartford, and New York.

English Operas

Early performances tended to be of *English opera*, most often ballad opera, which was very much like a musical, with a plot brought forth as speech heightened with musical numbers. The first American composers of opera used the British works as models. By 1820, a real American school of opera composition was strong on the East Coast. Philadelphia was probably the liveliest operatic town, but performances could be anywhere that a company could be brought together. In 1783, *Columbus: or, The Discovery of America* was performed in Baltimore; in 1787, *May Day in Town: or, New York in an Uproar* in New York; in 1794, *Slaves in Algiers: or, A Struggle for Freedom* in Philadelphia; in 1798, *Americania and Elutheria; or, A New Tale of the Genii* in Charleston; about 1801, *Federation Triumphant in the Steady Hearts of Connecticut Alone: or, The Turnpike Road to a Fortune* in Hartford; and in 1812 *Yankee Chronology: or, Huzza for the Constitution* in New York. (All of these works are of unknown composership.) The dates and titles tell their own story of American concerns in the early years. As time went on, performances became more common and more widespread, touring companies went the rounds of the towns that would welcome them, and subjects fanned out to the international. But American opera retained a pithy nationalism, often in a matrix of freedom of style and humor.

AMERICAN COMPOSERS

The composers working in the United States in its early decades were, for the most part, born abroad. Many were born in England. Raynor Taylor (1747–1825) was born in London, trained there, and came to the United States in 1792. His London opera, *Buxom Joan*, of 1778, was produced in Philadelphia in 1801; he composed seven others in the United States, including *The Irish Taylor: or, The Humours of the Thimble* (1796), produced in Charleston, and *The Æthiop: or, The Child of the Desert* (1814), produced in Philadelphia, and, unusually, published.[2]

Alexander Reinagle

Alexander Reinagle (1747–1809) was a Scottish-educated son of Austrian parents born in England; he emigrated to America at the age of thirty, after a long tour in Europe. He settled in Philadelphia, where he was extremely busy and was held in high esteem. He directed plays and operas, supervised the construction of the New Theatre (1793–94), and produced concerts, for which he wrote a good deal of music. He composed piano *sonatas*, violin/piano *sonatas*, incidental music to several plays, including Susanna Rowson's play *Slaves in Algiers: or, A Struggle for Freedom*, and twenty-eight operas of several types, all produced in Philadelphia, such as *Auld Robin Gray: or, Jamie's Return from America* (1795); *The Wife of Two Husbands* (1805); and *Pizarro: or, The Spaniards in Peru* ("celebrated tragedy in 5 acts"), composed with Raynor Taylor (1800).

Benjamin Carr

Benjamin Carr (1768–1831) was born and trained in London, and came to the United States in 1793, where he proved to be just the sort of energetic entrepreneur needed by the young country. He was extremely popular as both singer and composer, and was also a shopkeeper (a music store in Philadelphia, owned together with his father and brother, with later stores in Baltimore and New York), publisher (*Musical Journal*, a weekly from 1800), pianist, and organist. His career is most strongly associated with Philadelphia, but his operas (he is known to have composed only four) were produced both there and in New York. They were *The Archers: or, Mountaineers of Switzerland* (1796, produced in New York); *The Patriot: or, Liberty Obtained* (1796, produced in both Philadelphia and Baltimore); *Bourville Castle: or, The Gallic Orphan* (1797, produced in New York); and *The American in London* (1798, produced in Philadelphia). He also composed a pantomime, *Poor Jack: or, The Sailors' Return* (1795, produced in New York). In addition to his works for the theater he composed a number of instrumental and vocal works, including the *Dead March for Washington* (i.e., *funeral music*) in 1799, and a cycle of songs on poems from Sir Walter Scott's *Lady of the Lake* (1810).

sonata: a multimovement work for one or two players

funeral music: music to be played at a funeral or memorial service

▶ Recommended Recordings and Video Cassettes

Borroff, Compact Discs contains a movement from Alexander Reinagle's Sonata in D Major, a piano work from 1786.

Columbia ML 6141. *The Birth of Chamber Music in America: John Antes's Three Trios.* Antes (1740–1811) was born near Philadelphia. He made his own instruments, and wrote a group of string trios (for violin, viola, and cello) during the years 1779–1781. The performance here is romantic, rather than classical; the last (fast) movements are particularly good.

James Hewitt

program music: music that
expresses nonmusical ideas
or images

James Hewitt (1770–1827), British born and trained, emigrated to New York in 1792 and became a central figure in the cultural life of that city. He produced concerts, directed operas, and introduced American subjects into both opera and *program music* for piano. Between 1794 and 1800, he composed eight operas, including *Tammany: or, The Indian Chief* (1794), *Flash in the Pan* (1798), and *Wild Goose Chase: or, Mad Cap of Age Tomorrow* (1800). In addition, he composed such patriotic works as the piano pieces *The 4th of July: A Grand Military Sonata* and *The Battle of Trenton*. He was also active as a publisher.

Anthony Philip Heinrich

Anthony Philip Heinrich (1781–1861) was born in Bohemia, came to New York in 1810 to become a businessman, but was already trained as a violinist and pianist and eventually chose music as a profession. He moved to Kentucky in 1818, and in 1820 produced his Opus 1: *The Dawning of Music in Kentucky: or, The Pleasures of Harmony in the Solitudes of Nature*, an instrumental work. He led a restless life, traveling to Europe twice (where his music was well received), and working in many jobs: as a theater director (in Philadelphia and Louisville), orchestral violinist, and finally, in New York, as an entrepreneur (producer, publisher, composer). He was much liked: the critics called him "The Beethoven of America" (though this epithet was for his orchestral adventuresomeness, not his style), and his audiences affectionately dubbed him "Father Heinrich." He composed songs, piano works, operas, and symphonic music. The imaginative titles of his works were archly romantic: one is titled *The Wildwood Spirit's Chant, or Scintillations of "Yankee Doodle," forming a Grand National Heroic Fantasia scored for a Powerful Orchestra in 44 Parts!* His two operas were *The Child of the Mountain: or, The Deserted Mother* (1821) and *The Minstrel* (date unknown).

Heinrich's works, however quirky the titles, were well wrought; his second symphony, which he entitled *The Ornithological Combat of Kings* (1838), has been recorded and is well worth hearing. Its four movements are subtitled "Conflict of the Condor in the Air," "The Repose of the Condor," "The Combat of the Condor on Land," and "Victory of the Condor"; these suggest the usual four movements of a symphony—fast,

▶○ Recommended Recordings and Video Cassettes

Anthony Philip Heinrich's works are slowly being published in modern editions and are entering the repertoire.

New World Records 208. Heinrich, Second Symphony: *The Ornithological Combat of Kings*. Together with Gottschalk's orchestral work, *Night in the Tropics*.

Sheet-music cover of *The 4th of July: A Grand Military Sonata*, by James Hewitt. (The John Herrick Jackson Music Library, Yale University.)

slow, agitated, and majestic. The style is basically *classical*, though the work follows the almost romantic formulas of orchestration and development.

classical music: music of the late eighteenth century

THE TEACHING OF MUSIC

William Robyn

The United States continued in the apprenticeship training that was the only method of preparing professional musicians from earliest times. A good example of such a musician was William Robyn, born in Holland

viola: the standard alto string instrument

cello: the bass member of the violin family

string bass: the very low bass string instrument of the orchestra

horn: the French horn

trombone: a bass brass instrument

in 1814, emigrated to the United States in 1836. Robyn had already been trained, from the age of four, and had started teaching the piano at sixteen, held a church job as an organist, and worked also with the clarinet and the flute. When one of his patrons emigrated to the United States, he took Robyn along as tutor for his children. The trip took six weeks: they sailed to Baltimore and went via Philadelphia to Pittsburgh; there they boarded the steamboat *Niagara* and sailed via Cincinnati to St. Louis, where Robyn made his home and his career. He formed a "band" almost at once, and within a year he had formed an orchestra of two violins, a *viola*, a *cello*, a *string bass*, a flute, two clarinets, two *horns*, two trumpets, a *trombone*, and a drum, "all good musicians." This was, in fact, the beginning of the St. Louis Symphony, which is the oldest orchestra still playing today. Robyn composed quite a few works, including the *Mass in C minor* (he became organist of a Catholic church in St. Louis); *Festival Vespers, Trio for piano, violin, and cello*; songs; and piano pieces. The works, plus a substantial autobiography, are in the St. Louis Historical Society. Most of the works are undated, but they are youthful works for the most part (the trio is from his European days, dated 1829). Robyn spent many years in the service of music in St. Louis and is still honored there; he died in 1905.

Robyn was also an apprentice master, training young musicians (including his own children) as he had been trained as a boy. He did not change the tradition; he embodied it.

Lowell Mason

Another musician, Lowell Mason (1792–1872), changed it. The son of a prominent Massachusetts politician and the grandson of a singing-school master, he was trained in a singing school and then in an apprenticeship with a local organist. He became a bank clerk, but he continued his music studies with a German immigrant composer who taught him the new European style. In 1827, he accepted the position of music director of a Boston church, and soon he became the most influential music educator and director in nineteenth-century America—in fact, we still feel his influence in the teaching of music in our schools.

Mason changed the singing-school tunes to put them into the European style; and he compiled hymns, songs, and anthems in several books. They included his own works as well as those of many others. The most successful of these anthologies were the *Handel and Haydn Society's Collection of Church Music* (seventeen editions from 1822), *Lyra Sacra* (1821), and *Carmina Sacra* (twelve editions from 1841).

Mason initiated the profession of music education, which was an American idea founded both on the apprenticeship system and on the educational ideas of Johann Heinrich Pestalozzi (1746–1827), a Swiss philosopher/educator who believed in the validity of children's personalities and had amazingly modern ideas about education. Mason's introduction of music into the public schools was an American answer to tutorial education, common in Europe, but not brought into nineteenth-century America except in the wealthy East Coast families (Franklin D. Roosevelt would be the product of tutorial elementary education).

Mason wrote apprenticeship-inspired texts for the use of the young, such as *The Juvenile Psalmist* (1829); but he also wrote a methods text that was the pioneer work of elementary and high school music education, equating vocal music with elementary education and instrumental music with advanced study. This dichotomy was, in fact, the old division of the amateur (trained in tutorials on the trivium), the scientist of music (trained in the university on the quadrivium—Harvard University at this time was still using the writings of the sixth-century philosopher Boethius as their music text), and the professional (trained in apprenticeship). What Mason accomplished was the bringing of apprenticeship methods into the school work that was replacing the tutorials of Europe. His methods book was seminal. Its title reflected the basis of Mason's ideas: *Manual of the Boston Academy of Music, for Instruction in the Elements of Vocal Music, on the System of Pestalozzi* (1834).

The importance of Mason's work is difficult for us, in the twentieth century, to grasp. For one thing, education in apprenticeship was a freely ranging personal interaction between master and apprentice, while nineteenth-century schools were extremely strict and students were severely disciplined. School teachers came from the colleges, where students were already mature at matriculation; the apprentice master began work with young children, typically five or six years of age in most professions, but more often three or four years of age in music. The teacher was thus seldom prepared to face the young, but tended to see children as miniature adults; the apprentice master not only saw children as children, but knew what children could absorb and how they could best absorb it. The bringing of apprenticeship methods into music in the schools often gave the children the most humane, warm, and relevant encounters of their school lives.

BANDS

From the eighteenth century, bands in America were a special strength: suited to the out-of-doors and to the American temperament, versatile, and characterized by a clarity and an energy that no other musical medium could muster. Bands provided dignity at civic and state occasions, excitement at parades, and an ideal force for social occasions, for listening and, perhaps more important, for dancing. Throughout our history, the United States has fostered the world's best bands, and, along with them, some of the most marvelous music ever written.

brass instrument: instruments made of brass, using a mouthpiece instead of a reed

brass band: a band made entirely of brass instruments (no woodwinds and usually no percussions)

reed instrument: an instrument sounded by the use of reeds

woodwind: an orchestral instrument (originally of wood) played by the breath

Development of something like the modern band had its beginnings early in the nineteenth century. There were already two kinds of groups: the one basically military and associated with marching, and, later, with park concerts; the other basically social, a more intimate group associated with dancing, and even with singing.

Military Bands

The military band in other countries was often based in (or even limited to) *brass instruments*. The British armies, for example, used *brass bands*; brass instruments are safer to carry into the field than *reed instruments*. The oboe double reed is difficult to keep in playable condition; the bassoon is too cumbersome to make a good field instrument, while having also a double reed and thus problems similar to the oboe's; the clarinet is safer, but still requires a single reed in good condition. The flute is the safest of the *woodwind* group, but the standard flute is a bit

"OUR COUNTRY IS SAFE"

T. Moore's Lith. Boston.

THE BERRY STREET RANGERS
QUICK STEP.

"The Berry Street Rangers," performed by the **Boston Brigade Band, 1837.** (The Newberry Library.)

too large for comfort in the field, and the smaller flutes, notably the *piccolo* and the fife, were the mainstay of military bands. The small flutes were also higher in pitch, more piercing in tone than the delicate normal flute, and were suitable in the field for that reason as well. The fife-and-drum corps was a military "natural."

piccolo: a flute higher than the soprano

The clarinet became tremendously popular quite early in its development in the second half of the eighteenth century, and it was very useful indeed to early Americans. It was perhaps the most versatile of the woodwinds, with the ability to play quite softly and sweetly and also quite loudly and dramatically; it also had the largest range of any of the wind instruments. So, the clarinet became the mainstay of American bands.

Wars required the expansion of army bands, not only for field maneuvers but also for parades and special events—and for recruitment. The War of 1812 is a good example of this expansion, and the importance of New Orleans in that conflict makes that city a good example.

The Louisiana militia, led by Andrew Jackson (who would become the seventh president in 1829) was called into the army for the defense of New Orleans against the British in 1814. There were two large bands in the militia. The famous one was made up of black players from the two battalions that consisted of "Men of Color," most of them Creoles (born in New Orleans of mixed African with French or Spanish ancestry). The First Battalion of Free Men of Color, as it was called, consisted of 353 men, in six companies, each commanded by one of their own, with the rank of captain—but the battalion as an entirety was under the leadership of a white major. The band of the First Battalion was the most well-known band of the war.

By regulation of the War Department, every unit was given a fife-and-drum corps, which gave the field signals necessary for fighting groups. Payrolls show the payment of nine dollars a month to a "musician" and eleven dollars a month to a "senior musician." The band was an expanded group and consisted of nine players, probably pairs of clarinets, horns, and bassoons, possibly oboes (or perhaps an extra clarinet or even an extra pair instead) or a fife (or piccolo) and/or a drum.[3]

The band had a lot to do. An important function was that of playing at ceremonies, including those in connection with Jackson's arrival in New Orleans on December 2, 1814. They were also important in recruitment and recreation. Also, bands were expected to play for the dances attended by soldiers, and in New Orleans dances were "epidemic";[4] over eighty dance halls would be established in that city by 1841. Interestingly, the visit of Jackson to New Orleans was commemorated for many years afterward by an annual ball. At any rate, the sound at New Orleans was described as joyful, when "the different military bands pealed forth their most animating strains."[5]

One of the band members, Michel Debergue (1795–1865), a wealthy cabinet maker who owned considerable property (including slaves), was

Kent bugle: a bugle with keys

bugle: a brass instrument like a trumpet but without valves

range: the extent of a melody in low and high pitches

a member of a prominent musical family: his brother became an orchestra conductor and a teacher of music. Another member, Louis Hazeur (c. 1792–1860), produced musical descendants: two of his grandsons became well-known clarinetists, and one great-grandson, Lorenzo Tio, Jr., also a clarinetist, would take that instrument into jazz.[6]

One of the happy postwar happenstances was that band instruments, no longer needed in such numbers by the military, were for sale second-hand and cheap. In addition, many men who were mustered out had sharpened musical skills—or even acquired them—during military service. Thus in postwar days bands were founded and musical careers were determined.

Frank Johnson

Francis (Frank) Johnson, a black musician born in Philadelphia in 1792, became the most famous bandsman in the United States, after his service as a musician in the War of 1812. Johnson was already a virtuoso on the *Kent*, or keyed, *bugle*; he was also a composer. He founded a band after the war, a concert band (a new idea) that was racially integrated; and he became a triple-threat man: conducting, playing solos, and composing.

In 1825, the cornet was invented. This instrument was similar to both the trumpet and the bugle: it had the *range* and control of the trumpet, but responded more easily and had a warmer tone quality. The cornet became the most popular instrument in park concerts, those outdoor festivals of small-town America (and big-city America as well—but the park concerts had little competition in the small towns) that were the mainstay of public entertainment for so many decades. The town gazebo would be the focus of family entertainment: political speeches, Fourth-of-July picnics, and promenade concerts (during which the audience could stroll around the area of the band). These concerts were given impetus in the band heyday following the War of 1812, and the American love of the band was confirmed.

Johnson switched his virtuoso life to the cornet in 1825 and he became the most famous cornet star in the country. He continued with his band and with his composing; he left over three hundred works: in addition

Cornet. The cornet was the most popular nineteenth-century band instrument.

▶◯ Recommended Recordings and Video Cassettes

Finally, we are getting to hear some of Francis Johnson's music, though recordings are still rare.

Music Masters 7029-2-C. *The Music of Francis Johnson and His Contemporaries.* Contains 22 concert marches and dances.

Borroff, Compact Discs contain the *Voice Quadrille* of Francis Johnson.

Newport Classic NPD 85516. *Listen to the Mocking Bird.* Band music played on instruments of the period.

**"The American Boy,"
by Francis Johnson.**
(The Library of Congress.)

to music for band and for solo cornet, he composed many songs, piano pieces, and dance pieces for the smaller band ensembles. His group was so famous that he was invited to bring them to England to be part of the festivities attendant to the coronation of Queen Victoria in 1838 (the only other group invited was that of Johann Strauss of Vienna).

America had defined her art and was coming into her own.

NOTES

1. James J. Fuld, *The Book of World-Famous Music* (New York: Crown Publishers, 1966), p. 481.
2. Edith Borroff, *American Operas: A Checklist*, Detroit Studies in Music Bibliography, no. 69 (Warren, Michigan: Harmonie Park Press, 1992), gives a comprehensive listing of operas by American composers.
3. Charles E. Kinzer, "The Band of Music of the First Battalion of Free Men of Color," *American Music*, vol. 10, no. 3 (Fall 1992), pp. 348–69. All of the information on this group comes from this excellent source.
4. Henry Kmen, *Music in New Orleans: The Formative Years, 1791–1841* (Baton Rouge, LA: Louisiana State University Press, 1966), pp. 1–41.
5. Ibid, p. 248.
6. Kinzer, "First Battalion," pp. 358–60.

BIBLIOGRAPHY

Benton, Rita. "The Early Piano in the U.S." *Music, Libraries, and Instruments.* Edited by Unity Sherrington and Guy Oldham. London: Hinrichsen Edition, 1961.

Borroff, Edith. *American Operas: A Checklist.* Detroit Studies in Music Bibliography, no. 69. Warren, MI: Harmonie Park Press, 1992.

Carson, Gerald. "The Piano in the Parlor." *American Heritage*: 17 (December, 1965).

Fuld, James J., *The Book of World-Famous Music.* New York: Crown Publishers, 1968.

Havighurst, Walter. *Land of the Long Horizons.* New York: Coward-McCann, 1960.

Kinzer, Charles E. "The Band of Music of the First Battalion of Free Men of Color," *American Music*, vol. 10, no. 3 (Fall 1992).

Kmen, Henry. *Music in New Orleans: The Formative Years, 1791–1841.* Baton Rouge: Louisiana State University Press, 1968.

Kull, Irving S. and Nell M. *A Short Chronology of American History, 1492–1950.* New Brunswick, NJ: Rutgers University Press, 1952.

Murphy, Jeanette R. "African Music in the United States." *Popular Science Monthly*, September, 1899.

Ritter, Frederic Louis. *Music in America.* New York: Charles Scribner's Sons, 1883.

3

A Nation Struggling
for Maturity
(1840 to 1880)

In the United States the years until about 1840 had been spent working out the final forms of government, creating what amounted to a national identity. The presidents had been men who understood the original impetus toward nationhood, toward the establishment of the first genuine democracy, toward the maintaining of a viable international stance.

The next forty years, from about 1840 to about 1880, were very different. The goal was, of course, the same: continuing to define a national identity, now in quite a different context, of national expansion and international imperialism. Two concerns were uppermost in the minds of Americans at the midpoint of the nineteenth century.

The first was westward expansion, the "manifest destiny" of a nation.[1] That nation's lands would eventually go from the Atlantic to the Pacific, "from sea to shining sea."[2]

In 1841, the first wagon train, of forty-eight wagons, headed for California via the Oregon Trail, and by the end of the decade gold had been discovered in that territory. But expansion was hardly limited to the California area: the states that were added to the nation between 1840 and 1880 began with consolidation of adjacent territories and then reached over the near West to the Far West.

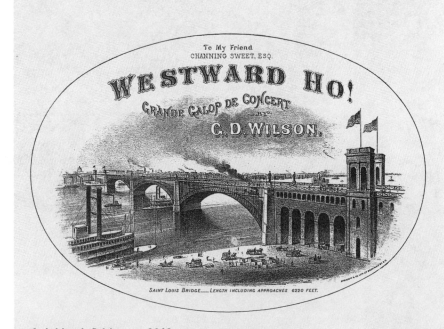

Saint Louis Bridge, c. 1860. (The Newberry Library.)

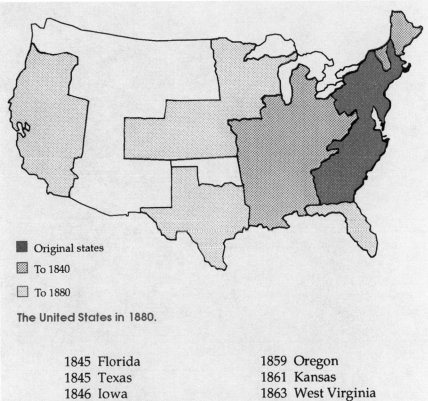

Original states
To 1840
To 1880

The United States in 1880.

1845 Florida	1859 Oregon
1845 Texas	1861 Kansas
1846 Iowa	1863 West Virginia
1848 Wisconsin	1864 Nevada
1850 California	1867 Nebraska
1858 Minnesota	1876 Colorado

The high point of the western expansion was probably in 1869, with the celebration, in Utah, of pounding in the golden spike that joined the Central Pacific and Union Pacific Railroads and completed the making of tracks from the East Coast to the West Coast. The annexation of Texas had caused a three-year war with Mexico (1846–48) and, of course, every opening up of new territory meant war—political or military—with the Indian tribes of the continent.

But the western movement was a national obsession, and in certain ways even an international one. The novels of James Fenimore Cooper (1789–1851) were the top draw of the mid-century in Europe, and Alexis de Tocqueville had published his keen observances of the new nation in his blockbuster *Democracy in America* in 1835. The idea, the adventure, the hope offered by the western expansion was a great unifying factor in the country.

But the second concern was so hugely disunifying that it led to

Bloomer Girl, 1850. (The Newberry Library.)

the great War Between the States and to the terrible question of whether or not the nation could survive. This was the problem of slavery. By 1836, over five hundred abolitionist societies had existed in the northern states, and the northern opposition to the practice of slavery grew from that point to galvanic proportions. The War for Bleeding Kansas (1854–58), the furor over the Dred Scott decision (1857), and, the final blow, the secession of South Carolina (1860) made war inevitable. From 1861 to 1865, the country was deep in the most horrendous of conflicts, a period of death and destruction surpassing that of any other war in which the United States has been involved.

The presidents of these forty years were opposite numbers to the statesmen of the Revolution that had preceded them. The issue of slavery in the territories (and hence in the new states) was the controversy that brought the two national concerns together and made the consideration of one automatically involve the other. All of the pre-Civil War presidents were engulfed in these issues: William Henry Harrison, nationalistic in his outlook, but who died of pneumonia one month after taking office in 1841; John Tyler (1841–45), a strict constructionist with Whig and later southern states-righter support; James K. Polk (1845–49), whose Manifest Destiny acquisitions enlarged the quarrel over the expansion of slavery; Zachary Taylor (1848–50), whose solution to the question of slavery in the territories ignored both the northern dislike of the

1840 Campaign song for the Whig ticket of William Henry (Tip) Harrison and John Tyler. (The Newberry Library.)

The Fort Sumter flag, 1861.

slave market in the District of Columbia and the southern demands for a stronger fugitive slave law; Millard Fillmore (1850–53), who signed the Fugitive Slave Act; Franklin Pierce (1853–57), who supported the Kansas–Nebraska Act, which reopened the question of slavery in the West, and James Buchanan (1857–61), the only president who never married, who urged the admission of Kansas as a slave state.

Abraham Lincoln (1861–65) was the president whose term almost exactly coincided with the war years—the Civil War ended at Appomattox on April 9, 1865, and he was assassinated on April 14. It was Lincoln's aim to preserve the Union; in pursuit of this goal he issued the Emancipation Proclamation, which forever changed the character of the nation.

The nation was not ready to accept the reality of Lincoln's Union, and the problems which arose from the reconstruction of the South occupied the postwar presidents: Andrew Johnson (1865–69), whose conciliatory policies regarding the South during the initial years of Reconstruction were ruthlessly attacked by the Radical Republicans; Ulysses S. Grant (1869–77), who allowed radical Reconstruction to run its course, bolstering it with military force; Rutherford B. Hayes (1877–81), the first president elected without winning the popular vote; and James A. Garfield (1881), who was assassinated after four months in office. All faced a nation licking its wounds and not ready to get down to business. Their successors would oversee that.

The presidents of this forty-year period make an interesting group: all but Lincoln and Grant were one-term presidents, and Grant was the only one of that period to serve two terms (Lincoln served only one month of his second term). And Garfield was the last of the presidents born in a log cabin of pioneer stock.

MUSIC ON THE FRONTIER

Cowboy Songs

The music of those forty years reflected the central national concerns. It was the era of the western song, which was a setting forth of both the exhilarating exploration and the lonely life of the ranchers who forged their lives on the huge spreads in the new territories, particularly of the workers who tended the herds on the prairies, shepherds of modern days, called "cowhands" or "cowboys." One of the most beloved of these songs was "Home on the Range," a Kansas song of 1872 or 1873, and now the state song of Kansas. Such songs as "Git Along, Little Dogies" talked of the cowboy life, and other songs such as "Oh Bury Me Not on the Lone Prairie" (from the 1850s—it is also known as "The Dying Cowboy") spoke of the loneliness. It is difficult to know the dates of many of these songs. They were eventually collected by poets and singers and scholars, when the literature began to fade and it was feared they might be lost. "Oh Bury Me Not on the Lone Prairie" was collected by John A. Lomax and published in a volume of *Cowboy Songs* in 1910. The cowboy songs were beloved of the American people, and they continued to be written—and still are written. About the time of the publication of the Lomax collection, for example, an American student, Zo Elliott, composed a western ballad for a fraternity banquet; he later went to England, and the song was published there in 1914—it was "There's a Long, Long Trail."

Canal, Railroad, and Mining Songs

Another result of the westward expansion was the popularity of canal and railroad songs. An early song, "The Erie Canal" reminds us that boats were led along the waters of the canal by mules. Probably the most famous was "She'll Be Comin' Round the Mountain When She Comes," an oldie collected by Carl Sandburg in *The American Songbag* (published in 1927).

The hard-working miners had their musical say as well, in such songs as the popular "Clementine," first known in 1863, but not published until 1884 with the attribution "words and music by Percy Montrose," an attribution doubted by some.[3]

▶◯ Recommended Recordings and Video Cassettes

Mid-nineteenth-century American music is easier to find on records than is the earlier American music, but authentic folk music is still difficult. Probably the best set is the Smithsonian Institution's collection, which is large (4 CDs), but is worth the investment. It contains over ninety items and comes with a "companion book." It deals essentially with the twentieth-century revival of interest in earlier folk music, but of course, no recordings were made in those early days.

Library of Congress 046 21489. *Folk Song America: A 20th Century Revival.* Another collection, more limited, but excellent, features folk songs and ballads.

Heritage Recordings AHR 009 (cassette). *Folksongs and Ballads, Volume 3.* Includes Civil War material and a Primitive Baptist hymn, along with songs on texts from *McGuffey's Reader.*

Fiddle Tunes

And the hoedowns continued. Everywhere that farmers farmed, fiddlers fiddled. Collections of fiddle tunes (most of them anonymous) are found in contemporary manuscripts; the manuscript book of James Gray, who came to Iowa territory from England, contains several anonymous tunes, including "Pleasures of the Town" and "The Devil among the Tailors."[4] Modern collections frequently include recordings of old fiddlers playing the traditional tunes, making history come alive with greater zest than the manuscripts can.

Songs of the Territories

The founding of new territories gave rise to music too, and many an old song gives tribute either to the territory or to the new state. "The Yellow Rose of Texas," first published in 1858, is an excellent example: it would

Concert Hall, Central City, Colorado, 1872. (Western History Department, The Denver Public Library.)

▶️ Recommended Recordings and Video Cassettes

Recordings of Civil War music are helpful not so much as wartime statements as for music that so incorporated the ideals of the day that it could be presented in support of wartime sentiments for a whole nation. New World Records features some useful items:

New World Records 202. *Songs of the Civil War.*

New World Records 202-2. *Songs of the Civil War.* Includes a narration by Tony Randall.

New World Records 80252-2. *Roots of the Blues.*

be a fighting song in the Civil War. Of course, many songs paid tribute to the conviction of both northerners and southerners, from "John Brown's Body" to "Dixie." The first had a fascinating history: known originally in 1858 as "Say, Brothers, Will You Meet Us?" it then became a Methodist hymn, as "Glory, Glory, Hallelujah," in 1859; and only after the firing upon Fort Sumter in 1861 was it joined to the poem written in that year by Julia Ward Howe and published in its final form in 1862. "Dixie" is equally interesting; it was written (words and music) by the violinist/director/composer Daniel Emmett (1815–1904), sung and danced by him in New York City in a performance with Bryant's Minstrels. The song, billed as "Dixie's Land," was used occasionally for the first year; then it caught on and was used from October, 1862, as Emmett's finale. It became so popular that it was issued by four publishers.[5]

URBAN MUSIC

Music in the cities was highly developed and multifarious. Between 1840 and 1880, more and more cities began to maintain an active, exciting musical life in the United States. There were, almost from the beginning, two main camps of musical awareness, musical predilection, and musical practicality. The first, and by far the richest, was that of American music, music developed by citizens of the New World for their own enlargement and daily pleasure; this was essentially a classical music in the historical sense, that is, music as practiced in the second half of the eighteenth century. It was characterized by clarity, melodic inventiveness, rhythmic interest, and a light, energized performance style, with harmony a servant of these dominant elements. The second, the more powerful politically, was that of European music transplanted to the New World; this was the art of music almost as a moral imperative, seen in romantic (rather than classical) terms. Romantic music, on the contrary, was characterized by grandeur of sound, harmonic inven-

Public Dance, 1852. (The Newberry Library.)

tiveness and strength, with rhythm, melody, and performance style all servants of that harmonic grandeur and strength.

The difference was not merely a scholar's definition: it was the very life of music. The first camp took music as a joy, as an entertainment (which means, something that holds one's attention entirely); the second took music with an almost religious seriousness. The entrepreneurs of the first said, "Come! You will be delighted! It will make your day!"; the preachers of the second said, "This is a holy grail! Enter its presence with trepidation and wonder!" The first of these musical genres could be heard anywhere: in a home, in a theater, at a park gazebo; the second would be heard in a concert hall or an opera house. The performers, the sponsors, the composers, the audiences would be different. But it was the nature of the first to be open-minded and to welcome the second; of the second to be exclusionary and to deplore the first. The first was finally called "popular" music, because people liked it; the second was called "classical" or "scientific" music. In 1843, *Dwight's Journal of Music*, a proponent of the second, deplored the mixing of the two, of "the classical with the frivolous; Beethoven, Mozart and Weber with Nini and Donizetti!"[6] In 1861, the same journal recognized that most people could not "find enjoyment in what some people sneeringly call 'classical' or 'scientific' music. We almost wish those terms had never been employed."[7]

But music in the parlor, or, as we would now call it, the living room, often included music of the second category, in addition to music that we in retrospect call "popular." Most young ladies, and many gentlemen, became singers or pianists (and many became both), and they performed European classical music alongside the American music they loved, and saw no contradiction at all.

Family Life, 1859. (The Newberry Library.)

Many songbooks were published for these amateurs. Some, like the *Song Book for the Million* (1848) contained texts only; others contained the music, too. The latter type included *The Forget-Me-Not Psalter* (from the 1850s), which concentrated on old songs, and *Catharine Hayes Swan of Erin Songster* (1851), which focused on new ones.[8] Humor was part and parcel of the musical art: in 1858, J. W. Turner (and others) issued *100*

"Rink Waltz" cover, 1868. (The Newberry Library.)

Comic Songs. There were many song books of many types published throughout the century, and they contained music from many sources: English, Irish, and Scottish songs, tried-and-true opera arias (including many names that we associate with "classical" music, like Donizetti in the middle of the century and Verdi at the end), new American songs (lyrical and theatrical), and, of course, songs that we now know but cannot date—but we can be sure that they were already well known when they were chosen for the books.

ELOCUTION

Many songs were written for a type of performance that we no longer have. There was in those early days training not only in music, in singing and playing of instruments (particularly the piano, the harp, and the flute), but also in an art known as *elocution*. In this art young people were taught to recite. The performance style was called "dramatic recitation"; it could be of Biblical texts, of poetry, or even of short short stories (anecdotes, we might call them), often written for elocution recitals. For there were indeed elocution recitals, just as there were music recitals, piano recitals by the students of a certain piano teacher, elocution recitals by the students of a certain elocution teacher, and often joint recitals of recitations and piano pieces, when teachers teamed up or had many students in common. [The elocution lessons remained until about 1940: I took part in more than one elocution recital as a child, reciting—among other items—John Greenleaf Whittier's "Barbara Frietchie," a poetic account of a Civil War incident (Whittier's book *Snowbound* was published in 1866), while other children recited the Twenty-Third Psalm and the Gettysburg Address. In 1992, I was invited to recite Clement C. Moore's "The Night Before Christmas" at a student recital at the State University of New York at Binghamton (now Binghamton University), where I was teaching, and used the old elocution style of recitation—and caused no little comment, since that style was by then a thing of the past!]

▶ Recommended Recordings and Video Cassettes

Little remains of the elocution recital. But the film Anne of Green Gables *contains part of an elocution recital, in which Anne recites the poem "The Highwayman" by Alfred Noyes.*

Walt Disney Home Video 642. *Anne of Green Gables* (1985 videocassette). The film takes place on Prince Edward Island, Canada, at the turn of the century, but the elocution recital is the same as one would have been in the United States. The recital takes place towards the end of the film.

Ballads and Story Songs

duet: a piece of music for two performers

dramatic song: a song that is acted as much as sung

group concert: a concert given by a group of singers, rather than one soloist

The singing of ballads and story songs, comic and character songs, was of course a special skill, a mixture of elocution and music, in which the singer was also an actor. The British entrepreneur Charles Dibdin (1745–1814) was called an "actor-singer";[9] that tradition was carried forth by such performers as Henry Russell (1812–1900), who was born in England, studied with Rossini in Italy, then came to Rochester, New York as an organist, but soon went into a performing career, over the years singing as many as eight hundred of his own songs. The most famous was "Woodman! Spare that Tree!," written in 1837.

Duet Singing

The nineteenth century was also a period of *duet* singing, and the *dramatic song*, of course, was particularly suited to performance by two singers, who could act out special songs written as dialogues. And one person could also act out two (or more) parts in a story song. Many duet story songs were presented to nineteenth-century audiences in both Europe and America; some were extended and were called farces— Arthur Sullivan (1842–1900) began his theatrical career with the farce *Cox and Box*, done in London in 1867 and in New York in 1875. The British farce may have preceded the American, but the American story and dialogue songs were particularly popular and could hit the national character with a force that purely musical songs lacked. On the other hand, although such dialogues could be sung at home and in amateur concerts, they demanded the skill of professional performance and were done most often in group concerts.

GROUP CONCERTS

The *group concert* was a phenomenon of the nineteenth century. In New York City in the decade of the 1840s, no fewer than twenty-seven singing groups were featured in concerts, of which the most famous was probably The Hutchinson Family Singers, originally from New Hampshire; three young men and a young woman made up the group, which was initially called The Aeolian Vocalists. They patterned their performances on those of Henry Russell: each member took on a character and sang story songs suited to that personification, but they also sang duets, trios, and quartets. They provided a variety of sounds and a variety of moods, and they proved immensely successful, touring in Europe as well as in the United States, and appearing in New York and other cities with regularity. Their personal appeal lay in their New

THE OLD GRANITE STATE,

A SONG,

Price 30 Cts Net

COMPOSED, ARRANGED AND SUNG BY

THE HUTCHINSON FAMILY.

First-edition sheet-music cover of the Hutchinson Family's theme song, "The Old Granite State," set to the revivalist tune, "The Old Church Yard." (Music Division, The New York Public Library.)

England speech, and they cashed in on that by ending their concerts with a brisk rendition of "The Old Granite State."

Other groups were various, but ranged from four to six members, and the "Family" concept was so widespread that they became known as "singing families." Many had specializations, such as the Bohannan Family "Mountain Vocalists" (who yodeled, as did the Hauser Family Tyrolean Alpine Singers) and the Raymond Family, who put on a show called "An Hour in Ireland."

Family groups were so successful that they were parodied relentlessly; as early as 1846, there appeared in New York City a group called The Unrelated Family (made up of four unrelated members of the Palmo

minstrel show: a musical show based on plantation entertainment

clog dance: a tap dance

tap dancing: dancing with metal tabs (taps) on the shoes to emphasize rhythms

ballad: a story song

Ethiopian song: a song in the African tradition

bones: two animal ribs held in one hand and clacked together

tambourine: a small open drum with mirlitons of circular metal disks

Burlesque Opera Company) which presented a parody that included takeoffs of both Henry Russell and the Hutchinson Family—they called the program a "Grand Burlesque Musical Soiree."[10] A humorous musical commentary on a humorous musical act is parody indeed!

THE MINSTREL SHOW

But the most successful of all mid-century American entertainments was the *minstrel show*. This type of production began to enter northern theaters about 1840, when Thomas Dartmouth Rice (1808–60) appeared in New York. The beginnings of this type of entertainment are lost in the past, but it is known that plantation slaves, not permitted to work on Sundays, put on shows that attracted huge amounts of attention and brought people from miles around to watch. They sang together and they danced together; they chanted their own songs, both lyrical and story songs, solo and chorus, and they danced alone, generally the *clog dance* (which has come down to us as *tap dancing*).

History leaves us little knowledge of these plantation shows, but we know that they must have been exciting and genuine. Imitation of these entertainments was based on their excellence, but soon became perversions of the splendid originals. Performers like Rice put on blackface and used the black musical idioms in their music. Rice wrote a great many comic scenes and sentimental *ballads*. These pieces were called *Ethiopian songs*. The entertainments were called *minstrel shows*. They featured parodies of the plantation events as well as imitations of them, increasingly so as time passed. Such stock characters as Jim Crow and Zip Coon might have begun as genial parodies, but they would soon become cruel ones.

By 1850, over two dozen minstrel companies had appeared in New York City and were touring the country. The most famous were the Christy Minstrels, the Virginia Minstrels, and the Ethiopian Serenaders.

The minstrel show was an American entertainment, but it was solidly based on the classical concepts of African music, mixed with foreign ideas, mostly British. The banjo, *bones*, and *tambourine*, which were used in the minstrel show, were truly African and had not been comic at first. The dialect was patterned on the pidgin English that had been used in the play *Robinson Crusoe and Harlequin Friday*, produced in London in 1786, and the "Negro type" was a variation on the traditional Irish buffoon. In the British play *The Triumphs of Love* (1795), which was brought to the United States and popularized here, an Irish comic role was switched, as written, to blackface.[11] In 1799, there was a revival in Boston of the old play *Oroonoko* (1695), by the British playwright Thomas Southerne (1660–1746). The play listed an "African prince" in its cast of

The stock character Jim Crow, as depicted in an American lithograph, c. 1830. (Picture Collection, The Branch Libraries, The New York Public Library.)

The showboat *Cotton Blossom*, docked at Cincinnati. (The Ohio Historical Society.)

characters, and for the revival, a new song, "The Gay Negro Boy," was interpolated and performed in blackface to a banjo. In addition, the blackface comic performances of Rice, particularly the "plantation songs and dances" (including the *shuffle*), popularized "Ethiopian" music and was probably the direct antecedent of the minstrel show.

In 1843, Daniel Emmett produced an "Ethiopian concert" with what he advertised as "the novel, grotesque, original and surpassingly melodious Ethiopian Band, entitled the Virginia Minstrels."[12] The group, which was four in number, played the fiddle, banjo, bones, and tambourine; they sat with the violin and banjo in the middle and the percussions on the side. They dressed in tattered costumes and were in blackface, and they introduced comic dialogue, acted out ballads, and danced in a parody of what they called plantation style.

By the mid-1840s, the minstrel show was the most popular entertainment in the United States. Large cities had permanent companies as well as those coming through on tour, while people in the outlying areas could come to the city or wait for a company to come through. The towns along the waterways, chiefly the Ohio and Mississippi Rivers, could count on the yearly showboat, which docked in town and called the people with trumpets and drums. (These boats provided also a circus, regular concerts, plays, and variety shows. In addition, they generally housed a small museum.)

It was in its formality and its beautifully balanced structure that the minstrel show was strongly linked to the African heritage. This heritage, in addition to working within a line of performers, often in a semicircle (as the minstrels sat), was concerned with spatial and *antiphonal* ele-

shuffle: a dance in which the feet are shuffled along the floor

antiphony: the sounding of music by two groups set apart in space

▶○ Recommended Recordings and Video Cassettes

The beauty of the original minstrel-show concept was entirely lost in its expansion and exploitation later in the nineteenth century and into the twentieth. It is much better to read descriptions of its classical form than to listen to or view present corrupt later versions.

interlocutor: the master of ceremonies of a minstrel show

first part: the first half of a minstrel show, featuring single acts and dialogues

olio: the second part of a minstrel show, featuring variety acts

variety show: a show of various acts

soft-shoe dancing: tap-style dancing without taps on the shoes

grand finale: the big final part of a show

general ruckus: the grand finale of the minstrel show, including the dance for the whole company; also called *walkaround*

afterpiece: a short section added to the end of a stage presentation

ments, along with a mix of sounds, of vocal and instrumental, of melodic and percussion music.

Form

In form the minstrel show was classically African as well. The form was aesthetically pure and deeply satisfying. The show began with a grand entrance of the entire ensemble, dressed elegantly in swallowtail coats. They were all in blackface (including black performers), except the master of ceremonies, called the *interlocutor*, who was in whiteface. After the opening chorus, during which the group formed a semicircle, the dignified interlocutor intoned, "Gentlemen, be seated!" and the show was underway. The interlocutor was the middleman of the semicircle. The two end men were Mr. Tambo and Mr. Bones, who, respectively, played the tambourine and bones, both percussion instruments. The other four members, called middlemen, were varying, but they sang and played melodic instruments rather than percussion; they varied even in the same show, perhaps fiddling or picking the banjo, and then later, singing.

In the *first part* the interlocutor would engage the linemen in (often humorous) dialogue, dividing his attention between the players to his right and to his left by alternation (never both at once). Some simple musical numbers were included.

The *olio*, or second part, was a *variety show* that featured bigger acts, such as quartet singing, *soft shoe* and clog dancing, acrobatic acts, and skits (often parodies of popular plays or Italian operas), a sketch (the comic dialogue "Reuben, Reuben, I've Been Thinking," of 1871, was one), or perhaps a plantation festival (Emmett's "Dixie" was one). The second part was based in music as the first part was based in comic dialogue. The varying performers moved occasionally in the second part, even dancing (particularly clog dancing), doing solos and duets more complex musically than the numbers in the first part. The end of the second part was a *grand finale* called the *general ruckus* or *walkround*, in which even the end men moved, and which involved everyone but the interlocutor. Sometimes after the walkaround, a one-act *afterpiece* would be presented with an intermission during which instrumentalists played and the scene was set. It was, in fact, as an afterpiece that Sullivan's *Cox and Box* was presented.

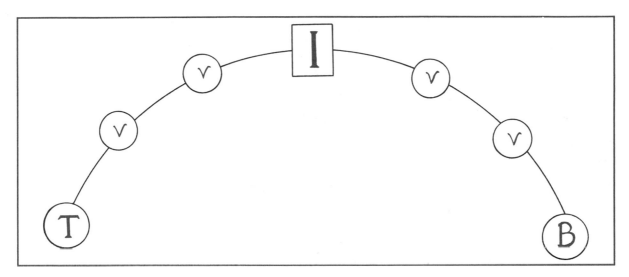

The classical minstrel-show line. I = Interlocutor, T = Mr. Tambo, B = Mr. Bones, v = varying members.

Thus, the classical minstrel show was a crescendo of activity: speech to song, song to dance, dance to parade and group finale.

Stephen Foster

Christy's Minstrels were perhaps the most popular of the New York troupes. Organized by Edwin Pierce (E. P.) Christy, they played in that city from 1846 to 1857; in 1853, Pierce began a second company in Philadelphia that would be in residence there for over seventy-five years. Most important, Christy connected with a young composer named Stephen Foster (1826–64), from Pittsburgh, who, at twenty listened to the black stevedores at the Pittsburgh levee and, with a servant, attended black church services. By 1849, with his song "Susanna," he became well-known (the song became popular with the gold rushers),

Christy's Minstrel's version of Stephen Foster's "My Old Kentucky Home."
(Picture Collection, The Branch Libraries, The New York Public Library.)

▶○ Recommended Recordings and Video Cassettes

Stephen Foster's music is generally performed in new and inflated arrangements, and is sung in the romantic style that was never Foster's intention. But they are still worth hearing.

Vox/Turnabout CT-4609. *Greg Smith Singers*, the New York Vocal Arts Ensemble.

University of Pittsburgh Stephen Foster Memorial. Cassette of Foster's music, by The Dear Friends, Jean Thomas, conductor. "Camptown Races," from this cassette, is included in Borroff, Compact Discs. This is undoubtedly the most authentic Foster sound available.

A romanticized painting depicting Stephen Foster, by Howard Chandler Christy. (Picture Collection, The Branch Libraries, The New York Public Library.)

and three years later, he wrote to Christy that he wanted to become "the best Ethiopian song-writer."[13] Foster's "Old Folks at Home" (1851) would become the most popular of all plantation melodies, with several others, such as "Camptown Races" (1849) and "My Old Kentucky Home" (1852), not far behind.

What made Stephen Foster's work so highly valued by his contemporaries was analyzed in an article in the *Atlantic Monthly* magazine of 1867.[14] Foster's songs, the article said, did not stoop to the caricatures so often found, even in the 1860s, in minstrel shows; his music "teemed with a nobler significance. It dealt, in its simplicity, with universal sympathies, and taught us all to feel with the slaves the lowly joys and sorrows it celebrated." The author felt that a debt of gratitude for this was owed to Foster; and time has validated this early appraisal.

LATER DEVELOPMENTS

But by 1870, the minstrel show was facing the greatest competition it could have: girls! On the legitimate stage, girls, dressed daringly in tights, danced the cancan and the ballet. And in *The Black Crook*, a musical extravaganza that opened in 1866 in New York (in a theater rebuilt for the production), they flew through the air on guy wires. The musical combined a German romantic story (related to Goethe's *Faust*) of an alchemist who sells his soul to the devil, with a French ballet. It was so popular that it ran for a year and a half in New York and then was on the road for over forty years after that.

Then there were the British Blondes, a troupe of variety artistes specializing in *burlesque* (parody), who arrived in 1869. A critic wrote, "It is impossible to give an idea of this sustained burlesque. It resembles an Irish stew as one minute they are dancing a cancan and the next singing a psalm tune. It is a bewilderment of limbs, belladonna and grease paint."[15] The public was faced with a moral question. Another critic summed up the dilemma and the American attitude: "The propriety of visiting the Blondes is a question which each individual must decide for himself. The number of individuals who have decided this question, by the way, is something astonishing."[16]

The variety show also was expanding to compete with the minstrel show. Formerly, the variety show had been a beer-hall entertainment for men only, with a few songs and dances to a honky-tonk saloon piano and a few girls to perform and act as hostesses. But by the end of the century, this entertainment was developing in three separate directions.

First was the parody minstrel show, which used girls instead of men. In 1869, Mme. Rentz's Female Minstrels appeared, and soon the producer began to present a new edition every year. The first part and the walk-around became girl shows and the comedy-centered olio continued as variety acts, with an occasional "added attraction." This variation of the minstrel show was to become the modern burlesque.

The second direction of the saloon show was the variety show as we know it: *vaudeville*. In the 1870s, saloon entertainment had been growing not only in scope but also in the degree of obscenity in its dialogue. Then, in 1881, one of the beer-hall managers, Tony Pastor, opened a "clean" show, with eight acts (or *turns*) of comedy, song, dance, acrobatics, and a female impersonator—in other words, an olio. The success of this venture was immediate. A special theater was built to house it, and by 1890, vaudeville would be firmly established on the American scene. Each show had an average of fifteen turns, including jugglers, knife throwers, contortionists, ventriloquists, animal acts, and musical specialists, such as accordionists and performers on the musical glasses.

burlesque: a kind of musical show based in parody

vaudeville: a show of various acts in a theater

dance hall: a hall where dances are held

The third direction of the saloon show was the *dance hall*, in which the entertainment was exclusively musical; it included both instrumental (small band or orchestra) and vocal solos—to be both listened to and danced to. Ballrooms were nothing new, of course, but these were democratic, not aristocratic, ballrooms, as their American predecessors had been (but not the European). In the United States, the vast majority of people went out to dance. By the end of the century, the club, particularly the nightclub, satisfied the public's desire to hear music and to dance.

The increasing popularity of the rival forms doubtlessly contributed to the decline of the minstrel show. But it had probably been doomed as soon as it lost its original directness and formal beauty. These were possible only when the concept was fresh and the ensemble small. From Emmett's handful to a dozen men a decade later and about twenty in Christy's company, expansion was swift. Troupes toured the country, and some were even sent to England. In addition, the Civil War ended the white man's near-monopoly of the shows. Black minstrel companies, playing in blackface (and whiteface) like their white rivals, soon started competing with the white companies.

Moreover, independent dance teams and comics, Irish tenors, and other dissonant elements entered the shows. In 1879, Haverly's Minstrels, a black company, played in New York. The playbill read:

> Splendid Achievement. The Success Unequalled in the Annals of Colored Minstrelsy. Haverly's genuine colored Minstrels: 100 performers, 20 end men, 3 middle men, 40 female jubilee singers, 20 [instrumentalists], 17 vocalists. . . . Gigantic First Part. Cotton field pastimes, canebrake frolics, flatboat varieties, plantation revels, levee comicalities, camp meeting refrains; the best ever seen, and at once gorgeous and immense.[17]

The black minstrels of the last third of the century contributed some lustrous names and enduring music to the theater, in spite of the exploitation of the classical concept by theatrical entrepreneurs, who knew a good thing when they saw it and who, quite in fashion philosophically, held the romantic notion that bigger was better. As early as 1848, the *New York Tribune* had smiled upon the "rampant rage" for minstrelsy and at the same time pointed the way to its gross romanticization: "We really believe that Negro Minstrelsy will expand itself into something sublime and grand."[18] Billy Kersands, who called himself "King Rastus," was a notable comedian, and James A. Bland (1854–1911), a freeborn black from Flushing, New York, was a star of Callender's Georgia Minstrels and the only postwar rival to Stephen Foster. Bland's songs included "In the Evening by the Moonlight" (date unknown), "Carry Me Back to Old Virginny" (1878), which was adopted as the official state song of Virginia and "Oh Dem Golden Slippers" (1879).

But even the gifts of James Bland could not save the minstrel show. It was not possible to think of Ethiopian music as it had been thought of fifty years before—and even in the early years, serious black musicians had found the minstrels galling. As early as 1836, Thomas J. Bowers, a renowned American *tenor*, wrote of the offense to his race, saying that in his own concert work he was "striving to give the lie to 'Negro sere- naders' and to show to the world that colored men and women could sing classical music as well as the members of the other race by whom they have been so terribly vilified."[19] Elizabeth Taylor Greenfield (called the "black swan"), who was compared to Jenny Lind, the "Swedish nightingale," also resented the minstrel stereotype. She left the United States, giving her farewell concert in New York to an enthusiastic crowd of four thousand, and attained a successful career in Europe.

tenor: a high voice of a male singer, or an instru- ment of that range

MUSIC OF THE AFRICAN-AMERICANS

The minstrel show was not an authentic black concept, though its best features were founded in the African heritage. True black music was found elsewhere.

Many black musicians continued in the tradition of dance music, which went back a century to the time when Sy Gilliat was the best fiddler in the Colonies and the official state fiddler of Virginia. In 1839, a traveler attending a dance in Virginia wrote that "the orchestra was filled by Negro musicians; the bands being almost always formed by coloured people."[20] The jazz musician George Morrison (born in 1891) said in a biographical interview:

> My father was a musician. In fact, as far back as you can trace the Morrison family, the men were all fiddlers—in those days instead of violinists they called them fiddlers. There was Uncle Jack and Uncle Alfred and my father, Clark Morrison. He was the king fiddler of the State of Missouri. He played those old time fiddling tunes like "Arkansas Traveler," "Devil's Dream," and "The Fisher's Hornpipe," for square dances [quadrilles]. The only thing they knew in those days was square dancing. They didn't play any concert music or anything. They couldn't read a note—never knew what a note looked like—played everything by ear. But they had the natural talent that God blessed them with.[21]

Morrison's father and uncles were of the generation after the Negro musicians described by the 1839 visitor to Virginia; these musicians doubtless knew music notation. At the end of the century, large ball- rooms were scarce and the education of black musicians much more haphazard.

work song: a song used to coordinate or energize work

patting juba: clapping complex rhythms

basse dance: a Renaissance dance for couples, performed with gliding steps

The music, both vocal and instrumental, practiced by the slaves had centered in *work songs*, Sunday dancing, and religious observances, which included both song and dance. The work songs of oarsmen and stevedores were described by several visitors to the docks, where blacks often had to wait for the arrival of boats and amused themselves while waiting. In 1876, a description of such entertainment was published in the *Cincinnati Commercial*, under the title "Levee Life: Haunts and Pastimes of the Roustabouts, Their Original Songs and Peculiar Dances." The author wrote of the "wild banjo thrumming" in the clear air.

> You may hear old Kentucky slave songs chanted nightly on the steamboats, in that wild, half-melancholy key peculiar to the natural music of the African race; and you may see the old slave dances nightly performed to the air of some ancient Virginia-reel in the dance-houses of Sausage Row. [In the dance house] a well-dressed, neatly-built mulatto picked the banjo, and a somewhat lighter colored musician led the music with a fiddle, which he played remarkably well and with great spirit. A short, stout negress, illy dressed, with a rather good-natured face and a bed shawl tied about her head, played the bass viol, and that with no inexperienced hand.
>
> The musicians struck up that weird, wild, lively air, known perhaps to many of our readers as the "Devil's Dream." . . . The dancers danced a double quadrille, at first, silently and rapidly; but warming with the wild spirit of the music, leaped and shouted, swinging each other off the floor, and keeping time with a precision which shook the building in time to the music. The women, we noticed, almost invariably embraced the men about the neck in swinging, the men clasping them about the waist. Sometimes the men advancing leaped and crossed legs with a double shuffle, and with almost sightless rapidity.[22]

As the music became wilder, "men *patted juba* and shouted, the Negro women danced with the most fantastic grace. . . . The white female dancers seemed heavy, cumbersome, ungainly by contrast."[23] And in conclusion, the author stated that "even the curious spectators involuntarily kept time with their feet; it was the very drunkenness of music, the intoxication of the dance."[24]

In European terms, the combination of fiddle, bass and banjo was baroque; in African terms, it was a combination of elements, of quality, rhythm, and pitches, indivisible from the instruments that produced them and creating a musical fabric indivisible from the tune or function of the occasion. It was the totality of the blacks' musical experience that Europeans could not comprehend, for by the second half of the nineteenth century, serious music had become so "civilized" in Europe that it was extrapolated from the stuff of everyday life.

The accompaniment of instrumental music by vocal interjections was also an African characteristic, but the shuffling step was akin to the European Renaissance *basse danse*, in which the feet seldom left the floor.

The leaping was the chief characteristic of the *volta*, a popular sixteenth-century southern European dance. And the wild turning, when the ladies held the men around the neck while being held at the waist, could be a description of the east European *polka*, about which a French dancing book of 1845 had said "to dance the polka men and women must have hearts that beat high and strong."[25]

The Cakewalk

The Sunday dance at the plantation, called the *cakewalk*, was a larger, more formal social occasion, but had fewer set patterns than the quadrille. One such event was described in later life by a son of freed slave parents in Tennessee.

> The cakewalk was originally a plantation dance, just a happy movement they did to the banjo music because they couldn't stand still. It was generally on Sundays, when there was little work, that the slaves both young and old would dress up in hand-me-down finery to do a high-kicking, prancing walk-around. They did a take-off on the high manners of the white folks in the "big house," but their masters, who gathered around to watch the fun, missed the point. It's supposed to be that the custom of a prize started with the master giving a cake to the couple that did the proudest movement.[26]

volta: a leaping dance from Provence, popular in Europe around 1600

polka: a fast dance originating in Bohemia, popular in nineteenth-century Europe and America

cakewalk: a dance by plantation slaves in which the owners were mocked

Cakewalk—poster and sheet-music cover. (Picture Collection, The Branch Libraries, The New York Public Library.)

Shouts

shout: an energetic singing of spirituals

spiritual: a folk or popular song with a religious text

The slaves' religious services, if they did not include dancing, were often followed by a song and dance session called a *shout*, a term of Biblical association.

The true "shout" takes place on Sundays, or on "praise" nights through the week. Very likely more than half the population of a plantation is gathered together. The benches are pushed back to the wall when the formal meeting is over, and old and young, men and women, all stand up in the middle of the floor, and when the "sperichil" is struck up begin first walking and by and by shuffling around, one after another, in a ring. The foot is hardly taken from the floor. Sometimes they dance silently, sometimes the song itself is also sung by the dancers. Song and dance are alike extremely energetic, and often when the shout lasts into the middle of the night, the monotonous thud, thud of the feet prevents sleep within a half mile of the praise-house.[27]

Spirituals

The *spiritual* song was the first authentic black music to be appreciated, written down, and studied. In 1861, "O! Let My People Go" was published (now it is known, to a tune published in 1872 as "Go Down, Moses"). "Roll, Jordan, Roll" followed in 1862. The first important collection, called *Slave Songs of the United States*, was published in 1867. By William Francis Allen, Charles Pickford Ware, and Lucy McKim Garrison, this book was a landmark in American musicology. Each spiritual was notated at its source and preceded by a commentary on the performance.

A portrait of the Jubilee Singers, which is the cover of *The Story of the Jubilee Singers with Their Music, 1883.* (Photo by R. E. Kalmbach.)

But the first significant contribution to the popular dissemination of the Negro spiritual was the tours of eleven young black singers. From 1871, they toured, in support of Fisk University in Nashville, as the Fisk Jubilee Singers. Changing personnel over the years, the group traveled in the United States first and later in Europe and Great Britain, remaining popular for many decades. Their collections, which were very important in the popularization of the spiritual, included *Jubilee Songs*, published in New York in 1872, and *The Story of the Jubilee Singers*, published in London in 1875. The former book contained "Swing Low, Sweet Chariot," and the latter included "Deep River."

But performance was highly embellished, and the notation, which was traditional, could not represent the pitches or rhythms. In 1899, an article in *Popular Science Monthly* attempted to present the spiritual "Mary and Marthy" with the notation of the actual performance, including the embellishments the blacks called "trimmings."[28]

Much of the style of the spirituals was African. But slave songs and dances had also been influenced by the singing-school music, which the blacks learned and evidently loved. The slaves took their religious instruction seriously, particularly in the second quarter of the century, and they attended camp meetings as well. In 1843, a visitor in Virginia noted that the blacks were singing at work and wrote that "all their tunes are psalm tunes."[29] In many cases, the spirituals could be easily harmonized in the traditional manner, and they were so presented by the Jubilee Singers in their publications.

MUSIC OF THE NATIVE AMERICANS

As the United States pushed the Indians aside to make room for the white man, the attitude toward the Indians was that they were to be elevated from savagery to civilization. The Indians were expected to react joyously to the white man's culture, because, in the nineteenth-century view, its superiority was self-evident. Thus, the music of the Indians was little studied; serious books dealt only with occasional, specific aspects of it. But this type of study was practically useless because the music was inseparable from the fabric of Indian life—song was used in virtually all activities. Like black music, Native American music was rhythmic and melodic. It used percussion that was important and often independent and was associated with the dance.

Indian music confounded the white scientists who studied it. The drums often beat a pulse different from that of the song they accompanied. Moreover, the voices frequently sang syllables rather than a verbal text. An observer late in the century wrote, in *A Study of Omaha Music* (1893), that many songs rearranged, fragmented, or modified the words "to make them more melodious."

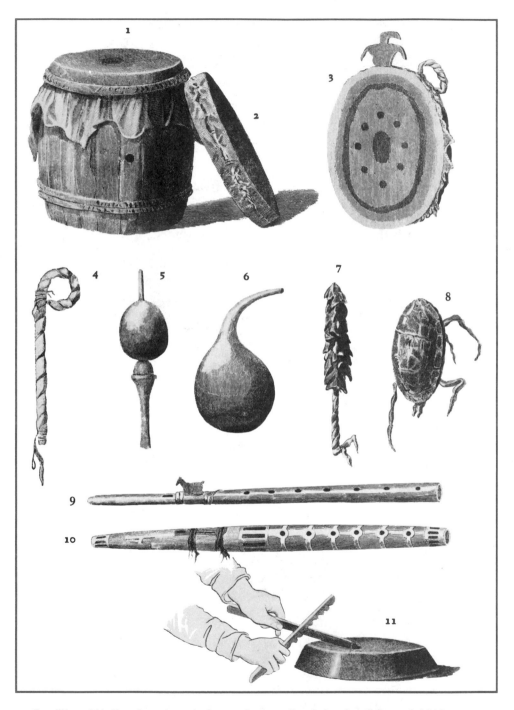

Traditional Native American instruments, from the *Schoolcraft Report,* 1844.
Key: 1–3, drums; 4, drumstick; 5, 6, gourd rattles; 7, rattle made of deer's hooves;
8, turtle-shell knee rattle; 9, 10, flutes; 11, scraper. (Mr. and Mrs. R. A. Rubovits. Photo
by R. E. Kalmbach.)

A majority of the songs, however are furnished almost wholly with syllables which are not parts or even fragments of words but sounds that lend themselves easily to singing and are without definite meaning; yet when a composer has once set syllables to his song, they are never changed or transposed but preserved with as much accuracy as we would observe in maintaining the integrity of a poem.[30]

Not only did the Omaha sing syllables, but they felt that a song with a text was a combination of two arts. The author continued, "Words clearly enunciated in singing break the melody to the Indian ear and mar the music. They say of us that we talk a great deal as we sing."[31]

The first extensive study of Indian music was written in Germany as a doctoral thesis in musicology at the University of Leipzig. *Über die Musik der Nordamerikanischen Wilden* (On the Music of the North American Savages, 1882), by a New Yorker, Theodore Baker (1851–1934), was based on the author's sojourn, during the summer of 1880, in western New York and in an Indian school in Pennsylvania. There he notated the music of the Seneca and the Iroquois. Baker's treatise included musical examples of interest to composers and analyses of value to musicologists, but the book was not translated and thus was not available to the general public.

However, interaction between the Indian and the white man was lessening, and influences that might have bent Indian music toward the white man's had not entered Indian life. The distance between European and Indian practice was too great, and after the turn of the century, when black music was winning a wider public, Indian music became more and more obscure. It would finally be of interest only to scholars.

WOMEN AND MUSIC

The place of women in American music is difficult for us to assess in retrospect. But it is clear that music was a significant part of women's education and that a young lady was expected to have elocution, music, and dancing lessons as a matter of course. The living room concert was to the nineteenth-century family what television is today, and women were its mainstays.

The professional life was denied to most women, simply because it was too difficult. And it was very difficult indeed: touring at least until her name was made, and then traveling either (impossibly) alone or (expensively) with chaperones, staying at flea-bag hotels and eating poor food. The establishment of a musical reputation has never been easy.

Many women were highly skilled, of course, since so many were trained. The living room music could be as good (or as poor) as any professional concert. What women could do successfully was compose, and

LESSONS for LADIES

Lessons for Ladies, c. 1860.
(The Newberry Library.)

a surprising percentage of the music popular in the nineteenth century was, in fact, composed by women. Scholars are just beginning to sift the women out—so many of them published under male pen names that it is not an easy task. But a few items, such as Harriet Mary Browne's "The Messenger Bird," which had appeared late in the 1820s (to a poem by Browne's sister, the well-known poet Felicia Hemans), were so popular that they are difficult to avoid. It was a duet in the dramatic/musical tradition, and it remained on the boards for over twenty years—and then it was parodied at least twice, by other women.

Augusta Browne

Two of the most popular songs of the mid-century were the products of women composers. One composer was Augusta Browne (1821–82), born in Ireland, but living in the United States by 1830. The family was of modest means and the young woman became a teacher, performer, composer, journalist, and organist of the First Presbyterian Church of Brooklyn, New York. She was referred to as a "professor" and she became quite well known as a composer (she issued a parody of Harriet Mary Browne's duet, called "Reply to the Messenger Bird"). Her works, like the works of many other composers of the day, reflected political events. Although she was known for sentimental ballads by 1840, with the publication of "The Stranger's Heart" in *Godey's Lady's Book* (a well-respected magazine—a good deal of music was published in magazines well into the twentieth century), she was perhaps best known for her musical response to the war with Mexico: a rousing dramatic/musical work (it is almost a *cantata*), "The Warlike Dead in Mexico" (1848). Like so many women composers, she transcended the common, limiting concept of "feminine" music, which often meant simply unskilled, amateur stuff.[32]

cantata: a piece in several movements for voice(s) and instruments

Caroline Norton

The other woman composer was Caroline Norton (1808–77). Norton and her sister were both typical living room musicians proficient in singing and in playing the harp and the piano. Norton composed several songs of great popularity, such as "Fairy Bells" (1839) and "The Officer's Funeral" (date unknown), but her sweeping success was a song still heard occasionally, "Juanita," first published in a Boston magazine called *The Melodist* in 1858, then in other journals as late as 1876.

Suzan Parkhurst

And women could get good, serious press coverage. One composer, Suzan Parkhurst (1836–1918), announced the publication of a volume of songs, and the *Brooklyn Eagle* reviewer wrote:

> We cheerfully call attention to Mrs. Parkhurst's advertisement of new music, which appears in our columns to-day. There are some ten or fifteen compositions in all, many of which are exceedingly meritorious, while all are above the average of such works. Mrs. Parkhurst is one of our most prolific native composers, many of her songs being familiar as household words. The fair author has a happy faculty of interblending words and melody, which results in most pleasing and memorable harmony.

Teresa Carreño

Certainly one of the most admired musicians of the period was Teresa Carreño (1853–1917), born in Caracas, Venezuela, but living in New York from the age of nine. She was active as one of the top concert pianists of the last third of the century and also as a composer (she composed a string quartet as well as piano music—some of it terribly difficult—and songs). When she was ten years old, she was already touring and presaging her renown as a virtuoso, and she gave a recital in Washington, D.C., that was attended by President Lincoln. In his honor she improvised a set of variations upon Lincoln's favorite piece of music, the song "Listen to the Mocking Bird"—by Dick Milburn, a free black barber in Philadelphia—which had been published in 1855. Not only was the concert given by a young female, but females were given an oblique compliment by that song: for the success of women in music was great enough that Milburn had published that song under a female pseudonym, Alice Hawthorne.

NOTES

1. Irving S. and Nell M. Kull, *A Short Chronology of American History, 1492–1950* (New Brunswick, NJ: Rutgers University Press, 1952), p. 115.

2. Katherine Lee Bates, "America The Beautiful," *Congregationalist* (Boston, July 4, 1895), p. 17. The poem, written at the end of the nineteenth century, was connected to Samuel A. Ward's tune "Materna" in the next decade and was published as a song for the first time in 1913.

3. James J. Fuld, *The Book of World-Famous Music* (New York: Crown Publishers, 1966), p. 148f.

4. Edith Borroff, *Music in Europe and the United States: A History*, 2nd ed. (New York: Ardsley House, 1990), p. 516.

5. Fuld, *World-Famous Music*, p.168.

6. Vera Brodsky Lawrence, *Resonances, 1836–1850. Strong on Music*, vol. 1 (New York: Oxford University Press, 1988), p. 197.

7. *Dwight's Journal of Music*, February 9, 1861, p. 367, in Paul Charosh, "'Popular' and 'Classical' in the Mid-Nineteenth Century," *American Music*, vol. 10, no. 2 (Summer 1992), p. 131.

8. Charosh, "'Popular' and 'Classical'", p. 124.

9. Percy A. Scholes, *The Concise Dictionary of Music* (Oxford University Press, 1960).

10. Lawrence, *Resonances*, p. 412.

11. Sterling A. Brown, "The Negro in the American Theatre,"*The Oxford Companion to the Theatre*, 2nd ed., Phyllis Hartnoll, ed. (New York: Oxford University Press, 1957), p. 565ff.

12. Chase, *America's Music,* p. 259.

13. Ibid, p. 289.

14. Robert P. Nevin, "Stephen C. Foster and Negro Minstrelsy,"*Atlantic Monthly,* vol. 20, no. CXXI (November, 1867), pp. 608–16. Robert was the brother of composer Ethelbert Nevin.

15. Bernard Sobel, *A Pictorial History of Burlesque* (New York: Bonanza Books, 1956), p. 19f.

16. Ibid, p. 20.

17. Walter Monfried, "Minstrel Show," *The Milwaukee Journal,* 8 February 1963, p. 1.

18. Lawrence, *Resonances,* p. 554.

19. John P. Davis, *The American Negro Reference Book* (Englewood Cliffs, NJ: Prentice-Hall, 1966), p. 751.

20. Ibid, p. 750.

21. Gunther Schuller, *Early Jazz: Its Roots and Musical Development* (Fair Lawn, NJ: Oxford University Press, 1968), p. 359.

22. Lafcadio Hearn, in Chase, *America's Music,* p. 436f.

23. Ibid, p. 437.

24. Ibid.

25. Curt Sachs, *World History of the Dance* (New York: W. W. Norton and Co., 1963), p. 434.

26. Chase, *America's Music,* p. 439.

27. Ibid, p. 256.

28. Jeannette R. Murphy, "African Music in the United States," *Popular Science Monthly,* September, 1899, p. 665.

29. Chase, *America's Music,* p. 236.

30. Natalie Curtis Burlin, *The Indians' Book* (New York: Harper & Bros., 1923), p. 413.

31. Ibid.

32. Judith Tick, *American Women Composers Before 1870* (Ann Arbor: UMI Research Press, 1983), p. 150ff.

BIBLIOGRAPHY

Benton, Rita. "The Early Piano in the U.S." *Music, Libraries, and Instruments.* Edited by Unity Sherrington and Guy Oldham. London: Hinrichsen Edition, 1961.

Brown, Sterling A. "The Negro in the American Theatre." *The Oxford Companion to the Theatre,* 2nd ed. Edited by Phyllis Hartnoll. New York: Oxford University Press, 1957.

Carson, Gerald. "The Piano in the Parlor." *American Heritage:* 17 (December, 1965).

Carosh, Paul. "'Popular' and 'Classical' in the Mid-Nineteenth Century." *American Music*, vol. 10, no. 2 (Summer 1992).

Chase, Gilbert. *America's Music: From the Pilgrims to the Present*. rev. ed. Urbana: University of Illinois Press, 1992.

Davis, John P. *The American Negro Reference Book*. Englewood Cliffs, NJ: Prentice-Hall, 1966.

Fuld, James J., *The Book of World-Famous Music*. New York: Crown Publishers, 1968.

Hamm, Charles. *Yesterdays: Popular Song in America*. New York: W. W. Norton & Co., 1947.

Kull, Irving S. and Nell M. *A Short Chronology of American History, 1492–1950*. New Brunswick, NJ: Rutgers University Press, 1952.

Lang, Paul Henry, ed. *One Hundred Years of Music in America*. New York: Schirmer, 1961.

Lawrence, Vera Brodsky. *Resonances: 1836–1850. Strong On Music*, vol. 1. New York: Oxford University Press, 1988.

Monfried, Walter. "Minstrel Show." *Milwaukee Journal*: 8 (February, 1963).

Murphy, Jeannette R. "African Music in the United States." *Popular Science Monthly*, September, 1899.

Nevin, Robert P. "Stephen C. Foster and Negro Minstrelsy." *Atlantic Monthly*, vol. 20, no. 130 (November, 1867).

Norton, Frank F., ed. *Historical Register of the Centennial Exposition, 1876*. New York: Frank Leslie, 1877.

Preston, Katherine K. *Opera on the Road: Traveling Opera Troupes in the United States, 1825–1860*. Urbana: University of Illinois Press, 1993.

Ritter, Frederic Louis. *Music in America*. New York: Charles Scribner's Sons, 1883.

Sachs, Curt. *World History of the Dance*. New York: W. W. Norton & Co., 1963.

Scholes, Percy A. *The Concise Oxford Dictionary of Music*. Fair Lawn, NJ: Oxford University Press, 1960.

Schuller, Gunther. *Early Jazz: Its Roots and Musical Development*. Fair Lawn, NJ: Oxford University Press, 1968.

Sobel, Bernard. *A Pictorial History of Burlesque*. New York: Bonanza Books, 1956.

Tick, Judith. *American Women Composers before 1870*. Ann Arbor: UMI Research Press, 1983.

Williamson, H. S. *The Orchestra*. London: Sylvan Press, n.d.

4

A Nation Coming of Age
(1880 to 1923)

As the United States emerged from the terrible ravages of the War Between the States, which had torn the nation virtually in two, the healing began under the shadow of dark times. After the healing came years of making the country into a competitive economy (roughly from 1881 to 1923). Americans had been inventive enough, certainly, and inventiveness continued; but the inventions of the past had to be put to constructive uses, a new working system instituted, a new sense of national identity created. This was, of all the periods in the history of the United States, the one in which the good and the bad, the healthy and the unhealthy, the idealistic and the cynical, were juxtaposed and brought into something like a facedown.

The territorial "manifest destiny" of the nation was to be fulfilled during this time; the sense of what America is and what it is to be an American came into a proud definition. But at the same time, big business and the labor movement hit head-on, and corruption in high places took its toll.

The fulfilling of the territorial pride in the country was carried out as the territories formerly straddled by the nation became full-fledged states.

1889	North Dakota	1890	Wyoming
1889	South Dakota	1896	Utah
1889	Montana	1907	Oklahoma
1889	Washington	1912	New Mexico
1890	Idaho	1912	Arizona

From the sheet-music cover of "Shores of the Ohio," by Adolph Pferdner. The picture depicts country life along the Ohio River in 1880. (The Newberry Library.)

The entry of these ten brought the continental nucleus to completion with forty-eight states, a number that would remain constant for well over four decades. The "near west" was filled in; the West Coast was completed; and Americans found in this an immense satisfaction.

Meanwhile, immigration continued at an accelerated rate, and the population of the country rose from 62,947,714 in the 1890 census to 105,710,620 in the 1920 census. In addition, the slave population (3,953,760 in the 1860 census) had to be reintegrated as part of the free population (part of the goal of Reconstruction), an integration fraught with difficulty upon difficulty and a continuing thorn in the national flesh.

The presidency turned from the generation of men who had served in the Civil War to those who were primarily interested in national identity, on the one hand, and big business on the other. In a way they were a more unified group; the twelve presidents who served in forty-one years (1841–81) were followed by nine who served in forty-three years (1881–1923).

The period began with the respected Chester A. Arthur (1881–85), who backed the Tariff Act of 1883, which adjusted rates downward, and in general, attempted to tidy up the national confusion of immigration, labor, and manufacture. His term was followed by those of Grover Cleveland (1885–89), the first Democratic president after the Civil War and the only president to be married in the White House, Benjamin Harrison (1889–93)—the grandson of William Henry Harrison—who, like Hayes, lost the popular vote but won in the electoral college, Cleveland again (1893–97), the only president to serve twice nonconsecutively, and William McKinley (1897–1901), the last president to have served in the Civil War. These presidents had seen the beginnings of the auto industry, the invention of the telegraph, the crossing of the continent by the railroads (putting the pony express out of business in 1862, only two years after it began full service), and the beginnings of years of devastating strikes—750,000 workers on strike in 1894.

McKinley was assassinated after six months of a second term, and the presidency was assumed by his vice president, Theodore Roosevelt (1901–09)—at 42, the youngest president ever to serve. He was reelected in 1905 in his own right. Roosevelt became a symbol of the expansive nation, and perhaps, because he had been sickly as a boy and was almost an adventurer in middle age, of the hope of robust health for a nation in harm's way. He was the first modern internationalist and is famous for his advice: "Speak softly and carry a big stick." He was a proponent of the national parks and national forests (and irrigation projects) and of the outdoor

The United States flag in 1912.

life, pulling visiting dignitaries along on hikes, and espousing activity and a full life. He believed in arbitration between labor and capital, and became the first politician to attack the huge monopolies or trusts, becoming a "trust-buster." He was the apex of those decades, incorporating virtually every American concern.

After Roosevelt, the financial concerns and the First World War took presidential energies: William Howard Taft (1909–13) was the prewar president, a man who quietly tried to do what was right in a noisy era, attempting to clean up the trusts as his predecessor had done, but without his predecessor's charisma and flair. Actually, his administration compared favorably with that of Roosevelt: in 1912, Taft wrote, "During the seven and a half years preceding this Administration forty-four cases against trusts were instituted. During the less than four years of this Administration twenty-two civil suits and forty-five criminal indictments have been brought under the Anti-Trust Law."[1] But the coming war absorbed national concentration; Woodrow Wilson (1913–21), the college president (of Princeton from 1902) became the war president who tried to heal international problems by (among other things) establishing a League of Nations. The administration of Warren G. Harding (1921–23) was characterized by scandal and corruption—or perhaps by the blindness of a peacemaker who would not see what was going on under his nose. Harding died of a heart attack in the third year of his term, leaving the country in the midst of the Teapot Dome Scandal and at the beginning of still another phase of national development. In 1922, over five hundred thousand coal miners were on strike; in 1923, U.S. Steel adopted the eight-hour workday, reducing it from the customary twelve hours for the first time.

The intellectual life of the country was still a frontier of a sort during these years. Such men as the Swiss naturalist Louis Agassiz (1807–73—in this country in his forties) brought new life to American college life; Agassiz taught at Harvard, changing the contours of American thought; he also did research on American glaciers, to that extent Americanizing himself. Botanist Asa Gray (1810–88), from Sauquoit, NY, devoted himself to American plant life, and in 1848, brought out his famous *Manual of Botany of the Northern United States*. Equally important, he was a convinced and articulate supporter of Charles Darwin, bringing Darwin's theory of the means of evolution to national attention (as Agassiz, a nonbeliever, did not). Romantic science was represented by the inspired, even excited inventor in his busy (and confused) workroom; the new, twentieth-century science would be represented by a cool technician in antiseptic and disciplined laboratory. These years were the bridge.

Perhaps the most significant American thinkers of the bridge years were William James (1842–1910) and John Dewey (1859–1952). James was from Albany, New York, a product of wealth, almost in the European sense, with leisure and self-indulgence always a possibility; but he also brought American energy into his life, traveling up the Amazon with Louis Agassiz at twenty-three, and earning an M.D. during an extended European sojourn, at twenty-seven (he studied in Bonn, Boulogne, Geneva, London, and Paris). He became many-faceted, publishing on philosophy, theology, and, most important for the future, on psychology—he created the basis of psychology as a university study (he taught at Harvard).

"Kissing Papa through the Telephone," by Thomas P. Westendorff, 1898. (The Newberry Library.)

John Dewey, from Burlington, Vermont, was also a broad-based thinker. He taught at the University of Michigan and the University of Chicago, where he developed his theories of education and wrote his influential book *The School and Society* (1899); he then taught at Columbia University, where he was a professor of philosophy but continued to define ideas in both psychology and education, writing *Democracy and Education* (1916). The influence of both of these men was huge in all fields, including music.

So these years were of widely ranging experience, even contradiction. Early in the period, the Indian wars had ceased; the capture of Geronimo in 1887, an Apache, symbolized the final defeat of the Native Americans. And late in the period the new technologies of radio, recordings, and motion pictures were already beginning a redefinition of American leisure. The seriousness of the earlier experience and the relative frivolity of the later phenomenon incorporate one more of the oppositions that beset this nation in the early years of the twentieth century.

INTERNATIONAL MUSIC

With their concentration on the fulfillment of manifest destiny, on the expansion of business interests and the labor movement, and, of course, on the great wars (the Civil War, 1861–65, and World War I, 1914–18) Americans allowed other affairs to lapse. Music was among the matters that were deflected, not into the background, but into an international arena. The fact that the United States was very different from any European country was often difficult for immigrants to realize. In 1900, for example, over 10 million people (of the approximately 76 million reported in the census) were foreign born, and in 1910, it was about 13.5 million (out of 92 million)—figures well over ten percent.

So it was easy enough for Americans to believe that their music was a branch of European music and to ignore the tremendous artistic energy of the American people. And their ignorance of their own music coincided with American philosophical, historical, and political developments. In the middle of the nineteenth century, romanticism was at its height in Europe, and that happenstance would prove of surpassing importance in the growth of musical consciousness in the United States. For romanticism was above all a German movement, and more German immigrants came to this country than those of any other country (6.9 million over the long haul, 1820–1975, as against 5.2 million from Italy, 4.7 million from Ireland, and 4.3 million from Austria-Hungary).[2] And

"The German Band," by J. G. Brown, N. A., an engraving in Harper's Weekly, April 26, 1879. (Picture Collection, The Branch Libraries, The New York Public Library.)

being the musical leaders of the romantic movement gave German immigrants the confidence to set up musical entertainments on the German model and to expect Americans to accept this ideal as American. Some Americans did and some did not, and that split in musical views between the German and American musical forces in the United States is still with us today. Oscar Sonneck (1873–1928), born of German stock in Jersey City, but trained in Germany, said in 1909, "We German-Americans . . . [have the] historical right: [sic] to be named joint godfathers of American musical life."[3] Sonneck, as the first music librarian of the Library of Congress (1902–17) and, later, as an executive of the music publisher G. Schirmer, was able to influence a generation of Americans. And Sonneck in these roles was representative.

Louis-Moreau Gottschalk

Perhaps the earliest American musician to be of importance in international terms, Louis-Moreau Gottschalk (1829–69) comprised an exception. Gottschalk was born in New Orleans of mixed German-Jewish, English, French, and Creole heritages, showed his gifts early, and at thirteen was sent to Paris to live with his mother's family; he made a great splash in the Paris of the 1840s, playing recitals and composing in both American and European styles—but never attempting to unite the two. He was famous for his "Negro" pieces, such as *Bamboula* and *The Banjo*, and these are indeed amazing works; but he was admired also for his highly romantic works, such as *The Dying Poet* and *The Last Hope*. He returned to the United States, toured during the 1860s (when the minds of Americans were focused on the Civil War), and continued to Cuba and South America, where he died of yellow fever.

Gottschalk was trained in the apprenticeship system, in which all composers were trained in his day. In that system performance and composition were strongly linked: a person was a whole musician. But soon after that, the formal training of musicians was taken, first into the hands of Germans who had recently immigrated (and who sent their students to Germany to complete their studies) and then into the university system, where practical musicianship was new and where students could study theory and even composition (at a few universities), but not performance. At the same time, other Americans continued in the apprenticeship system, which was dominant in the United States everywhere but on the East Coast.

Thus, a rift sprang up among American musicians: between those trained in the European (German) tradition and those trained in American apprenticeship. Gottschalk was firmly on the apprenticeship side, and, further, what European experience he had was not in Germany but in France. But he was extremely successful in France and also in Spain, and, later, as a pianist, in the United States, Cuba, and South America.

▶◯ Recommended Recordings and Video Cassettes

American composers enter record catalogues beginning with Louis Moreau Gottschalk, whose piano music is becoming more and more known to performers and audiences.

Vanguard Classics OVC 4051. *The Banjo: Piano Music of Gottschalk.* An excellent album by Eugene List.

Vox Box CDX 5009. *Music of Gottschalk.* This album includes orchestral and vocal music as well as music for four hands (two players at one piano).

New World Records 208. Gottschalk's orchestral work, *Night in the Tropics*, together with Heinrich's Second Symphony, *The Ornithological Combat of Kings*.

By the time Gottschalk's career was over, a strong generation of Americans had been born who would commit professional musical training and practice to the German tradition. They defined concert music in the United States at the end of the nineteenth and the first quarter of the twentieth centuries. Most of them were important both as professional musicians (performers and composers, for the separation into specialties did not take place in their generation, but in the next) and as teachers.

symphonic poem: a one-movement orchestral work

incidental music: the music to a play

quintet: five people playing or singing together

suite: a set of pieces to be played as a group

John Knowles Paine

John Knowles Paine (1839–1906), born in Portland, Maine, was trained in Berlin (1858–61) and returned to the United States to compose and to teach at Harvard, as instructor from 1862, working his way up to a professorship in 1875, and retiring in 1895. As a composer he left two exciting symphonies, *symphonic poems*, a choral Mass (composed in Berlin), cantatas, songs, piano works, two operas, and *incidental music* to *Oedipus Rex* of Sophocles and *The Birds* of Aristophanes. He was capable of a broad range of musical statement and mood: his *Fuga Giocosa* (1884) is a saucy work written upon a well-known musical phrase.[4] As a professor—the first professor of music at any university in America—Paine exerted a lasting influence upon both the university system and upon concert music in this country.

George Whitefield Chadwick

George Whitefield Chadwick (1854–1931), born in Lowell, Massachusetts, studied in Germany and returned to become an important organist/composer/teacher in Boston. As a composer, he worked in a variety of forms and media, leaving three symphonies, five string quartets, a piano *quintet*, symphonic *suites*, and a good many short works, vocal and instrumental. As a teacher he was of enormous influence: he

George Whitefield Chadwick. (Picture Collection, The Branch Libraries, The New York Public Library.)

▶ Recommended Recordings and Video Cassettes

John Knowles Paine is underrepresented in record lists, but a few items are available.

New World NW 374-2 and 350-2. (compact discs). The first and second symphonies, the first, from 1875, paired with the concert overture *As You Like It*.

New World NW 80262-2. *Mass in D, for Choir, Soloists, Organ and Orchestra.* This remarkable work was composed in 1866 when Paine was a student in Germany, where it was first performed.

Premier Recordings PRCD 1019. *American Piano, Vol 2.* This exceptionally fine album, by pianist Ramon Salvatore, contains music by Paine, George Whitefield Chadwick, Amy Cheney, and several other composers from this and later periods.

taught at the New England Conservatory of Music in Boston and for a considerable time served as its director. More than any other person, he established the German-American romantic tradition of music composition and performance.

Edward MacDowell

Edward MacDowell (1861–1908) who was born in New York City, studied piano with Teresa Carreño, and then at the Paris Conservatory; then he went on to composition study in Frankfurt and Darmstadt. Returning to New York after several years in Germany, he settled in Boston, but was invited in 1895 to become the first Professor of Music of Columbia University in New York, and he taught there until 1904, when his health failed. As a composer he was prolific and his music was often played; it included symphonies, two piano concertos and four sonatas, plus many short piano pieces such as the *Sea Pieces* and the *Woodland Sketches*. The latter contained the most popular of his works, the pieces "To a Wild Rose" and "To a Water Lily," very American in their classical directness and simplicity (these pieces are still often played). He also composed songs, symphonic poems (notably in the romantic tradition of strong association with literary works—his *Hamlet and Ophelia* and *Six Idyls after Goethe* are representative), and other works. As a teacher he also exerted enormous influence.

▶◯ Recommended Recordings and Video Cassettes

The string quartets of George Whitefield Chadwick are excellent.

Northeastern Records 234, 235, and 236. All center on the string quartets; number 235 is particularly recommended because it combines the *Quintet for Piano and Strings* with the String Quartet No. 3, thus giving the listener two chamber-music sounds.

Edward MacDowell's professorship at Columbia University gives him a higher place in historical studies than many other composers, and his music is excellent.

Pro Arte/Fanfare CDS 3412. Both of MacDowell's piano concertos plus the *Poem erotique* for orchestra alone.

Teldec 9031. *Songs.* Along with songs by Charles Tomlinson Griffes and Charles Ives. MacDowell's songs are to German texts.

Elektra/Nonesuch 71411-4. *Woodland Sketches* for piano. These are perhaps MacDowell's best-known compositions.

Delos DE-1019. *Twelve Virtuoso Etudes for Piano.* These works are more difficult, and hence were limited in performance to professional pianists, as the *Woodland Sketches* were not. Fine etudes.

Nuova Era 6821. *American Indian Music ca. 1900.* An album of piano music by MacDowell, Charles Wakefield Cadman, and others, based on native American materials.

Horatio Parker

Horatio Parker (1863–1919) was born in Auburndale, Massachusetts; he studied with Chadwick in Boston, then went to Germany, where he studied organ and composition in Munich. He was the first Professor of Music at Yale University, teaching there from 1894 until his death. He left three operas, one of which, *Mona*, completed in 1911, was performed at the Metropolitan Opera in New York in 1912 and won the Metropolitan's ten thousand dollar award for the best opera in English by a native-born composer. But he composed in a variety of media: one symphony, other works for orchestra, chamber music, and *oratorios*. His oratorio *Hora Novissima*, performed in New York City in 1893, became popular at the British oratorio festivals, and was sung at these festivals many times (Worcester in 1899, Chelsea in 1900, and so forth)—and he was awarded an honorary doctorate by Cambridge University in 1902.

> **oratorio:** a large work telling a story, for soloists, choir, and orchestra

Amy Marcy Cheney

Amy Marcy Cheney (Mrs. H. H. A. Beach; 1867–1944) was born in New Hampshire, but made her life in Boston from 1875 to 1905. She studied piano with a teacher from Leipzig, but was largely self-taught in composition. She joined herself with German organizations from the start, however, and an early performance (1892) with the Handel and Haydn Society of Boston of her *Mass in E-flat* was written up in the Society notes in glowing terms: the Mass "may well be considered a wonder. . . and is certainly matter for hearty congratulations and great national and local pride."[5] Her most important works were composed

▶ Recommended Recordings and Video Cassettes

The music of Amy Marcy Cheney (Mrs H. H. A. Beach), certainly one of our top composers, is becoming more widely available.

Northeastern (Classical Arts) NR 223 and 9004. Two albums of piano music played by Virginia Eskin. The first combines with music by Arthur William Foote, a student of John Knowles Paine at Harvard; the second is all Cheney, including a violin sonata and several songs.

Northeastern Records NR 202 (LP). *Amy Beach: Songs and Villin Pieces.* Eleven songs, two violin/piano pieces, three piano solos (again by Virginia Eskin).

Vox/Turnabout PVT 7196. An excellent performance of the piano concerto (1899) by M. L. Boehm, paired with the quintet for piano and string quartet (1907).

Library of Congress OMP 105. The "Gaelic" Symphony (1896). Paired with Arthur William Foote's *Four Character Pieces after the Rubiyat of Omar Khayyam*, from about the same year.

early in her career, notably, the *Gaelic Symphony* (1896), performed in that year by the Boston Symphony Orchestra and then later performed by other orchestras, including those of Philadelphia, New York, Chicago, Detroit, Minneapolis, and San Francisco. This work is often cited as the first symphony by an American woman. The *Piano Concerto*, which she performed with the Boston Symphony Orchestra in 1900, was one of her finest works.

Beach flourished at the turn of the century, but after the First World War, her output declined in amount and (because of post-Romantic stylistic change) relevance. In 1932, she composed the opera *Cabildo*, and she received a significant recognition—a medal presented at the Chicago International Exposition—in 1933. She also composed chamber music, piano pieces,[6] songs, and choral works, including anthems composed for St. Bartholomew's Episcopal Church in New York City, where she was a member for many years.

Other Composers

Henry F. Gilbert (1868–1928) was MacDowell's earliest composition student. MacDowell had become interested in the use of Native American materials in symphonic forms, and Gilbert became interested in the use of African-American materials, also in symphonic forms.

Arthur Farwell (1872–1952) studied first to become an engineer, but then went to Berlin to study music composition. He taught in several American universities, but he became a renegade to the Germanization of American music, and was not comfortably received in any of them. As a teacher, he espoused both French and Russian traditions, and in his music he used Native American and Hispanic idioms.

▶◯ Recommended Recordings and Video Cassettes

Ramon Salvatore's album of American piano music (Premier Recordings PRCD 1019) includes two pieces by Arthur Farwell in the tradition of music influenced by Native American elements: "Pawnee Horses" (1904) and "Navajo War Dance No. 2" (1908).

Laurel Records LR-112 (LP). *The Western Arts Trio.* Volume 4. Rubin Goldmark: *Trio in d minor* (1892). Goldmark (1872–1936) was born in New York, studied with Antonin Dvorak (among others) and taught at Juilliard. His influence on American music was huge.

Vocal music might include:

Northeastern Records 207 (LP). *Charles Martin Loeffler: Songs.* Sung by D'Anna Fortunato, mezzo-soprano.

APPRENTICESHIP COMPOSERS

At the same time that certain American composers were creating a German-American tradition, others were continuing with the apprenticeship tradition. In this tradition, children were started very early (usually by the age of three) and were trained at singing and playing and, above all, in music as a language. Specialization had already begun in the universities when Paine and Parker began teaching at Harvard and Yale, but apprenticeship changed only in *venue*: apprenticeship musicians founded conservatories of music in which children were trained as well as adults, and in which composition followed performance as part of unified linguistic skill—like reading and writing in English.

venue: the location and special musical profile of a particular kind of music

pit orchestra: a small orchestra playing in the theater pit during stage performances

John Philip Sousa

John Philip Sousa (1854–1932) was a consummate apprenticeship composer. He was trained from early childhood, was playing in the Marine Band by 1867, and was directing the *pit orchestra* in a vaudeville theater in 1871. At twenty-five, he was appointed director of the Marine Band; he conducted it for a dozen years and then founded his own group,

An advertisement for Sousa's band. (Picture Collection, The Branch Libraries, The New York Public Library.)

◖◗ Recommended Recordings and Video Cassettes

John Philip Sousa was undoubtedly our most exciting composer for band. It is important to try and hear the authentic Sousa sound in the famous marches, but also to savor orchestral and vocal music of this master.

Delos DE 3102. *Keith Brion & His New Sousa Band.* A remarkable recording, with excellent interpretations of thirteen marches. Just as important: the album contains a 35-second radio announcement by Sousa himself, along with high-quality reissues of Sousa's original band in seven marches conducted by the master between 1917 and 1923.

ESS. A. Y 1003. *Sousa for Orchestra.* Two orchestral works plus six songs from one of his operettas.

Premier Recordings PRCD 1011. *Concert, Theater & Parlor Songs.* Contains six songs for soprano, seven for baritone, and five duets by Sousa.

New World Records 266. *The Pride of America: The Golden Age of the American March.*

which would become the most famous band in the world—in fact, making a world tour in 1910–1911. The band's repertoire was broad: it included transcriptions of well-known orchestral works and solos by voice and violin as well as cornet and trombone virtuosos. Sousa composed over one hundred and forty marches, plus other works for band, and he generally concluded the extremely varied programs with one of his own works. He was a man of great intelligence combined with great energy; he composed in many media besides band (over 500 works, including opera); he wrote a novel and an autobiography. His marches are still in the repertoire; the most famous are *Semper Fidelis* (1888), *The Washington Post* (1889), and of course *The Stars and Stripes Forever* (1897).

Alfred G. Robyn

Alfred G. Robyn (1857–1935) was the son of William Robyn, the "founder" of the St. Louis Symphony, and was born and raised in St. Louis. His first public appearance was at the age of nine, when he played in a piano trio; at ten, he took over his father's organ job for a year (the pedals had to be built up so that he could reach them). He concertized as a pianist, both solo and with chamber groups. His compositions spread out over many media, including a symphonic poem (*Pompeii*), two oratorios, a piano concerto, piano pieces, a piano quintet, a symphonic poem, and over two hundred songs. But he was best known for his fourteen operas and one musical comedy, *Princess Beggar* (1906). *The Yankee Consul* (1903), a comic opera, was one of the most successful works of any composer in that decade. It was premiered in Boston in 1904 and the review called it a delight; . . . the audience rose to it like hungry fish to the flies cast by a dexterous angler. . . [The work is] honestly artistic and sanely amusing. . . . A great success and it won legitimately. . . . The music is ambitious throughout, gracefully, strongly, characteristically written, capitally suited to the action, and situations and the players.[7]

The sequel, *A Yankee Tourist* (1907), was equally successful. Robyn also composed grand opera, in particular *Jacinta* (1894), which he called a "Romantic Mexican Opera" and *The Bandit* (c.1915); these works, contrary to the norm, were published in piano scores for the general public to enjoy. And they did!

microtone: a musical interval smaller than a half step

chorus: a large group of singers performing together; also, music for such a group

Charles Ives

Charles Ives (1874–1954), of Danbury, Connecticut, was a businessman who wrote music technically as an amateur. But his father was a musician, and he studied with him as an apprentice; later, he studied with Horatio Parker at Yale University. He was an experimenter, an iconoclast, and a musical freethinker who wrote many invigorating scores that were largely ignored during his lifetime but are now much under scrutiny by music scholars. His experiments included using layers of music (that is, having two completely different musical entities going on at once, synchronized only loosely), *microtones*, optional parts, and surprises (such as having a flute sound at the end of a piano sonata, or the sudden interpolation of a patriotic tune). He composed five symphonies, of which his third (from 1911) brought him the Pulitzer Prize in 1947; other orchestral works, piano works, including the *Concord Sonata* (1919), *choruses*, a large amount of chamber music, and a volume of 114 songs, which Ives himself published. Whatever his value to future generations, he was a maverick and a loner in his own day.

🔊 Recommended Recordings and Video Cassettes

Charles Ives has been the subject of considerable study in the university community, and his recordings are of substantial number.

Pro Arte CDD-102. Contains Ive's *The Unanswered Question* (an orchestral work of 1908), along with items by Samuel Barber, Henry Cowell, Aaron Copland, William Schuman, and Leonard Bernstein. A useful album.

Unicorn-Kanchana DKPcd 9111. H. Herford, baritone, and R. Bowman, piano, presenting songs by Ives.

Cedille CDR 900000 005. The Ives *"Concord"* Sonata paired with a sonata by Copland.

Pro Arte CDD-140. Ives's *Three Places in New England*, paired with Copland's *Appalachian Spring*.

Charles Ives in 1948.
(Picture Collection, The Branch Libraries, The New York Public Library.)

R. Nathaniel Dett

chord: a group of notes sounding together as an entity

chromatic: using notes close together in pitch

diatonic: the normal ("do-re-mi") scale type

R. Nathaniel Dett (1882–1943) began an apprenticeship as a youth in Quebec, then at Oberlin Conservatory, Harvard and Columbia Universities, the Eastman School of Music, and then back to apprenticeship again when he decided to put his black heritage into music in a definitive way. He worked in a variety of places, ending in Battle Creek, Michigan, where he instituted a highly successful program of musical exchanges between white and black churches. He composed *Magnolia Suite* (1911) and *In the Bottoms Suite* (1913) for piano—the latter contained the "Juba Dance," which became extremely popular and is still heard occasionally. Representative of Dett's work is *Listen to the Lambs* (1914), which he called "A Religious Characteristic in the Form of an Anthem." It calls for an eight-part chorus of mixed voices without instruments and is based on a spiritual. It alternates between partial and full choir, between spare and thick *chordal* deployments, and between *chromatic* and *diatonic* usage. The contrasts are heightened not only by immediate juxtaposition, but also by exaggeration. It uses both African and European elements, the black reaching into the white, rather than vice versa. Dett was a highly respected musician in both camps.

Marie Bergersen

Marie Bergersen (1894–1989) was, in a real sense, the opposite of Amy Marcy Cheney. Cheney, a New Englander, was enamored of the German school and worked to enter it. Bergersen, born and brought up in Chicago, was trained in apprenticeship from her third birthday, giving piano recitals eighty-nine years apart and working on French, Italian, Russian, Polish, and American, as well as German music. She was sent to Vienna to study with Leopold Godowsky (1870–1938, a Polish pianist of renown), but he was truly an apprenticeship performer and taught music of many lands. Like Cheney, Bergersen composed for the most part in her youth, but, unlike Cheney, she was known almost entirely for her extraordinary gifts as a performer and composer of piano music,

Youthful photograph of Marie Bergersen.

 Recommended Recordings and Video Cassettes

Little music of R. Nathaniel Dett has been recorded, but some of the piano music remains in the repertoire.

New World NW 367-2. Piano music, including suites (*In The Bottoms* and *Magnolia Suite*) and the *Eight Bible Vignettes*. The "Juba Dance" from *In The Bottoms* is included in Borroff, Compact Discs.

Although Marie Bergersen's Theme and Variations *was performed as part of the United States Bicentennial Celebration (in Washington DC), it has never been commercially recorded. The* Three Silhouettes *(1911) are included in Borroff, Compact Discs.*

which she played both in the United States and abroad. Her most famous works were her *Three Silhouettes* (1911)[8] and *Theme and Variations* (1912), which she played in Vienna in 1913, but she also composed songs and choral works, plus some chamber music.

conductor: the musical director of a performing group

rubato: the pushing and relaxing of the beat for expressive purposes

CONCERT LIFE

Formal concerts in these years became more and more a part of the German-American system, which was an interrelated one of composers, performers, critics, and managers. As the university began to cover more and more of the operations of criticism and, particularly, publishing, the apprenticeship composers were squeezed more and more into the edges of concert life. Critics and publishers were, by and large, university trained. The bastions of the apprenticeship system were popular music (which was already in apposition to the formal-concert world) and all music having to do with theater, including opera. Performance had not yet been subsumed into university studies, and in any case, training for performance has always been, and probably will always remain, to a large extent a learning-by-doing, hands-on, one-on-one, master/student matter.

The Orchestra

The most German of the performing groups was the orchestra. Romantic philosophy was based to a certain extent upon the idea of a musical hierarchy, with the symphony at the top. Three performing media were recognized in all: the orchestra, the piano, and the operatic voice. All three of these were quite different in the nineteenth century from their eighteenth-century predecessors. The orchestra had grown from a group of twelve or eighteen to a group four times that large, and the instruments themselves had been developed to be more imposing in sound and easier, surer, in negotiation. The increasing size of the orchestra made necessary a *conductor*, which the eighteenth-century orchestra had not needed: not only was the earlier group smaller and more able to interreact, but the style of the music had been more straightforward. The ups and downs of rhythm (in a changing beat, using speed-ups and slowdowns, sometimes constantly shifting within individual phrases— called *rubato*) and of dynamic level (in a changing amount of sound, louder and softer within the phrases) made coordination impossible without a conductor. Individual subtlety had been turned into group subtlety, and the group no longer needed simply to begin together with the same speed, which the first violinist had seen to, but required an interpreter, who would oversee the small interpretive niceties that the new scores required.

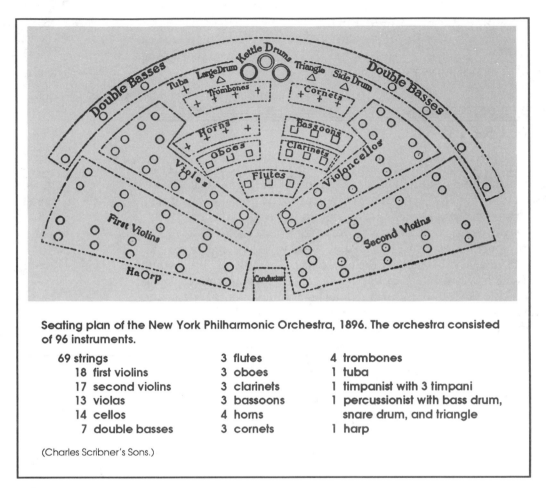

Seating plan of the New York Philharmonic Orchestra, 1896. The orchestra consisted of 96 instruments.

69 strings	3 flutes	4 trombones
18 first violins	3 oboes	1 tuba
17 second violins	3 clarinets	1 timpanist with 3 timpani
13 violas	3 bassoons	1 percussionist with bass drum,
14 cellos	4 horns	snare drum, and triangle
7 double basses	3 cornets	1 harp

(Charles Scribner's Sons.)

The Piano

concert grand: the largest piano, eight or nine feet long

The piano became the modern *concert grand*, an instrument whose crowning glory of having the longer strings cross over the middle-sized strings, releasing that added resonance to build a more robust tone, had been developed by Steinway and Sons of New York. Their instrument was exhibited at the Paris Exposition of 1867, was called "extraordinary" in the exhibition's report, and was awarded the grand prize. The American attitude toward piano playing was mixed; it was based more in the apprenticeship than the concert tradition—whereas the European-trained pianists thought of themselves as above playing for dances or contributing to the evening living room entertainments, the Americans were urged to be more practical. In 1851, *Harper's Magazine* published "Mems for Musical Misses," a set of instructions for playing the piano, instructions very, very American.

"The Orchestral Galop," songwriter unknown, 1867. (The Newberry Library.)

Sit in a simple, graceful, unconstrained posture. Aim more at pleasing than at astonishing. Be above the vulgar folly of pretending that you cannot play for dancing; for it proves only that if not disobliging, you are stupid. Although you must be strictly accurate as to time, it should sometimes be relaxed to favor the expression of Irish and Scotch airs. Never bore people with ugly music merely because it is the work of some famous composer, and do not let the pieces you perform before people not professedly scientific be too long.[9]

So even the art of the piano joined the schism between the apprenticeship and the concert traditions. Actually, few living rooms had a concert grand piano; most had smaller models, *uprights* or *spinets*. The music composed for the two sides overlapped, with the short pieces by Paine and MacDowell turning up in both camps.

upright piano: a piano with its mechanism in a vertical position

spinet: a small harpsi-chord; later, a small piano

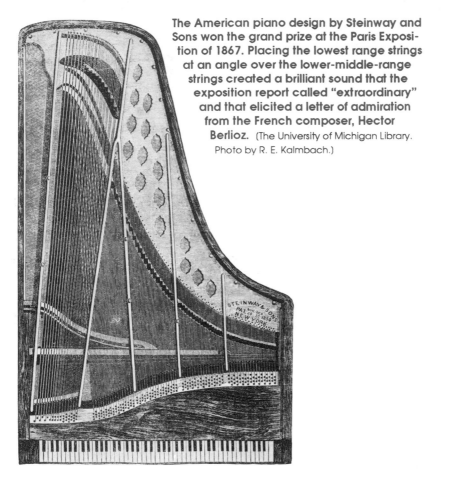

The American piano design by Steinway and Sons won the grand prize at the Paris Exposition of 1867. Placing the lowest range strings at an angle over the lower-middle-range strings created a brilliant sound that the exposition report called "extraordinary" and that elicited a letter of admiration from the French composer, Hector Berlioz. (The University of Michigan Library. Photo by R. E. Kalmbach.)

Heinrich Steinway, founder of Steinway and Sons. (Picture Collection, The Branch Libraries, The New York Public Library.)

The Operatic Voice

The romantic operatic voice developed in the second third of the nineteenth century, but here too the schism dictated a continuation of eighteenth-century ideals for American music and a switch to the romantic voice for the concert crowd. The classical ideal for the professional had been, as a writer put it in 1705, that "a perfect voice should be sonorous, of wide range, sweet, exact, lively, flexible."[10] That would remain the American ideal, the ideal of the singers of Stephen Foster's songs and, later, it would be the ideal of blues and swing singers. But the operatic ideal was quite different: loud, voluptuous, dramatic. The singer of European grand opera had to compete with an orchestra of size and splendor—one European composer, Richard Strauss, called for a group of 108 instrumentalists for his opera *Salome*, produced in Dresden in 1905 and in New York in 1907—and had to project into an immense space. (The Metropolitan Opera House in New York, which opened in

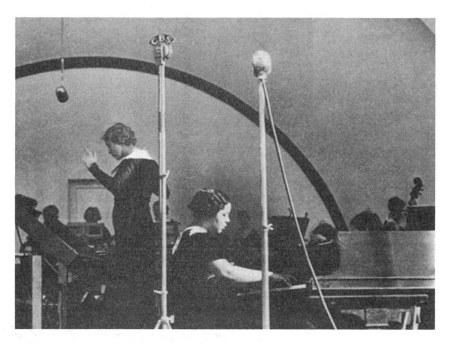

Ebba Sundstrom conducting the Woman's Symphony Orchestra of Chicago, with Margaret Bonds as soloist, 1934. (Music Division, Library of Congress.)

1883, sat 3,500 people and had standing room for 600 more.) The singers had to be athletic to overpower such odds, and they were called *Heldensinger*, hero-singers, by the Germans.

European Influences

So the European concert life was based in the symphony, the virtuoso, heroic piano literature, and the opera. In addition, combinations of these were admitted to the hierarchy: the opera was already a combination of voice and orchestra; the piano concerto was a combination of piano and orchestra; and the *Lieder* (German: *songs*) recital combined piano and voice.

It was an uphill battle for the German-Americans. The Germania Society, founded in New York in 1847, established a small group (of two dozen players) called the Germania Orchestra, but the German ideal did not immediately win the public. "That the Germania [orchestra] did not succeed in attracting audiences was repeatedly regretted in the newspapers."[11] Nonetheless, they won a permanent berth eventually, in Boston.

Women

Women fared better in apprenticeship than in the European concert system. Women, after all, had been part and parcel of the apprenticeship

Heldensinger: "hero-singer," one able to sing in the lush romantic style

Lieder: songs (German), commonly referring to German "art songs"

song: a melody sung to words

corps de ballet: the dancers of a ballet company performing together

English opera: British ballad opera, a stage work in which speech and song, action and dance, were mixed

system even before there were written records: in Egypt, the Pharaoh's instrumentalists had been about half and half male and female; and Sappho had been a famous poetess in Greece in the seventh century B.C. In New York in 1899, Amy Fay (1844–1928), a Mississippi-born pianist who studied in Berlin and Weimar, and her sister, founded the Women's Philharmonic Society, with more than two hundred members. In 1908, Charles Martin Loeffler (1861–1939), a British-born, Berlin-trained violinist (a member of the Boston Symphony Orchestra), formed a group of his women students into The American String Quartette—their debut in 1909 was successful and they were on their way.[12] The Fadette Women's Orchestra of Boston was active from 1888 to 1920. The number of competent women must have been very high for such groups to be formed, to keep in business, and to succeed.

Also, in 1898, Helen May Butler founded an "all-ladies' concert band" billed as "An Adamless Garden of Musical Eves." Butler was a cornet soloist and conductor who once was the guest conductor of the Sousa Band.[13]

OPERA

Americans have always liked opera. From earliest days, the electricity of the combined theatrical arts has appealed to them, and as cities were founded and developed in the United States, opera companies have thrived—in the early days mostly on tour—but also, as it proved practicable, opera houses have been built. American opera, however, was for the most part unlike European opera, which, in the nineteenth century, entered the romantic spirit, with long productions, large orchestras, and the heavy singing voice of the *Heldensinger*. Americans preferred shorter works, small orchestras (known as *pit orchestras*, generally of twelve to sixteen players), and a classical singing voice. This texture was livelier, quicker, and allowed the text to be heard; it threw the action of the opera from the European voice-and-orchestra to the American singer-and-singer. In addition, it emphasized dancing in a more direct way: in European opera, any dance element was generally provided by a separate *corps de ballet* attached to the opera house; in American works, the chorus members both sang and danced, and sometimes even danced while singing.

American operas had begun as an offshoot of *English opera*. English opera was not simply opera in the English language, but was a special kind of stage work in which speech and song, action and dance, were mixed. That type of theater was brought here by British musicians and taken to the bosom of American audiences. In Europe a stern judgment took place: opera with no speech was called *grand opera*, and other kinds were looked down upon. But grand opera also dealt with mythology and royalty, gods and kings, and the Americans liked homier subjects—and humor. Some operas had very little spoken performance, and others had a great deal, virtually a play with songs interjected here and there. There is no real dividing line; the subject matter and the text (called the *libretto* or *book*) decided the ratio of speech and music, the ratio between song and dance.

Almost at once in the United States, the Americans established a strong tradition of opera of all kinds, and the European-trained composers began a much smaller tradition of grand opera. The first was by the Philadelphia composer-critic William Henry Fry, whose opera *Leonora* was produced in Philadelphia in 1845. Another from his pen followed: *Notre Dame de Paris*, in 1864. The European subject matter of these works is obvious—the heroine Leonora had been the subject of operas by three European composers, including Beethoven.

By the end of the century the Metropolitan Opera had been founded in New York City (in 1883), and companies were working both in home cities and on the road. But the Metropolitan Opera was (and still is) basically a European house in New York, and American composers who aspired to having their works produced there had to compose works in the European mold.

So once again a schism established itself. And once again the purveyors of the European tradition declared that tradition superior; in fact, they refused to call other works "operas" at all—they were called *comic operas*, *light operas*, and, at the end of the century, *operettas*, and, still later, *musicals* or even *shows*.

The American vein was rich. The 1850s were abundant in productions of American opera. Examples are George Frederick Bristow's *Rip Van Winkle* (1855) and George Frederick Root's "operatic cantatas," including *The Haymakers* (1857). The Civil War, of course, dampened all projects as expensive as opera production, but within a generation after the war, production had begun again. Emma Roberts Steiner (1850–1929) was an opera conductor; she conducted over 6,000 performances of operas in America (not all of them American works, of course), and composed nine of her own, including *Fleurette* (1889). John Philip Sousa's *El Capitan* was produced in New York in 1895, in Boston in 1896 (it ran for four years), and in London in 1899 (for 140 performances)—and it has recently been revived, by the Mississippi Opera in 1989 and the Skylight Opera of Milwaukee in 1990. Rosalie Balmer Cale was noted for humor; her *Love, Powder, and Patches*, produced in St. Louis in 1897, was called "fascinating" by one critic. Her opera *Four Pecks or a Bushel of Fun* was also produced in St. Louis, in 1907, and later in New York as *Cupid's Halloween*. In a more serious vein, Bruce E. Knowlton composed six operas, all produced in Portland, Oregon, from *The Monk of Toledo* (1915), to *Montana* (1933). The most prolific of the composers was doubtless Harry Lawrence Freeman (1869–1954), who composed twenty-seven

libretto: the text of an opera

book: libretto

THE DEATH OF MINNEHAHA.

WORDS FROM
LONGFELLOW'S NEW POEM
HIAWATHA.
MUSIC BY
CH. C. CONVERSE.

"The Death of Minnehaha," music by Ch. C. Converse, c. 1867. (The Newberry Library.)

operas between 1892 and 1944, on his own librettos, including *The African Kraal*, produced at Wilberforce University in Ohio in 1903, *Voodoo* (set in Louisiana) in New York in 1914, and *Vendetta* (set in Mexico) in New York in 1923. His first big success, *The Martyr*, was premiered in Denver in 1893, but also was done in Chicago that year, in Cleveland (where Freeman was born) in 1897 and 1900, at Wilberforce University in 1904—and in New York in 1947! Several of Freeman's works were grand operas.

But grand operas were few; there were few houses in which to mount

No nineteenth-century American operas have been recorded except Scott Joplin's Treemonisha, *which is available on records and on video cassette. The latter is highly recommended.*

Kultur International Films Ltd., VCR 1240. Scott Joplin, *Treemonisha*. An excellent performance.

them. The Metropolitan Opera in New York produced very few American operas, notably Horatio Parker's *Mona*, in 1910, Victor Herbert's *Natoma*, in 1911 (by the Met, in Philadelphia; it was also done in Baltimore, Chicago, Los Angeles, and San Francisco); and Charles Wakefield Cadman (who composed ten operas, from 1912 to 1932) was represented by *Shanewis* in 1917. John Knowles Paine, who had composed a comic opera in Italian in 1862, composed *Azara* (on a French story) in 1898, but it received only a concert performance (that is, not staged, but sung rather like an oratorio, without costumes or sets). George Whitefield Chadwick composed six operas from 1884 to 1917, but they were performed in Boston and Chicago, not at the Met.

Perhaps the most exciting of the American operas of that era were Scott Joplin's *A Guest Of Honor* (1903) and *Treemonisha* (1911). With their melodic grace, the rhythmic vitality of *ragtime* elements, and harmonic leanness, so contrary to romantic concerns, they paved the way for the future.

ragtime: an African-American musical style characterized by high energy and off-rhythms

"Indian Operas"

Many American operas were produced on Native American subjects during those years; it amounted to a fad. Indian music had come into popularity in good part through statements (verbal and musical) by the Czech composer Antonin Dvorak (1841–1904), who served as director of the National Conservatory in New York from 1892 to 1895. He had fostered the music of African–Americans, women, and Native Americans, and, in 1893, produced his famous *New World Symphony*. The challenge of bringing Native American musical idioms into the European traditional forms was a fascinating one. Edward MacDowell composed an orchestral work, the *Indian Suite*, in 1898. Thurlow Lieurance (1878–1963), an Iowa-born bandmaster, brought out several volumes of songs based on Indian themes, including items from Cheyenne, Sioux,

Black Hawk Waltzes, by Mary E. Walsh, was first printed in 1872. This cover is from 1902. (Duke University.)

⊃ Recommended Recordings and Video Cassettes

| *The piano album cited on page 100 contains items of Native American materials.*

Navajo, Crow, and Omaha cultures.[14] And, of course, Arthur Farwell was composing music on Indian themes.

But operas on Indian subjects were not new. In 1858, Lucien H. Southard had produced *Owano* (in a concert performance); in 1859, Eduard Sobolewsky immigrated from Germany to Milwaukee, largely a German-speaking community, and produced *Mohega, die Blume des Waldes* (Mohega, the flower of the fields—about a Native American woman). William Legrand Howland (1873–1915) composed the opera *Sarrona: or, The Indian Slave*; it was produced in New York in 1901 and 1910, in Bruges, Belgium, in 1903, and in Philadelphia in 1911—and it had over two hundred performances in twenty-one houses in Italy and Austria. Mary Carr Moore (1873–1957) composed ten operas, including *Narcissa: or, The Cost of Empire* (1911), and *The Flaming Arrow* (1920).

BAND MUSIC

Americans were holding their own in the concert field. The piano music of Gottschalk, Paine, MacDowell, Dett, Cheney, and Bergersen (among many others) stood up proudly alongside the European-trained traditionalists. The symphonies of Paine and Chadwick, the piano concertos of Robyn and Cheney, the symphonic poems of such composers as John Alden Carpenter (*Adventures in a Perambulator*, 1915) and Charles Tomlinson Griffes (*The White Peacock*, 1917—a strangely French work)— all of these works, and many more, did America proud.

But the band in the United States was a national glory. The smiles of summer evenings in the park, the excitements of the Barnum and Bailey Circus (from 1871, "The Greatest Show on Earth"), the high-stepping of the dance hall, the panoply of political and military parades, the dignity of presidential inaugurations all were energized by that most American of musical groups, the band.

Patrick Gilmore

Patrick S. Gilmore.
(Picture Collection, The Branch Libraries, The New York Public Library.)

Patrick Gilmore (1829–92) was an Irish-born cornetist who settled in Massachusetts and formed Gilmore's Grand Boston Band in 1859; in 1861, the whole group joined the Union Army. When the Civil War ended, Gilmore snatched up musicians as they were mustered out, and

A quintette from Gilmore's band. (Picture Collection, The Branch Libraries, The New York Public Library.)

he produced a number of Jubilee spectaculars: in 1864, a Grand National Band festival in New Orleans, with five hundred army musicians, plus added drums and bugles and a chorus of five thousand children, ending with a performance of "Hail, Columbia!" that included bursts from thirty-six cannons; in 1869, the National Peace Jubilee, in Boston, a five-day affair with an orchestra of one thousand, six bands, and a chorus of ten thousand. In 1872, he mounted the World Peace Jubilee, also in Boston, with an orchestra of two thousand, a chorus of twenty thousand, and a performance of Verdi's "Anvil Chorus" that featured one hundred Boston firemen with real anvils. But Gilmore's lasting fame as a musician dated from 1873, when he took directorship of the 22nd Regimental Band, turned it into a fine concert group, and toured the United States, Canada, and Europe.

Gilmore's Successors

Gilmore's successors were less monumentally inclined, but they made the concert bands of America the best in the world. Notable were those of Giuseppe Creatore, Edwin Franko Goldman, Bohumir Kryl—and, of course, John Philip Sousa, one of those larger-than-life figures who appears, armed with tremendous talent and determination, just as the wave crests, and rides it with great flair to immortality.

▶○ Recommended Recordings and Video Cassettes

Some excellent recordings have been made recapturing turn-of-the-century bands. See also the Sousa albums mentioned on page 102.

Angel CDC-54131. *The Great American Main Street Band.* A turn-of-the-century park band concert. It includes early jazz.

RCA RCD-4336. *The Village Band.*

Philips 434276-2. *Red, White & Brass.* Featuring The Canadian Brass.

New World 80266. The Goldman band, in concert items.

harmonium: a reed organ

carillon: a set of bells or chimes

pipe organ: an organ whose sounding elements are pipes controlled by a player at a console

chimes: tubular bells

The Johnson band of the first half of the century had been at home in the park gazebo, the Gilmore band in the festival arena, and the Sousa band found its home in the concert hall. Sousa as an international figure was as important as anyone else in his day; and the band became for the United States what the orchestra was for Germany.

The National Centennial

A representative use of the band in America, its symbolic participation in the national life, was the celebration of the national centennial, in Philadelphia, from May to November of 1876, with attendance of well over nine million. The exposition was concerned almost entirely with mechanical and commercial exhibits, and the only musical exhibits were pianos, *harmoniums*, and the centennial *carillon* (of thirteen bells to represent the thirteen original states). But band concerts were frequent.

The huge opening ceremonies went to the heart of the nation. An immense platform had been erected to hold the band, an orchestra, and a choir, and a *pipe organ* had been built. The ceremonies began with the band playing thirteen national anthems, beginning with that of the United States and ending with that of Russia. Next came a newly commissioned "Inaugural March" by the renowned German composer Richard Wagner. (It fell far below the standards for marches set by American band composers—it is as difficult for an orchestral composer to write for band as it is for a band composer to write for orchestra.) Next, after the invocation, was a new hymn by John Greenleaf Whittier, with music by John Knowles Paine, performed by the choir, organ, and orchestra (Paine, of course, as a German-trained composer, would not have used the band). A cantata by the poet-composer Sidney Lanier preceded the opening speeches. Finally, President Grant declared the exposition officially open. The climax of the occasion occurred as the flag of the United States was unfurled: George Frideric Handel's "Hallelujah Chorus" was sung with orchestra and organ accompaniment, and a salute of 100 guns was fired from George's Hill, together with the ringing of *chimes* from different parts of the grounds.[15]

NOTES

1. *The Saturday Evening Post*, October 19, 1912, in *The United States Presidents* (Indianapolis: The Curtis Publishing Company, 1980), p. 97.

2. Eric Foner and John A. Garraty, eds., *The Reader's Companion to American History* (Boston: Houghton Mifflin Company, 1991), p. 534.

3. William Lichtenwanger, ed., *Oscar Sonneck and American Music* (Urbana: University of Illinois Press, 1983), p. 60.

4. This work is contained in the *Anthology of Musical Examples* accompanying Edith Borroff, *Music in Europe and the United States: A History*, second edition (New York: Ardsley House, Publishers, Inc., 1990), pp. 407–10.

5. Christine Ammer, *Unsung: A History of Women in American Music* (Westport, CT: Greenwood Press, 1980), p. 77.

6. Borroff, *Anthology*, pp. 411–15 for Cheney's piano piece, "Dreaming" (1892).

7. *The Boston Herald*, 22 September 1903.

8. Borroff, *Anthology*, pp. 416–27.

9. Arthur Loesser, *Men, Women, and Pianos* (New York: Simon and Schuster, 1954), p. 509.

10. Le Cerf de La Vieville, in Oliver Strunk, ed., *Source Readings in Music History* (New York: W. W. Norton & Co., 1950), p. 501.

11. Lawrence, *Resonances*, p. 548.

12. Ellen Knight, "The American String Quartette," *Sonneck Society Bulletin*, vol. 18, no. 3 (Fall, 1992), pp. 98–101.

13. Patricia Backhaus, "The Female Sousa," *Sonneck Society Bulletin*, vol. 18, no. 3 (Fall 1992), p. 120.

14. Borroff, *Anthology*, pp. 466–70.

15. Frank F. Norton, ed., *Historical Register of the Centennial Exposition, 1876* (New York: Frank Leslie, 1877), p. 78.

BIBLIOGRAPHY

Ammer, Christine. *Unsung: A History of Women in American Music*. Westport, CT: Greenwood Press, 1980.

Borroff, Edith. *American Operas: A Checklist*. Detroit Studies in Music Bibliography, no. 69. Warren, MI: Harmonie Park Press, 1992.

————. *Music in Europe and the United States: A History*, 2nd ed. New York: Ardsley House, Publishers, 1990.

————. *Anthology of Musical Examples—Music in Europe and the United States: A History*, 2nd ed. New York: Ardsley House, Publishers, 1990.

Chase, Gilbert. *America's Music: From the Pilgrims to the Present*. rev. ed. Urbana: University of Illinois Press, 1992.

Foner, Eric, and John A. Garraty, eds. *The Reader's Companion to American History.* Boston: Houghton Mifflin Company, 1991.

Knight, Ellen. "The American String Quartette." *Sonneck Society Bulletin,* vol. 28, no. 3 (Fall 1992).

Lawrence, Vera Brodsky. *Resonances: 1836–1850. Strong On Music,* vol. 1. New York: Oxford University Press, 1988.

Lichtenwanger, William, ed. *Oscar Sonneck and American Music.* Urbana: University of Illinois Press, 1983.

Loesser, Arthur. *Men, Women, and Pianos.* New York: Simon & Schuster, 1954.

Norton, Frank F., ed. *Historical Register of the Centennial Exposition, 1876.* New York: Frank Leslie, 1877.

Slonimsky, Nicolas. *Baker's Biographical Dictionary of Musicians,* 8th ed. New York: Schirmer Books, 1990.

Strunk, Oliver. *Source Readings in Music History.* New York: W. W. Norton & Co., 1950.

———. *The United States Presidents.* Indianapolis: The Curtis Publishing Company, 1980.

5

Other Venues
(1880 to 1923)

A lthough the difference in training between the American apprenticeship and the European traditions was, at first, chiefly a matter of method rather than content, the gap was beginning to widen in the matter of content as well—not yet a dissonance, but noticeable just the same.

A gap was spreading much more quickly and widely, however, between what we now call "classical" and "popular" music. These two types of music, through the last several hundred years in Europe, had diverged and then come back together several times; most notably, in late eighteenth-century Europe the two types had come so closely together that composers could write music of both types in the same style. But with the romantic movement, the two diverged once again.

By the last third of the nineteenth century, romantic music had diverged from the eighteenth-century norm in the matters of size, dynamic level, *tempo*, and *texture*. Romanticism went off toward grandeur: big orchestras, louder sounds both individually and corporately, slower tempos, and smooth textures. This new musical ideal required special performance techniques, and therefore it demanded new teaching techniques to implement the ideal.

Concert apprenticeship went along with much—although not all—of the new ideal. Sousa's band, for example, was a large one compared to earlier concert bands (except for the giant bands of Gilmore): it ranged from thirty to forty-five players over its many years. Concert pianists were still trained in apprenticeship but used the new, more forceful, instruments. The universities still did not teach practical music—that is, the art of performance—except for choirs, which paralleled church choirs in significant ways.

But much of American music remained with the old ideal: small groups, less encompassing sounds, livelier tempos, and more animated textures. Music of the old tradition changed in content too, but on its own terms, designed for the place, the occasion, and the audience. This unified concept, of the music appropriate to a certain architecture, a certain audience, and a certain purpose, is called a *venue*, from the Latin "to come." Park concerts, for example, comprised a venue: an outdoor concert, which means a need for carrying power of instruments and voices; a presentation where the audience moved around, or would come and go, with many people sitting on blankets on the grass, eating sandwiches or popcorn. The churches also comprised a venue: the services themselves (of almost all churches) included substantial musical components. And churches also maintained social institutions that included everything from regular choir concerts to special appear-

120

Bandstand at Edgerton Park in Rochester, New York. (Picture Collection, The Branch Libraries, The New York Public Library.)

ances of solo singers, instrumental groups, or visiting virtuosos. In the smaller communities that could not support a concert hall, churches provided good performance spaces. And in the larger towns, even when they supported concert halls, special musical events often took place in churches, which generally had higher vaulting, and often had pipe organs, which the concert halls did not have.

And, of course, as the cities grew, they built concert halls, opera houses, and theaters, which, along with saloons and dance halls, offered musical excitements to the townspeople. Each venue developed its own music, suitable to its place, its purpose, its audience—that was inevitable. And those types of music most strongly bound to a particular type of occasion were the most strongly bound to the apprenticeship system of training.

THE LIVING ROOM

transcription: the adaptation of a composition to a medium other than its original one

trimmings: spontaneous decoration in music

variations: trimmings

The one exception to this was probably the living room. For one thing, different families wanted different music. Some families had more than one pianist, and they played four-hand music. Some family musicians played for singers, others for dancing; some played only for the family, others for company or even for larger groups of people when their reputation led to it—fiddlers often began at home and earned their initial reputations in the living room. Four-hand piano music and fiddling are at the opposite poles of European and apprenticeship music. For the music printed for two players—i.e., piano four hands—most likely consisted of *transcriptions* of symphonies and string quartets from the European tradition, whereas fiddle music was seldom written down at all, often improvised, and even if written down, not played "straight." European music was to be taken literally, but fiddle tunes were to be dolled up in performance, enlivened by embellishments called *trimmings* or *variations*. These would be done on the spur of the moment; they were not written down, but were added by individual singers, fiddlers, pianists, clarinetists, or any other soloists, as an enrichment that added presence, immediacy, and excitement.

Both could be found in the living room. Actually, *anything* could be found in the living room. One family might have a fiddler cousin, and abound in *extempore* trimmings. Another might have a minister for a father, and reverberate with hymn singing, either straight or with trimmings, or, in the same evening, both. Still another family might love concert music and concentrate on staid performances of well-known European songs and violin/piano or piano *solo* sonatas (or other pieces) in straightforward performances of variable skills, depending upon the family members currently making music. Another might have a visiting harmonica player who could play for dancing almost like a fiddler, present a popular song with trimmings, or offer folk music, like an old-timer on the trail in the West. Many songs would be performed just as they were published; others might be done *by ear*, that is, without written music, but presented as the memory dictated (as someone might read a story or tell it from memory—with trimmings!). The same was true of the piano literature: in the 1890s, for example, a young person (or an older man or woman) might play a piano piece by MacDowell, exactly as published, or a popular piece such as "The Missouri Waltz" by Frederic Knight Logan (popular in the nineties, and the official song of the state of Missouri), with whatever skill the player's personality, training, and aptitude allowed.

No venue was as free, as varied, or as full of imagination as the living room, which remained the center of the American musical art through most of the first half of the twentieth century.[1]

THE THEATER

Almost as rich a vein was the popular theater. Vaudeville had expanded and given way to musical shows, particularly *musical comedy* and the *revue*. No two scholars agree on the exact origin of these musical types, but they seem clearly related to the two halves of the minstrel show: the first part, with its dialogues and skits, to the musical comedy; and the second part, or olio, to the revue. The first type dealt with situations and responses to situations; the second was a series of acts, starring opera singers, clog dancers, acrobats, singers in the popular style, magicians, dog acts, and anything else that could intrigue (and lure) an audience. All of the acts used music, in more than one way: such features as acrobats, jugglers, and animal acts used music to coordinate movement, give energy to the performers, and suggest moods or responses to the audience (to overlay but not to synchronize with their activities); dancers used music in a much more precise way, in exact synchrony not only of beat but of meaning, not only to coordinate but to define; and singers, fiddlers, or harmonica players (to name but three) used music essentially, presenting not an action heightened by music, but music itself. The pit orchestra of such a production had to be extremely versatile, perhaps playing the orchestral counterpart of a grand-opera aria, then *background music*, then *essential music*, one after the other in quick succession and without dropping a beat.

Vaudeville had contained elements of both, and it was still going

musical comedy: a play or movie in which the story is developed with song

revue: a musical production made of various segments or acts, usually without a unifying dramatic element

background music: music behind dramatic action

essential music: music presented for itself alone

A vaudeville theater.
(Picture Collection, The Branch Libraries, The New York Public Library.)

strong, but vaudeville had been a gathering of acts, any one of them dispensable, and the individual show might change kaleidoscopically over a long run, with acts leaving and new ones coming in; the idea was that of a variety show, and the producer's job was to offer a balance of types and interests, while at the same time starring personalities whom the public were interested in and would pay money to see.

The musical comedies had plots, of course, even if loose ones; the revues had general themes. But the stars often owned their own music, and star appearances were often added without much thought of relevance or appropriateness of mood.

The musical comedy was related also to comic opera, and often it is not easy—or even possible—to tell which category a work fell into. The dividing lines between opera and comic opera and musical comedy were never precise. The deciding issue was venue: at the end of the nineteenth century the opera houses were already using singers trained in the European romantic style of singing, and the popular-music houses were still using singers trained in the old classical voice techniques, including the singing/acting combination of song and recitation. So by the turn of the century, singers sang either in opera houses or concert

A scene from *An American Beauty*, 1897. (Picture Collection, The Branch Libraries, The New York Public Library.)

The Belle of New York,
1897. (Picture Collection,
The Branch Libraries, The
New York Public Library.)

halls (both European venues), or theaters or dance halls (apprenticeship venues). The different names attest to this distinction, and there were other differences. Speech was simply "spoken dialogue" in the musical comedy, but in opera, speech (or the half-spoken, half-sung style related to elocution) was given the Italian name *recitativo* (or, in English, *recitative*); the printed-out text of a musical comedy was the book, but in opera it was the *libretto* ("little book" in Italian); in musical comedy the vocal solo was simply a "song," but in opera it was an *aria* (Italian for "song")—for grand opera was as Italian as the symphony was German. The orchestra was still called the orchestra, though the musical comedy and revue had pit groups and opera orchestras were as large as the house and the budget would allow. The *producer*, director, and conductor were given the same names and had the same jobs, although the demands of their jobs were very different, and an opera producer would not have been able to produce a revue (and vice versa). They represented two different theatrical and musical worlds.

It is believed that the term *musical comedy* was first used as a designation for a theatrical work on the score of *The Belle of New York* by Gustave Kerker in 1897. The term *revue* was probably later: the impresario Florenz Ziegfeld (1867–1932) produced his first New York revue in 1907, and by 1911, was calling the new editions the *Ziegfeld Follies*, defined as "an elaborate, richly costumed theatrical revue consisting of a series of musical or dance skits,"[2] and of course, these productions too included a variety of acts, including comedy skits. Ziegfeld was known for the finale of his shows, in which extravagantly dressed beauties proceeded down an elaborate stairway—certainly with resonances of the minstrel show's walk-around.

By the early 1920s, Ziegfeld was probably at the top of the theatrical

recitativo: vocal music more spoken (recited) than sung

aria: a song, particularly in an opera

producer: the person in charge of the finances and practical arrangements for a musical event

▶◯ Recommended Recordings and Video Cassettes

Albums of old-time Broadway shows are available; some are reworkings of old recordings.

New World NW 215 (LP). *Follies, Scandals, & Other Diversions, from Ziegfeld to the Schuberts.* Contains "Mister Gallagher and Mister Sean," sung by those two in the *Ziegfeld Follies of 1922* and recorded in that year; George Gershwin's "I'll Build a Stairway to Paradise," from the *George White Scandals of 1922*, played by Paul Whiteman and His Orchestra, originally issued as a Victor record in 1922; Jimmy McHugh's "Doin' the New Low-down," from *Lou Leslie's Blackbirds of 1928* (but representative of earlier shows), sung and tap-danced (you can hear it!) by Bill Robinson; and "Shine On, Harvest Moon" by Nora Bayes and Jack Norworth, sung by Bayes in the *Ziegfeld Follies of 1908*, but recorded in 1931 by Ruth Etting, impersonating Bayes.

New World 80387. *Sitting Pretty* by Jerome Kern. This show was produced in 1924, but it was at the end of the era in which Kern collaborated with British novelist P. G. Wodehouse.

heap, but other showmen, such as George White, had entered the arena. George White's Scandals, the chief rival of the Ziegfeld Follies, were notable in that they introduced the music of the young George Gershwin, music that would be important in the two decades to follow. Both Jerome Kern and Irving Berlin were involved in shows in the first two decades of the twentieth century. In fact, one of the strong points of the apprenticeship system was that it allowed young composers to have a chance at introducing just one number into a show, often sponsored by a performer of renown. (On the other hand, one composer had to write an entire opera, a difficult task for a young composer trying to get started.) An excellent example of this process is the use by Al Jolson, the last of the blackface entertainers, of Gershwin's song "Swanee" in the show *Sinbad* in 1919. Jolson brought the song into the show; it became his signature song, and it pulled Gershwin into the limelight.

SONGS

Songs are always part of cultural expression. (All of the arts are always a part of it.) But at certain times in history one type of expression becomes more important than others, and songs are no exception. At the end of the nineteenth century (as at the end of the sixteenth), songs became a principal means of that expression in the United States. Speculation about causes is extremely interesting to scholars, and perhaps also to the people who love songs, but speculation proves nothing, however interesting it is. It seems clear, for example, that the popularity of songs comes in cycles: a cycle of musical style, in which a new style is defined elsewhere and moves into song late in the formulation; and a cycle in which words predominate, then music, and, for a brief lovely time between, both are equal in importance.

tearjerker: a popular song of the 1890s, generally with several stanzas, with a sad, melodramatic text

Songs of the Late Nineteenth Century

Songs in the last two decades of the nineteenth century were for the most part either folk songs, patriotic songs, or *tearjerkers*. The folk songs were declining in number as the coast-to-coast expansion of the country was more and more taken for granted; "Polly-Wolly-Doodle" is an example (it was published in 1883, but probably dated from twenty years

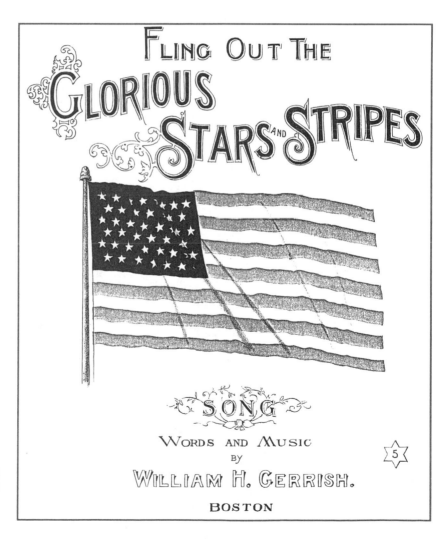

"Fling Out the Glorious Stars and Stripes," by William H. Gerrish, 1897. The flag had 45 stars, following the statehood of Utah the preceding year. (The Newberry Library.)

earlier). The patriotic songs were also declining in number, not because patriotism itself was in decline, but because the Civil War had brought out so many; "America the Beautiful," published in 1895, is an example.

The tearjerker was a singing/acting story of a hard life, extremely emotional (the dictionary says "mawkish"),[3] generally a song of several stanzas depicting not only events, but reactions to events; such songs as "The Little Lost Child" (by Marks and Stern, 1894), "The Picture that Is Turned toward the Wall," and "My Mother Was a Lady" were favorite vaudeville numbers, often sung pathetically, with illustrations projected from slides. "Sometimes I Feel like a Motherless Child" (published in 1899 in *Old Plantation Hymns*) and "She's Only a Bird in a Gilded Cage" (1900)—it sold two million copies—may have been the final ones.

The tearjerker "Bid Me Good Bye," music by F. Paolo Tosti, 1888. (The Newberry Library.)

Just listing the songs of the "Gay Nineties" reveals the scope and joy of American life in those years. In the 1890s, there was "After the Ball" by Charles K. Harris (1892), a banjo player from Poughkeepsie, New York, a waltz tune of sweet sadness, but not a tearjerker. Other songs in the Gay Nineties were already heading toward the future: "Daisy Bell" (known as "A Bicycle Built for Two," by Harry Dacre) in 1892 told of the joys associated with the bicycling fad of those years; "The Band Played On" by John F. Palmer (1895) is a tribute to the dancing days—and these would become stronger in their appeal as the decades went on. "A Hot Time in the Old Town Tonight" (by Cad L. Mays, 1896) suggests a more raucous side.

"Oh Aint He Sweet on Me," music by Emile Chandos, 1871. (The Newberry Library.)

Harry von Tilzer

Tin Pan Alley: a nickname for the song business, centered on lower Broadway, at the beginning of the twentieth century

sheet music: short pieces or songs in separate publications

The writer of "She's Only a Bird in a Gilded Cage" was Harry von Tilzer (1872–1946), who came to New York from his native Detroit and became an important entrepreneur in the music business. As musician, composer, and publisher, he was a chief founder of the lower Broadway group called *Tin Pan Alley* (the term was first used in 1908). The selling of *sheet music* was an essential business when living rooms had pianos and the family all played and sang. Tilzer reflected public taste and also influenced it. His songs were many and extremely popular; they included "Wait 'til the Sun Shines, Nellie" (1905) and "I Want a Girl (Just like the Girl that Married Dear Old Dad)" (1911). These later songs told of more modern American interests, were often straightforward love songs, and, in general, spoke of a proud people pleased with what they had become.

Tin Pan Alley, 1916. (Picture Collection, The Branch Libraries, The New York Public Library.)

The cover for "All the Boys Keep Looking Down," by Harry von Tilzer, 1926. (The Newberry Library.)

ALL THE BOYS KEEP LOOKING DOWN

WORDS & MUSIC BY HARRY VON TILZER

Harry Von Tilzer Music Pub Co 1587 BROADWAY NEW YORK

WITH UKULELE ACCOMPANIMENT

Recommended Recordings and Video Cassettes

The best recordings of period songs are those by Joan Morris, accompanied by her husband, composer William Bolcom.

Nonesuch H-71304 (LP). *After the Ball.* Joan Morris and William Bolcom. Songs by Charles K. Harris, James Weldon Johnson, and Harry von Tilzer. The album includes "She's Only a Bird in a Gilded Cage" (1900) and "Wait Till the Sun Shines, Nellie" (1905) by von Tilzer, and "Under the Bamboo Tree" (1902) by J. W. and J. Rosamund Johnson and Bob Cole.

Nonesuch H-71330. *Vaudeville: Songs of the Great Ladies of the Musical Stage.* Also by Morris and Bolcom, including "May Irwin's 'Frog' Song" (1896) by Charles E. Trevathan; "In the Baggage Coach Ahead" (1896) by Gussie L. Davis; and "Shine On, Harvest Moon" (1908) by Nora Bayes and Jack Norworth.

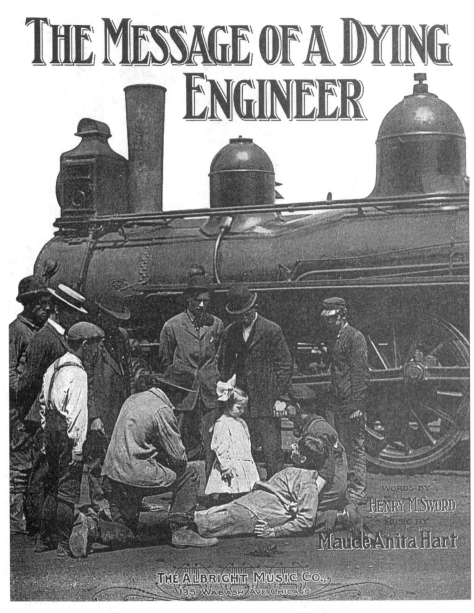

The tearjerker "The Message of a Dying Engineer," music by Maude Anita Hart, **1908.** (The Newberry Library.)

Songs of the Early Twentieth Century

A list of songs of the first decades of the twentieth century can only suggest the genuineness of experience and the joy in it which characterized them.

1903 "Ida Sweet as Apple Cider" by Eddie Munson

1903 "Sweet Adeline" by Henry W. Armstrong, probably the most popular work for barbershop quartet—it sold four million copies

1905 "The Whistler and His Dog" by Arthur Pryor
1908 "Shine On, Harvest Moon" by Nora Bayes and Jack Norworth
1909 "Put on Your Old Grey Bonnet" by Percy Wenrich
1910 "Down by the Old Mill Stream" by Tell Taylor
1910 "In the Shade of the Old Apple Tree" by Beth Whitson and Leo Friedman—with a sale of over eight million copies perhaps the biggest seller of them all
1911 "Oh, You Beautiful Doll" by Nat D. Ayer
1912 "When Irish Eyes are Smiling" by Ernest R. Ball
1913 "Too-Ra-Loo-Ra-Loo-Ra" by J. R. Shannon
1914 "By the Waters of Minnetonka" by Thurlow Lieurance
1918 "K-K-K-Katy" by Geoffrey O'Hara
1920 "Margie" by Con Conrad and J. Russel Robinson

But this happy list was interrupted by World War I, with such songs as "Pack Up Your Troubles in Your Old Kit Bag" by a Welshman, Felix Powell, but published in both London and New York in 1915; "You're in the Army Now" by Victor Ormond (1917); "Over There" by George M. Cohan (also 1917, but with a verse adapted from the 1886 song "Johnny Get Your Gun" by M. H. Rosenfeld); and "The Caissons Go Rolling Along" by Edmund L. Gruber (1918).

SHOWS

There were a great plenty of songs in those years, of which the list is representative. A glance at them reveals that they were composed by a large number of men and women, most of them now forgotten. A smaller number, of men for the most part, became famous for their musical shows. It is important to acknowledge, however, that a clear distinction cannot be made between songs published on their own, as part of the song literature, and songs that appeared in musical shows. First of all, the styles were the same, and the character of a song cannot place it in one venue or the other. And secondly, songs were put into and pulled out of shows with freedom, so that in the business there was no musical distinction to begin with.

Gus Edwards

Gus Edwards (1879–1945) was a German-born composer/producer, an important Tin Pan Alley man, who is known for his topical songs as well as those in shows. In addition to "In My Merry Oldsmobile" he composed "School Days" (1906) and "By the Light of the Silvery Moon" (1909).

George M. Cohan in *The Tavern*, 1921. (Picture Collection, The Branch Libraries, The New York Public Library.)

George M. Cohan

lyrics: the words of a song

dialogue song: a duet song based in exchanges between singers

Songs were often composed by the people who sang them. George M. Cohan (1878–1942) was an important example—and he wrote the *lyrics* as well. Perhaps he was most famous for his "Give My Regards to Broadway," which he performed in the revue *Little Johnny Jones,* in 1904. But he was also known for "Mary's a Grand Old Name" from *Forty-Five Minutes from Broadway* (1906), and "You're a Grand Old Flag" from *George Washington, Jr.* (also 1906). "Over There," already mentioned, was not in a show.

The Follies and Scandals

In addition to these important musicians, a host of stars appeared in the Follies and Scandals. After World War I, they made records and we can hear them still: Bert Williams singing "The Moon Shines on the Moonshine" by Robert Hood Bowers in *Broadway Brevities of 1920*; Fannie Brice

▶○ Recommended Recordings and Video Cassettes

> *Recordings of music from the Victor Herbert operettas are rare now, though songs from the productions were immensely popular on records for half a century; it wasn't until the development of LPs that entire musicals were recorded. See also the Recommended Recordings and Video Cassettes on page 218.*
>
> Arabesque Z-6529, Z-6547, and Z-6561. Victor Herbert songs from three shows, the last one of *The American Girl.*

singing "Second Hand Rose" (an acting/singing song) by James F. Hanley in the *Ziegfeld Follies of 1921*; and (Ed) Gallagher and (Al) Shean singing "Mister Gallagher and Mister Shean," a *dialogue song* which they wrote—words and music—and performed in the *Ziegfeld Follies of 1922.*

A new generation of songwriters was beginning to be heard. They included Jerome Kern, whose shows with British author P. G. Wodehouse included *Leave It to Jane* (1917); Irving Berlin, whose early songs were featured in the Ziegfeld Follies, including "A Pretty Girl Is Like a Melody" in the 1919 *Follies*; and George Gershwin, with early songs in *George White's Scandals*, "South Sea Isles" in 1921 and "I'll Build a Stairway to Paradise" in 1922. They were young, still tentative voices, but they would be vital in the music of the next decades.

ragtime: an African-American musical style characterized by high energy and off-rhythms

Victor Herbert

In addition, there were the forty-eight operas and operettas by Victor Herbert (1859–1924), an Irish-born cellist, whose career in New York began when he became a cellist in the Metropolitan Opera Orchestra. His stage works (he wrote other works, such as a cello concerto) included *Babes in Toyland* (1903), *The Red Mill* (1906), *Naughty Marietta* (1910), which included "Ah, Sweet Mystery of Life," *Sweethearts* (1913), *Angel Face* (1919), and *Orange Blossoms* (1922). He competed successfully with the Europeans working in New York, such as Franz Lehar (*The Merry Widow*, 1907), Sigmund Romberg (*Maytime*, 1917), and Rudolf Friml (*Rose Marie*, 1924).

RAGTIME

But perhaps nothing summed up the music of the turn of the century so much as *ragtime.* Modernism in the arts took on many forms during the first years of the century; Americans were feeling their oats, and new forms, whether or not they originated on our shores, were being enjoyed here. The New York Armory Show, in New York City, was a fine example; 1,400 feet of wall space held over 1,600 works of art, many French but also many American. The opening night, February 17, 1913, was an American production at its most exuberant: 4,000 guests attended to see the works of art, to hear speeches, and to listen to the Sixty-Ninth Regimental Band play from the balcony. Before the show closed, about 70,000 people had paid admission to see it, and the reviewer in the *Globe* had said, "American art will never be the same again."[4]

W. C. Handy

American irreverence for staid tradition was never far from the surface and never richer than in music. Many Americans recognized the excellence of the music of the blacks, which was so strongly African—to Europeans an exotic folk tradition. The dancing on the plantations, which was so admired by the visitors at the Sunday cakewalks from the beginning of the century, continued to develop. W. C. Handy (1873–1958) would speak of his early experience listening to the fiddler known as Uncle Whit Walker, who "stomped" as he played:

> Uncle Whit could stomp the left heel and the right forefoot and alternate this with the right heel and the left forefoot, making four beats to the bar. That was real stomping. . . . We Handy's Hill kids made rhythm by scraping a twenty-penny nail across the teeth of the jawbone of a horse that had died in the woods nearby. . . . We sang through fine tooth combs, . . . and made rhythmic sounds rattling our teeth.[5]

The body and the use of the mirliton (comb) came directly from Africa, as did the strong rhythmic motivation and the combination of body movement and instrumental technique.

W. C. Handy. (Photofest.)

"The Gravel Rag," by Charlotte Blake, 1908.

Scott Joplin

Handy was joined early in his work by Scott Joplin (1868–1917), who played the piano at the Chicago Columbian Exposition, bringing "ragged time" to the attention of an eager public. At the piano, ragging was the playing of sharply *syncopated* (off-accented) rhythms in the right hand against a steady beat in the left hand; by the time Joplin introduced it in Chicago, it was no longer new, but at the piano it took on a particular character, and the ragging of the right hand against the left gave it its name. Such rhythms had long been played, sung, and danced by more than one person (it was the heart of the cakewalk). Ragtime was piano music: music for the most romantic European instrument that introduced the African-American beat, rhythm, and strong melody—all played on one instrument by one person.

But ragtime, though named for its piano style, was not limited to that instrument: when Joplin moved to Missouri after his Chicago appear-

syncopated: on the off-accents

Recommended Recordings and Video Cassettes

More and more good recordings of ragtime music are available. The best recordings of solo piano are probably those of Scott Joplin, whose piano rolls are being made available at last.

Biograph BCD-101 and BCD-102. *The Entertainer*. 14 piano rolls, three played by Joplin.

Angel 4XS-36060. The New England Conservatory Ragtime Ensemble playing ragtime.

Nebula NU-5008. Ragtime played on guitar.

Northeastern (Classical Arts) NR 225-C. (cassette) *Pickles and Peppers and Other Rags by Women*. Played wonderfully by Virginia Eskin. Six composers of ragtime from the first decade of the twentieth century, with one modern item.

The "Maple Leaf Rag" is in Borroff, Compact Discs, which also contain the rag "That's Good Enough for Me" from *All in Fun* (1938) played by the composer, Baldwin Bergersen, in 1940 and then again in 1980, showing how performance varies (even of the same work) in the popular field.

The best of banjo ragtime is:

Banjar Records BR-1781. *Banjo Ragtime*.

"The Matinee Girl," by Jerome Basye, 1894. This two-step was played by Sousa's band. Note the wasp waist, in fashion at the time. (The Newberry Library.)

"La Rumba," danced by Ted Shawn and Ernistina Day. (Picture Collection, The Branch Libraries, The New York Public Library.)

ances, he founded a band in Sedalia and played there at the Maple Leaf Club, from 1897. It was a five-man band: cornet, clarinet, baritone horn, *tuba*, and piano—with Joplin at the piano. Joplin was an innovator; in addition to his composing some of the most famous of the rags (*Easy Winner, Original Rag*, and, his most famous, the *Maple Leaf Rag*, published in 1899—it sold three million copies), he wrote six piano studies of considerable difficulty, called *The School of Ragtime* (1908) and two operas: *A Guest of Honor*, produced in St. Louis in 1903, and *Treemonisha* (1911)—first produced in 1972 with an orchestration by composer T. J. Anderson. *Treemonisha* was truly experimental; it was ahead of its time in juxtaposing traditional recitatives and arias with ragtime choral dances.

The Dance Craze

But even more than instrumental musicians, Handy and Joplin were dance musicians. In the first decades of the twentieth century there was a dance craze in the United States. The *maxixe, turkey trot, one-step, two-step, shimmy, Charleston, conga, rhumba*, and *fox-trot* laid the foundation for social dancing since then, from the *jitterbug* and *big apple* to the *twist* and the *frug*.

tuba: the lowest-pitched brass instrument

maxixe: a rapid, syncopated Latin American dance adopted from the polka

turkey trot: an early twentieth-century round dance to ragtime for couples, consisting of a springy walk accompanied by swinging body motions

one-step: an early twentieth-century dance performed to ragtime

two-step: an early twentieth-century dance featuring sliding steps

shimmy: a dance step popular in the 1910s and '20s characterized by rapid

Ragtime Bands

movement of the two shoulders in opposite directions

Charleston: a vigorous, rhythmic dance that was the most popular one of the 1920s

conga: a Cuban dance performed in a single line, consisting of three steps forward, followed by a kick

rhumba: a Cuban dance with complex rhythms

fox-trot: a social dance with various combinations of slow and fast steps that was popular in the first half of the twentieth century

jitterbug: a popular strenuous dance of the 1930s

big apple: a social dance in the 1920s and '30s

twist: a popular dance in the 1960s and '70s featuring strong rhythmic turns and twists of the body

frug: a dance derived from the twist, popular in the 1960s

saxophone: a reed instrument invented by Adolph Sax about 1840 for use in military bands; a "woodwind" made of metal

snare drum: a small drum with a mirliton

In the years before World War I, dance bands in the new tradition were called *ragtime bands*. The small dance combo was representative of the small living room group, expanded not by numbers, but by professional skill and know-how. The instruments of the ragtime bands were diverse, including drums, banjo, and *saxophone*, as well as the trumpet, cornet, trombone, string bass, and piano. And instead of working toward homogeneity, the band was working toward individuality of line, apposition rather than blend.

Ragtime bands were playing in many cities, but New Orleans was the largest center; this New Orleans music was called "Dixieland." Brass bands had been popular in the second half of the nineteenth century, along with the more typical bands that included woodwinds and percussion along with the brass instruments. Most American parks still had bandstands (gazebos) for summer concerts, and in New Orleans that tradition was still strong. Gilmore's great Jubilee had been held there, and at the end of the Civil War a large number of military instruments had flooded the New Orleans secondhand shops—so instruments were cheap. Schools and orphanages had bands, and white, Creole, and black clubs maintained them as well.

> All we had in a band, as a rule, was bass horn, trombone, trumpet, an alto horn and maybe a baritone horn, bass and snare drum—just seven pieces, but, talking about noise, you never heard a sixty-piece band make as much noise as we did.[6]

In New Orleans and other cities, bands were used in funeral processions. A ragtime musician who grew up at the turn of the century wrote,

> Joe Blow would die, and maybe he belonged to some society, so they would get the money together and have a band for his funeral. . . . They sure played ragtime on the way back from the graveyard. There were dozens of fine musicians who played ragtime in the parades and at the funerals. . . . We called the music ragtime, whether it was a piano or a band playing. We never heard the word jazz until many years later.[7]

A bandsman who had played in New Orleans toward the end of the century told of playing in "parades and advertising wagons and, excuse me the expression, honky tonks."[8] Parades and wagons draw crowds, and the New Orleans bands had an almost Elizabethan color and energy,

▶◯ Recommended Recordings and Video Cassettes

The New Orleans "Dixieland" bands were originally parade bands, often playing to and from funeral services.

Cambria Records. *Pebby Gilbert and The Dixie Belles.* Recaptures the "Dixieland" sound splendidly.

with *buskers* (street musicians) and children, and frank acceptance of bawdiness. (Many ragtime players began their careers in New Orleans bawdy houses.)

busker: a street musician

folk ballad: a story song in the folk tradition

Vocal Art

But the vocal art of the blacks was also actively developing. The voice contrasted with instruments not only in medium, but also in its soulful, introverted style, which balanced the kinetic, extroverted style of ragtime. The *folk ballad* and the slow tune had ancient traditions; what was new was that ballad singers—and women ballad singers at that—

Ma Rainey with her Rabbit's Foot Minstrels. From left to right: Gabriel Washington, drums; Al Wynn, trombone; Dave Nelson, trumpet; Ma Rainey; Eddie Pollack, saxophone; Thomas A. Dorsey, piano (and gospel songwriter). (Picture Collection, The Branch Libraries, The New York Public Library.)

solo: the performance of any piece or part by one person

blues: a vocal type featuring "blue" notes

response: the final line of a three-line poetic stanza that contrasts with the opening line and its repetition

phrase: a unit of melody comparable to a short sentence

improvise: to make up, extemporize

break: a contrasting section

key: a flap, generally metal, for playing brass and woodwind instruments

meter: the regular grouping of rhythmic beats

off-accent: the accenting of unexpected beats, particularly beats two and four of four

toured with bands to spell the dances with *solo* song. Basing their music on the long sorrow of their people's heritage, they sang ballads of rejection and loneliness, which they called *blues*. Ma Rainey (1886–1939) and her student Bessie Smith (1894–1937), who toured in their teens and were famous before World War I, brought the blues to an early height. They sang simple songs, often a three-line poetic stanza, made up of an opening, its repetition, and a final, contrasting line called the *response*.

The Blues

The classic blues consisted of three short *phrases*. Separation of phrases gave the singer a spot to *improvise* or to think of the next phrase while one of the instrumentalists interjected a solo, also called a *break*. The first published blues song was Handy's "Memphis Blues" in 1912; the more famous "St. Louis Blues" followed in 1914. Both titles cite cities in which the tradition of the blues was strong.

Vocal decoration was intense. By providing *key* (the pitch center of the melody) and *meter* (the regular grouping of beats), the European art provided the musicians with a sturdy basis on which to superimpose African techniques. Complex proportional rhythms pulling against a metric frame produced syncopations and tense *off-accents* (unexpected beats), and variable intonations produced the *"blue" notes* (inflected notes). Long phrases often used fragmented words and syllables chosen for sound.

Bessie Smith.
(Photofest.)

The Original Dixieland Jazz Band in London. From left to right: Billy Jones, Larry Shields, Nick La Rocca, Emile Christian, Tony Spargo. (Picture Collection, The Branch Libraries, The New York Public Library.)

Scat Singing

The technique of singing sounds, called *scat singing* (singing to sounds, rather than to texts), enabled the singer to dispense with the acting-out of a ballad text and to take part in a *combo* as one of the instruments. Instruments reciprocated with the solo techniques of talking a tune, of shaping it with *inflections* (subtle changes of pitch) and rhythms associated with speech. In the trumpeter's use of the *mute*, which softened sound, vocal emulation could be uncanny.

"blue" notes: the inflection of notes, generally a lowering, for expressive purposes

scat: singing to sounds rather than to texts

combo: a small group of varied instruments

inflection: the subtle raising or lowering of pitch

mute: a device to soften the sound

▶◐ Recommended Recordings and Video Cassettes

Several vintage blues records have been issued; the best is probably:

New World Records 80252-2. *Roots of the Blues.* Old records reprocessed, with a booklet.

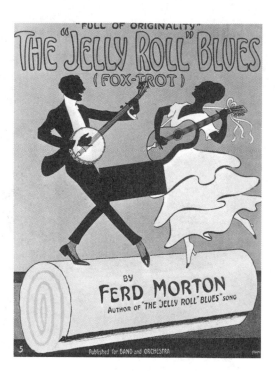

"The 'Jelly Roll' Blues," by Jelly Roll Morton, 1915. The picture illustrates Morton's conviction that both the African and the Spanish heritage were present in ragtime. (Melrose Music Corp.)

Jazz

jazz: a twentieth-century popular development from ragtime, combining

In 1917, a new spirit that had been growing in the ragtime movement culminated in the development of a style called *jazz*, which was characterized by a faster beat and an expanded melodic improvisation. The

Eubie Blake. (Photofest.)

word *jass* was Creole for "speeding up," but it was also a "four-letter word" common in the New Orleans brothels. As late as 1970, the ragtime pianist Eubie Blake (1883–1983) declined to use it in a lecture, replying to a questioner, "It's a bad word, you know; I never say it in front of ladies."[9] The first jazz group comprised five white New Orleans musicians (piano, drums, cornet, clarinet, and trombone) and was led by Nick La Rocca (1889–1961), the cornetist. By 1919, the group, touring abroad, was advertised as "The Original Dixieland Jazz Band, the Creators of Jazz," a claim widely disputed, but restated by La Rocca as late as 1959.

The year 1917 witnessed not only the organization of the first jazz band but also the introduction of jazz recordings. Thus, the change from easy ragtime to the high-powered jazz style that would dominate and symbolize the Roaring Twenties was the first musical style to be documented from its beginning. Also in 1917, the New Orleans brothels and honky-tonks were closed, bringing the heyday of New Orleans to an abrupt close. However, the country was eager for the new style, and the large number of jazz musicians who left New Orleans established jazz colonies in northern cities. Ferdinand Joseph La Menthe (1885–1941), the Creole pianist who took the name Jelly Roll Morton, was playing *stomp tunes* and rags in New Orleans sporting houses; Louis Armstrong

African, American, and western European influences

jass: early spelling of *jazz*

stomp tune: a melody intended to be danced to

Jelly Roll Morton. (Picture Collection, The Branch Libraries, The New York Public Library.)

▶○ Recommended Recordings and Video Cassettes

Early jazz is immortalized in several historical series. Most of them concentrate on later dates and are listed in Chapter 8. But some early ones that are appropriate include:

Biograph 12005 (LP). *Chicago Jazz (1923–1925).*

Bluebird 6752-2. *Chicago/New York Dixieland.*

It might also be worthwhile to inquire about forthcoming releases by "Original Jazz Classics," a company which is reissuing early cuts.

hymnal: a book of hymns

sacred harp singing: a style of nineteenth-century hymn singing

(1900–71), who had been a busker in New Orleans at the age of seven, was studying cornet at the Waif's Home and playing parades and picnic gigs; and Edward Kennedy ("Duke") Ellington (1899–1974), the son of a Washington, D.C., Navy blueprint maker, was in high school, studying piano and listening to the ragtime pianists who came to his city. The ragtime lessons of these young men would come to fruition in the jazz decade.

RELIGIOUS MUSIC

The churches of the United States comprised another venue. Or, more properly, a number of venues, for churches differ from denomination to denomination and from one part of the country to another. Primarily, towards the end of the nineteenth century, there was a considerable difference between city and country churches.

The country churches were the backbone of American religious life at its start, and throughout the time of expansion, country churches still outnumbered city churches. When the country was small, however, it was easy for churches to keep in touch with one another, and they had an unusual unity of spirit. This was increased by the use of common materials; published books were not as common as they are now, and a single publication could reach a large percentage of potential users.

In 1855, the Rev. William McDonald and S. Hubbard's *The Wesleyan Sacred Harp* was published in Boston, a center of religious activity throughout the century. Hymn-tune composing was primarily an apprenticeship art, and early *hymnals* reprinted many of the old singing-school tunes—and the singing of these hymns was called *sacred harp singing.* A strong school of apprenticeship hymn composing continued through the nineteenth century and well into the twentieth. New Yorker William B. Bradbury, for example, composed hymns still well-known today, such as "Just As I Am" (1849), and anthems, such as *And It Shall Come to Pass in the Last Days* (1857).

The choir of the First Congregational Church of Aurora, Illinois in 1854. (Picture Collection, The Branch Libraries, The New York Public Library.)

Lowell Mason

But Bostonian Lowell Mason was the most influential hymn composer of the nineteenth century—and indeed his influence is still being felt. His work in grammar school education, with the *Manual of the Boston Academy of Music*, remained in constant use: the eighth edition was published in 1861. But his grammar school work had been associated with the place of music in elementary (i.e., basic) studies in the trivium of the liberal arts, which included a genuine respect for the integrity of children because music can be felt very early in life (in the nineteenth century, many teachers believed that babies could respond to music *in utero*). Young children are especially affected by the human voice, so Mason's commitment to vocal music was strong. His work with church choirs was strongly related to that essential commitment. But he was equally committed to the German romantic view of music, and his books were, in that sense, in an opposite camp. As early as 1839, Mason had issued "Joy to the World" (ascribed to the British composer George Frideric Handel, "adapted" by Lowell—but not to be found in Handel's

Lowell Mason. (Picture Collection, The Branch Libraries, The New York Public Library.)

gospel song: a song whose text is based on a Biblical theme

work), and, in 1841, "Nearer, My God, to Thee." In 1859, he, together with Edwards A. Park and Austin Phelps, produced *The Sabbath Hymn and Tune Book*. And even after his death in 1872, Mason's hymns abounded: a century later (1966) it was said of him that "no [other] American has ever written so many hymn tunes that have endured."[10]

In the *Hymnal of the Methodist Episcopal Church with Tunes* (1878), Mason had by far the largest number of entries: forty-six original tunes and twenty-two arrangements. The next was Bradbury, with sixteen. And still, as late as 1935, the *Methodist Hymnal* would contain thirty-two entries by Mason.

Apprenticeship Hymn Composers

Perhaps the most important apprenticeship hymn composers at the end of the nineteenth century were Philip P. Bliss (1838–76) and Ira D. Sankey (1840–1908). Both were involved with what was called *gospel songs*. Sankey was the musician in charge of the revivalist services of evangelist Dwight L. Moody (1838–99), where Bliss's hymn "Hold the Fort For I Am Coming" was featured in the campaign of 1875 and won international acclaim.[11] In 1876, Rev. E. J. Goodspeed brought out a huge (743 pages) *Full History of the Wonderful Career of Moody and Sankey.*[12] Bliss's hymns would make up a significant part of *The Baptist Hymnal* of 1883. Charles H. Gabriel (1856–1932) would become the musical counterpart of Sankey when he worked closely with revivalist Billy Sunday (1862–1935), with hymns like "By and By," "There Is Glory in My Soul," and "O That Will Be Glory for Me." And in recent times, the evangelical meetings of Billy Graham would feature his favorite hymn, "Blessed Assurance" (1873), by Phoebe Palmer Knapp.

Other Composers of Religious Music

Anglican churches, such as Christ Church Episcopal in Chicago, and Catholic churches also made use of such Protestant materials, and were going abroad with missionaries of virtually all denominations. "From Cairo to Honolulu, and from São Paulo to Madras, American evangelical missionaries have so thoroughly imbued converts with this kind of song that 'gospel' music now dominates nearly every foreign language hymnal."[13]

But the European-trained musicians were composing religious music too, not so much for churches as for concerts. Concerts featuring religious music, such as those at the Handel and Haydn Societies of the large cities, stayed with European works for the first fifty years or so—Handel's *Messiah* was the most frequently performed work of the European school in the United States for many years. As early as 1822, Lowell Mason had brought out a collection of suitable materials, published as the *Boston Handel and Haydn Society Collection of Church Music,* which was virtually a group of German offerings. But in the last quarter of the nineteenth century, a number of American composers offered successful works in that venue.

One of the most successful was Dudley Buck (1839–1909), a church organist from Hartford, Connecticut. He worked both in the East and in the Middle West; Theodore Thomas, from 1891 conductor of the Chicago Symphony Orchestra, said that Buck "stood more nearly for a distinctive style of American Church music than any other composer."[14] Buck wrote several religious works, most importantly, the cantata *The Legend of Don Munio,* in 1874.

Other important works were Eugene Thayer's *Festival Cantata* and Paine's oratorio *St. Peter,* premiered in Paine's native city, Portland, Maine, in 1873; one critic said of it that Paine was "the first American who has shown the genius and the culture necessary for writing music in the grand style" and another wrote that "*St. Peter* is without doubt the most important music work yet produced in this country."[15] Important also was Horatio Parker's oratorio *Hora Novissima* of 1893, which was performed by the Church Choral Society of New York, then at both the

Handel and Haydn Society and the Cincinnati Festival (under Theodore Thomas) in 1894. It was to be the first American work to receive recognition at the British festivals, where it was "acclaimed in the English press as a work worthy of comparison with the best that Europe was producing."[16] Amy Marcy Cheney's *Mass in E-flat* had already been sung in Boston in 1892.

By the end of the century, this genre of music was yielding place to other genres, but Horatio Parker's *The Legend of St. Christopher* was sung in 1898; in 1900 his work *A Wanderer's Psalm*, commissioned in England, was sung there; and in 1915, he produced a final oratorio, *Morven and the Grail*.

SPIRITUALS

The blacks contributed to the literature of religious music as well. The publication of spirituals, in the 1867 collection *Slave Songs of the United States*, had coincided with the development of scholarly methodology; according to Lucy McKim Garrison, one of the collectors, "the greater part of the music here presented has been taken down by the editors from the lips of the colored people themselves."[17] However, even the scholars had little tolerance for the rhythm-centered, nonharmonic music of the ex-slaves, much less their rhythmic motions, which they sometimes thought of as dance and sometimes as a rightful part of the music. In 1862, a woman who had seen some of these motions asked an ex-slave about them (she had heard and seen a "wild song," the motions of which included the clapping of hands and stomping). The man had replied that it was part of the song, part of the worship.[18] The Fisk Jubilee singers continued to be popular, in part because they worked as concert performers and behaved appropriately to that venue. According to a missionary of the day,

> they have also received considerable musical instruction and have become familiar with much of our best sacred and classical music, and this has modified their manner of execution. They do not attempt to imitate the grotesque bodily motions or the drawling intonations that often characterize the singing of great congregations of the colored people in their excited religious meetings.[19]

A Brooklyn pastor, having seen and heard the singers, wrote of them:

> I never saw a cultivated Brooklyn assemblage so moved and melted under the magnetism of music before. The wild melodies of these emancipated slaves touched the fount of tears, and grey-haired men wept like little children. In the program last evening were not only the well-

known slave songs "Go down, Moses," "Roll, Jordan, Roll," and "Turn back Pharaoh's army," but a fresh collection of the most weird and plaintive hymns sung in the plantation cabins in the dark days of bondage. One young negress—exceedingly "black yet comely"—sang a wild yet most delicious melody, "I'll hear the trumpet sound in the morning," which was the very embodiment of African heart-music.[20]

Henry T. Burleigh

The next development was the setting of spirituals in the European tradition, to be used as anthems and as concert pieces as well. The black performer/composer Henry T. Burleigh (1866–1949), a *bass* player and singer from Erie, Pennsylvania, had been in New York during the tenure of Antonin Dvorak at the National Conservatory there, and Dvorak and Burleigh can truly be said to have influenced each other: Burleigh introduced Dvorak to music of the black traditions, and Dvorak encouraged him to value them. As a singer, Burleigh was employed both at a church and a synagogue in New York City, a practice not uncommon at that time; two Christians became *cantors* in the Midwest, where Jewish singers of traditional chant were a rarity. (The author's grandfather, Albert Borroff, though a practicing Episcopalian, studied Hebrew for many years and served as cantor of Sinai Temple in Chicago for thirty-six years. A doctoral dissertation at Yeshiva University, New York, was written about these Christian cantors, and I was interviewed on this subject in the mid-eighties. The other midwestern Christian cantor practiced in Minneapolis.) Burleigh was encouraged also by the black English composer Samuel Coleridge-Taylor (1875–1912), who had used both American Indian themes (in his trilogy of oratorios dealing with the Hiawatha legend) and African subjects (such as his *Symphonic Variations on an African Air*). What Burleigh accomplished, aside from composing a considerable amount of fine music in the European tradition, was to arrange spirituals for European consumption. The disadvantage was, of course, making them less themselves; the compensating advantage was of producing a richly harmonic piece with a stronger melodic element than the romantic style generally allowed.

One of Burleigh's arrangements was of the spiritual "Deep River," made in 1913. Unlike European music, which at that time put the tune in the *soprano* voice, this arrangement has the tune in the *alto*, so that it is surrounded in the harmonic fabric. The harmony is rich, romantic stuff—but the alto is directed to be medium loud and the rest of the parts soft, so that the domination of the melodic element is never in doubt. And, unlike the European music of that day, it is *a cappella*, that is, unaccompanied by an orchestra, as in Coleridge-Taylor's oratorios, letting the voices fulfill themselves without competition. It makes a stunning choral piece.[21]

bass: a low voice of a male singer, or an instrument of that range

cantor: the chief singer and prayer leader of a synagogue

soprano: a high voice of a female singer, or an instrument of that range

alto: a low voice of a female singer, or an instrument of that range

a cappella: choral music without instruments

THE END OF AN ERA

semiclassical music: a concept including both formal and informal music

baritone: a middle voice of a male singer, or an instrument of that range

One other style of music was important through this period: the music of composers of the apprenticeship tradition who wrote music in the European style, called *semiclassical* by the Europeans. They were a lively group who composed some highly successful music. Among the best-known of their works are:

Chauncey Olcott (1858–1932): "My Wild Irish Rose" (1899), a song popularized by the tenor John McCormack; and "Mother Machree" (1910)

Reginald De Koven (1859–1920), a Connecticut composer of nineteen comic operas, two grand operas, and many songs, including "Oh Promise Me" (1889)

Ethelbert Nevin (1862–1901), a Pennsylvania composer of piano music and songs: "The Rosary" (1894); "Mighty Lak' a Rose" (1901)

Carrie Jacobs Bond (1862–1946), a Wisconsin composer who composed both music and texts: "I Love You Truly" (1901) has sold over a million copies and has been sung at thousands of weddings; "[When You Come to the End of] A Perfect Day" (1910)

Oley Speaks (1874–1948), an Ohio singer (*baritone*) and composer of songs and anthems: "On the Road to Mandalay" (1901); "Sylvia" (1912)

But these composers too gave way to new styles and interests that would characterize the coming decades. The end of World War I saw that the German hold on American music had been weakened; in 1917, Karl Muck, the German conductor of the Boston Symphony Orchestra, refused to conduct "The Star-Spangled Banner," and was arrested and jailed. At the end of the war, the band of James Reese Europe toured in France to great popularity, which heralded a universal interest in ragtime and jazz. Ragtime and jazz became the music of the hour, and dance took over as the number-one musical interest from the choral music that had dominated the second half of the nineteenth century. Not all music was published with words; a two-step called "The Winner . . . Salute" was published without a text in 1906 or 1907 (scholars disagree), and soon thereafter was published as a patriotic song with the words "Anchors Aweigh." The very popular "Nola" by Felix Arndt was published as a piano solo in 1915 and not given words until 1924; it is still heard today, more as an instrumental than as a vocal work.

But ragtime outdid them all, with such works as "Bill Bailey, Won't You Please Come Home?" (1902), by Hughie Cannon; "Chicken Reel, or Performer's Buck," by Joseph M. Daly, published as "A Two-Step and Buck Dance" in 1910; "Alexander's Ragtime Band" (1911), by Irving

Berlin; "Waiting for the Robert E. Lee" (1912), by Lewis Muir; "Ballin' the Jack" (1913), by Chris Smith; "The Darktown Strutters' Ball" (1917), by Shelton Brooks; "Limehouse Blues" (1922), by Philip Braham; and "Charleston," from the show *Runnin' Wild* (1923), by Cecil Mack and Jimmy Johnson.

The men and women (for there were indeed many women) who made ragtime music, and those who began the jazz era were everywhere. In Chicago in 1921, the Friar's Inn hired a group that styled themselves The New Orleans Rhythm Kings; trombone and clarinet played behind the lead trumpet, Paul Mares, and his "inspired solo flights" ushered in a new era.

NOTES

1. Edith Borroff, "An American Parlor at the Turn of the Century," *American Music*, vol. 4, no. 3 (Fall, 1986).

2. *The American Heritage Dictionary of the English Language* (Boston and New York: Houghton Mifflin Company, 1973).

3. Ibid.

4. Richard McLanathan, *The American Tradition in the Arts* (New York: Harcourt, Brace & World, 1958), pp. 402–06.

5. Chase, *America's Music: From the Pilgrims to the Present*, rev. ed. (Urbana: University of Illinois Press, 1992), p. 459.

6. Jelly Roll Morton, in Chase, *America's Music*, p. 476.

7. Eubie Blake, in Leonard Feather, *The New Edition of the Encyclopedia of Jazz* (New York: Bonanza Books, 1962), p. 22.

8. "Bunk" Johnson, in Chase, *America's Music*, p. 471.

9. Rutgers University, lecture-recital, June, 1970.

10. Robert Stevenson, *Protestant Church Music in America* (New York: W. W. Norton & Co., 1966), p. 80.

11. Ibid, p. 111.

12. Ibid, p. 127.

13. Ibid, p. 111.

14. Ibid, p. 113.

15. Ibid, p. 115.

16. Ibid, p. 116.

17. Ibid, p. 96.

18. Ibid, p. 99.

19. Ibid, p. 101.

20. Ibid.
21. Borroff, *Anthology*, pp. 471–74.

BIBLIOGRAPHY

Borroff, Edith. "An American Parlor at the Turn of the Century." *American Music*, vol. 4, no. 3 (Fall, 1986).

———. "Origin of Species: Conflicting Views of American Musical Theater in History." *American Music*, Vol. 2, No. 4 (Spring, 1985).

Chase, Gilbert. *America's Music: From the Pilgrims to the Present*. rev. ed. Urbana: University of Illinois Press, 1992.

Feather, Leonard. *The New Edition of the Encyclopedia of Jazz*. New York: Bonanza Books, 1962.

Fuld, James J., *The Book of World-Famous Music*. New York: Crown Publishers, 1968.

Lewine, Richard, and Alfred Simon. *Encyclopedia of Theatre Music*. New York: Bonanza Books, 1961.

McLanathan, Richard. *The American Tradition in the Arts*. New York: Harcourt, Brace & World, Inc., 1958.

Morgan, Thomas L., and William Barlow. *From Cakewalk to Concert Hall: An Illustrated History of African-American Popular Music from 1895 to 1930*. Washington DC: Elliot & Clark, 1992.

Raymond, Jack. *Show Music on Record: The First 100 Years*. rev. ed. Washington DC: Smithsonian Institute Press, 1992.

Schwartz, H. W. *Bands of America*. New York: Da Capo Press, 1975.

Stevenson, Robert. *Protestant Church Music in America*. (New York: W. W. Norton & Co., 1966)

6

The Business and
Dissemination of Music

Music is an art. The living room, the street on parade day, the park of a summer evening, the concert hall, the church, the popular theater, the opera house—all are venues for hearing marvelous music. The United States is unusual among nations in that all of our venues have produced strong musical offerings, none of them more splendid than the rest. Or, to put it another way, each of them more splendid than the others. The living room was the most versatile, the street, the most invigorating, the park, the most romantic, the concert hall, the most edifying, the church, the most inspirational, the popular theater, the most whole-heartedly of the present, the opera house, the most symbolic; each had its own ambiance and its own stars, and each was a business in itself. The publisher who brought out church music did not bring out popular songs; the publisher of European piano music did not bring out ragtime.

But the music in the United States had two industries that pulled across virtually all of the musical venues: the manufacture of musical instruments and education in music of both the professionals in their craft and the nonprofessionals in the ability to enjoy the music provided by the professionals. Both of these industries took on particularly American emphases and methods in the years before and after the turn of the twentieth century.

INSTRUMENT MANUFACTURE

All instrument makers were trained in apprenticeship—and still are. They limited themselves to certain categories of instruments—nobody, no company could make all of them. Many people came to the New World with small instruments in their luggage, and others made their own instruments, simple ones, like flutes, and even the more difficult ones, like fiddles.

The Piano

So it is natural that the earliest instrument makers in America were piano makers. Piano making requires special materials, special equipment, and considerable expertise. Also, the piano was at the cusp of modernity and therefore was strange to the builders and impossible for the Colonists to have brought with them—even if there had been room. The first public piano recital anywhere was in London in 1768, and the first piano produced in America was made in 1769. The builder was John Harris of Boston.

Boston and Philadelphia were the first centers of piano building, with two builders in each city before the end of the century. Already the American builders had brought an innovative energy to bear upon their trade, and by 1825, Babcock of Boston had invented the complete cast-iron frame that would give the instrument the strength that it needed if size and sound were to be expanded—and size and sound were of utmost importance in the coming romanticism.

By the middle of the nineteenth century, the piano makers of the United States were competing with those of Europe; before Steinway (founded in 1853) won the grand prize at the Paris Exposition of 1867, Jonas Chickering (founded in 1823) had paved the way by winning a gold medal in the Great Exhibition of 1851 (in London) for technical improvements in the mechanism.

The piano led a charmed life in the nineteenth century and the early part of the twentieth: the piano spanned the styles of the century as no other instrument did. It was the instrument of the living room, becoming more and more common there as more and more people managed to afford one, so that the great years of the piano at home were the 1920s. It was the instrument of the concert hall, played by visiting European virtuosos (and, later, a few American virtuosos as well). It was the instrument of the high-class dance hall and also of the honky-tonk. But of course, pianos of different sizes and capacities had to be built for the different venues: theater pianos were the mainstay of pit orchestras, but the pit was small and the upright models, which took less room than the grands, were most often used in the pit. Many homes had small instruments, too, uprights or the even smaller spinets. Dance halls and

A spinet piano. (Picture Collection, The Branch Libraries, The New York Public Library.)

Expert craftsmen at the Mason & Hamlin piano factory, 1937. (Picture Collection, The Branch Libraries, The New York Public Library.)

bars also had small pianos. The upright was invented by Hawkins of Philadelphia in 1800, but did not become standard for another half-century. The concert grand was the largest piano, and still is. The greatest number of pianos built by any maker in the world have been built by the Kimball Company of Chicago, founded in 1871 and quick to respond to cultural changes and needs.

The pianos of today are virtually the same as those of a century ago; ideas of tuning have changed, and the strings are stretched a bit, the tension causing a slightly higher pitch and a more striking tone. Thus, the piano reached its zenith in the late nineteenth century, a romantic zenith that musicians of the eighteenth century would not have admired, but which the musicians and audiences of the early twentieth century thought was superlative.

The developments of the piano after the zenith were mechanical: first,

▶◯ Recommended Recordings and Video Cassettes

> Biograph Records BLP 10000Q, "Happy Days Are Here Again." This player-piano recording includes such items as "Life is Just a Bowl of Cherries" and "Singing in the Rain."
>
> *See also* The Entertainer *in the Recommended Recordings and Video Cassettes on page 138 and* George Gershwin Plays the Rhapsody in Blue *in the Recommended Recordings and Video Cassettes on page 220.*

the *player piano*, which contained an automatic mechanism and was played with paper rolls punched with information. The first keyboard automated instruments date from the 1880s; by the turn of the century a pneumatic system had been invented which defined the player piano and *orchestrion*, an automatic instrument that included sounds other than those made via piano keys—one even had an automatically activated violin. For historians the most important development was the *"reproducing piano,"* invented in Germany in 1904 and first made in the United States by the American Piano Company as the Ampico, and by the Aeolian Company as the Duo-Art, both in 1913. The Duo-Art was a player piano whose punched paper rolls captured the subtleties of performance, such as slight variations in tempo and loudness, so that it could personalize performances. The pianists of the day, such as Sergei Rachmaninoff, recorded for Duo-Art and spoke favorably of the capacity of the instrument to present each artist as an individual stylist.

player piano: a piano activated mechanically rather than by a pianist

orchestrion: an automatic instrument using a player piano and other instruments to produce the sounds of an orchestra

reproducing piano: an early player piano

String Instruments

Orchestral instruments were made in the United States from early days. The strings are the only orchestra members not also in bands, and they were at the top of the romantic hierarchy, almost as highly esteemed as the piano. Violins were also fiddles, and fiddlers often made their own instruments. But orchestral violinists did not make their own instruments, and violin makers increased at a slow, steady pace in this country until about 1930, when over five hundred American violin makers were in business. Then performers began to prefer old instruments. Although there continued to be a few good violin makers (such as George Germunder, who made violins in New York from 1851 to 1899, and William Lewis & Son in Chicago, from 1874), by 1930, repairmen and dealers outnumbered makers.

The violin is not a likely instrument for automation; yet, in addition to the orchestrion, the Violano Virtuoso was made in Chicago from 1904. It combined a paper roll with electromagnets, activating the violin and the piano accompaniment. A few of these mechanisms still exist, but they are rare.

Band Instruments

sousaphone: a circular tuba played upright; named for John Philip Sousa

bells: hollow cup-shaped units struck in the inside by a clapper

hand bells: small-handled bells held in the hand

sleigh bells: small bells affixed to a sleigh or to the halters of horses pulling a sleigh

Band instruments were much more an American strength: by 1850, there were many wind-instrument makers, many of whom introduced new designs. The Midwest seems to have been the location of most of the wind-instrument activity. Brass instruments were more popular than woodwinds in the mid-nineteenth century, in part because of the success of the cornet virtuosos, and in part because of the Civil War, when brass instruments were much more in demand for the army bands. In 1875, C. G. Conn opened a factory in Elkhart, Indiana, and for two generations, that company was in the forefront of band-instrument design and manufacture, though not without strong competition. Conn manufactured the first American saxophone in 1889 and the first *sousaphone* in 1892; the company has remained active through the twentieth century.

Percussion Instruments

Orchestral percussion instruments were the province of drum manufacturers, who had been making military drums since the middle of the nineteenth century. And a number of Philadelphia manufacturers began to make tambourines and bones for use in minstrel shows, switching, during the Civil War, to military drums, and banjo heads (which, unlike the bodies of guitars, were made like drumheads). At the same time, a company in Connecticut specialized in *bells—hand bells, sleigh bells,* and the like.

The exception was the J. C. Deagan Company, organized in St. Louis, but soon in Chicago, which manufactured pitched percussion instru-

Sousaphone.

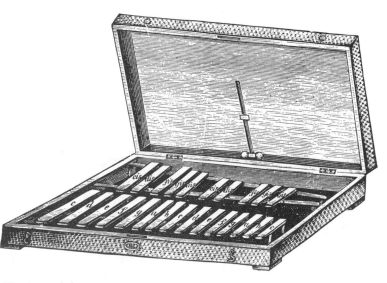

Glockenspiel.

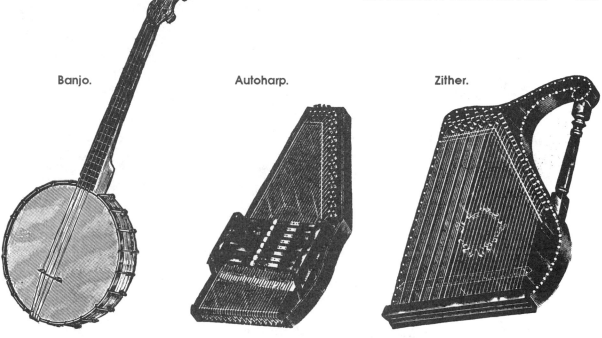

Banjo.   Autoharp.   Zither.

ments. Deagan made *orchestral bells*, *glockenspiels*, xylophones, and other such instruments. They also manufactured *carillons*, sets of bells or chimes, generally to be housed in church steeples or municipal towers. Carillons were used to alert citizenry of everything from the death of a mayor to the wedding of a church member. Music was played on the carillon and a carilloneur (a performer on this instrument) was a respected member of the community. By 1925, there were a number of carillon manufacturers, two in New York State alone.

Apprenticeship Instruments

Instruments played only within the apprenticeship tradition intersect here: banjos and bells were much more apprenticeship-bound, along with *guitars* and harps. These instruments were widely built in the United States, with banjo makers active from 1830; the most successful was probably William Boucher of Baltimore, who made banjos from 1845 to 1870.

But there were other apprenticeship instruments as well. The *dulcimers* and *zithers* were of many kinds. The *hammered dulcimer* was at its peak, with five hundred instruments a year, in the 1850s; the *Appalachian dulcimer* followed about twenty years later. *Autoharps* became almost a fad in the 1890s, with one company in New York making three thousand a week. In 1890, a small Portuguese guitar was introduced in the Hawaiian Islands and soon developed into the *ukulele*.

After 1900, instruments were developed that were being demanded

orchestra bells: small bells on a stand, played with hammers

glockenspiel: orchestral bells

carillon: a set of bells or chimes

guitar: a plucked string instrument

dulcimer: a shallow box with strings to be plucked or struck with small hammers

zither: a set of strings in a shallow box, played by plucking

hammered dulcimer: a dulcimer

Appalachian dulcimer: a dulcimer modified in the Appalachian region

autoharp: a zither with keys for playing chords

ukulele: a small guitar popular in Hawaii

trap drum set: a group of drums plus cymbals

vibraphone (vibes): an instrument of metal bars played with soft mallets

Grand Harmonicon: musical glasses

Aeolian harp: strings placed in a box and activated by the wind

wind chimes: pieces of glass, metal or other substances strung up so as to hit each other and sound in the wind

pipe organ: an organ whose sounding elements are pipes controlled by a player at a console

reed organ: an organ with a reed mechanism, rather than pipes

console: the organ keyboards and control at which the organist sits

pedalboard: the low keyboard of the organ console, played with the feet

by the ragtime bands: the *trap drum set* was perfected in the first two decades of the century; in 1923, Deagan brought out the *vibraphone*. From 1900 to 1930, keen interest in plucked string instruments gave great impetus to the manufacture of mandolins, guitars, and, in a new thrust of popularity, banjos.

For the musical hobbyist, there was, in the third quarter of the eighteenth century, Franklin's *glass harmonica* (*see* page 20). (People had played on partly filled crystal glasses on a table for a long while.) Musical glasses were mounted in 1825 as the chromatic *Grand Harmonicons*. Perhaps more furniture than musical instrument, the *Aeolian harp*, strings placed in a box in such a way that they would be activated by the wind, was made in New York from 1833 (such apparatuses had been common in Europe since the end of the sixteenth century). These harps were related to *wind chimes*, popular in the twentieth century, and were oriental in origin; they were made of activating pieces (of wood, metal, glass, or other substances) that strike against a musical entity, generally a sounding tube, in the wind. Wind chimes are still made and are still popular.

The Organ

Pipe-organ manufacture was largely apprenticeship, since organs were originally built for churches, and church organists were trained in apprenticeship (and would be until the middle of the twentieth century). Church organs have been fairly steady in manufacture, from the eighteenth century to the present, though changing styles in organ types have influenced the details of manufacture.

The *reed organ*, which was small and could be used in the home, was invented in 1809 and was made steadily from the second decade of the nineteenth century; it enjoyed its apex in the 1850s, but was made until about 1920.

The trend after the Civil War was for pipe organs that in sound came as close as possible to the orchestra. Many makers changed the architectural layout and the physical makeup of the instrument so that sets of pipes could sound like trumpets or clarinets, or even string instruments.

It is difficult to conceive the size of pipe organs. The place where the organist sits, the *console*, is not the instrument, but rather, the control site; the console may have one, two, three, or, exceptionally, more keyboards plus a *pedalboard*. The instrument itself is the sets of pipes, arranged by the builder to conform to the architecture. An instrument built by George Jardine & Son of New York for the Catholic cathedral in Mobile, Alabama, and installed in 1858, had thirty-six sets of pipes, mostly traditional ones, designed specifically for organs. St. Luke's Church of Germantown, Pennsylvania, bought an organ built by Cole & Woodberry and Mitchell, installed in 1894, which had thirty-eight sets of

Trap-drum set.

pipes and included orchestral instrument imitations: violin, viola, flute, piccolo, oboe, clarinet, trombone, and trumpet.

In 1902, an organ was commissioned for the 1904 St. Louis Louisiana Purchase Exposition; the original commission was from M. Harris, but the organ was completed by the Los Angeles Art Organ Company. It was built in Los Angeles, and the parts required ten railroad cars for shipping to St. Louis for assembly. It contained over 10,000 pipes in 128 sets, and its manufacture required 80,000 feet of timber, 20 tons of zinc, 3 tons of soft metal, and 115 miles of wire. It had five manual keyboards and a pedalboard. The cost of this instrument was $105,000.

After the Exposition closed, John Wanamaker bought the organ for his Philadelphia department store. It was installed in 1909, and it would be played by master organists from all over the world. And it was expanded and expanded; by 1930, it had 30,067 pipes in 469 sets, and was the largest musical instrument in the world.[1]

Chicago

Chicago, at the end of the nineteenth century, was the leading American city in the manufacture of musical instruments. It was built around Fort Dearborn in the early 1830s and was incorporated in 1837. The city had a musical life almost from the start: instruments—even pipe organs—were brought in, but the making of instruments on any kind of commercial basis began only about 1850. The first company was probably G. A. Helmkamp, which began in 1851 as "maker of organs, pianos, guitars, and violins."[2] That company was followed by R. G. Green, a reed-organ

Organ.

The ferris wheel was first introduced at the Chicago Exposition, 1892. (Illustration by Harry Jenks.)

concertina: a small accordion

maker, in 1854; Green manufactured some three hundred instruments a year. In 1857, Julius Bauer & Co. set up shop, and in the 1860s, was turning out banjos, tambourines, guitars, violins, *concertinas*, accordions, and reed organs. In 1857, Wallace W. Kimball (1828–1904) began his business, at first simply as a seller of musical items. Kimball had been born in Maine and had come to Chicago in 1857, but was a very modern businessman: he began manufacturing instruments only when he realized that he could sell more of them than he could obtain from current manufacturers. In 1880, the Kimball Company began the manufacture of reed organs (selling over 400,000 of them before 1922, when they went out of style and were discontinued); in 1888, he began the manufacture of pianos (to become the biggest manufacturer in the world); and in 1890, the firm began the manufacture of the Portable Pipe Organ, a concept of Kimball's devising. A magazine, *The Organ*, described it as "one of the most remarkable instruments now before the public." It was only one manual of six sets of pipes, and a pedalboard with two sets, and it would "go through any door or window affording a space three feet six, by six feet. It requires no expert to set it up."[3] It was so successful that it was developed in several sizes, including a model with two manuals and pedalboard.

In 1864, the firm of Lyon & Healy opened its doors, like Kimball selling, then manufacturing. They began making plucked string instruments from 1880, and soon they added brass instruments, drums, organs, and pianos. Their most famous invention was probably the *orchestral harp*, first built in 1889, designed "to withstand the rigors of the American climate." This harp quickly became standard in orchestras both in the United States and Europe. In the 1890s, Lyon & Healy produced more than one hundred thousand instruments yearly. They remained an important part of the life of Chicago, long enough to celebrate their centennial with three radio shows featuring their own instruments—Marie Bergersen, the Chicago pianist, was the featured artist on all three programs.

In 1880, Chicago had fourteen instrument factories; by 1890 there were thirty-one. By 1900, there were twenty-one piano factories (producing 16% of all American-made pianos), nine organ factories (18%), and fifteen manufacturing other instruments. By 1925, over 180,000 pianos were being made in Chicago every year; J. C. Deagan was making more carillons and vibraphones than any other company in the world; Carl Geyer's French horns were considered the finest in the country; and the Ludwig Drum Company had "revolutionized" the design of drums and other percussion instruments. In 1927, Deagan presented the *vibraharp*, like a vibraphone, but with such desirable features as the capacity to control the duration of the sound and to produce a *vibrato*; in the 1930s, such musicians as Chicagoan Lionel Hampton were using this instrument—perhaps the only one to have been invented in the United States.

The George P. Bent Company, in business from 1881 to 1949, manufactured a player piano called the Combinola. And in the 1920s, Chicago was the scene of the earliest electromagnetic instrument concerts. The Choralcelo Company produced instruments unlike any other: generally with a piano keyboard, one organ manual, and a pedalboard, it had five or six units (hard wood, soft wood, aluminum, steel, and a bass made of buggy springs—and sometimes glass) that were activated by electromagnets. Depression of a key activated a magnet of the required pitch, causing the bar of wood or metal or glass to vibrate. Concerts were given in a North Side mansion, by invitation, for some of the world's most famous people. Principles of manufacture became commonplace in the 1930s, and in 1935, the Hammond Organ Company began manufacture of a totally synthesized sound (the Choralcelo had had a synthesized unit); before long, that company made more small electronic organs than any other company in the world.

Chicago was not typical. Because it was a railroad center—*the* railroad center of the country—the city was ideally situated for shipment of large

orchestral harp: a large harp used in a symphony orchestra

vibraharp: a vibraphone

vibrato: a tremulous, quick, continuous, subtle variation of pitch

items and for the quick sending of goods around the country. Companies were common in nearby towns as well (Elkhart, Indiana, and Milwaukee, Wisconsin, were two), and those companies could use the Chicago railroad systems to good avail.

MUSIC PUBLISHING

Music publishing in the United States followed the country's development. The first book known to have been printed in the northern colonies was the Protestant *Bay Psalm Book* (1640), containing the texts of hymns without the music, but this had been preceded by Catholic music books printed by the Spaniards in Mexico from the 1540s. The first music printed in the northern colonies was an eight-page supplement of tunes, done as woodcuts, for the ninth edition of the *Bay Psalm Book*, in 1698.

Engraving was the process of choice from the early eighteenth century, common in tune books as late as *The New-England Psalm-Singer* by William Billings, engraved by Paul Revere for publication in 1770. The Moravians who settled in Pennsylvania brought movable type with musical notes already on staff lines with them; this was processed the same way as alphabet letters. These publications were not all of a religious nature, however; among the tune books was *The Youth's Entertaining Amusement*, issued in Philadelphia in 1754.

Engraving was used widely until recent times. Alexander Reinagle's anthologies, vocal and instrumental, beginning about 1786, and Francis Hopkinson's *Seven Songs*, published in 1788, opened up the way for the copious literature that followed.

"Chester," by William Billings, was included in *The New-England Psalm-Singer*, 1770.

Broadsides (single sheets sold on the street) and sheet music were also engraved. A patriotic tune, the "New and Favourite Liberty Song," was the first music broadside, issued in Boston in 1768. A sheet music magazine, *Monthly Numbers*, was begun in Philadelphia in 1793, and other such publications followed in Boston, New York, and Baltimore.

Lithography had a brief vogue in the 1820s and 1830s, but that process was much coarser, so publishers went back to engraving. Baltimore became an important music publishing center, and then Pittsburgh, Cincinnati, Chicago, St. Louis, New Orleans, and San Francisco, following the path of the country's expansion. New York and Boston continued in prominence as well.

After the Civil War, publishing split along the lines of European and American traditions. German immigrants founded houses: G. Schirmer was already in New York before the war, joined by Carl Fischer in 1872; Arthur P. Schmidt set up in Boston in 1876 and Theodore Presser in Lynchburg, Virginia, in 1883 (but soon moved to Philadelphia). These publishers served professional musicians in the European tradition, issuing symphonic scores and parts, difficult piano works, and some easier pieces for the students of professionals in that tradition. All of them are still in business.

At the same time, a great many smaller companies began bringing out theater turns and popular songs, popular music for the general public, in a "happy expansion" that lasted until about 1970.[4] Engraving remained the rule until the 1980s, when photolithography began to dominate in music publishing.

Publishing in Chicago was representative, rather than outstanding. But between 1850 and 1930, over three hundred music publishers were active in Chicago, and many famous songs were originally issued there: "They Buried Her Under the Old Elm Tree" (1855, an early tearjerker), "Kingdom Coming" (1862), one of Henry Clay Work's most popular—he also composed the famous "Grandfather's Clock," but that was published in 1876, after he had moved to New York—"Down by the Old Mill Stream" (1910), "Let Me Call You Sweetheart" (1910), "Some of These Days" (1910, made famous by singer Sophie Tucker), "A Perfect Day" (also 1910), by Carrie Jacobs Bond, who set up her own company for publishing her hits—this one sold over five million copies in its first twenty years—"Green River" (1920), "That Old Gang of Mine" (1923), "The Sweetheart of Sigma Chi" (1927), and "When You're Smiling, the Whole World Smiles with You" (1928).

broadside: a song, lyrics, or an ad for a song, printed on a single sheet of paper, generally hawked on the street

EDUCATION IN MUSIC

The United States was vibrantly alive musically, a vast American apple pie with a European upper crust. The musical art was rich in scope and rich in detail; it was made up of many venues and styles, from the apprenticeship arts of living room acting/singing and community dances to European *Lieder* recitals and symphony concerts, from the minstrel show and revue to ballet and grand opera. They were all wonderful, creating an amazing and vital juxtaposition of many musical types and venues.

Even more amazing was the system—indeed, the systems—of education that developed in the United States. This country has been unique in the world in its public education; the concept of equality of oppor-

"The School-House in the Lane," music by Edwin Christie, 1871. (The Newberry Library.)

tunity would have had little meaning if it were not embodied in an open educational structure. Whereas most European children either had tutorial education or no education, American children went to the schoolhouse, which was open to all.

The Apprenticeship System

The apprenticeship system had come with the settlers: fiddlers taught the next generation of fiddlers, singers taught the next generation of singers, and music was passed down through generations—as was the skill of composing new music. So fiddle tunes and songs entered the repertoire and left it, in a cultural fluidity that we still have in our bones, a piece remaining until people no longer want to hear it.

Formal apprenticeship—that is, training for a professional career as a musician—began early, generally at the age of three, and often with a child either born into a family of musicians or placed with one. In small towns and in city neighborhoods, contact was sufficient without the child actually moving in with the master. Training would be initially the hearing of music and the objectification of sound, but would soon move to technical and theoretical matters, so that early professional work (at nine or ten) was the rule rather than the exception. Full musical capacity would be reached in the early teens.

A lesson by William Mason, the third son of Lowell Mason, at Steinway Hall, New York.
(Picture Collection, The Branch Libraries, The New York Public Library.)

In general, apprenticeship consisted of in-depth daily work from the earliest years, with daily supervision by the apprentice master in a context of fairly constant musical stimulation of rehearsals, concerts, conversation, and criticism. It was very much a hands-on, learning-by-doing system, with respect for the young musical experience and appreciation of youthful professionalism and enthusiasm.

All of this was true in Europe too. What was different in America was the education of potential audiences. In Europe, the layperson's concept of music had been instilled in children by tutors, but in the United States the tutorial system gave way very early, and, in addition, the family became a very different social structure. Even well-to-do mothers raised their own children; governesses and tutors were rare on the East Coast and virtually nonexistent on the frontier. So music in the American living room became a family recreation, as reading aloud was a family recreation.

Children's Music

In the United States, a remarkable literature developed for small children: wonderful books, not just those by Mark Twain (1835–1910), such as *Tom Sawyer* and *Huckleberry Finn*, but the adventure stories of Horatio Alger (1834–99), the *Uncle Remus* stories of Joel Chandler Harris (1848–1908), the Oz books of L. Frank Baum (1856–1919), beginning with *The Wizard of Oz* (1900), and the Tarzan books of Edgar Rice Burroughs (1875–1950).

A parallel flowering of music literature also went into the American living room. A great deal of children's music was composed, comparable to the reading material for children, from "Rock-a-Bye Baby," composed by Effie I. Crockett (a relative of Davy Crockett), about 1872 (when she was fifteen), to piano pieces such as the *Peter Pan Suite* of Louise Robyn (niece of Alfred G. Robyn). Two things were remarkable about these many pieces: one was the ability of the mother (or other companion) to play fairly difficult accompaniments on the piano, and the other was the contribution to this literature by composers not associated with children's work, such as Walter Damrosch, conductor of the New York Symphony Society from 1885 to 1927, George Whitefield Chadwick, and Arthur Foote, a student of John Knowles Paine and a respected composer of orchestral works. In 1885, for example, the Century Company published an album of 100-odd songs, probably as a special issue of a children's magazine. The album contains game songs, songs about the weather, lullabies—and talk songs in the elocutionary tradition.

"Riding on the Rail" by Homer N. Bartlett specifies "Recitation," without pitch notation but with rhythm exactly specified. It is to be recited very fast and synchronized precisely with the piano; the voice imitates the sounds of a train, aided by the driving repetitions of the text

("Jiggety, joggety, bumpity bump, Crickety, crackety, humpity hump"). Many collections of such songs were published from about 1875 to 1930, and many living rooms reverberated with mothers playing and children reciting and singing, alone or for guests.

Some of this teaching material was related to apprenticeship teaching, which at the end of the nineteenth century was as much influenced by the writings of Italian physician and educator Maria Montessori (1870–1952) as the work of Lowell Mason had been influenced by the writings of Johann Heinrich Pestalozzi. This influence led to inclusion of music in the kindergarten.

Mason's Influence

Meanwhile, the work of Lowell Mason was bearing fruit. The grade schools expanded their music study, in vocal music, to which Mason was devoted, and finally in instrumental study. This was more questionable, since it was associated in Mason's mind (and in many other people's minds) with advanced work, symbolized in the quadrivium of the liberal arts and therefore suited for the level of college and graduate school. At any rate, such advanced studies were associated with professionalism and were not taught at a school; yet they were still part of the apprenticeship system. Nonetheless, in a few schools instrumental work was taught fairly early.

In apprenticeship, learning began in the preschool years, was gradual, and was one-on-one; in schools, new teaching materials had to be developed since the work began later, allowed less time, and was done in groups or classes. The materials thus had to be very different. This movement began in New York with the publication of Lewis A. Benjamin's *Musical Academy* (the title a tribute to Mason!), a collection of dances for violin, cello, clarinet, flute, and other instruments. Next was a violin method for class teaching by Joseph Howell of Arkansas, in 1859. Howell's was basically a fiddling book for playing and dancing, as was one by Frank T. Benjamin (a nephew of Lewis A.) in 1889, the *Free Violin School*. From 1883 to 1891, Frank T. Benjamin put on programs (he called them "Children's Carnivals") that amounted to variety shows; they drew audiences over three thousand strong and used instrumentalists the way other schools were using vocalists—as a choir of instruments.[5]

Vocal Music

Vocal music continued, not only in grade schools, but also in high schools and colleges, often with three or four choirs: perhaps a choir for young men only, one for young women only, a large chorus open to any student (to do easier music), and a smaller choir open only by audition to those more advanced in music. And combined choirs were part of the romantic love of size; in Chicago, churches joined in the production of

An illustration of a church choir, by Randolph Caldecott, that appeared in an 1875 printing of *Old Christmas, from the Sketchbook of Washington Irving.* (Picture Collection, The Branch Libraries, The New York Public Library.)

festivals, as many as a dozen churches all learning the same choral works and then combining in concert. And the same was true of schools. In 1928 in Chicago, choirs came from east and west and south to join in a concert at Orchestra Hall as the National High School Chorus. Their program was remarkable—beginning and ending with presentations by the entire company, and including a Zuni Indian song and a Chilean folk song (sung by all the girls with orchestra): the *Mexican Serenade* by George Whitefield Chadwick (sung by the full choir with orchestra); "Were You There?," a spiritual arranged by Henry T. Burleigh (sung by the choir alone); the song "Sylvia" by Oley Speaks (sung by a soloist with piano); the "Spinning Chorus" from *The Flying Dutchman* by Richard Wagner (sung by all the girls with orchestra); and "Listen to the Lambs" by R. Nathaniel Dett (sung by the entire choir alone). The critic of the *Daily Tribune* wrote of it that "it was about the finest piece of singing ever done by a high school group."[6]

School Bands

Town bands were in their golden age from about 1870 to about 1930; in 1889 there were 10,000 bands in the United States—it was said in Illinois in 1915 that there were more bands than there were towns.[7] From about 1900, there were girls' bands. And there were "kid" bands, often of mixed gender. Young people on stage were common enough, with the apprenticeship system active in the theater as much as in music—in 1875, a children's company of Gilbert and Sullivan's *H.M.S. Pinafore* had been mounted in New York City, for example. It seems remarkable then that school bands were so rare, but Mason's dictum on their place as advanced studies plus the strength of the apprenticeship system account for this situation.

The secondary school bands that existed before the First World War were rare. In 1884, the Christian Brothers High School in Memphis, Tennessee, founded a band and accepted members from any level of school, from elementary to college level. The band stayed in business until World War I; when the college-level players joined the army (as a group!), it went out of business.[8] Other bands were being run in Greenville, South Carolina, from 1893; in Live Oak, Florida, from 1896; in Connersville, Indiana, from 1907 (they allowed only twenty players and had another twenty on the waiting list); and at the Oberlin Academy, in Ohio, from 1913 (in 1914 they went on tour and played at the White House for President Wilson).

In 1912, the Music Supervisors' National Conference (MSNC) was still saying that vocal music outranked instrumental music and that the orchestra outranked the band. They published a position paper stating that the hierarchy of musical types in the schools should be (in ranking order, from top to bottom): the full chorus, music appreciation, orchestra, girls' chorus, band, boys' chorus, and glee club.[9] In 1914, the organization held another meeting on bands, but the officers were still against them. The same was true in 1916.

But the First World War, like the War of 1812 and the Civil War, had promoted bands, and at the 1919 meeting of MSNC in St. Louis, an argument for the "democratizing" of music was put forth successfully. A school questionnaire was sent out, 352 schools replied, and the results revealed that 79% of the schools had orchestras and 24% had bands. In 1921, MSNC created the Committee on Instrumental Affairs; it started work in 1922, and in 1923, the band was validated and took off.

Proponents had long felt that the band was an ideal teaching group. As early as 1877, the magazine *Trumpet Notes* had run an article stating that a band gets more benefit from a single contest "than from months of the ordinary routine of band practice."[10] That year, fifteen cornet bands met in Portage, Wisconsin, marched, and gave concerts. Contests were held in Arapahoe, Nebraska, in 1896; in Ottawa, Kansas, in 1897; and in Ruggles Grove, Ohio, in 1899. The contests became more frequent after the First World War, and in 1923, the first of a series of National School Band Contests was held in Chicago (and they would continue until World War II), sponsored by the C. G. Conn Company and the Band Instrument Manufacturing Association. In 1925, regional contests opened up; in subsequent years they grew much more common, remained successful, and became so essential to secondary-school education that in 1931, only one band canceled because of the Depression.

Music Appreciation

Music appreciation was from the beginning connected with the German tradition in music. First, because Lowell Mason put himself into that tradition, and second, because so many German immigrants took jobs in the teaching profession. And although music had been taught to children long before Mason's day, his work with the Boston Academy was vital because it put music into the budget and therefore made it a permanent and vital factor in public education. Music appreciation was in America what the tutorials had been in Europe; nevertheless, it was strongly associated in method with the apprenticeship system.

Music appreciation in the public schools moved forward with the times. Elementary-school books were readied in the 1840s by Charles Aikin of Cincinnati, Ohio. By the end of the century, Aikin had issued a graded series, *The National Music Course* (1898); by then, he had moved to Boston, where his influence could become nationwide, and indeed, his books were adopted around the country. After the turn of the century, the influence of psychology was strongly felt in music education, and many tests of musical aptitude were developed, chiefly the *Measures of Musical Talent* by Carl Seashore, published in 1919 and offered in revised editions in 1939 and 1960.

During the 1920s, a general background in music became a require-ment for most junior high school students; in the '30s, music courses related music to other disciplines, such as history and literature; in the '40s, educators turned to the goal of encouraging the growth of musical skills rather than musical knowledge; in the '50s, this trend turned to the establishment of large performing groups; in the '60s, criticism of music education led to a series of studies at Yale University and seminars sponsored by the Music Educators' National Conference (formerly the Music Supervisors' National Conference), promulgating the idea that popular music and the music of other cultures should be included in music education in the schools. The Ford Foundation joined in with grants for a Contemporary Music Project and a Comprehensive Musi-cianship Project, which encouraged and supported music teachers to introduce new and more relevant materials; in the '70s, the National Foundation on the Arts and Humanities expanded on a John D. Rocke-feller III Fund Arts in Education grant, with a view to reaching younger children; and in the '80s, the United States took stock of the develop-ments in music education, which was serving some 90% of the children in the country. The statistics are mind-boggling: over 1.6 billion students were in school bands; about one billion dollars of the nation's $2.3 billion music industry was being spent for school programs.

Colleges

The European tradition established itself in American universities through John Knowles Paine, at Harvard, and Horatio Parker, at Yale; that tradition would come to dominate virtually all college and university music programs in the United States. It is hard to believe that an anti-American stance has characterized our higher education, but as early as 1900, when publisher Macmillan Co. invited scholars to write a history of American music, the scholars replied that there was "not enough" American music to warrant such a book.[11] The contempt for "popular music" was almost violent: Daniel Gregory Mason (1873–1953), grandson of Lowell Mason and Professor of Music at Columbia from 1910, called urban music "the sweeping of our streets."[12]

Although some courses are offered to general students, little, if any, American music is given to music majors, and it was possible even after World War II to go through college from freshman year to a Ph.D. degree in music without ever encountering an American work. The courses offered to general students, influenced by music education, have concentrated upon popular music, and that too is misrepresentation. And since the colleges and universities prepare teachers, those teachers who do present American music to their classes view it not as the rule but as the exception.

The brass band of Meharry Medical College, Nashville, Tennessee, c. 1910. (Picture Collection, The Branch Libraries, The New York Public Library.)

Oscar Sonneck

musicology: the study of music from a technical point of view

Probably the most significant influence on the offerings of music to college students was Oscar Sonneck, an American born, German trained scholar who became the first Chief Music Librarian at the Library of Congress (1902–17) and then, after he was dismissed because of strong anti-German feeling during the First World War, director of the publications department for music publisher G. Schirmer in New York. He defined the position of the European tradition relative to the teaching of music in graduate school, which was for the introduction of *musicology* as a Ph.D. subject. Sonneck coined the American term "musicology," taking it directly from the French *musicologie* (study, theory, or science of music) rather than from the German *Musikwissenschaft* (science of music), and yet he considered it a German study: We should institute "such German cultural achievements . . . as we lack here. One of these undertakings should be to create in our colleges and universities a place for musicology, in the German sense and along German lines";[13] and he espoused and reiterated the hierarchical idea that a basic schism existed between the "democratic masses" and an "aristocratic minority."[14]

Musicology

The first doctoral dissertation in musicology was written at Harvard in 1905 by Louis Adolphe Coerne (1870–1922); it was *The Evolution of Modern Orchestration* and was later published as *The Evolution of the*

Modern Orchestra. Coerne had studied in Munich and presented the romantic European orchestra as the highest point of musical evolution (in Darwinian terms).

The first chair in musicology in the United States was established at Cornell University in 1930, and its first incumbent was Otto Kinkeldey, born in New York City, trained at Columbia by Edward MacDowell, and a professor at the University of Breslau, Germany, before accepting the professorship at Cornell. Kinkeldey contributed not only his university teaching, but also wrote books for grammar school children.

By the mid 1950s, fifty-six universities in the United States were offering doctoral degrees in musicology; a great number of German professors taught at American schools, refugees during the Second World War, and slowed the acceptance of American music in the schools. But in the '70s and '80s, the study of American music opened up, music appreciation courses began to include it, and the 4,000 odd doctoral dissertations a year (in the mid '80s) included more and more studies on the music of our own country.

NOTES

1. Orpha Ochse, *The History of the Organ in the United States* (Bloomington: Indiana University Press, 1975), p. 356f.

2. Robert L. Brubaker, *Making Music Chicago Style*, Chicago Historical Society, 1985.

3. Ochse, *History*, p. 302.

4. D. W. Krummel, "Publishing and printing of music," *The New Grove Dictionary of American Music*, H. Wiley Hitchcock and Stanley Sadie, eds. (London: Macmillan & Co., 1986).

5. James A. Keene, *A History of Music Education in the United States* (Hanover and London: University Press of New England, 1982), p. 275f.

6. Ibid, p. 321f.

7. Ibid, p. 285.

8. Ibid, p. 286.

9. Ibid, p. 287.

10. Ibid, p. 294.

11. Alan Howard Levy, *Musical Nationalism: American Composers' Search for Identity* (Westport, CT: Greenwood Press, 1983), p. 128.

12. Ibid, p. 128.

13. William Lichtenwanger, ed., *Oscar Sonneck and American Music* (Urbana: University of Illinois Press, 1983), p. 74.

14. Ibid, p. 88.

BIBLIOGRAPHY

Borroff, Edith. "The Choralcelo: One Uniquely American Instrument." *Symposium,* Fall, 1982.

———. *Music in Europe and the United States: A History,* 2nd ed. New York: Ardsley House, Publishers, 1990.

Brubaker, Robert L. *Making Music Chicago Style.* Chicago Historical Society, 1985.

Hitchcock, H. Wiley, and Stanley Sadie, eds. *The New Grove Dictionary of American Music.* London: Macmillan Press, Ltd., 1986.

Keene, James A. *A History of Music Education in the United States.* Hanover and London: University Press of New England, 1982.

Krummel, D. W. "Publishing and Printing of Music," *The New Grove Dictionary of American Music,* H. Wiley Hitchcock and Stanley Sadie, eds. London: Macmillan Press, Ltd., 1986.

Levy, Alan Howard. *Musical Nationalism: American Composers' Search for Identity.* Westport, CT: Greenwood Press, 1983.

Lichtenwanger, William, ed. *Oscar Sonneck and American Music.* Urbana: University of Illinois Press, 1983.

Ochse, Orpha. *The History of the Organ in the United States.* Bloomington: Indiana University Press, 1975.

Sadie, Stanley, ed. *The New Grove History of Music and Musicians.* London: Macmillan Press, Ltd., 1980.

Thompson, Kevin. *Wind Bands and Brass Bands in Schools and Music Centers.* Cambridge, MA: Harvard University Press, 1985.

Boom, Depression, and War
(1923 to 1961)

I t seems impossible for one country to have gone through so much in so short a time, but in the thirty-eight years beginning in 1923, when the reverberations of the First World War had ended and the corruption that led to the Teapot Dome Scandal was being put to rest, the United States went from boom in the 1920s, to the Great Depression in the '30s, to the Second World War in the '40s, to a post-War period of searching for completeness (Alaska and Hawaii became states in 1959). Yet those decades, for all their seeming differences, were strangely one, creating a period of coming to know the strength of the nation and of feeling at last that Americans were the equals of any other people in the world.

There were only five presidents in those thirty-eight years, and each of them in his way summed up the significance of his years in office.

Calvin Coolidge, president from 1923 to 1929, succeeded upon the sudden death of President Harding in August of 1923. One politician of the time recognized the task that Coolidge had faced: "His great task was to restore the dignity and prestige of the Presidency, when it had reached the lowest ebb in our history."[1] Coolidge, feeling that too much government had, in fact, been the undoing of past presidents, undertook to cut drastically the involvement of government in business. Journalist Walter Lippmann wrote that "This inactivity suits the mood and certain of the needs of the country admirably. . . . It suits all those who have become convinced that government in this country has become dangerously complicated and top-heavy."[2] He seemed to be right because the country was enjoying a boom time, living it up, dancing the Charleston, feeling its oats. The Volstead Act, forbidding the manufacture and sale of liquor (any beverage with an alcoholic content over 0.5%), had led to bootlegging, trafficking in illegal beverages, to the tune of $3,600,000,000 in 1926. Movies had become profitable, and the silent films had given way to talkies with the production of *The Jazz Singer* in 1927. In that same year, the fifteen millionth Ford car had come down the assembly line, and Charles A. Lindbergh in a monoplane, *The Spirit of St. Louis*, had flown alone from New York to Paris nonstop, and had become a national hero.

Herbert Hoover (1929–33) was a Quaker who had achieved respect as a government official in charge of such drastic necessities as relocating Americans caught in Europe at the beginning of World War I (he got more than 120,000 of them home in six weeks) and taking charge of the Food Administration during the remainder of the war, then heading the American Relief Administration to

Al Jolson in the title role of *The Jazz Singer*. (Picture Collection, The Branch Libraries, The New York Public Library.)

help feed starving Europeans after the fighting had ceased. Hoover believed that the boom would last: "We in America today are nearer to the final triumph over poverty than ever before in the history of any land," he said.[3] Yet within a year of his inauguration, in October of 1929, came the famous Wall Street crash, leaving the country desperate and without stabilizing mechanisms. From the free-wheeling Roaring Twenties, the country was plunged into the depths of the Great Depression.

Franklin Delano Roosevelt, known as FDR (1933–45), a fifth cousin of Theodore Roosevelt, took over the reins of the nation at the height of the Depression. In March of 1933, 13 million Americans were unemployed, and banks were closing. Roosevelt began with his first "Fireside Chat," broadcast to the country; he proposed, and Congress enacted, many programs—so many that his New Deal was called "Alphabet Soup." The NRA (National Recovery Administration) was perhaps the most important, providing for the setting of standards by industry. Many of the initials stood for work programs, such as the CCC (Civilian Conservation Corps), which was begun in 1933 and functioned for nine years, putting people to work at jobs of general benefit to the country—the Corps planted over three billion trees, for example. The WPA

(Works Progress Administration) was established under the Emergency Relief Appropriation Act in 1935, and gave jobs to about two million people in its seven years, doing such work as building bridges, expanding electrical service, and making new highways. The NYA (National Youth Administration) gave jobs to about a million students, and, more important for music in the country, brought works of art, including music, to many small communities, created a federal theater for the production of plays and musical events, and commissioned murals and paintings. It also produced travel brochures encouraging travel within the country.

Signs of war were perceived early in Roosevelt's administration. German dictator Adolf Hitler had created the Rome/Berlin Axis in 1936, and had invaded Czechoslovakia's Sudetenland in 1938; in 1939, he took the rest of Czechoslovakia, all of Bohemia and Moravia, and then Poland. Travel to Europe by Americans was restricted. When Great Britain and France declared war on Germany, entry into the war was inevitable for the United States as well. In 1940, Germany captured Paris, the Battle of Britain began, and the Selective Service (draft) law required registration of all American men of fighting age. In 1941, Roosevelt said, in his Fourth of July address, that "the United States will never survive as a happy and fertile oasis of liberty, surrounded by a cruel desert of dictatorship."[4] On December 7, the Japanese bombed Pearl Harbor; the next day the United States declared war on Japan, and then on Germany on December 11. In 1942 and 1943, the war increased in scope, reaching its acme in 1944. In 1945, the war was won, in Europe in May, in the Pacific in August; but Roosevelt died suddenly of a stroke on April 12, the day before the liberation of Buchenwald concentration camp. Hitler's suicide came on May 1.

Harry Truman (1945–53), Roosevelt's last vice president, was thus at the helm at the end of the war in the Pacific, brought to a close by the dropping of the atomic bomb, on Hiroshima on August 6 (after a plea for peace and a threat to bomb had been ignored), and on Nagasaki on August 9 (again, after a warning delivered by dropped leaflets). Truman's first year celebrated the peace, with a ceremony of capitulation aboard the battleship *Missouri* on September 2, but it would take many years for the United States to recover from the horrors of World War II. From 1941 to 1945, 15,493,657 members of the armed forces (Army, Navy, and Marines) had faced incredible odds: 325,464 had died, 669,429 had come home wounded, and the cost had been $330,500,000,000, with another $46,070,000,000 in military aid to other nations.

A sailor on leave, 1942. (Picture Collection, The Branch Libraries, The New York Public Library.)

On the domestic front, Truman's administration faced a new series of strikes, at Westinghouse, General Electric, General Motors, and at coal and steel plants, among others, with over 4,600,000 workers idle in 1946 alone. At the same time, the Servicemen's Readjustment Act (the G.I. Bill, 1944) was providing a college education for about nine million veterans (from 1945 to 1949), which meant expansion and new respect for many colleges and universities. In 1947, the Cold War between the U.S.S.R. and the United States was named, came to a head, and loomed menacingly; the Cold War would mean problems for presidents to come.

In 1949, Truman's administration was named the Fair Deal; it was an eventful year spanning the first nonstop round-the-world airplane flight (23,452 miles in 94 hours, 1 minute, in an Air Force Superfortress B-50, *Lucky Lady II*, from Fort Worth, Texas), and the development of strong anti-Communist sentiment that brought forth the witch hunt led by Senator Joseph McCarthy, to go on until he would be censured by the Senate in 1954.

By 1940, over 29,500,000 homes had radios; within a decade, over 45,000,000 would have them, and by 1950, 8 million homes would have television sets.

Truman's administration would end as it had begun—with war, this time the Korean War. Again, the numbers were daunting: 1,800,000 members of the armed forces served, of whom 52,400 were killed, 103,000 were wounded, and 8,200 were missing in action. The peak of the fighting came in 1952, the grudging peace in 1953. The armed forces were desegregated during this conflict, and the results of that would carry over into the next administration.

Dwight D. Eisenhower (1953–61), Texas born and Kansas raised, was the post-World War II president as Grant had been the post-Civil War president. Eisenhower, a graduate of West Point, was a career soldier who was beloved of the people not only because he had been the supreme commander of the European theater in World War II, but because he obtained the Korean truce in 1953. He worked for continued desegregation in the armed forces, and he saw the two important school cases go before the Supreme Court: *Brown* v. *Board of Education of Topeka* in 1954; and *Aaron* v. *Cooper* in 1958, which ordered the immediate desegregation of a high school in Little Rock, Arkansas. Eisenhower was a middle grounder on domestic issues, wanting peace above everything, as Grant had. His last public pronouncement was for peace.

During Eisenhower's administration, the United States reached its current size of fifty states.

1959 Alaska
1959 Hawaii

The United States flag since August, 1959.

THE LITERATURE OF THE PERIOD

All of the arts reflected the nation's attitudes during the buffeting of this long back-and-forth between peace and war, boom and bust. In literature, Anne Nichols's play *Abie's Irish Rose* incorporated the bright side of things—it was produced in 1924 and ran for 2,532 performances; F. Scott Fitzgerald saw the other side in *The Great Gatsby* (1925); Willa

Ernest Hemingway with Sylvia Beach in front of her Parisian bookstore.
(Picture Collection, The Branch Libraries, The New York Public Library.)

Cather's novels included *My Antonia* (1918), about pioneer life; *A Lost Lady*, also about pioneer life (1923); *Death Comes for the Archbishop*, about the southwestern missions (1927); and *Sapphira and the Slave Girl* (1940), based on an incident in Virginia in 1856. The Depression was represented in such books as Erskine Caldwell's *Tobacco Road* (1932); John Steinbeck's *Tortilla Flat* (1935); *Of Mice and Men* (1937); and *The Grapes of Wrath* (1940)—it won a Pulitzer Prize; while such plays as Thornton Wilder's *Our Town* (1938), also a Pulitzer Prize winner, presented an idealized America that sparked patriotic unity important in the war about to come. Drawing on the European modernist tradition, William Faulkner experimented with the form of the novel in such works as *The Sound and the Fury* (1929), and *Absalom, Absalom!* (1936). The American expatriate writer Ernest Hemingway became famous for the clipped, colloquial style exemplified in his novels *A Farewell to Arms* (1929), and *For Whom the Bell Tolls* (1940). Lillian Hellman reflected national prewar despair in such works as *The Little Foxes* (1939), and *The Watch on the Rhine* (1941). Then such works as John Hersey's *Hiroshima* (1946) and

conservatory: a school for the training of musicians

James Michener's *Tales of the South Pacific* (1947) commented on the war; and items like W. H. Auden's *Age of Anxiety* (1947), Norman Mailer's *The Naked and the Dead* (1948); Herman Wouk's *The Caine Mutiny* (1951), a Pulitzer Prize winner (and adapted by the author as a play, *The Caine Mutiny Court-Martial*, 1954), Rachel Carson's *The Sea Around Us* (also 1951), and Arthur Miller's play *The Death of a Salesman* (1953, a Pulitzer Prize winner)—incorporated the postwar malaise. Finally, in the mid- and late 1950s, such works as J. D. Salinger's *Catcher in the Rye* (1951), Arthur Miller's *Crucible* (1953), Saul Bellow's *The Adventures of Augie March* (1953), and Eudora Welty's *The Ponder Heart* (1954) rocked the boat of national satisfaction and led directly to the unease of the 1960s to come. A remarkable group of poets made these years radiant: Robert Frost, Langston Hughes, Edna St. Vincent Millay, James Weldon Johnson, Sara Teasdale, Marianne Moore, and Theodore Roethke are examples.

THE EUROPEAN TRADITION IN MUSIC

Such authors as Gertrude Stein and Ernest Hemingway were in Paris after the First World War, part of a general rejection of the Germanic intellectual hegemony; and many American composers were in Paris as well. And a substantial contingent studied in Italy. The French attitude was one of amused tolerance of just about anything, and life among the American expatriates was both negative and positive: negative in rejection of a good deal of the national pomp and pride, but positive in the reaffirmation of creative drive and power. The Italian attitude was less insouciant, and, in any case, the Americans were more sequestered there, in the American Academy in Rome, in particular. The results were extraordinary in art as a whole and in music in particular. The result was not seen immediately, but made a crescendo of purpose, particularly in the 1930s.

University Composers

For the first time, composers were studying their art at universities in the United States, the first fruits of the appointments of composers to the faculties of Harvard, Yale, and Columbia. But these schools did not offer performance, which was still taught only in *conservatories*, so composers branched off from the concept of the "musician" and became specialists for the first time. The early generation of university composers, however, transferred from apprenticeship to university training and brought with them their performance skills.

Walter Piston

Walter Piston (1894–1976) was a pianist and saxophonist from Rockland, Maine, who studied with John Knowles Paine at Harvard, then in Paris; he became a member of the Harvard faculty in 1940. He was noted as a composer of orchestral works (including seven symphonies, the last in 1961), chamber music (including three string quartets), and, perhaps the most famous, a ballet, *The Incredible Flutist* (1938), from which he drew an orchestral suite that is still in the repertoire. He was known as a theorist and wrote texts on *Harmony* (1941) and *Counterpoint* (1947).

counterpoint: the study of combined melodies

Roger Sessions

Roger Sessions (1896–1985) was born in Brooklyn, New York, and studied with Horatio Parker at Yale, then at the American Academy in Rome; he spent five years in Europe, beginning in 1926, and returned a staunch supporter of European leadership in American music. One of the most influential teachers of those years, he taught at many schools, including Smith College, the Cleveland Institute of Music, the University of California, Berkeley, and finally Princeton University. His works include nine symphonies (the last in 1980), two operas, several string quartets, choral works, some pieces for organ, and some for piano.

Aaron Copland

Aaron Copland (1900–90), also born in Brooklyn, was a pianist in his youth, studied with Rubin Goldmark (a native New Yorker who had studied with Dvořák in New York and then in Vienna) and finally, at the

▶◯ Recommended Recordings and Video Cassettes

American composers of the European tradition are well represented in record listings. The following recordings balance vocal and instrumental music, chamber music, and song with orchestral and choral music.

RCA (Red Seal) 60798-2. Walter Piston's *The Incredible Flutist* with Symphony No. 6 (1955).

Premier Recordings PRCD 1006. *American Winds.* Piston's Woodwind Quintet (1956) along with quintets by Elliott Carter, Irving Fine, and Elie Siegmeister, played by the Boehm Quintet.

New World NW-368-2. Roger Sessions's orchestral suite *The Black Maskers* (1928), along with Aaron Copland's *Connotations* and William Schuman's *In Praise.*

CRI CD 587. String quartets of the modernist school, by Sessions (No. 2, 1951), Milton Babbitt, and Stefan Wolpe.

Aaron Copland. (Picture Collection, The Branch Libraries, The New York Public Library.)

American Academy at Fontainebleau, near Paris, before returning to a life of lecturing (at Harvard, among other schools, in 1934, 1943, and 1951–52), composing, and working for the cause of American music (he founded the American Composers Alliance, an organization still functioning as a conduit for American music shunned by publishers). Many schools and styles are represented in his works, from the severe European style of the 1920s, in his *Variations* (for piano, 1930), to Latin American folk idioms, in *El Salon Mexico* (1936), and *Three Latin Sketches* (1972); but he is most widely known for his American folk idiom,

Recommended Recordings and Video Cassettes

Doubtless the most important of Aaron Copland's music for a study of American music are his most deeply American works.

Delos DE 3104. *Out West: Tone Poems of the American West.* Copland's *Billy the Kid* (1938), along with his *Rodeo* (1942) and Ferde Grofe's *Grand Canyon Suite.*

CBS MK-42431. *Appalachian Spring* (1944), the original version, with *Lincoln Portrait* (1942) and *Billy the Kid.*

Delos DDC-1013. Piano music of Copland: *Passacaglia* (1922), *Variations* (1930), *Fantasy* (1957), and *Night Thoughts* (Homage to Charles Ives, 1972). Excellent in its span of a half-century of changing American styles.

Virgin Classics 59207 (2 CDs). *The Tender Land* (1955, full opera in three acts).

especially in ballet. His western-idiom ballets, *Billy The Kid* (1938) and *Rodeo* (1942), choreographed by Agnes De Mille, brought that idiom into the European tradition; his culminating *Appalachian Spring* (1944), choreographed by Martha Graham, was awarded a Pulitzer Prize. His two books, *What to Listen for in Music* (1938) and *Music and Imagination* (1952), were influential in the teaching of music appreciation.

William Schuman

William Schuman (1910–92), born in New York, studied at the Juilliard School of Music and in Salzburg, Austria. He taught at Sarah Lawrence College from 1935 and was able to take years off to concentrate on composition after winning Guggenheim Awards in both 1939 and 1940. In 1945, he composed *A Free Song*; it won the Pulitzer Prize. After the years devoted to composition, he entered administration and served as president of the Juilliard School for almost twenty years (from 1945 to 1962), then as president of Lincoln Center for seven (until 1969). He retired from this position in 1969 and devoted himself to composing again. His works include ten symphonies, four string quartets, choral works, and theater music, including four ballets.

Samuel Barber

Samuel Barber (1910–81) was born in West Chester, Pennsylvania. He was trained by his aunt, a famous singer, and then studied at the Curtis Institute of Music in Philadelphia, beginning in 1924. After that, he studied in Europe on fellowships: The Rome prize in 1935 and a Guggenheim Fellowship in 1945. (He also won the Pulitzer Prize in both

▶◯ Recommended Recordings and Video Cassettes

RCA (Red Seal) 61282. William Schuman's *New England Tryptich* (1956), along with the *American Festival Overture* (1939) and Symphony No. 10 ("American Muse"—1975).

Premier Recordings PRCD 1009. *Three American One-Act Operas*. *The Mighty Casey* (1953) by Schuman, along with Marc Blitzstein's *The Harpies* (1931) and Samuel Barber's *A Hand of Bridge* (1958). An excellent introduction to American opera in the twentieth century.

Chandos CHAN 8958. *American Series, Vol. 1*. Samuel Barber: Overture to *The School for Scandal* (1933) and Symphony No. 1 (1936); with Amy Beach's "Gaelic" Symphony (1896).

Sony Masterworks (Portrait) MPK 46727. Vocal music of Barber sung by Elanore Steber (soprano): *Knoxville: Summer of 1915* (1947); *Dover Beach* (1933), for baritone and string quartet, sung by Dietrich Fischer-Dieskau; and the *Hermit Songs* (1953). Some of the best vocal music of the century.

adagio: slow

1935 and 1936.) *Dover Beach* (1931, for voice and string quartet) and the overture *School for Scandal* (1933), brought him early success, confirmed by the *Adagio for Strings* (1938), a lush movement drawn from his *String Quartet* of 1936, rescored for string orchestra. Barber's ability to develop an original harmonic language from traditional elements made his music exciting, yet accessible to listeners uncomfortable with dissonant modernism. From 1939 to 1942, Barber taught at Curtis, and from 1942 to 1945, he served in the United States Army Air Force. Upon his return, he produced his most successful works with a remarkable creative intensity: *The Serpent Heart* (1946), a ballet choreographed by Martha Graham; *Knoxville: Summer of 1915* (1948), for soprano and orchestra, which turned a nostalgic text by James Agee to a plangent lyricism; many works for piano (*Excursions*, 1945; *Souvenirs*, 1953) and voice (*Hermit Songs*, 1953); and three operas: *Vanessa* (1953, produced at the Metropolitan Opera in New York), *A Hand of Bridge* (a short—nine minutes—comedy, 1960, produced at the Spoleto Festival, Italy), and *Antony and Cleopatra* (1966, also produced at the Met).

The German Hegemony

These composers worked within the European tradition, coming to grips with American ideas only occasionally and tangentially, devoting themselves, within the American university system, to the international ideal. That ideal, initially German a century before, was still basically German (in spite of the stylish study trips various composers took to France and Italy), and German theory texts, either in English translation or in new books based upon and infused with German theoretical desiderata, were used in virtually all of the colleges and universities offering professional music study. This theoretical intransigence was heightened by specialization within music, which took not only "composers" and separated them from "musicians" but also took "theorists" and separated them as well; in fact, composers were more inclined to American materials than theorists were.

Apprenticeship musicianship died out during these decades. Apprenticeship teaching had settled into nonaccredited conservatories of music, where musicians and nonmusicians alike studied music and became musically literate. Just as it was not considered that learning to read and write would of necessity result in the profession of authorship, so it was not considered that the study of music, even in depth, should result in professional musicianship. There were many knowledgeable and highly competent amateurs. Conservatories had thus trained—and honed—audiences as well as performers. They had trained—and honed—prospective patrons as well. The universities had not trained musicians, but had taught music in the quadrivium of the liberal arts, theoretical music as opposed to the theory of music, that is, philosophy rather than practical grammar. Their training of audiences had been relegated to music appreciation courses, where they stayed throughout this period: courses telling students what they ought to like, and who were the composers at the apex of German romanticism. If a college-educated American was asked to name five composers, he or she would probably name at least four Germans; few college-educated Americans knew of American concert music at all. American composers of concert music were thus caught in a most curious web: since the art of music was European and Americans were *ipso facto* exceptions, Americans were foreigners in their own country.

EUROPEANS IN THE UNITED STATES

The situation in Europe brought many European composers, threatened (or just sickened) by Nazism, to our shores. These composers varied considerably, but as a group they did little or nothing to help American composers find their way; they very strongly confirmed the idea that music was a European matter and that Americans could be acolytes, but could never be central to musical reality. Early composers emigrated in large part because they were modernists in a musical environment inimical to anything that opposed the traditional European romanticism. But later composers came because of Nazi persecution, which reached a dangerous level by the mid-1930s.

Edgard Varèse

The first of the Europeans of the modern school to move to the United States was Edgard Varèse (1885–1965). He arrived in 1915, settled in New York, and became a citizen of the United States in 1926. As a radical modernist, he worked for new sounds and new techniques in music, and devoted himself to a multi-national life. He founded a Composers Guild in 1921 and a Pan American Society in 1926, taught in New York, but was a European composer and an American teacher, in support of European musical radicalism in the United States.

Arnold Schönberg

Arnold Schönberg (1874–1951) arrived in 1933, one of the first of those escaping Nazi persecution. He accepted a professorship at the University of California at Los Angeles (1936–44), became a citizen in 1941, and continued to live in California after he retired. He made an English edition of his early theory text *Harmonielehre* (1911), issued as *Theory of Harmony* in 1947. He too remained a German composer teaching in the United States.

Paul Hindemith

Paul Hindemith (1895–1963) was a professor in Berlin, left Germany in 1935, and taught in several countries, including the United States; his teaching here included stints at Yale, Harvard, and Aspen (a summer school in Colorado). He wrote his book *The Craft of Musical Composition* in the United States; it was published here in 1937. At the outbreak of the Second World War, he returned to Europe, accepting a professorship in Zurich, Switzerland.

Béla Bártok

Béla Bártok (1881–1945), a Hungarian working in Budapest, came to the United States in 1940 to participate in a conference on folk music, a longtime interest; he decided to remain, and lived in New York City until his death five years later.

Darius Milhaud

Darius Milhaud (1892–1974), a French composer, also came to the United States in 1940, and moved to California, where he accepted a professorship at Mills College. After the war he became binational, continuing his work at Mills but also teaching at the Paris Conservatoire, commuting between his two homes, remaining essentially French.

Igor Stravinsky

Igor Stravinsky (1882–1971), a Russian who had already emigrated to France and become a French citizen in 1934, visited the United States in 1925 and 1935. He moved to the United States in 1939, living in Beverly Hills, California, until 1969—and a citizen from 1941. He was an early proponent, along with Milhaud, of the use of ragtime and jazz elements in concert music (see p. 233). Stravinsky continued to be active as a composer well into his old age, but he remained a French-enamored Russian until the 1950s, when he turned to German techniques.

The Germanic Position

Hindemith, Schönberg, and the later Stravinsky continued to assume the natural leadership of Germany in twentieth-century music, teaching this to Americans as a matter of course. Milhaud and Bártok, and the earlier Stravinsky (before he arrived in the United States) espoused a more open palette, with folk music and jazz prominent in their work. Varèse was the modernist, the iconoclast who wanted to break with the past quickly instead of slowly, who acknowledged German theory as that musical thought against which he was working.

Igor Stravinsky. (Drawing by David Zuckerman.)

There were radical departures from German romantic thought in American composers as well. And as time went on, the iconoclasts were more and more honored.

THE ICONOCLASTS

Henry Cowell

Henry Cowell (1897–1965) was a Californian who went his own way, experimenting with the unification of oriental and occidental styles of music, an idea that won strong support after World War II and the

▶○ Recommended Recordings and Video Cassettes

The piano music of Henry Cowell illustrates the search for new sounds.

CRI ACS 6005. Music of Henry Cowell. "Tone Cluster" Pieces (for piano); plus *Hymn and Fuging Tune* (1946), for orchestra; and *Persian Set* (1957), also for orchestra.

New World 80405. Music for Percussion, by Cowell, John Cage, Lou Harrison, Lukas Foss, and Harvey Sollberger.

Cowell's *Banshee* (1925), for prepared piano, is included in Borroff, *Compact Discs*.

octave: an interval encompassing eight tones on a musical scale

kithara: a large harp of ancient Greece

scale: an orderly listing of musical pitches

indeterminacy: music that makes deliberate use of chance or random elements

Korean War, when so many returning soldiers came home having heard oriental music. Cowell was one of the first to compose music for a piano that was "prepared" for a work by having objects (paper, metal objects, pieces of wood) placed on the strings to elicit strange sounds; *Banshee* (1925) was an example of such a work, in which astonishing sounds are created.[5] But the idea of form cannot follow from sound alone—like most of those works, it was brief (less than two and a half minutes). Cowell was tremendously prolific, and wrote a great deal of music in traditional forms as well—including twenty symphonies.

Harry Partch

Harry Partch (1901–74), who worked and taught in several areas of the United States, built an array of instruments that could produce not only new sounds but new scales. These included an adapted cello (with brads for thirty-seven notes to the *octave*, 1928), a huge *kithara* (ancient Greek harp) about six feet tall, with seventy-two strings tuned variously (1938–43), and adapted guitars, one with six strings tuned in unison (1935–53). Partch favored a *scale* of forty-three notes to the octave, which he derived from American and oriental speech patterns.

John Cage

John Cage (1912–92) was a Californian who studied with Schoenberg, Cowell, and Varèse. He devoted himself to experimentation, writing for prepared piano and mounting a vast scope of musical effects from random noise to total silence. He experimented with computers and also with oriental philosophy, writing on the *I Ching* and its applications to the production of music. He proposed a theory of *indeterminacy*, using random sounds, giving performers basic choices of procedure and often retaining for himself only the specifications of overall length, locale, personnel, and instruments. Cage claimed that "My purpose is to eliminate purpose." The piano piece 4'33" presented four minutes and

John Cage. (Picture Collection, The Branch Libraries, The New York Public Library.)

thirty-three seconds of silent contemplation of the open piano by the soloist, a work that angered a British audience but delighted the Italians—Cage had the piano bench wired so that at the end of the piece he would be wafted off the stage, and the irrepressible audience, far from impressed with the philosophic statement, yelled "Arrivederci, Giovanni!" at his departing figure. The *Theatre Piece 1960* "was based on a scheme of simultaneous incoherent actions and 'happenings.' The performers shot at balloons filled with paint; one of them had a shave while the March from [Wagner's] *Tannhäuser* issued from a loud-speaker and the contralto sang Lucienne Boyer's twenties hit *Parlez moi d'amour.* . . . The whole affair was cheerful rather than outrageous. . . . "[6]

Recommended Recordings and Video Cassettes

The music of Harry Partch and John Cage illustrates the twentieth-century search for new means of making music.

CRI 193. *From the Music of Harry Partch* (LP). A good survey of Partch's instrumental inventions. An excellent booklet accompanies the record.

New Albion NA 035. *Singing Through: Vocal Compositions by John Cage.*

Etcetera KTC 2016 (2 CDs). *26'1.1499 for a String Player* (for solo cello, transistor radio, two record players, and voice—1955). Also contains *Lecture on Nothing* (1959), solo for cello, and variations for several cellos.

The Iconoclastic Position

All of these composers were iconoclasts, not of an American music, but of the European tradition. To an extent, iconoclasts are self-motivated, putting themselves in a position of opposition to what they have been taught. And to an extent, they must work out their own musical procedures, in a practical thrust that shares a hands-on philosophy with apprenticeship. But they were attacking the European tradition specifically and defining their art in terms of a very particular negation. The true apprenticeship composers were found elsewhere.

THE END OF APPRENTICESHIP IN THE CONCERT TRADITION

Apprenticeship was still widely practiced in the 1920s, but as more and more European performers came to the United States, the concert venues dried up as places where new American works could be performed. A few orchestra conductors, like Frederick Stock in Chicago, German born and trained, encouraged composers native to the United States; and a few European soloists played works by composers native to the United States. But such opportunities were rare, and, with the influx of wartime refugees, became rarer. The welcoming of the refugees was a marvelous cultural generosity that had long-term negative results musically. Unaccredited conservatories still functioned during the Second World War, though much weakened; after the war, the G.I. Bill, by granting free tuition to returning veterans only to accredited institutions, killed off all competition for college and university music departments. Even in the late 1950s, the National Association of Schools of Music was dominated by conservatories. But over the next twenty years "conservatories merged with universities, and by the end of the 1970s, conservatories in the old sense were no longer of measurable significance in American secondary-school education."[7]

So the last generation of apprenticeship composers was born about the turn of the century, and, after having twenty or thirty years of good fortune, fell upon hard days.

David Guion

David Guion (1895–1981) was a Texan who studied piano in Vienna with Leopold Godowsky. He taught at several Texas institutions: the Daniel Baker College School of Music in Brownwood, the Fairmount Conservatory in Dallas, and at Southern Methodist University, also in Dallas. (He also taught briefly at the Chicago School of Music.) The bulk of his work comprised the bringing of American and African music into

🔊 Recommended Recordings and Video Cassettes

Most of the music of the apprenticeship school is on old recordings, which might be found in the college record archives. But a few are readily available.

Premier Recordings PRCD 1024. *Prairie Echoes: Piano Music of David Guion.* An excellent selection, including two of the *Alley Tunes*, plus the transcriptions of "Home on the Range," "Turkey in the Straw," and "The Arkansas Traveler."

the piano, vocal, and orchestral literature. In 1929, he composed a ballet suite with an African subject that dealt with African musical entities; he was commissioned to compose a work in honor of the Texas centennial celebration in 1936, a "musical panorama" that he called *Cavalcade of America*; and he composed a *Texas Suite* for band in 1952. But above all, he was known for his piano works, and, within those, for the writing of variations on well-known American tunes. These were in the tradition of the piano *transcription* (that is, the putting into piano technique a work composed for another medium), and, in the case of a virtuoso pianist, the transcription would be highly ornamental and very difficult to play. He composed piano transcriptions that amounted to sets of variations on such tunes as "Home on the Range," "The Arkansas Traveler," and "Turkey in the Straw." He composed a volume of *Alley Tunes*, including "The Harmonica Player," and two suites for piano, *Southern Nights* and *Mother Goose* (for children). He had a radio show in 1932 and 1933 called "Hearing America with David Guion," performing his own works, playing for guest singers (who sang Guion's songs), and telling "colorful stories" of his life as a musician.[8]

transcription: the adaptation of a composition to a medium other than its original one

cacophonic: sounding unpleasant or ugly

Irwin Fischer

Irwin Fischer (1903–77), born in Iowa, studied at the American Conservatory in Chicago (an unaccredited apprenticeship school) during the 1920s and made that city the focus of his career. He was a consummate apprenticeship musician, a pianist, organist, conductor, composer, teacher, and writer, called by a musicologist "a kind of twentieth-century Bach,"[9] though his music was an idiosyncratic mixture of German and French styles. Reviews of his music were entirely enthusiastic, one saying that his *Piano Concerto*, which he had performed with the Chicago Civic Orchestra in 1936, was "entirely modernistic, but not *cacophonic*, . . . [displaying] talent and inspiration that teachers alone cannot give." Other critics spoke of his "shining talents" and his "genuine originality."[10] But after the Second World War, when the universities had taken over, his work was dismissed by scholars who had never heard it, and his early success was followed by later rejection by the university musical community, now in power, though never by the organizations with which he worked.

Irwin Fischer. (The Newberry Library.)

Recommended Recordings and Video Cassettes

A few of Irwin Fischer's works were issued on CRI, and are probably still available on LP.

CRI-122. Fischer's *Hungarian Set* ("*Pearly Boquet*"—1938), on Hungarian folk tunes heard when he was a student in Budapest in 1936.

Louisville Series LOU-676. Fischer's *Overture on an Exuberant Tone Row* (1964). Certainly one of the most accessible of serial works.

Two of Fischer's songs are included in Borroff, *Compact Discs*, along with a madrigal by James Ming (born in 1918).

Radie Britain

rhapsody: a romantic instrumenal piece

song cycle: a group of songs constituting a musical entity

Radie Britain (born in 1903), a Texan, studied at the American Conservatory in Chicago. The focus of her works, as evidenced in their imaginative titles, closely parallels our history, with an early orchestral work, *A Heroic Poem* (1927), about Lindbergh's transatlantic flight—the work won a prize in 1932; another prize-winner, *Light*, about Edison, dates from 1935 (it was performed by the Chicago Women's Symphony); and the *Translunar Cycle*, celebrating the lunar landing of 1969. Her earthy titles, such as the *Cactus Rhapsody*, a piano trio of 1953, and the *Cowboy Rhapsody* (1956) reflect her Texas heritage. And her chamber work, *Chipmunks*, for woodwinds, harp, and percussion shows imagination and wit. She also branched out from American subjects, composing such works as the *Pyramids of Giza*, performed in New York in 1976. She composed two string quartets (one of them, in 1978, titled *Musical Portrait of Thomas Jefferson*, was premiered in Sacramento, California) and a number of *song cycles*.

Abram Chasins

Abram Chasins (1905–87) was a gifted pianist and composer whose career exemplifies the problems of apprenticeship composers in this university-dominated country. Tremendously successful in the 1920s, Chasins taught at the Curtis Institute (Philadelphia) from 1926 and published four volumes of marvelous piano *Preludes* plus a great many other works before 1930; his *Three Chinese Pieces* became extremely

 Recommended Recordings and Video Cassettes

Nothing by Radie Britain is listed currently, but, again, college record archives may well contain some materials. Of Abram Chasins, only the "Rush Hour in Hong Kong," from the Three Chinese Pieces *is currently listed.*

Nimbus NI-5020. "Rush Hour in Hong Kong" is included in an otherwise European piano album.

Abram Chasins. (Drawing by David Zuckerman.)

popular among concert pianists. He composed two piano concertos, both of which he played with the Philadelphia Orchestra under the baton of Leopold Stokowski; the first of these was the first American piano concerto to be performed in Europe. But from the mid-1930s, Chasins's career was finished. By 1941, he had taken an executive job at radio station WQXR in New York City, from which he retired and went to the radio station of the University of Southern California, where he directed the music from 1972 to 1977.

These composers all found themselves at the end of their open road after World War II, when universities closed ranks upon them. There were exceptions, of course, chiefly musicians who changed course, going from one system to the other.

William Grant Still

William Grant Still.

William Grant Still (1895–1978) was a musician of multiple heritage, and his scope of musicianship reflected not only his racial background (African-American, Indian, Spanish, Irish, and Scottish), but also the main roads of music in his native country. He was born in Mississippi, but was raised in Little Rock, Arkansas, where his mother was a high school teacher and his stepfather a mail carrier (his own father, a college teacher, died before the son was born). He was brought up on German romantic music, but entered the profession of music via work with W. C. Handy and swing bands, such as Artie Shaw's, for which he made over one thousand arrangements. In concert music he studied with both Chadwick and Varèse, and he made sincere attempts to make himself into the German acolyte that they asked him to be. But he broke away, returned to apprenticeship, and composed in his own unique African-American style. His *Afro-American Symphony* (1930) was probably the most widely played symphony by any American, done by over 38 different orchestras in America and Europe in its first twenty years. He lived in New York until 1934, when he was awarded a Guggenheim Fellowship and moved to California, where he wrote the choral work, *Kaintuck'*, 1935, and the tone poem *Dismal Swamp*, 1936. He also composed eleven operas, several ballets, a song cycle, the choral work, *A Psalm for the Living*, 1954, a good deal of chamber music, and several movie scores, plus TV show scores (the "Perry Mason" show, for example).

Ruth Crawford

Ruth Crawford (1901–53) was born in Ohio; her father was a minister who moved around a good deal, and the child was brought up in a number of places: in Missouri, Indiana, and finally, in Jacksonville, Florida, where she was educated. She taught at the School of Musical Arts, a conservatory in Jacksonville, from 1918 to 1922, and then went to Chicago to study at the American Conservatory. In 1929, she moved to New York, where she met Charles Seeger (1886–1979), an American musicologist and *ethnomusicologist* (one who studies the music of cultures other than one's own), who was a Harvard graduate and had lived two years in Cologne, Germany. From 1912 to 1919, Seeger had taught at the University of California, Berkeley, and there introduced the first course in musicology in the United States. From 1919, he was in New York, and, with Henry Cowell, had taught the first class in ethnomusicology in the United States. He took Ruth Crawford as his second wife; he introduced her to the German tradition of university music, to which tradition she switched. She was never prolific, but her *String Quartet* of 1931 is a magnificent work of the new tradition. In the 1940s, Crawford began working with folk songs, coming out with two books: *American Folk Songs for Children* (1950) and *American Folk Songs for Christmas* (1953).

▶️◯ Recommended Recordings and Video Cassettes

Several recordings of music by William Grant Still are available.

Mercury (Living Presence) 434324-2 PM. *Sahdji* (1930). The best of the early recordings.

Library of Congress OMP 106. *Our Musical Past, Vol. 5.* Still's *Afro-American Symphony* (1930), paired with *Salome* (1906) by Henry Hadley.

Bay Cities BCD 1033. *Songs of Separation* (a song cycle—1949). With instrumental music: *Lenox Avenue* (1937), a ballet suite for orchestra and speaker; and a *Suite for Violin and Piano* (1943). A nice variety.

New World 80399-2. *Ennaga, for String Quartet, Harp, and Piano* (1956); with other instrumental works and songs.

Glendale Legend Recordings GL-8011. *William Grant Still Conducts William Grant Still.* Contains the ballet *Lenox Avenue* (1937), two movements of *Symphony in G minor* (1937), and *La Guiablesse* (1927).

Borroff, *Compact Discs* includes Still's "Hard Trials," a spiritual.

Ruth Crawford has only three listings.

Delos DCD-1012. *Two Movements for Chamber Orchestra.* Along with works by Thea Musgrave (an American resident) and Joyce Mekeel.

Cambria DCD-1037. *Five Songs, for Solo Voice and Piano* (1929), sung by L. Field, soprano; together with songs by other American composers—Florence Price, Patsy Rogers, Miriam Gideon, Nancy Van de Vate, and Dorothy Klotzman.

Gramavision R21S-79440. *String Quartet* (1931). With a mixture of other American works (by Conlon Nancarrow and Roger Reynolds) and foreign ones.

The Two Camps

Such careers as those of Still and Crawford were not peaceful, but showed the strain of being in two camps. That kind of confusion was probably inevitable at the end of the apprenticeship period in the history of music. Change to the university system was probably inevitable also. But the apprenticeship system had certain advantages: among them was the acceptance of women, none of whom were permitted as composers in the university system until quite recently—the first woman to receive a doctorate in composition (standard for males) at an accredited institution would do so only in 1975. African-Americans also were trained more frequently in apprenticeship, though their entry into the university system was earlier than women's. One thinks of Burleigh, studying with Dvořák in New York City in the apprenticeship system, with its one-on-one give-and-take, and the many women trained at the American Conservatory in Chicago, with a certain regret for a system that gave a great deal to music over thousands of years—and now is found only in the training of theater and popular-music professionals.[11]

CONCERT LIFE

impressionism: a late-romantic development featuring responses to places and people

expressionism: a post-romantic development featuring musical objectivity

serialism: a composition technique developed early in the twentieth century

neoclassicism: the use of classical elements in postromantic music

Concerts in the United States after the First World War were for the most part European in personnel and in content. Members of orchestras were often Americans, but the conductors and the soloists were always European, and the works performed centered in the European tradition. Certain conductors, like Frederick Stock in Chicago and Leopold Stokowski in Philadelphia, included a small amount of American music in their expansive European repertoires, but the sense that the country was musically equal to Europe was totally lacking, even when evidence to the contrary was to be heard.

This anti-American prejudice was exacerbated by the state of confusion of the art of music in general: romanticism was failing, and various "isms" were proposed to succeed it, most of them using the very materials that were central to the romantic aesthetic, exaggerating rather than changing the *basis operandi*. Works became longer, orchestras got bigger, and harmony became richer. But gradually, antiromantic styles emerged: *impressionism, expressionism, serialism,* and *neoclassicism* were four among many, the most important, perhaps, in a period that in general was called postromantic. The really marvelous music of the best of romanticism was no longer exciting (as it had been when it was being born), but nobody knew which way to turn, and each composer in the European tradition was on his own (remember, women were not welcome in that tradition—although they persisted), basically dealing with the problem of what to do next. Wagner had gone so far as to say that he could not be topped. The Darwinists believed in progress, but not in any change of the fundamentals of the romantic style: bigger was better, and as early as 1889, a Darwinist responded to the invention of the phonograph with an impossible dream. As complicated as Wagner's music was (in romantic terms), the dreamer dreamed on:

> In the far-off future, when our descendants wish to compare our simple little Wagner operas with the complex productions of their own days, requiring, perhaps, a dozen orchestras, playing in half a dozen different keys at once, they will have an accurate phonographic record of our harmonic simplicity.[12]

So not only was bigger better, but more complicated was better. The result was a school of modernism built on intellectual, rather than musical, developments; mathematical, rather than intuitive, creative elements; the production of a music-of-the-eye, rather than music-of-the-ear; of the quadrivium, rather than the trivium. Concerts of the modern music were given more and more frequently as the decades passed, but they were produced in modernist enclaves rather than mixed with older, well-known works, in concerts of traditional venues.

Pianists in the 1920s programmed more and more works by American composers, and such Americans as Guion and Chasins braved the European monopoly to become concert artists, playing their own works as a matter of course. But in the 1930s, this changed, as orchestral music did, and American music disappeared from piano recitals, with few exceptions. Marie Bergersen, in her only recorded recital (in 1965), played fourteen works, of which seven (exactly half) were American, mostly of the 1920s and '30s—and she included works of both literal rendition and transcription. But by then, that was eccentricity.

Band Concerts

Band concerts were still a national strength in the 1920s and '30s; after Sousa's death in 1932, they began to change substantively. Leading bandsmen, such as Edwin Franko Goldman (1878-1956), began commissioning new band works. A concert in Carnegie Hall, New York City, in 1948, in honor of Goldman's seventieth birthday, consisted of ten such works, nine of them European (including one by Schoenberg); the one American work was Henry Cowell's *Shoonthree*, composed in 1941. Goldman had studied with Dvořák in New York City, was a cornet virtuoso of the "old school," and had been a member of the Metropolitan Opera Orchestra when he founded his own band in 1911; the band functioned for over sixty-five years, with his son Richard Franko Goldman (1910–80) the assistant conductor from 1939 and the conductor upon the father's death.

By 1940, there were over ten thousand secondary-school bands in the United States, along with seventy-five hundred other vocal and instrumental ensembles, with over five hundred thousand students taking part.[13] Bands were more and more important in high school and college concerts and football games, playing at halftime in skillfully choreographed walking designs, thrilling to watch as well as to hear. But the old-fashioned concert band became important in schools as well. William Revelli (born in 1902), from Colorado, studied at the Chicago Musical College, was a high school band director in Hobart, Indiana (winning the national championship contest six years in a row), and then band director at the University of Michigan from 1935. In his thirty-six years there, Revelli developed an entire band program, which included seven bands at different levels of competence. His principal band toured many times, including a tour of the Middle East, under State Department aegis, in 1961.

Bands were still vital to civic events and expositions, and expositions remained important in unifying Americans in patriotism: in 1926, Philadelphia held its Sesquicentennial Exposition. But the Depression gave rise to many more, as part of the pulling together of the New Deal, to give work to some and pleasure to many. Chicago held the Century of

The Fort Lee, NJ, High School band at the New York World's Fair, 1940. (Picture Collection, The Branch Libraries, The New York Public Library.)

sinfonietta: a small orchestra often used for the performance of semiclassical music

pops concert: an informal concert for large audiences, often outdoors

arranger: the musician who adapts a composition for a medium other than the one for which it was originally intended

Progress Exposition in 1933 and 1934; Cleveland, the Great Lakes Exposition in 1936; Dallas, the Pan American Exposition in 1937; and New York City, the World's Fair in 1939 and 1940. Bands were very much a part of those projects.

Pops Concerts

But orchestral pops concerts began to supplant band concerts; these were modeled after the park concerts of a century before, with orchestras playing in outdoor gazebos, now with the benefit of microphones and loudspeakers, so that the less penetrating sounds could be heard. Arthur Fiedler (1894–1979), a violinist and, later, a violist in the Boston Symphony Orchestra, who had worked with his father and then gone off for the obligatory study in Berlin (1909–13), founded the Arthur Fiedler *Sinfonietta* in 1924, using players of the Boston Symphony Orchestra. In 1929, he began the free summer concerts in a Boston park along the Charles River; in 1930, the *Sinfonietta* became the "Boston Pops," and from then until Fiedler's death, it virtually defined the park concert of the twentieth century, offering lively performances of both traditional literature and music from other venues, orchestrated and put into the more prestigious hands of musicians in the European tradition.

Pops concerts brought forth a host of *arrangers* and transcribers, who produced a literature that was unique to the pops concerts. Composer Leroy Anderson (1908–75), with apprenticeship training, then study at Harvard and a stint (1932–35) as Harvard's band director (in the physical education department), became an important composer in this vein.

▶◯ Recommended Recordings and Video Cassettes

Several recordings have been made by the Boston Pops Orchestra, under both Arthur Fiedler and John Williams.

RCA 61237-4. *Leroy Anderson's Greatest Hits.*

Mercury (Living Presence) 432013-2. The best-known of Anderson's pieces, including *The Syncopated Clock, Fiddle Faddle,* and *The Typewriter.*

He began as an arranger for the Boston Pops, then wrote such works as *The Syncopated Clock, Fiddle Faddle, Sleigh Ride, A Trumpeter's Lullaby,* and *The Typewriter.* He was an engaging melodist, and also brought humor and imagination into his music.

The Boston Pops concerts were the best known, but there were many more, such as the Ravinia Concerts in Chicago and the Hollywood Bowl series in California. Some pops series were discontinued during the Second World War, but they returned after the war to be even more popular than before, both to attend and to hear on radio, and then later, to see on television.

Arthur Fiedler. (Picture Collection, The Branch Libraries, The New York Public Library.)

OPERA

But the strongest creative efforts of Americans, strongest in the number of performances and the amount of public support and enthusiasm, lay in the musical theater.

Opera already had an impressive history in the United States, and that history continued through the twenties and the Depression, slumped during the years of the Second World War, when such expensive productions were out of the question, and then returned to popularity. Of course the "big" houses, like the Metropolitan Opera in New York City, mounted European works almost entirely, with a few exceptions, but throughout the country theaters were producing operas by American composers. Fewer were on American topics, and many were downright exotic, such as *Yolanda of Cyprus* by Clarence Loomis (1889–1965) which was composed in 1926 and produced in Chicago in 1929, then in New York and in twenty-eight other productions throughout the country. Loomis (who had studied in Vienna with Leopold Godowsky) composed nine operas in all, and became more American as time went on, with *Susannah Don't You Cry* in New York in 1931 and *The Fall of the House of Usher* (based on Edgar Allan Poe's story of 1839) in Indianapolis in 1941.

Loomis won the David Bispham Medal in 1926 for *Yolanda of Cyprus*. That medal was established by Eleanor Freer and Edith Rockefeller McCormick in Chicago in 1924; it was given to over sixty composers of opera before it was discontinued, after Freer's death during World War II. Chicago was, in fact, a leading city in the performance of American music, much more so than New York, which had such a large immigrant population still in tune with their European roots. But over 175 American cities featured opera productions by the end of the 1960s.

Composers whose operas were performed at the Metropolitan were few, and they were the most European of Americans, who wrote long operas with big orchestras, in the European style. Deems Taylor, a composer and writer on musical topics for the layman, was the only one to have two operas performed at the Met: *The King's Henchman* in 1927 (it had won the Bispham Medal in 1926) and *Peter Ibbetson* in 1930. Marc Blitzstein's *The Cradle Will Rock* was produced in 1937, Gian-Carlo Menotti's *The Island God* in 1942, and Bernard Rogers's *The Warrior* (about Samson) in 1944.

But probably the most important one was Howard Hanson's *Merry Mount* of 1933. It was given a concert performance (that is, like an orchestra concert, without costumes, scenery, or action) in Ann Arbor, Michigan that year, and then produced at the Met the following year. Hanson was a prolific composer and also a well-known educator—he

▶ Recommended Recordings and Video Cassettes

Not many American operas have been recorded. Only an orchestral suite is available from Howard Hanson's Merry Mount.

Delos DE 3105. Suite from *Merry Mount.* Along with other works by Hanson, including *Symphony No. 4* ("Requiem"—1943).

directed the Eastman School of Music from 1924, and "he elevated" that school "from a provincial conservatory to one of the most important musical institutions in America."[14] *Merry Mount* was based on the story "The Maypole of Merrymount" (1842), by Nathaniel Hawthorne, and dealt with Puritan New England. The Met opening was extraordinarily successful; there were fifty curtain calls. But the place of American composers was made clear: "Despite this popular reception and favorable critical reviews, the opera had only four performances, and was not retained in the repertoire, a fate not unlike that of other American operas produced at the Metropolitan."[15]

Howard Hanson. (Picture Collection, The Branch Libraries, The New York Public Library.)

It is formidable to list the American operas of these years, but they were bountiful. Eleanor Freer (1864–1942), co-founder of the Bispham medal, had eleven operas produced between 1921 and 1936. *The Legend of the Piper* (1921) was given productions in Chicago, Boston, and Brooklyn (and it won the Bispham Medal!). She encompassed Native American, Spanish, and chivalrous subjects, in addition to American ones, such as *Scenes from Little Women* (1934, on Louisa May Alcott's novel of 1869). Julia Smith (1911–89), a Texas composer, had six operas performed in Dallas, Amarillo, Denton, Fort Worth, and Austin. Charles Sanford Skilton (1868–1941), a Kansan, composed three operas between 1927 and 1936—*The Sun Bride*, produced for an NBC radio broadcast in 1930, was based on a Native American legend. Charles Edward Hamm (born in 1925), a Virginian, had six operas performed between 1952 and 1961, in Cincinnati and Athens, Ohio; San Francisco; Bristol, Virginia; and New Orleans.

Douglas Moore (1893–1969), from upstate New York, composed the popular work *The Ballad of Baby Doe*, which told the true story of Baby Doe Tabor, a Wisconsin woman in Colorado, and was premiered in Central City, Colorado, in 1956; it has been produced by several companies since then, including the New York City Opera in 1976. Aaron Copland's *The Tender Land* was performed by the New York Opera in 1954, the same year as George Kleinsinger's *archy and mehitabel* and Evelyn Pittman's *Cousin Esther*. Pittman's work was produced twice in New York, once in Paris, and then broadcast as part of the American Music Festival in 1963. Virgil Thomson, a Harvard graduate, one of the Paris group in the 1920s and later a critic for the *New York Herald Tribune*, composed two operas to librettos by Gertrude Stein: *Four Saints in Three Acts* (Bispham Medal), performed in Ann Arbor, Michigan, in 1933 and Hartford, Connecticut, in 1934; and *The Mother of Us All*, performed at Columbia University in 1947. (These works would be revived for later performances: the first in 1973 and 1986; the second in 1986.)

The vein was rich and would get richer.

▶◯ Recommended Recordings and Video Cassettes

Douglas Moore's Ballad of Baby Doe, *for some unknown reason, is not available. But two of his other operas are.*

Phoenix PHCD 103. *The Devil and Daniel Webster* (folk opera in one act—1938).

Bay Cities 2-BCD-1012 and 1013 (2 CDs). *Carry Nation* (opera in two acts—1966).

The works of George Kleinsinger and Evelyn Pittman have not been issued on commercial discs. But those of Virgil Thomson have been.

Elektra/Nonesuch 79035 (2 CDs). *Four Saints in Three Acts* (1937).

New World NS 288-289 (2 CDs). *The Mother of Us All* (two acts—1947).

NOTES

1. Alfred E. Smith, in Frank Freidel, *The Presidents of the United States of America* (Washington, DC: National Geographic Society, 1964), p. 65.

2. Ibid.

3. In his nomination acceptance speech, 1928. Irving S. and Nell M. Kull, *A Short Chronology of American History* (New Brunswick, NJ: Rutgers University Press, 1952), p. 245.

4. Ibid, p. 267.

5. *Banshee* is included in Edith Borroff, *Compact Discs to Accompany Music in Europe and the United States: A History.*

6. H. H. Stuckenschmidt, *Twentieth-Century Music* (New York: McGraw-Hill, 1968), p. 223.

7. Edith Borroff, *Three American Composers* (Lanham, MD: University Press of America, 1986), p. 10.

8. Steve Buchanan, "Guion," *New Grove Dictionary of American Music*, H. Wiley Hitchcock and Stanley Sadie, eds. (London: Macmillan & Co., 1986).

9. F. Joseph Smith, in Borroff, *Three American Composers*, p. 29.

10. Ibid, p. 21.

11. Edith Borroff, *Compact Discs to Accompany Music in Europe and the United States: A History*, contains works of both the university and apprenticeship systems.

12. Philip G. Hubert, Jr., "The New Talking-Machines," *Atlantic Monthly*, vol. 42, no. 1 (February 1889), p. 260.

13. James A. Keene, *A History of Music Education in the United States* (Hanover and London: University Press of New England, 1982), p. 275f.

14. Nicolas Slominsky, *Baker's Biographical Dictionary of Musicians*, 8th ed. (New York: Schirmer Books, 1990).

15. Ibid.

BIBLIOGRAPHY

Borroff, Edith. *American Operas: A Checklist*. Detroit Studies in Music Bibliography, no. 69. Warren, MI: Harmonie Park Press, 1992.

———. *Music in Europe and the United States: A History*, 2nd ed. New York: Ardsley House, Publishers, 1990.

———. *Three American Composers*. Lanham, MD: University Press of America, 1986.

Friedel, Frank. *The Presidents of the United States of America*. Washington, D.C.: National Geographic Society, 1964.

Haas, Robert Bartlett, ed. *William Grant Still and the Fusion of Cultures in American Music*. Los Angeles: Black Sparrow Press, 1975.

Hitchcock, H. Wiley, and Stanley Sadie, eds. *New Grove Dictionary of American Music*. London: Macmillan Press, Ltd., 1986.

Hubert, Philip G., Jr. "The New Talking-Machines." *Atlantic Monthly*, vol. 62, no. 1 (February, 1889).

Kull, Irving S. and Nell M. *A Short Chronology of American History*. New Brunswick, NJ: Rutgers University Press, 1952.

Lang, Paul Henry, ed. *One Hundred Years of Music in America*. New York: Schirmer Books, 1961.

Pendle, Karen, ed. *Women and Music: A History*. Bloomington: Indiana University Press, 1991.

Sachs, Curt. *World History of the Dance*. New York: W. W. Norton & Co., 1963.

Schwartz, H. W. *Bands of America*. New York: Da Capo Press, 1975.

Slonimsky, Nicolas. *Baker's Biographical Dictionary of Musicians*, 8th ed. New York: Schirmer Books, 1990.

Stuckenschmidt, H. H. *Twentieth-Century Music*. New York: McGraw-Hill, 1968.

8

Other Venues
(1923 to 1961)

Theater was a strength of American music from the start. And in the middle of the twentieth century, the theater became even stronger. The scope of what the theater encompassed, in setting, meaning, and production, expanded; in addition, the theater stayed with the apprenticeship system even as other professions were losing that connection. Guthrie McClintic, noted actor and director, talked of learning his craft at the side of a master, detailing both the intense work, with its personal involvement, and something of the process:

> And there I was, emerging from the flotsam and jetsam of the theater, sitting at [the master's] elbow across the prompt table, writing down his directions and absorbing as much as the days gave. This was the beginning of my theater doctorate—or apprenticeship—or whatever you choose to call it. It was to continue eight more years. Hours? There were none for me. . . . I had few diversions—no cocktail parties, no social life—just the supreme satisfaction of discovering that which I had always somehow known was there, and, to top it all, for this extraordinary enlightenment I was being paid.[1]

This was an intense experience, master to apprentice, but in musical theater, apprenticeship was more a learning-by-doing, with whatever chance advice a young performer received along the way. Larry Adler, a harmonica player of the vaudeville circuit, spoke during an interview of his apprenticeship, particularly of a contract for forty-four weeks of work that he was granted at the age of fourteen.

> I truly think that if I were starting in show business today with whatever talent I had—the same today as it ever was—I don't think I'd last six months. Because it's a different kind of show business. There isn't the chance to *learn* your trade. Remember when I told you I got this contract at Paramount, we went around to forty-four cities doing four and five and six shows a day. The monotony was unbearable, but you *learned your trade*. You learned to walk on and off a stage, you learned to cope with an audience that didn't like you.
>
> And incidentally this reminds me of something that Jack Benny said to me, probably the best advice a performer could ever get: "Don't press." Isn't that great? That means that the audience is cool—when I say cool, I mean unfriendly. You're not getting anywhere with them. The impulse is to work harder to make them like you. And Jack said, "No; relax. Wait for them to find you." Now that is a lesson that is terribly difficult to learn. . . .[2]

Recommended Recordings and Video Cassettes

Larry Adler's playing is available on disc, but the album contains a preponderance of European music. An older LP is perhaps still available.

Angel CDM-64134. *Larry Adler in Concert*. It contains an arrangement of George Gershwin's *Rhapsody in Blue*.

RCA (Gold Seal) AGL 1-1391 (LP). *Larry Adler Plays*. Includes Morton Gould's "Nightwalk" and Gershwin's rag "Merry Andrew," the latter, a splendid performance of a wonderful piece.

Chandos CHAN-8645. *Thanks for the Memory*. Fifteen American pop standards for harmonica and piano, played by Tommy Reilly (with James Moody at the piano).

Larry Adler. (Picture Collection, The Branch Libraries, The New York Public Library.)

Adler's words speak particularly of the variety show, in which acts could be substituted and the *esprit de corps* was not of an entire company unless, by chance, an entire company stayed together for an extended period of time. The African-American productions tended to bond more effectively because there were fewer performers and they played together more often. The minstrel shows gave way to revues; Eubie Blake was probably the most sought-after composer of such productions: *Shuffle Along* (1921), which featured his wonderful song "I'm Just Wild About Harry" (far from the stereotypical minstrel-show item), *Blackbirds of 1930* (one of a series composed by a number of men), and *Swing It* (1937). The African-American revue gave way to parodies of standard works, with jazzed-up scores and all-black casts, such as *The Swing Mikado* (1939), *The Hot Mikado* (also 1939), a lavish production starring Bill Robinson, which was the hit of the New York World's Fair, and *Carmen Jones* (1943). Finally, musical plays featuring all-black casts arrived on Broadway: *Cabin in the Sky* (1940) by Vernon Duke and *Carib Song* (1945) by Baldwin Bergersen (nephew of Marie Bergersen) were notable.

Although revues such as *New Faces* (1934, 1936, 1943, 1952, and 1956) still appeared, they were less frequent and less lavish, and by the 1960s, they were more likely to turn up on television than on Broadway.

THE MUSICAL

musical comedy: a play or movie in which the story is developed with song

musical: a popular twentieth-century form of musical theater; also, a film in which the action stops occasionally for formal musical numbers

But opera-like musical theater expanded and prospered through the decades. The system used in the production of revues was put into danger, and although it has never disappeared, it is much less important; what happened is that through the 1920s and '30s, the revue was supplanted in large part by the *musical comedy* (or just *musical*). In the musical comedy, a plot gave rise to the production: sets, costumes, songs, dances, and virtually all other details. Individual numbers were not mounted for guest stars, and, most important for the composer, one person produced the music for the entire evening. The one-shot numbers that had given experience to young composers were no longer the rule, and the exceptions grew more and more sparse.

Attendance at theaters declined in these years and so did the number of productions. The popular appeal of radio, the movies, and, finally, television, may have been responsible for this decline in the number of productions on Broadway; whatever the cause, the 1920s was the decade of the revue, with an average of thirty-eight openings a year, fifteen a year during the 1930s' Depression, then under a dozen from the 1940s on.

And yet this reduction of offerings came with the development of a new kind of production, which would become an American triumph: this was the musical comedy. Musical comedy established a new direction for stage works; it was not a collection of unrelated acts but the mounting

The Swing Mikado, 1940.
(Picture Collection, The Branch Libraries, The New York Public Library.)

of a single unified musical evening, dealing with dramatic events, characters, and plots. As this type of theatrical offering developed, the taste for comedy (but not farce) changed from delight in zany satirical plots, in which stereotypes served the satire, to a savoring of stories of significance in human terms.

Many composers incorporated this remarkable unfolding, but five displayed unusual theatrical and musical vigor.

Jerome Kern

Jerome Kern (1885–1945) was an early leader: he composed over sixty musical shows, which traveled a sure path from the giddy works he produced with the stylish British author P. G. Wodehouse, such as *Oh, Lady! Lady!* (1918) to the landmark musical play *Show Boat* (1927), with Oscar Hammerstein II (but with the lyrics to one song—"Bill"—still by Wodehouse). Kern was educated in both the United States and Germany, and his shows were produced in London as well as New York. He was the first Broadway composer to be responsible for an entire show (*The Red Petticoat*, 1912), when that idea was too new to be successfully carried out, and continued with *Sally* (1920) featuring the long-limned "Look for the Silver Lining" (lyric by B. G. de Sylva), and *Very Warm for May* (1939), containing "All the Things You Are" (lyric by Hammerstein).

Oh, Lady, Lady!, by **Jerome Kern and P. G. Wodehouse, starring Carl Randall and Vivienne Segal, 1918.** (Picture Collection, The Branch Libraries, The New York Public Library.)

A scene from *Show Boat*, by Jerome Kern and Oscar Hammerstein II, 1927. (Picture Collection, The Branch Libraries, The New York Public Library.)

His final work was done for the screen, with such movies as *Swing Time* (1936), which contained the song "The Way You Look Tonight" and *Cover Girl* (1944) with "Long Ago and Far Away." His graceful melodic lines and charming rhythms blended European and American elements.

Irving Berlin

Irving Berlin (Israel Baline, 1888–1989) was brought to the United States in 1893; his father, a cantor, died three years later, and the boy worked as a busker and a singing waiter, then as a *song plugger*—song pluggers were either singers or pianists who worked in stores, letting customers hear songs as a stimulus for sales. Berlin had no training in music and never learned to read it. But when he began writing songs in his late teens, this minus became a plus: he wrote music of simple, direct, energy that directed itself to basic statements. He wrote both lyrics and music, which added a deep artistic integrity to the force of his art. He wrote over eight hundred songs, nineteen Broadway shows, and eighteen movie musicals. The songs include "Alexander's Ragtime Band" (1911), "Oh, How I Hate to Get Up in the Morning" (1918), "Always" (1925), and "God Bless America" (1939), made famous by singer Kate Smith. His most popular shows were *Annie Get Your Gun* (1946), which included the blockbuster song "There's No Business Like Show Business," belted out by Ethel Merman; and *Call Me Madam* (1950), again

song plugger: a singer or pianist who sang or played songs in a store as a stimulus for sales

Irving Berlin. (Picture Collection, The Branch Libraries, The New York Public Library.)

with Merman, and with such songs as "The Hostess with the Mostes' on the Ball" and "It's a Lovely Day Today." The movies encompassed *Top Hat* (1935), with Fred Astaire and Ginger Rogers, and *Holiday Inn* (1942), in which Bing Crosby introduced the megahit "White Christmas."

Cole Porter

Cole Porter (1892–1964) was the grandson of an Indiana millionaire, and his opulent lifestyle entered his songs as an insouciant sophistication. His early songwriting was done for his university shows, at Yale as an

Cole Porter. (Picture Collection, The Branch Libraries, The New York Public Library.)

◖◗ Recommended Recordings and Video Cassettes

The recordings of musicals are legion. It is much, much better to get an original-cast album than a revamped version: the style of popular music changes and performance changes with it. In the 1930s, several of Victor Herbert's operettas were filmed, usually starring Jeanette MacDonald and Nelson Eddy. In these operettas, the older (authentic) style of performance was maintained in the film adaptation. But later movie versions of musicals changed the performing style. For example, tempos got slower and textures heavier. The difference between the original of Frank Loesser's Guys and Dolls *(1950) and the movie version (1955) is huge: the spare, energetic musical was presented in a "lavish Hollywoodization" (according to Leonard Maltin in his* Movie and Video Guide 1993) *that turned it into something quite different. Others, such as Rodger's* Oklahoma! *and Meredith Willson's* The Music Man *fared better. Wherever possible, a video cassette is preferable to a disc. Jerome Kern's work largely predated recordings, and his stage songs appear here and there.* Showboat *(1927), however, has been redone many times, by both show-business and grand-opera personnel. The best recording may be a recent one made after the original orchestration was found.*

Angel 3-A23-49108. *Showboat.*

But the older style of singing is to be found in:

RCA-1126. *Showboat*, with William Warfield and David Wayne among the stars.

See also, Sitting Pretty, *in the* Recommended Recordings and Video Cassettes *on page 126:*

Irving Berlin, too, made his fame before the time when recordings of musicals were common. The later shows are more completely recorded, and have the advantage of being made with the original stars, who included, most importantly, Ethel Merman. She shines in both:

MCA Classics MDAC-10047. *Annie Get Your Gun* (1946).

MCA Classics MDAC-10521. *Call Me Madam* (1950).

Cole Porter's recorded shows are his later ones as well.

Columbia CK-4140. *Kiss Me, Kate* (1948).

SONY Broadway SK-48223. *Out of This World* (1950).

undergraduate and at Harvard as a graduate student (law, then music). For many years he traveled in Europe, known as something of a *bon vivant*. But in 1928, he returned and began a serious career on Broadway. He wrote both lyrics and music, and was considered a particularly masterful lyricist. His shows included *The Gay Divorcee* (1932), with the song "Night and Day"; *Anything Goes* (1936); *Panama Hattie* (1940); and *Kiss Me, Kate* (1948), which combined a contemporary love story with Shakespeare's *The Taming of the Shrew*. Porter also wrote for films, such as *Born to Dance* (1936), which included the song "I've Got You under My Skin" and *Broadway Melody of 1940*, which included "Begin the Beguine." Such songs testify to his subtle unity of lyric and music, for which he was so deeply appreciated.

George Gershwin

George Gershwin (Jacob Gershvin, 1898–1937) was the son of a moderately well-to-do immigrant family, who exposed him as a young child to jazz and concert music as well as to the music of the synagogue. His family also gave him the desire to learn, and he studied with several composers, including Henry Cowell. But Gershwin had to make his own path, and he began by becoming a rehearsal pianist and song plugger.

George and Ira Gershwin.
(Picture Collection, The Branch Libraries, The New York Public Library.)

***Porgy and Bess*, by George Gershwin, with Todd Duncan and Ann Brown, 1935.** (Picture Collection, The Branch Libraries, The New York Public Library.)

 Recommended Recordings and Video Cassettes

George Gershwin is now considered a fine all-round composer; his music is listed along with concert composers. His shows were also too early for authentic recordings, but one early show has been recorded with its rediscovered orchestration:

CBS-2-M2K-42522. George Gershwin: *Of Thee I Sing* (1931). The musical in its original orchestration was recently discovered, together with excerpts from *Let 'Em Eat Cake* (1933) whose orchestrations were discovered at the same time.

Sony Masterworks (Portrait) MPK 47681. *Rhapsody in Blue,* the Concerto in F. Played by Oscar Levant (in 1942). Levant, a friend and admirer of Gershwin, is the most authentic of performers. This recording is with Andre Kostelanetz and the New York Philharmonic.

Columbia M 34205. *George Gershwin Plays the Rhapsody in Blue* (the 1925 piano roll with the Columbia Jazz Band).

Mark 56 Records. *Paul Whiteman: "A Tribute to George Gershwin"* (1938). A reissue.

Further, an album has been issued of Gershwin playing items from one show, including "Fascinating Rhythm":

World Record Club SH 124 (LP).

And finally, many recordings have been issued of music from Porgy and Bess *(1935). This work was composed as a grand opera and performed as a Broadway musical, so the recordings span the vocal and instrumental styles of those venues. Perhaps the best recording of* Porgy and Bess *is by the Houston Grand Opera:*

RCA 3-RCD-2109. *Porgy and Bess.*

He started composing songs in his teens and he placed them in several revues: these included "Swanee" (sung by Al Jolson in 1919). He composed all of the music for *George White's Scandals of 1920*. But he branched out also, composing a string quartet in 1919 and the short opera *Blue Monday* (later called *135th Street*) in 1922. This led to the commissioning of the piano concerto *Rhapsody in Blue* from Paul Whiteman, the bandleader (it was orchestrated by Ferde Grofé). Teaming up with his brother Ira, Gershwin led musical comedy into its heyday, with shows like *Lady Be Good* (1924), with its song "Fascinating Rhythm," *Strike Up the Band* (1927), and *Girl Crazy* (1930). The 1931 show *Of Thee I Sing* was a political satire (it was called a "burlesque") whose book won a Pulitzer Prize. But Gershwin's most significant outward reach lay in the opera *Porgy and Bess* (1935), on a story by Du Bose Heyward, who wrote the libretto and worked with Ira Gershwin on the lyrics. This work was rejected by European-minded opera houses and was produced as a musical; it would be a half-century before this marvelous work would be presented as the grand opera that Gershwin composed.

A scene from *Of Thee I Sing*, by George Gershwin, 1931. (Picture Collection, The Branch Libraries, The New York Public Library.)

This photo of Richard Rodgers appeared in the New York P.M. to commemorate the 2,000th performance of *Oklahoma!*, with Rodgers conducting the orchestra. (Picture Collection, The Branch Libraries, The New York Public Library.)

Richard Rodgers

Richard Rodgers (1902–79), a New Yorker, began composing as a boy, continued as a student at Columbia University, then at Juilliard, where he teamed up with writer Lorenz Hart. Their first post-student show, *The Garrick Gaieties* (1925), established their reputation. Their 1936 show *On Your Toes* introduced the jazz ballet *Slaughter on Tenth Avenue*, in a pithy choreography by George Balanchine, and changed both ballet and the Broadway show indelibly. The Rodgers-Hart show *Pal Joey* (1940), on stories by John O'Hara, included the song "Bewitched, Bothered, and Bewildered." Two events in the early 1940s gave Rodgers a new direction of lyrical depth and patriotic fervor: one was Hart's death in 1943; the other was World War II, which led to a new examination of life in general and the American character in particular. His new teammate was Oscar Hammerstein II, who joined Rodgers in such shows as *Oklahoma!* (1943) and *South Pacific* (1949). Then they expanded into internationalism, perhaps inspired by the exotic elements in *South Pacific*, but always aware of the basic human condition which all people share in common. *The King and I* (1951), *Flower Drum Song* (1958), and *The Sound of Music* (1959) exemplified Rodgers's litmus-paper musical response to scene and character.

▶ Recommended Recordings and Video Cassettes

Richard Rodgers, being younger than Kern, Berlin, Porter, and Gershwin, was the luckiest in obtaining cast recordings of his shows. Several have been recorded well and are still available.

MCA Classics MCAD-10046. *Oklahoma!*

Columbia CK-32604. *South Pacific.*

MCA Classics MCAD-10049. *The King and I.*

The Garrick Gaities by Richard Rodgers and Lorenz Hart, with Philip Loeb, Sterling Holloway, and Romney Brent as the Three Musketeers, 1925. (Picture Collection, The Branch Libraries, The New York Public Library.)

CHARACTER SONGS

By the 1940s, songs began not only to incorporate an overall balance of musical types and moods, as those of comic opera had always done, but also to delineate and deepen awareness of character and situation. In that sense, songs and dances were no longer parenthetical, but could and did advance the dramatic thrust of the work through clarification of the characters, their perceptions, their realizations, and their responses. Thus, a love ballad in a revue was one act among many, a one-shot song featuring a star performer; its relation to the show as a whole lay entirely in overall balance of acts—the producer would not put two similar acts in succession, and probably would not have included two competingly similar ones in one show at all. In a comic opera a love ballad was part of an overall balance of musical elements, providing a slow, pleasant lyrical moment. In an early musical play it would balance the score, but it would also be a poignant lyrical moment that enlarges the audience's knowledge of love. And in a fully developed musical play the ballad balanced the score, enlarged the audience's knowledge of love, and also portrayed the character who sang it as a particular individual in a particular moment of self-realization. The song "Many a New Day," from *Oklahoma!*, for example, created a woman's solo and women's chorus number of a medium-fast tempo and upbeat mood, told of the feelings of sadness that anyone has when a relationship does not work out as anticipated, and also portrays the heroine as miffed and independent, as well as hurt.

Influences from the Past

Added to the character song that had developed in the 1940s was a conscious incorporation of techniques and musical types from a wide swath of past genres. The score as a totality stopped striving for an obvious homogeneity and became musically polylingual, increasing its interest and scope, while supporting differentiation of character and mood, and moving toward dramatic and musical integrity. Frank Loesser's *Guys and Dolls* (1950) incorporated a dance tune, a ballad, a burlesque tune, a Gilbert and Sullivan type of duet, a folk song, a spiritual, a straight popular song, and a Salvation Army march; Meredith Willson's *The Music Man* (1957) used *Sprechstimme* (a modern German concert technique in which a singer is given very specific instructions for rhythm, but not for pitch), a *barbershop quartet*, a hoedown, a fast "gossip song" combined with the traditional "Goodnight, Ladies" (a technique popular in the sixteenth century), a Sousa-style march, and a gentle *waltz-ballad*, "Goodnight, My Someone," a character song that is transformed by change of meter into the march "Seventy-Six Trombones" (another sixteenth-century technique known as a *double*).

Sprechstimme: speech accompanied by instruments, with rhythm specified, but not pitch

barbershop quartet: four men of varying voices singing a capella

waltz-ballad: a song with a waltz-like rhythm

double: the repetition of a song in a different meter

▶◯ Recommended Recordings and Video Cassettes

> Warner Home Video: Musical 11473. Meredith Willson's *The Music Man* (musical 1957, movie 1962). This deals with the establishment of a town band, which, in spite of the humorous negatives in the plot, did happen in a serious way in many towns. (Willson had been a flute player in Sousa's band.) It might be interesting to discuss the opening up of the story from the spatial limits of the stage to the spatially unlimited film. In much of the movie this opening up is an artistic advantage, but the creation of the train onstage by the salesman (at the start) cannot be duplicated on film, since the train is actually there.

The musical plays that most forcefully incorporated these ideals spanned the years 1943 to 1957. After World War II, they reflected the two complementary aspects of postwar America: there were works that looked affectionately inward at the American character and works that looked admiringly outward in a new appreciation of other cultures and other times. Irving Berlin's *Annie Get Your Gun*, Loesser's *Guys and Dolls*, Willson's *The Music Man*, and Harvey Schmidt's *The Fantasticks* (1960) represent the inward American musical; Cole Porter's *Kiss Me, Kate*, Frederick Loewe's *Brigadoon* (1947) and *My Fair Lady* (1956), Rodgers's *The King and I*, and Loewe's *Camelot* (1960) represent the outward or exotic counterpart, while Rodgers's *South Pacific* reached in both directions at once.

America as World Leader

Few women were represented in the Broadway milieu as composers, but Kay Swift's *Fine and Dandy* (1930), with its plaintive "Can This Be Love?" and its rousing "Fine and Dandy" title song, showed the world what women could do when given the opportunity.

All in all, American musical theater was a splendid medium. It was, in fact, the world leader in such productions; its tunes were played and recognized everywhere. The music was a true amalgam of everything valued in the American tradition of earthy, rhythmically motivated music. The styles were not consistent, even with a single composer, and the roots of the style were many and varied. The music was varied and had the single aim of communication; anything that communicated was acceptable. It had elements of many traditions, yet was very much itself.

▶◯ Recommended Recordings and Video Cassettes

> RCA AGK-1-4363 and ARK-1-0508. *30's Hits* and *50's Hits*. Played by the Boston Pops Orchestra.

> RCA 3201-2. *Fiedler on the Roof*. The Boston Pops Orchestra in Broadway hits.

> *(See the listings of Recommended Recordings and Video Cassettes in Chapter 11 for musicals originally composed as movies.)*

It was not concert music, it was not ballet, and it was not jazz, blues, or *swing*. Those styles led their own lives and enjoyed their own triumphs.

swing: a slower, popular, dance-oriented, big-band jazz style that used more than one player on many of the parts

EARLY JAZZ AND BLUES

With the emergence of jazz on the national scene, the advent of Prohibition, and the rise of the speakeasy, the generation after World War I created the Roaring Twenties with energy and free-wheeling insouciance.

The Roaring Twenties. From a painting by Otto Dix. (Picture Collection, The Branch Libraries, The New York Public Library.)

black bottom: a popular dance characterized by emphatic, sinuous hip movements

The decade was characterized by its music as strongly as any short period in history: high society frequented the Diamond Horseshoe of the Metropolitan Opera, real opera lovers all over the country went to hear native operas, the flapper did the Charleston at the dance hall, and everyone listened to the new jazz artists, idealized the stars of the *Ziegfeld Follies*, listened to the radio, and went to the movies every Saturday night.

The Roaring Twenties

The Roaring Twenties was the Golden Age of jazz. Dancing was still essential, and new dances—the *shimmy, Charleston, black bottom, rhumba*—were being continually introduced. A dance critic said that "the twentieth century has rediscovered the body; not since antiquity has it been so loved, felt, and honored"; the generation of the twenties wanted "to exchange stereotyped movement for something genuinely of the soul."[3] Although musicians served as disseminators of jazz techniques, even more important were phonograph records, which made new techniques and sounds available in all areas and at low cost. The years 1926 to 1929 were the great years of jazz recording.

The materials and performance style were those of ragtime, and the bands were small, generally six to ten men. The leader was also a per-

King Oliver. (Picture Collection, The Branch Libraries, The New York Public Library.)

Jelly Roll Morton and his Red Hot Peppers. (Picture Collection, The Branch Libraries, The New York Public Library.)

former, and his personal style, as much as his instrument, characterized his group. King Oliver (1885–1938), a cornet player who left New Orleans for Chicago in 1918, recorded in 1923 with six *sidemen*; these included Louis "Satchmo" Armstrong, another New Orleans musician. In 1924, Armstrong moved to the Roseland ballroom in New York, where he built his own legend as trumpeter, singer (particularly, scat singer), and bandleader. In 1926, Jelly Roll Morton was recording in Chicago with a group he called the Red Hot Peppers; the group was representative in that all but one member had been active in New Orleans ragtime.

sidemen: jazz players who accompany a soloist

release: the contrasting section of a popular song

bridge: release

bar: a unit of beats; a measure

measure: the regular grouping of beats

Blues Songs

Jazz was essentially a semi-improvised variation on a preexisting tune. The standard form of a popular tune was of two statements of the main phrase (*AA*), a contrasting line called the *release* or *bridge* (*B*), and a restatement of the first unit (*A* again), creating a four-section form (*AABA*). Since all of the phrases were four *bars* (*measures*) long, the popular tune was sixteen bars long.

twelve-bar blues: a blues song of three four-bar sections

melodic embellishment: variations on a melody

rhythmic embellishment: the enhancement of a melodic line through spontaneous variation

But the blues form was shorter, made of the same two statements of the main phrase (*AA*) plus a single contrasting phrase to complete the thought (*B*), making blues a three-section form (*AAB*). This form was called the *twelve-bar blues*.

Jazz groups organized their performances through an orderly rotation of solo players, but this rotation was extremely subtle, with three players assigned to the four-section form and four players assigned to the three-section form. This changing of the sound (and even of the personality) of the music contrasted with the steady beat and the simple harmonies that together provided the frame for the *melodic* and *rhythmic embellishment* of the soloists.

The early blues singers were women—Ma Rainey, Bessie Smith (the "Empress of the Blues"), and Ella Fitzgerald (the "First Lady of Song"). They were virtuoso artists of the blues and were important figures in a

Ella Fitzgerald. (Picture Collection, The Branch Libraries, The New York Public Library.)

long and many-faceted heritage. The songs themselves went back to the nineteenth century, to the beginnings of slavery, but black field workers in the twentieth century still sang *work songs* and *hollers*; the heritage was old but was constantly being reborn. The lyric was central to blues, and a blues man was actually singing his poem.

Son House's *Depot Blues* (recorded in 1942), a twelve-bar blues with guitar, was representative. The falling line of the phrases, the talking style, and the banjo-like guitar style were all from the African-American heritage. Like other examples of jazz and the blues, this piece has more in common with medieval music than music of any other Western period.

Basic Jazz

Basic jazz was more complex, because the jazz group contained more elements. Actually, the group was composed of soloists, who alternated in improvising variations on the song phrases, and a rhythm section, using combinations of piano, bass, guitar, and drums (generally two or three). As notated, the song line was *straight*; embellished, it was called *hot*.

Jazz Techniques

Jazz techniques were those of performance; Jelly Roll Morton said that jazz was a style, not a composition. Repeated harmonic patterns, called *riffs*, and extended virtuoso breaks pulled the music forward, set up frames for soloists, and helped shape the performance, but did not contribute to the form *per se*.

An interaction of players was basic to the music, as was its strong rhythmic impulse. Most striking and highly motivating was the equal strength of four beats with percussion emphasis on the second and fourth; they were called the *back beats*.

The relationship between voice and instruments was lively and inimitable. *Scat* singing was a technique in which the voice used instrumental attacks and embellishments and virtually became an instrument. And conversely, instruments used vocal imitations—laughing (clarinet), crying (trombone), sliding, growling, and *wa-wa* and other muting techniques. The basic instrumental style of jazz with its incorporation of vocal elements is a chief characteristic of the art.

To the jazz purist, the *jam session*, a spontaneous improvisation by professionals after work, was the truest form of jazz. All other types of performance were lesser, with the completely orchestrated arrangement at the opposite pole. The popular theater could, and often did, provide tunes for jazz, but a theater performance, which had to be carefully synchronized and rehearsed, lacked the essential freedom, even when emulating jazz.

work song: a song used to coordinate or energize work

holler: a popular song style, originating outdoors (the field holler)

straight: as written, without variation

hot: having strong rhythm and inspired improvisation

riff: a repeated harmonic unit

back beats: accents on the notes not generally accented

scat: singing to sounds rather than to texts

wa-wa: a mute for a brass instrument

jam session: improvisation by jazz players, characteristically in informal meetings

Jazz and Popular Music

In spite of the use of jazz techniques in the musical theater and of show tunes in the jazz traditions, jazz and popular music were not joined. Their differences of technique, place and purpose of performance, and type of audience led to a mutual disdain. Jazz players looked on the traditionally schooled musicians as *squares*; pop musicians called the jazz players illiterate; and both were dismissed by "serious" musicians of the European tradition.

A few popular musicians were trying to give jazz validity in concerts as symphonic jazz. In a strange amalgam of orchestral music, theater music, and jazz, the bandleader Paul Whiteman (1890–1967) sponsored George Gershwin's *Rhapsody in Blue* (1924), for solo piano and jazz orchestra, at a concert in Aeolian Hall in New York.

American critics were nonplussed by the confusion of styles repre-

 Recommended Recordings and Video Cassettes

The Library of Congress has issued useful histories of jazz and the blues.

Columbia/Legacy C2K 47091 and 47471. *Bessie Smith: The Complete Recordings, volumes 1 and 2.*

Biograph BCD 121. *Johnny Shines: Traditional Delta Blues.*

Verve 00902. *Charlie Parker: The Essential Charlie.*

Blue Note 11000. *The Best of Miles Davis—The Capitol/Blue Note Years.*

Almanac Record Co. QSR 2404. *Jelly Roll Morton.* This fine album contains thirteen items, including "The Pearls," "Melancholy Baby," and the "King Porter Stomp."

Folkways RF-3 (LP). *History of Jazz: The New York Scene.*

Oscar 301. *Chicago Jazz (1927–28).*

Videos are also useful, particularly in historical summaries and in interviews.

Viewfinders, Inc. *Always for Pleasure.* New Orleans parades (including a jazz funeral) and Mardi Gras, 1977.

Educational Audio Visual, Inc. *EAV History of Jazz.*

Jamey Aebersold Jazz Aids. *New Orleans: 'Til the Butcher Cuts Him Down.* Dixieland and marching bands.

Jamey Aebersold Jazz Aids. *Sarah Vaughan and Friends.*

Jamey Aebersold Jazz Aids. *After Hours.* Features Coleman Hawkins.

Jamey Aebersold Jazz Aids. *The Coltrane Legacy.* Documentary.

Sony Video Software. *Bird.* Documentary on Charlie Parker.

Sony Video Software. *Jazz at the Smithsonian: Art Blakey.* Features Wynton Marsalis.

sented by such a work, and the American public was biased by its association of jazz with dance and its prejudice toward African-Americans. Europeans had a very different reaction, seeing jazz either as authentic folk art to be honored and classified as another transitional technique or as a low musical form beneath the whole hierarchy of musical types. The latter view kept jazz out of music schools, but at the same time added to its glamour in the minds of the public. No less a figure than the French minister of national education said, "Jazz is the only accomplishment of collective imagination since the end of the art of conversation."[4]

Paul Whiteman. (Drawing by David Zuckerman.)

Benny Goodman. (Photofest.)

European Attitudes

Europeans studied jazz with appreciative seriousness. In France, Stravinsky had utilized ragtime elements in the theatrical chamber work *l'Histoire du soldat* (The Soldier's Tale, 1918) and in *Piano Rag Music* (1920), and Darius Milhaud utilized jazz sounds in the ballet *la Création du monde* (The Creation of the World, 1923). In Germany, experiments in new sounds were entering both "serious" and popular music, and jazz was added as one more technique. The most popular new opera of the period was *Jonny spielt auf* (Johnny Gets Hot), by Ernst Křenek (born 1900). It was first performed in Leipzig in 1927 with a black hero; later (1929) it was produced at the Metropolitan in New York in blackface. Eventually, this work was produced in eighteen translations throughout the world.

More important, Europeans were following the jazz movement by means of imported phonograph records, so touring jazz groups found themselves public figures. In France and England, jazz was considered worthy of a large critical literature, and the jazz public on the Continent was well informed on many details of both general and individual styles. The French were the most ardent followers of the movement, and French record companies began very early to issue their own records, both of French editions of American performances and performance by their own practitioners.

big band: a swing band that used more than one player on some of the parts

SWING AND THE BIG BANDS

In the 1930s, the radio and movies were bringing popular music into the daily lives of people throughout the United States. Like all arts when they are diffused and popularized, jazz took on some aspects of the older tradition. Musicians with traditional training were attracted more and more to careers in popular music, and they created a slower, larger, and simpler style, which they called *swing*. Jazz had been an elite art, practiced and savored by a few connoisseurs, but for an exciting decade, swing was the musical passion of a whole nation. The years from 1935 to 1945 comprised the peak years of the "era of the *big bands*."

Perhaps the most representative of the big bands were those of Benny Goodman (1909–86) and William "Count" Basie (1904–84). Goodman, a clarinetist from Chicago, was a radio musician in New York who formed his own band in 1934. His success came the following year, overnight, during an engagement at the Palomar Ballroom in Los Angeles, and in that same year he made his first record, "The King Porter Stomp." Count Basie also started his career on radio but in Kansas City. He took over the Bennie Moten Band after Moten's death in 1935 and moved the band to New York in 1936. By 1937, the band was recording under Basie's name.

jazz combo: a performing group (combination), generally small

Many bands reached stardom in the decade after 1935. Artie Shaw's (born 1910) fifteen-piece band became popular in 1937, and Glenn Miller (1904–44) formed his first band in 1937 and was popular by 1939.

Instead of the sharply etched sound of the small *jazz combos*, the bands used doublings and created a fuller, smoother effect. Most had fourteen to sixteen members, though some had twenty or more. The big bands used a slower beat in a four-beat bar, without back beats, and strove for an intense energy that was compelling and danceable. The thirties were a decade of dancing, with bobby-soxers doing the big apple and the jitterbug in theater aisles.

Benny Goodman's Band in 1937	Count Basie's Band in 1940
3 trumpets	4 trumpets
2 trombones	3 trombones
4 saxophones	4 saxophones
1 clarinet (Goodman)	4 rhythm instruments
4 rhythm instruments (piano, drums, guitar, bass)	(piano [Basie], drums, guitar, bass)
14	15

More than other big bands, the Duke Ellington (1899–1974) band was true to the roots of jazz; yet his work transcended both jazz and swing, with chromatic harmony, complex rhythms, and longer forms characteristic of the concert tradition. Ellington's association with Harlem's Cotton Club (1927 to 1932) was a jazz apprenticeship, and he never

 Recommended Recordings and Video Cassettes

Many collections by swing musicians have been issued. Probably the most useful is:

Columbia/Legacy C3K 52862 (3 CDs). *Swing Time! The Fabulous Big Band Era, 1925–55.*

Some good videos are available that deal with swing bands and their creators. But movies such as The Glenn Miller Story *(1953), with Miller played by Jimmy Stewart, and* The Benny Goodman Story *(1955), with Goodman played by Steve Allen, are also instructive. Swing bands played in many musicals as well: Miller in* Orchestra Wives *(1942), Goodman in* Hollywood Hotel *(1938) and* Sweet and Lowdown *(1944)—among many others. Perhaps Duke Ellington is the most important of these bandleaders, and also there are video cassettes that summarize his career (as there are for some others).*

American Express Special Offer Center. *The Duke Ellington Story.*

American Express Special Offer Center. *Count Basie Live at the Hollywood Palladium.*

A program from the Cotton Club. (Picture Collection, The Branch Libraries, The New York Public Library.)

yielded to the heavier lines of the swing bands, but achieved an amazingly rich world of color and sonorous shadings in the "tonal tapestry"[5] of atmospheric beauty that owed much to the clarity of solo playing. Swing was in a sense the white culture's way of responding to the raw materials of black music—a bridge between two musical concepts. Ellington was able to take a position on that bridge and to create an art of integrity: the band became his instrument—critic E. J. Hobsbawm ranks it as "the greatest band in the history of jazz"[6]—and he created a vibrant community of musicians who articulated and ramified its expression.

The swing sound was ideal for Hollywood musicals and for singing, and the hit songs of the decade were movie songs. As early as 1929, the movies had begun to pull songwriters westward. "In Tin Pan Alley and

Ginger Rogers and Fred Astaire in the motion picture *Roberta*, **1935.** (Picture Collection, The Branch Libraries, The New York Public Library.)

on Broadway," an observer reminisced, "1929 is remembered as the year of the California gold rush."[7] Over fifty musicals a year were produced from 1934 to 1944; bands were heard in all of them and featured in many. Louis Armstrong was in *Pennies from Heaven*, Duke Ellington was in *The Hit Parade of 1937*, and Benny Goodman was in *The Big Broadcast of 1937*. The Hollywood musical at its height used such stars as Fred Astaire and Ginger Rogers and such innovative directors as Busby Berkeley, whose production numbers explored the camera's ability to see in a new way.

Louis Armstrong. (Photofest.)

Sarah Vaughn.
(Photofest.)

boogie-woogie: a pre-World War II jazz-piano type of music with a strong bass

eight-to-the-bar: eight beats to the measure

ostinato: a single phrase used over and over

Jazz singers were co-creators of the music they sang. They included Nat "King" Cole (1917–69), who formed his own trio of piano, guitar, and bass; Ella Fitzgerald (born 1918), who sang with Chick Webb (1907–39); Sarah Vaughan (1924–90), who sang with Earl Hines (1905–83) and Billy Eckstine (1914–93); Peggy Lee (born 1920), who sang with Goodman; and Frank Sinatra (born 1917), who sang with Harry James (1916–83). Their styles ranged from the rich instrumental style of Sarah Vaughan and the smooth elegance of Nat "King" Cole to the jazz-based improvisation of Peggy Lee. These singing artists led to the next generation of singers who composed the songs they sang.

The last big craze before World War II was *boogie-woogie*. It was based on a revival of the "Honky Tonk Train Blues" (1929) beat of Meade Lux Lewis (1905–64), which had a fast, *eight-to-the-bar ostinato* pattern exploiting the flat seventh. Boogie-woogie was a good foil for the swing sound; together they entered the forties.

Post-World War II Jazz

The postwar years began with a many-faceted popular tradition—of swing, boogie-woogie, and vestiges of hot jazz and the blues. Western and gospel music also became popular. Many of the postwar figures were familiar—from the thirties or even the twenties. Duke Ellington was still the most popular musician; touring Europe after the war (in 1948 and 1950), he won a series of popularity polls. Blues singer Huddie Ledbetter (1888–1949), known as Leadbelly, enjoyed a comeback and recorded "Goodnight, Irene," which was later popularized by the Weavers (1950); he toured in France the last year of his life. Louis Armstrong toured in both Europe (1948–49) and Japan (1954). And popular singers carried on in the big-band tradition: Tony Martin, Teresa Brewer, Johnny Mathis, and Tony Bennett joined Nat "King" Cole and the other singers

Huddie "Leadbelly" Ledbetter. (Picture Collection, The Branch Libraries, The New York Public Library.)

A xylophone player. (Picture Collection, The Branch Libraries, The New York Public Library.)

cool jazz: a lighter jazz style of the 1940s and '50s

bongo drums: small drums of Afro-Cuban origin, played in pairs

of swing, even after the big bands were on the decline. Singing groups such as the Ames Brothers climbed in popularity.

The first notable new style of the postwar years emerged in the music of Miles Davis (1926–92), a trumpet player. He worked with a group of five, six, or nine, but rejected the big-band sound and sought a lighter style, called *cool jazz*. By 1948, Davis was popular in the United States, and in 1949 he was touring in France.

Jazzmen were seeking new sounds and were examining historic and exotic practices. *Bongo drums* and other Latin rhythm instruments were popular, as were the flute, violin, vibraphone (vibes), xylophone, and French horn. A few individual experiments pointed to a broader reference. The New Friends of Rhythm, a sextet consisting of a string quartet together with guitar and harp, recorded paraphrases of classics, such as Wolfgang Amadeus Mozart's overture to *The Marriage of Figaro* (1782) and variations on Niccolò Paganini's *24th Caprice* (1838). In 1953, a New York composer who styled himself "Moondog" (1917–93), a percussionist in the jazz tradition, composed a string quartet in collaboration with Tony Schwartz, a sound engineer who recorded the night noises of the New York docks; together they produced *Piece for String*

▶◯ Recommended Recordings and Video Cassettes

The Moondog recordings mentioned are out of print, but a retrospective of his work has been issued.

CBS MK-44994. *Music of Moondog.*

Quartet and Harbor Sounds, a haunting evocation of the city at night. Moondog also produced *Tell It Again*, a setting of nursery tunes for soprano, baritone, flute, and percussion: it had isorhythmic structures, a *polyphony* of elements in an African technique, *tabla* rhythms deriving from India, and a fast beat in units of three and seven (as well as three and four).

Jazz critics, from 1950, became increasingly serious about their subject, ignoring "popular" music, but supporting jazz by writing scholarly articles in newspapers and magazines and by covering the jazz festivals at Newport, Rhode Island (from 1954), Monterey, California (from 1958), and other cities in the United States and abroad. In 1959, seventy thousand people attended a three-day jazz festival in Chicago, indicating that interest in jazz was widespread. Since the 1970s, attendance at jazz events has greatly increased.

polyphony: an interplay of elements—in particular, the simultaneous combination of melodies

Charlie Parker

A culmination of the pure, hot-jazz style came in the mid-1940s, in the improvisations of Charlie Parker (1920–55), called "Yardbird," a master of the alto sax. A critic summed up many concurring opinions.

> In bringing the art of improvisation to a new peak of maturity, Parker had an inestimable influence on jazz musicians regardless of what instrument they played. From the mid-40s on, it was almost impossible for any new jazzman anywhere in the world to escape reflecting to some degree, consciously or unconsciously, a Parker influence; his work set a new standard on every level—harmonic, tonal, rhythmic and melodic.[8]

The sweep of Parker's improvisation cannot be written down in musical notation, which does not illustrate spontaneity. Instrumental skill of consummate virtuosity is at the bottom of Parker's improvising; it left him free for rhythmic subtlety and expansiveness as well as for melodic shape and embellishment, the hallmarks of top-level jazz playing. Improvisation itself is an art to be wondered at: classical musicians valued it from the earliest days through the eighteenth century and into the nineteenth, but recent concert music has valued the literal. One of the marvelous aspects of the singing of spirituals and of the blues, ragtime, and jazz is the maintenance of the improvisational skills. In this art, the distinction between composer and performer is blurred, and it is impos-

Charlie Parker. (Drawing by David Zuckerman.)

sible to say whether an imaginative improvisation, even on somebody else's tune, comes under the rubric of performance or composition. Certainly, jazz maintained this unity most creatively. This movement away from the literal page was enriched by the long African-American tradition, which used techniques that were closer to the universal concepts of living music than the overrefined extremes of the European romantic tradition, with its restriction to the printed page.

Bebop

Jazz from the 1940s, in its new style, was called *bebop*. Bebop was so multi-faceted a development that scholars have spoken of its origin as "confused":

> One of its leaders, . . . "Dizzy" Gillespie, said it was a device to shake off white plagiarists, but its most gifted practitioner, Charlie Parker, . . . explained it in strictly technical terms. By evoking a system of substituted chords superimposed on the original ones and by playing in double-time of the tempo being asserted in the rhythm section, Parker . . . changed the face of jazz.
>
> Although technically he made jazz more complex, emotionally he cleansed it, and his famous blues recordings looked back to Armstrong's achievements.[9]

"Emotionally he cleansed it" is perhaps the most important statement here. For jazz, like most popular forms of music, is essentially classical, rather than romantic, free of the weight of the romantic association of music with verbal elements. This concept of musical classicism is old indeed: Johannes Tinctoris, a fifteenth-century theorist, called music "the noblest among the mathematical arts,"[10] and in the early eighteenth century, Gottfried Willhelm von Leibniz defined music as "a kind of counting performed by the mind without knowing that it is counting."[11] That this argument, central to the quadrivium of the liberal arts (see page 11), should continue into the jazz world, is illuminating.

The discussion of bebop begun above continues:

> Throughout its history jazz has been abstract, in the sense that, subconsciously informed though it may be by race memory [of the African heritage], it has been guided less by concrete or living factors than by mathematical precision of the march from discord to resolution, the soloist being like a man working out an algebraic equation. For this reason Duke Ellington was unique, in that he moved toward that ideal where authentic jazz performances may reflect the nuances of personality. . . .
>
> Ellington thus attempted to make his music measure up to a constant dual standard, for he intended it to be not only fine jazz but also intelligible program music.
>
> Nothing comparable has been attempted in jazz by anyone else, although the work of *"progressive"* jazz musicians such as Thelonious Monk and The Modern Jazz Quartet [of John Lewis] in the 1950s and 1960s hinted at extramusical connotations through the relentless Europeanization of its theme titles. . . . Ellington attempted to make his jazz mirror the people and places that led him to the extreme sophistication of his old age.[12]

▶○ Recommended Recordings and Video Cassettes

American Express Special Offer Center. *Dizzy Gillespie's Dream Band* (video cassette).

bebop: a jazz type developed in the late 1940s and '50s, featuring highly complex solos, dissonant chords, and extreme tempos; also called *bop*

progressive jazz: modern jazz in the 1950s

Baron Gottfried Willhelm von Leibniz. (IBM Archives.)

Thelonius Monk.
(Photofest.)

Thus, Ellington can be seen as having attempted a fusion of classical and romantic elements in his music. He can also be seen as a clarifier of jazz reality for wider and wider audiences (such as in his Carnegie Hall appearances).

Coleman Hawkins

Improvisation seems to have been the true inner life of jazz from its very beginning. Improvisation is, of course, a highly personal art. Coleman Hawkins (1905–69), a tenor saxophonist, was another musician highly valued for his improvising. A jazz critic felt that Hawkins's improvising was the essence of jazz, embodied in his "musical adventurousness" and "unstemmable creativity." For Hawkins, creativity was always spontaneous.

He spent most of his life *improvising,* which means that he altruistically gave part of himself away night after night, month after month, year after year. A sculptor can touch his work, a painter can stare at his finished canvas, but improvisation—except in the rare instance when it is recorded—is borne away the second it is uttered.[13]

Jazz climaxed at the end of the 1950s. Swing was in the past, and Broadway was at its peak. But the social channels of music were shifting. The postwar "baby boomer" generation had been brought up with the radio, the movies, and records.

RADIO

Radio's heyday began in the mid-1920s and lasted a generation or longer. The directing of radio broadcasts to the country as a whole began, not with regular programs, but rather with the bringing of special events—symphony concerts and operas, for example—to people who could not attend them. But soon regular programming developed; WSM in Nashville began broadcasting "Grand Ole Opry" as early as 1925—it yielded to television when that medium became strong enough.

An early NBC broadcast from the Metropolitan Opera House, 1932. Deems Taylor is at the microphone.
(Picture Collection, The Branch Libraries, The New York Public Library.)

The Depression Years

Radio was the perfect medium for the Depression, serving as an inexpensive entertainment and a cohesive force, uniting the nation before and during World War II. The first part of the minstrel show, a mixture of song and comic dialogue, became the basic format for radio shows. Bob Hope's weekly program was representative. A half-hour long, it included an opening monologue, comic dialogue, musical numbers, a guest spot, and as an afterpiece, Robin and Rainger's tune "Thanks for the Memory" (from a 1938 movie). New, topical words were written for it each week, and it became Hope's signature song. The show's format was lively, varied, and versatile, and it lasted through World War II.

In 1935, "Your Hit Parade" began, a weekly show presenting the best-selling songs of the week, often in new arrangements. This show maintained a stable of performers and arrangers, but it also welcomed guests. If a song remained popular, it might be presented several times on "Your Hit Parade," but of course, each program's line-up was unique.

Much greater change in mood was evidenced in such shows as the "Lux Radio Theater" (sponsored by Lux Soap), in which producer Cecil B. De Mille each week introduced a one-hour radio version of a movie, with movie stars as guest actors. Sometimes the stars were the same as in the movie version, sometimes not. *The Scarlet Pimpernel* (1935), which starred Leslie Howard and Merle Oberon as a movie, was broadcast starring Leslie Howard and Olivia De Havilland; *Dark Victory* (1939), which starred Bette Davis and George Brent as a movie, was broadcast starring Bette Davis and Spencer Tracy (De Mille proudly announced that they had both won Academy Awards that year—Davis for *Jezebel*, Tracy for *Boys Town*). New music was composed for these broadcasts, in part because the timing in a one-hour show was so different from that in the much longer movies, but in part because the show used an orchestra, and the action was sumptuously cushioned by the lush background.

There were other kinds of shows as well: news, sports events, and, most important, dramatic shows. Those with continuous action were often inspired by pulp novels; because of their highly charged emotional

▶◯ Recommended Recordings and Video Cassettes

It has become stylish to offer old radio broadcasts on cassette tapes and LPs (with some CDs).

Jabberwocky. This company has issued both Lux Radio Theater productions mentioned in the text: *Dark Victory* (0-88142-105-7) and *The Scarlet Pimpernel* (0-88142-053-0).

MARK 56 Records. LP 583. An original broadcast of *Fibber McGee & Molly*, a comedy show in the dialogue-comedy tradition. A half-hour show, complete with original music.

A broadcasting studio in the 1920s. (Picture Collection, The Branch Libraries, The New York Public Library.)

content, they were dubbed *soap operas* (the sponsors were often soap companies). The comedy and adventure stories were most often fifteen-minute shows, broadcast five days a week. "Amos 'n' Andy," the last vestige of the minstrel show, was the longest-running radio series; it would be soon followed (from 1969) by the "Cosby Show" on TV. Second in radio endurance was "Jack Armstrong, the All-American Boy," a modernized western.

Recommended Recordings and Video Cassettes

A recording of a Jack Armstrong show proved not to have either the original actors or the music, but another radio show album, for Sky King, *proved to be authentic, with music composed by Marie Baldwin (Marie Bergersen).*

MARK 56 Records. LP 703. *Sky King.* Two fifteen-minute broadcasts: "Lady Alice" and "The Mark of El Diabolo."

Radio Music

sound mix: the mixture of sound elements in radio

theme song: a song associated with a particular show or performer

musical interlude: music in radio used to connect sections of dialogue or to announce changes of scene

background music: music behind dramatic action

The shorter shows didn't have orchestras; their music was provided by a single musician at a Hammond electric organ. In fact, the musician was part of a *sound mix*: the whole of radio was made of nothing but sounds mixed together creatively. Dramatic shows, of course, used speakers: the announcer, who presented introductions (and commercials), and the actors, whose readings suggested mood, emotion, and even gestures—heavy breathing could suggest hard work, or excitement, or perhaps fatigue after running. Two microphones might be used by the speakers; one scene was done at one microphone, while the people in the next scene gathered at the other.

The musical contributions were vital, and they would inaugurate a new way of mixing sounds and even of perceiving them. A *theme song,* always the same and generally a recording, served as an identifying introduction. *Musical interludes* were used to connect sections of dialogue and to announce changes of scene by setting the mood; these interludes were the products of an organist/composer, who composed them during rehearsals, generally on the same day as the broadcast (and all broadcasts were live), and who used a separate microphone. The organist/composer also provided *background music*, as demanded by the script—music suggesting the rhythm of the gallop in a scene of horses, for example, or tense chords to suggest an emotional crisis.

Sound Effects

And to provide aural illusions, *sound effects* were used. These were of three kinds, and the soundman (or two men for a very busy script) used three microphones in presenting them. First were props, such as a door in a frame, which could be opened in a number of ways (slowly, quickly, with difficulty—or perhaps closed with a slam), door and telephone bells, or two baseball bats to be struck together to suggest a hit ball. Second were special-effects devices, such as suspended wood blocks, which could be lifted and dropped rhythmically to suggest marching feet, or a piece of cellophane, which, when slowly crinkled right at the microphone, simulated the sound of frying eggs. And third were recordings with a record player, recordings of such background noises as the hum of people talking in a restaurant, or a coming thunder storm, with or without crickets, with or without rain. The record collections of radio stations were voluminous: some numbered in excess of thirty thousand. The sound-effects men worked from a central position, surrounded by their props, mechanisms, records (all chosen for the day), and two or more record turntables with their own microphones.

Thus, there were typically five or six microphones in use at once for a broadcast: two for the actors and announcer, one for the organist/composer, and three for the soundmen (when the action called for all

A broadcast in progress, 1936. A group of actors is at one microphone and sound-effects men, using a device to simulate the sound of hoof beats, are at another. The musicians' microphone, not in the picture, is probably to the right of the sound mike. In the background, the sound engineer is controlling the mix of sounds to create the whole. A large cast would necessitate the use of another mike for actors, and still another mike would be required for the sound men if the script called for an unusual number of effects or if recorded sounds were used. (Picture Collection, The Branch Libraries, The New York Public Library.)

three types of sound effects). And the producer, in the *control room* (or *control booth*), mixed these sounds, bringing one up, muting another, flowing from one scene to another.

Collaboration between the organist/composer and the soundman was vital and vitalizing. The sound effects could pick up rhythmic features from the music, and "the organ could pick up the pitch of a ringing telephone,"[14] for example, and give it a musical background that suggested the emotional implication of the telephone call.

The musical interludes were measured in seconds, generally lasting from five to ten seconds, depending on the psychic distance to be bridged. The interlude could be discrete, that is, parenthetical to the script, beginning and ending with autonomous musical elements, or it could rise into prominence from behind the action or fade into the next scene, suggesting what that scene would be, melting into night sounds, footsteps, or galloping horses. The length of time for each piece of background music could be even shorter; often it consisted of only a single chord to suggest a sudden realization or to underline an implied action. In these cases, the timing of the music would be crucial. The shortest sound was a single accented chord called a *stinger*, which the organist would achieve by opening the volume pedal and then playing the chord while closing the pedal quickly. The organist "improvised from the script, working from short melodic, rhythmic, and harmonic units jotted down during rehearsal in musical shorthand."[15]

stinger: a sudden accented chord, especially on an organ

A broadcast was controlled by the director from the control room with gestures very like those of an orchestra conductor, which were observed by the sound engineer and translated into the desired effects. The director created the tempo of speech and action for all participants, cuing their entries and indicating the length of musical interludes and sound effects, the relative loudness of background music or sounds and speech, and indicating fades and other interrelations. The mix of the sounds of the five or six microphones was thus the province of the sound engineer, who created layers of sound by regulating the various elements into foregrounds and backgrounds. This was a new reciprocity between layers of sound and between music and nonmusical sounds.

Radio, then, was essentially the layering of sound elements into a satisfying integrity. Another kind of layering was begun by guitarist Les Paul; in the mid-1940s, perhaps inspired by radio techniques, he created the guitar/voice recording of "How High the Moon," twelve layers of guitar and twelve of voice.[16] He also created the "Walkin' and Whistlin' Blues" (issued on the reverse side) of three layers: footsteps, guitar, and whistle. All had to be done with two disc recording machines, going from one to the other, playing the record while adding another layer, and so forth. So many jazz festivals had been featured on the radio; in this technique, radio returned the favor.

THE MOVIES

Silent Movies

The movies got off to a fairly slow start; they entered the United States (from France) in 1896; it was 1903 before the first American film, longer than a kiss or a sneeze (both filmed by Edison), appeared. This was *The Great Train Robbery* (1903), an eleven-minute film directed by Ernest S. Porter. In 1915, D. W. Griffith made *The Birth of a Nation*; this was the first film epic (about Reconstruction and the Ku Klux Klan). His film *Intolerance* (1916) was even more serious. But comedy was not long in coming. Charlie Chaplin started making short films in 1914, developed the Little Tramp in 1915, and quickly expanded to such movies as *The Kid* (1920), *The Gold Rush* (1924), and *Modern Times* (1936). Chaplin had good company: Buster Keaton, the Keystone Kops, Our Gang, and Laurel and Hardy followed, creating a firm foundation for film comedy as well.

Until the late 1920s, film was silent. Sound was provided by a pianist, an organist, or an orchestra, depending on the budget of the theater showing the films. Jerome H. Remick & Co., of New York and Detroit, published the *Remick Folio of Moving Picture Music*, a series whose first volume appeared in 1914, and which provided suitable excerpts for the

A French poster, by Auglemarie, advertising a Charlie Chaplin film, 1916. Chaplin was so well-known that his full name and the film title were omitted on many posters. (Picture Collection, The Branch Libraries, The New York Public Library.)

film **score:** the music of a
film

accompaniment of films; some pianists and organists also improvised. But the Remick publications were available with orchestra parts as well—orchestras cannot improvise. In 1927, sound was added to movies, and the business of composing music for films was underway.

Sound Tracks

Movies had sounds similar to those of radio programs; but movies did not require artificially produced sound effects, since the action of the cast produced them naturally. The technical process of producing sound in films was the creation of a *sound track*, a band that runs parallel to the pictures on the edge of the film strip. Two problems to be dealt with in making a sound track were mix and synchrony. *Mix* involved essentially the same problems as it did in radio, and it was handled in the same way. *Synchrony* involved the precise matching of all sound—musical and vocal—with the visual images.

In early sound pictures, independently activated recordings were used, and inevitably there were difficulties in synchrony. But soon, the sound equipment was synchronized electrically with the cameras, and a sound track was made by transforming the sound frequencies into light waves running sideways on the film-strip margin. The major disadvantage of the technique was that only frequencies of from fifty to eight thousand vibrations per second could register, whereas human beings can perceive sounds of from about thirty to twelve thousand vibrations per second. However, this disadvantage was outweighed by the possibility of achieving exact sound-image synchrony, an innovation that was crucial to the future development of the cinema.

Film Scores

Movie composers had to think in both theatrical and musical time. A *bit*, a short piece of stage business, might be as short as a glance and call for a single orchestral loud chord in imitation of the organ stinger; an *action sequence*, such as a chase, might consume six minutes and require a complete musical entity in itself. But as the glance might be part of the chase, the chase was also part of the larger rhythm of the film as a whole—and the film might last ninety minutes. Composers could use the sound track for timing music, cutting the track to synchronize the score with the action. With twenty-four frames per second, time could be measured precisely in inches of track.

Thus the composing of *film scores* was quite a different task from composing for the concert hall. The first score preceded the invention of the sound track, however, and was produced in the theater with the movie. It was an orchestral score by Victor Herbert to be played live and

◑ Recommended Recordings and Video Cassettes

The music composed by Victor Herbert for D.W. Griffith's The Fall of a Nation *(1916) has been found and issued.*

Library of Congress OMP 103. Film score to accompany the silent film *The Fall of a Nation*, by Victor Herbert (1916).

synchronized with *The Fall of a Nation* (Griffith's 1916 sequel to his 1915 blockbuster).

Since about 1930, when the profession locked into place, a number of outstanding composers have produced film scores.

Max Steiner

Max Steiner (1888–1971) was born in Austria but came to the United States in 1924. He went into the business of scoring for films at the inception of the profession, and he produced more than fifty movie scores, including *Cimarron* (1931), *The Informer* (1935, for which he won

Max Steiner composed the film score for *Cimarron*, 1931, starring Estelle Taylor and Richard Dix. (Picture Collection, The Branch Libraries, The New York Public Library.)

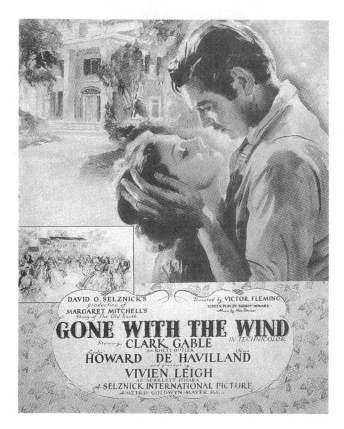

Steiner also composed the film score for _Gone with the Wind_, 1939. (Picture Collection, The Branch Libraries, The New York Public Library.)

an Academy Award), _Gone with the Wind_ (1939), _Now, Voyager_ (1942, another Academy Award winner), _Since You Went Away_ (1944), _The Treasure of the Sierra Madre_ (1947), _The Fountainhead_ (1949), _The Caine Mutiny_ (1954), _Band of Angels_ (1957), and _The Dark at the Top of the Stairs_ (1960). He was known for his lush underlining of the emotional meanings in the films he scored.

Erich Wolfgang Korngold

Erich Wolfgang Korngold (1897–1957) was a Czech composer who had worked with the German director Max Reinhardt; he came to Hollywood to score Reinhardt's Hollywood production of Shakespeare's _A Midsummer Night's Dream_ (1935), and he stayed to do many more. Korngold was associated with swashbucklers, and his action scenes were notable, filled with rhythmic verve. He was unusual in scoring _Robin Hood_, the Errol Flynn classic, in 1938, composing the action-scene scores before the filming—the action was directed to synchronize with the music instead of vice versa, leading Korngold to refer to that film as an opera. (The music won an Academy Award.) His list of movie credits

▶ Recommended Recordings and Video Cassettes

A few compendiums of film music have been issued.

Bay Cities BCD 1014, 1021, and 1037. *Classical Hollywood.* 3 CDs, of which the first and third contain music by Erich Wolfgang Korngold.

RCA 7890-2-RG. *Film Music.* This contains excerpts from the music for several films.

But, of course, the best evidence is the thing itself! Recommended excerpts from film scores:

CBS/Fox Video 4540. *Robin Hood* (1938), Award winning score by Erich Wolfgang Korngold. (102 minutes). The first half is particularly good.

MGM/UA Home Video M201264. *Casablanca* (1942), score by Max Steiner. (104 minutes). About two-thirds through the film, the French national anthem is superimposed upon a German drinking song in a symbolic and highly effective musical moment.

A Midsummer's Night's Dream, 1935, film score by Erich Wolfgang Korngold. (Picture Collection, The Branch Libraries, The New York Public Library.)

is long and includes *The Prince and the Pauper* (1937), *The Sea Hawk* (1940), *Kings Row* (1941), *Of Human Bondage* (1946), *Escape Me Never* (1947), and *Magic Fire* (1955).

Dimitri Tiomkin

Dimitri Tiomkin (1899–1979) was a Russian-born pianist who had played in a movie theater before coming to the United States in 1925. He composed over sixty scores before winning his first Academy Award, for *High Noon*, in 1952. His films include *Lost Horizon* (1937), *The Moon and Sixpence* (1942), *Duel in the Sun* (1946), *Portrait of Jennie* (1948), *The High and the Mighty* (1954, his second Academy Award), *Friendly Persuasion* (1956), *The Old Man and the Sea* (1958, his third Academy Award), and *The Guns of Navarone* (1961).

Portrait of Jennie, film score by Dimitri Tiomkin, starring Joseph Cotten and Jennifer Jones, 1948. (Picture Collection, The Branch Libraries, The New York Public Library.)

Melodramas and Musicals

The music of films comes in two categories of motion pictures: melodramas and musicals. The *melodrama* is action with spoken words, synchronized with music (this dramatic form was popular in the nineteenth century, when romanticism gave it such an emotional charge that the word "melodramatic" came from it—but it is a technical term); almost all movies are thus melodramas. The *musical* is action that stops occasionally for formal musical numbers, like a Broadway musical, except that the action part has music behind it (and on Broadway it does not). Thus, a Broadway musical brought to Hollywood becomes a *musical melodrama*, and this transformation is not always successful—nor do music directors always know how to deal with the double whammy of background music and musical numbers. The list of Broadway musicals that have been recast as films is long; Victor Herbert's *Naughty Marietta* (1910) was produced as a movie in 1935; but the 1950s was the chief decade, with *Oklahoma!* and *Guys and Dolls* in 1955, *The King and I* in 1956, *The Music Man* in 1957, and Irving Berlin's *Call Me Madam* in 1959.

More important, musicals were produced directly for film. The most famous of these were the Fred Astaire/Ginger Rogers movies made for RKO from 1933 to 1939, including *Top Hat* (1935) with music by Irving Berlin, and *Swing Time* (1936) with music by Jerome Kern. Richard Rodgers composed the score for *State Fair* (1945), Gershwin's music was used in *An American in Paris* (1951), Frederick Loewe composed the score for *Gigi* in 1958 (it won an Academy Award), and Gene de Paul composed the score for *Seven Brides for Seven Brothers* (1959).

These movie musicals followed the developments of the United States as a nation in the same way that operas and Broadway musicals did. But

melodrama: a play or film consisting of action with spoken words, synchronized with music

musical: a popular twentieth-century form of musical theater; also, a film in which the action stops occasionally for formal musical numbers

musical melodrama: a play or film with music coordinated with the action

Recommended Recordings and Video Cassettes

MGM/UA Home Video M600371. Victor Herbert's *Naughty Marietta* (1910). The movie, starring Jeanette MacDonald and Nelson Eddy, was issued in 1935; it runs 106 minutes. The middle part is the best musically.

The most important film musicals are those for which the music was written directly for the screen.

VidAmerica 929. *Top Hat* (1935), score by Irving Berlin. (99 minutes). Excellent for many reasons. The unreal get-away world of elegant hotels in the depression era is comparable to a fairy tale. Astaire's dances fit perfectly with the music.

MGM/UA Musicals M700091. *Seven Brides for Seven Brothers* (1954), score by Gene de Paul. (102 minutes). About two-thirds of the way through comes a real hoedown.

MGM/UA M700050. *Gigi* (winner of 9 Academy awards, including Best Picture—1958), score by Frederick Loewe. (117 minutes).

Walt Disney's *Bambi*, film score by Frank Churchill, 1942. (Picture Collection, The Branch Libraries, The New York Public Library.)

the movies manifested this in special ways. The Depression musicals tended to be lavish, with simple plots and fairy-tale settings (the hotel rooms in *Top Hat* are as fabulous as the castles of the Brothers Grimm); the music balances that with discipline and dignity. But in the wartime musicals, the scene opened out, first in semirealistic sets like *State Fair*, with wholesome, almost folklike music; and the postwar musicals presented sweeping views combined with music of great energy and verve, as in *Seven Brides for Seven Brothers*.

And the Walt Disney films followed the dream worlds, aided by the sparkling music of Frank Churchill (1901–42): the short film *The Three Little Pigs* (1933), and full-length movies *Snow White and the Seven Dwarfs* (1937), and *Bambi* (1942).

NOTES

1. Guthrie McClintic, *Me and Kit* (Boston: Little, Brown, 1955), p. 125.
2. "The Joe Franklin Show," syndicated for release in June, 1987.
3. Curt Sachs, *World History of the Dance* (New York: Norton, 1963), p. 447.
4. André Francis, *Jazz* (Paris: Solfèges, 1958), p. 188.
5. I am much indebted to Gilbert Bond, who generously shared his authoritative views on Ellington with me in a phone conversation, 10 January 1988.
6. E. J. Hobsbawm, "Slyest of the Foxes," a review of James Lincoln Collier's biography, *Duke Ellington*, in *The New York Review of Books*, vol. 34, no. 18 (19 November, 1987), p. 6.
7. Jack Burton, *The Blue Book of Hollywood Musicals* (Watkins Glen, NY: Century House, 1953), p. 11.
8. Leonard Feather, *The New Edition of the Encyclopedia of Jazz* (New York: Bonanza Books, 1962), p. 376.
9. *The New Encyclopedia Britannica*, 15th ed. (Chicago: University of Chicago, 1992), 24:647.
10. Ian Crofton and Donald Fraser, *A Dictionary of Musical Quotations* (New York: Schirmer Books, 1985), p. 48.
11. *The Monadology*, 1714, in Crofton and Fraser, *Musical Quotations*, p. 48.
12. *Encyclopedia Britannica*, 15th ed., 24:647.
13. "The Talk of the Town," *The New Yorker* (31 May 1969), p. 27.
14. Marie Baldwin, letter to Edith Borroff, 1 June 1969.
15. Ibid.
16. Edith Borroff, *Music in Europe and the United States: A History*, 2nd ed., p. 640.

BIBLIOGRAPHY

Borroff, Edith. *Music in Europe and the United States: A History*, 2nd ed. New York: Ardsley House , Publishers, 1990.

———. "Origin of Species: Conflicting Views of American Musical Theater in History." *American Music*, vol. 2, no. 4 (Spring 1985).

Burton, Jack. *The Blue Book of Hollywood Musicals*. Watkins Glen, NY: Century House, 1953.

Feather, Leonard. *The New Edition of the Encyclopedia of Jazz*. New York: Bonanza Books, 1962.

Francis, Andre. *Jazz*. Paris: Solfeges, 1958.

Hobsbawm, E. J. "Slyest of the Foxes," *The New York Review of Books*, vol. 34, no. 18 (19 November 1987).

Lang, Paul Henry, ed. *One Hundred Years of Music in America*. New York: Schirmer Books, 1961.

Lewine, Richard, and Alfred Simon. *Encyclopedia of Theatre Music*. New York: Bonanza Books, 1961.

McClintic, Guthrie. *Me and Kit*. Boston: Little, Brown, 1955.

Sachs, Curt. *World History of the Dance*. New York: W. W. Norton & Co., 1963.

Slonimsky, Nicolas. *Baker's Biographical Dictionary of Musicians*, 8th ed. New York: Schirmer Books, 1990.

"The Talk of the Town." *The New Yorker*. 31 May 1969.

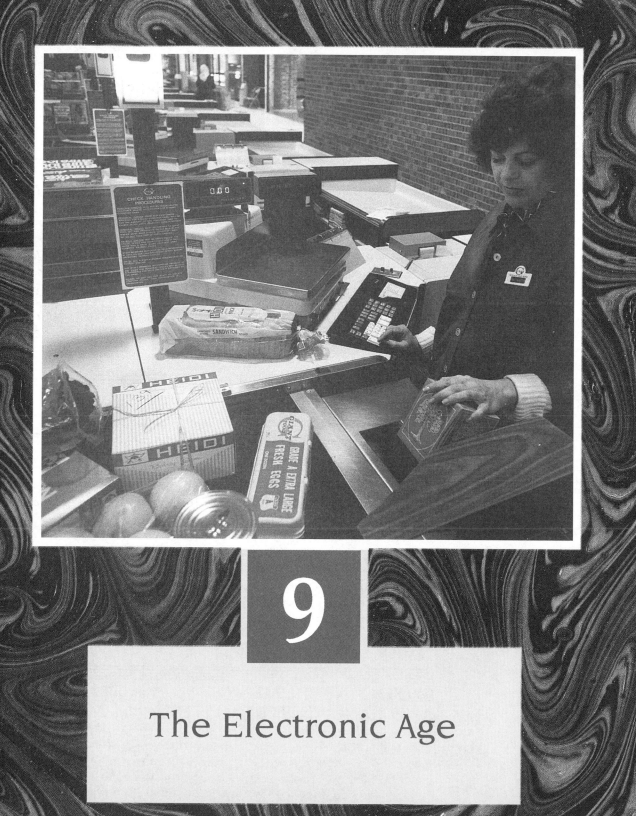

9

The Electronic Age

player piano: a piano activated mechanically rather than by a pianist

gamelan: a Javanese instrumental group

The old days had known instruments and machines. They had known instruments such as the violin, which was at first beloved in concert music because of its singing quality; the voice (an instrument too) was loved because of its inseparable closeness with the very breath of life; woodwind instruments were also activated by human breath—they were loved for that and they were loved because they could reach notes that no normal voice could reach and play intricate patterns that only a few singers could match; brass instruments were loved because of the dignity that they imparted to social and political functions; and percussion instruments were the heartbeat of life as melodic instruments were the breath, and loved because they could mix the throbbing of the heart with the complicated mathematics of rhythm. Instruments didn't substitute another function for human function; they expanded upon a basically human function and ennobled it.

THE PLAYER PIANO

But a *player piano* was a machine. Machines took over human jobs and did them, substituting for the person and for personal function, not working with the person and expanding the human melodic or rhythmic reach. A regular piano was played by man or woman, girl or boy, or perhaps two of them at once, but the only human function with a player piano was simply to activate it, start it, get it on its way and stand back. The paper roll which was pumped through the machine, at first by foot pedals, but later by machinery—machinery to activate machinery—could be made literally from a performance, note for note, but a performer could add perforations to the roll (Gershwin is known to have done that, for example) so that the piano would sound forth more notes at once than any pair of human hands could manage.

EXOTIC INSTRUMENTS AND EARLY INSTRUMENTS

Instruments had by no means disappeared from the scene. In fact, new instruments were welcome. New percussion came to the United States after the Second World War; servicemen had heard Indochinese *gamelans* and had attended Japanese Kabuki and Bunraku (puppet) per-

The Starr Piano
PRE-EMINENTLY THE PIANO OF AMERICA

NO artist has ever achieved finer interpretations of the great masterpieces in music than may be obtained by intelligent manipulation of the Starr Player Piano.

From an ad for a player piano, 1913. (Picture Collection, The Branch Libraries, The New York Public Library.)

formances; they had heard Hawaiian *uli uli* (rattles) and Maori chanting, and they had brought memories of these experiences home with them. This meant that suddenly the United States was able to listen outwards in a way it never could before.

Instruments previously considered exotic began to be popular here; the *Flamenco guitar* is just one of many *folk instruments* that began to be heard, along with the *country-western guitar* and, of course, the banjo. Folk music of the United States, which had been of relatively little interest for half a century, became popular again, and banjo sales went up.

At the same time, the new historical studies of earlier music, the daily bread of musicologists, had opened up the desire to hear this earlier music played on its own instruments; harpsichord makers began to turn out elegant twentieth-century copies of eighteenth-century instruments. The *recorder*, a Renaissance and baroque wooden end-blown flute, had already enjoyed the hobbyist's popularity, but now professionals strove to be virtuosos on that instrument. Pipe-organ builders began to pro-

uli uli: Hawaiian rattles

Flamenco guitar: a Spanish Gypsy folk guitar

folk instrument: an instrument used by nonprofessionals

country-western guitar: a traditional six-string acoustic guitar

recorder: a wooden flute with a whistle head, blown from the top rather than across

Electric guitar.
(Yamaha Corporation of America.)

Acoustic guitar.
(Picture Collection,
The Branch Libraries,
The New York Public
Library.)

harpsichord: a keyboard instrument with strings plucked by the key mechanism

clavichord: a keyboard instrument in which the strings are touched by the key mechanism

finger cymbals: a pair of small disks attached to the fingers and played by clicking them together

Krummhorn: an obsolete instrument with an encased reed

duce copies of early instruments. Do-It-Yourself kits were developed so that amateurs could build some of the smaller instruments—notably small *harpsichords* and *clavichords*—for themselves at home. And the more obscure medieval and Renaissance instruments (the *finger cymbals,* the *Krummhorn*—a capped reed instrument obsolete since the seventeenth century) began to appear, as scholarly musical groups, called *Collegia Musica,* began to concertize.

The expanding scope of instruments went the other way as well, from a studied authenticity of the old to a spontaneous combustion of the new. *Electric* guitars became standard in the 1970s. Whereas the old, authentic instruments, for the most part, produced softer sounds than their modern opposite numbers, the new instruments were louder, and in the 1960s, the sounds became even louder when *amplification systems* were invented. *Amplified* guitar became the mainstay of popular music.

But by far the most important developments in recent decades have taken place in the category of electronic machines.

RECORDINGS

In one sense, reproduction of sound was not new when Edison invented his cylinder machine in 1877; Queen Victoria had had a bustle that played "God Save the Queen" when she sat down![1] What Edison had invented was the analog system, which created not an original sound, like a *music box* or a player piano, but a parallel, an analogy, of the original sound. The sound then needed a machine to reactivate it, in Edison's case, with a needle, which played the reactivated sound through a horn for augmentation, so that a group of people could hear it. This was ideal for the living room, with just a few people to listen.

Disc Recordings

Disc recordings followed, and by the 1920s, these were ten-inch 78 RPM (revolutions per minute) with up to three minutes on a side; by the 1930s discs were twelve-inch 78 RPMs that played up to four-and-a-half minutes on a side. A symphony might require four or five discs in a set, sold in an album, and the discs were heavy and cumbersome. Machines were invented that would play them one by one, stacked, so that a person did not have to reload every four or four-and-a-half minutes, but could play all the records on one side, then turn the stack over and play all the records on the other side.

The postwar period brought *stereophonic sound* (two speakers) and later *quadraphonic sound* (four speakers). Stereo was hugely successful, but quadraphonic did not sell, possibly because it was difficult to distinguish the speakers—we have only two ears, after all. And in the 1950s, 33 RPM records, or LPs (long-playing) were supplanting 78 RPMs.

Tapes and Compact Disks

Digital systems came first in movie sound tracks, but were soon in recordings as well. In a digital system, many sample sounds are recorded and then turned into binary numbers, then put on tape. The *compact disk* (CD) came only in the 1980s, following the digital mastering of tapes in the 1970s, with the first truly digital machines (i.e., not transferred to tape but played with lasers) in 1983.

But for the composition of music, the *tape deck* is by far the most manipulable kind of machinery, and tapes can be used much more easily than disks. So the invention of the tape recorder was a landmark for composition. Tapes were developed in the popular music world in the 1940s, and by 1948, tape manipulation was being taken into the composers' field of expertise. Composers could use tapes as they could

Collegium Musicum: a group devoted to performing early music

electric instrument: an instrument played normally but amplified electrically

amplification system: a mechanism for making music louder electrically

amplified instrument: an instrument made louder electrically

music box: a box containing a cylinder with metal teeth that sound musical pitches when the cylinder is rotated

stereophonic sound: sound from two or more speakers placed apart to obtain a richer effect

quadraphonic sound: recording equipment providing four speakers

compact disk: a recording device of the 1980s and '90s in which music is digitally encoded on one side of a 5-inch disk

never use disks: tapes could be mixed, made into a loop (in which case the same bit of music would be repeated over and over again until it was stopped), spliced, combined, played backwards, sounded at any number of different speeds (which change the pitch: the faster the speed the higher the sound), and of course played at any dynamic level.

The consumer of music also benefited from the inventions of new recording devices. The *cassette* overtook LP sales in the United States in 1982. For one thing, the tapes and the compact disks contain the greatest amount of music packaged in the smallest amount of space; tapes and disks are lightweight and the playing equipment is lightweight as well, and easily managed, so that joggers and other itinerants can use playing devices attached to their clothing and enjoy music while in motion. More important, the blind can get the use of recorded books and other literature in an efficient and cost-effective manner.

TELEVISION

Radio gave way to television as the national entertainment medium, gradually, during the 1950s and 1960s. In 1949, there had been 940,000 television sets in homes in the United States (and five times as many radios); by 1953, there were over 20,000,000 television sets. Radio personalities had been the common coin of home entertainment as movie stars were of public entertainment. But soon, television had its own stars, its own programs, its own strengths; sets were more reliable, they were increasingly variable in size, and they received telecasts in color.

Television brought about many changes in American life. Most important, politicians were seen as well as heard, and live telecasts brought them into the home in a direct and stunning way that had never been possible before. Daily news coverage greeted the tired mother and father after the day's work, and in times of crisis brought continuing coverage of both disasters and triumphs into the home—from the Kennedy assassination of 1963, to the Watergate hearings in 1973 and the Iran-Contra hearings of 1988, to Olympic Games and inaugural celebrations throughout the decades. Radio didn't disappear, but it yielded to television the role it had played in unifying and characterizing the nation.

In addition, television developed its own language and literature. The language was a visual one as radio's had been an aural one: serials in radio had dealt with the spoken word and that which sound effects could suggest; television dealt with the deed witnessed and that which the eye would savor more than the ear. This fed car chases and violence on fast-action series, relegating the joys of conversation to the wastebasket; yet in the late 1980s, talk shows began to proliferate and conversation began a return.

The movie star yielded to the popular-music star as the American unifying symbol, and television developed the video presentation of popular-music performance. In addition, popular music was featured on the VCR (video cassette recorder) tape, so that the visual aspects of performance could be recaptured on television as they had been on the screen. So, television became in part a replacement for radio and in part a replacement for the movie theater. The movies had always been a social phenomenon, however, as radio had been a private (or family) phenomenon; young people on dates still go to movies in larger numbers than can sit around a radio comfortably.

SYNTHESIZERS AND COMPUTERS

Synthesizers

In 1906, Lee De Forest invented the triode vacuum tube, enabling waveforms to become repetitive (through oscillators) and thus achieve pitch, which is vibration at one speed over a long enough time for it to be perceived as regular. The *Choralcelo* and the *Ondes Martenot*, in the early and middle 1920s, had incorporated the manufacture of waveforms in musical instruments. The *synthesizer* was not far off: in fact, one was exhibited at the Paris Exposition of 1929, made by the French, the *Coupleux-Givelet*. It was activated by a paper roll, which opened electronic circuits that generated waveforms. It could control pitch, *tone color*, time, and dynamic level. After the invention of the tape recorder in the 1940s, the French also invented *musique concrète*, in which sounds from the radio library of sound effects were put together by the manipulation of tapes and worked into satisfying integrities as works of music.

Choralcelo: an early electronic instrument

Ondes Martenot: a French electronic instrument

synthesizer: a mechanism that manufactures sound waves directly, without a musical instrument

Coupleux-Givelet: an early synthesizer, exhibited at the Paris Exposition of 1929

tone color: timbre

musique concrète: music created by combining recorded elements

Synthesizer. (Yamaha Corporation of America.)

analog synthesizer: a machine that creates sounds directly, rather than recording them

digital synthesizer: a computer system for combining, modifying, and reproducing sounds

music system: a computer program for music

In Chicago, meanwhile, the Manert Electrical Orchestra, made by the Hammond Organ Company in 1945, was produced; this was a synthesizer that consisted of "a roomful of electronic tone-generating equipment controlled by an elaborate, motor-driven scanner."[2] In the 1950s, RCA developed a more practical synthesizer, and one was established at a composer's workshop in 1959 at Columbia University in New York, in cooperation with Princeton University. Synthesized sound was a combining of a sum of different elements made possible in practicable, smaller consoles through the development of low-cost silicon transistors. In 1964, Robert Moog and Donald Buchla developed a music center for the production of synthesized music on disc records, issuing Morton Subotnik's *Silver Apples of the Moon* in 1966 and his *Sidewinder* in 1970.

By 1980, these were called *analog synthesizers* because they directly produced simulated waveforms as analogies to actual waveforms. After 1980 the *digital synthesizers* and *music systems* were in operation; these were programmed with numbers that were then converted to waveforms. But these synthesizers to be effective had to be part of a general-purpose computer in order to create systems that could result in works of music.

Computers

The computer is not as new as the synthesizer. In 1801, French inventor Joseph-Marie Jacquard (1752–1834) devised a weaving process wherein punched cards would activate a loom so as to incorporate a woven design indicated by the cards. The Jacquard loom thus used the basic tools of computers: the mechanism that would activate a machine through the use of many punched cards, cards punched with holes or notches to represent data to be fed to and used by the machine. Still, this was a loom, not a computer.

Perhaps the first computer was invented (although never built) by the English mathematician Ada Augusta Byron, the Countess of Lovelace (1815–52—younger sister of the poet George Gordon, Lord Byron). She certainly opened the way for modern computer programming. She was first a student, then a colleague of the mathematician Charles Babbage, who worked to produce a calculator; he put Jacquard's punched cards to use in a new direction by deploying them in mathematical formulations. But Lovelace reached further, seeking to make the basic procedures programmable and, in fact, to develop viable programs. Her success is still applauded: the United States Pentagon Department of Defense systems today use the computer language ADA, named after this remarkable woman.

By the end of World War II, computers were being used in industry, still activated by punched cards like Jacquard's. Those computers were huge; most were the size of a garage—they could be walked into for

The Jaquard loom.
(IBM Archives.)

repairs, and they were slow, even ponderous, in use. But development was swift, with the smaller and smaller size of the machines in inverse proportion to the greater and greater capacity: the size was gradually reduced so that by the end of the 1980s "laptop computers" were being manufactured; and the piles of punched cards were replaced by a single disk containing a program, a set of instructions that served as a link between the capacity of the machine and the mind of the human being who wanted to use that machine.

The computer developed first with the management of numbers. It was used for account-keeping in industry; the numbers gradually became refined and translated to other systems, so by the end of the 1940s,

Charles Babbage. (IBM Archives.)

The ENIAC, the first electronic computer, 1946. (Smithsonian Institute.)

it was possible to link numbers, through the punched cards, to nonnumerical elements. This meant that statistical reports and business summaries could be made. These capacities were sharply refined in the next two decades.

The step from handling numbers to handling words was the next stride. The computer was no longer linked simply to a calculator and the management of numbers, as Babbage had foreseen, but to the typewriter, and to the concatenation of ideas, as Ada Lovelace had envisioned. Word processors began a spiral of increasingly complex machinery interacting with increasingly sophisticated programs.

In 1970 for the first time, a computer composed a poem. This was *The Meditation of IBM 7094-7040 DCS*, the product of a programming experiment by my sister, Marie Borroff, poet and Sterling Professor of English at Yale University.

Borroff spent last spring feeding the machine simple grammar, assorted stanzaic patterns and a vocabulary of 950 words that she selected by letting her finger fall blindly on poems in classical and avant-garde anthologies. Then she had the computer's random-number generator make the word selections and let it rip—at two stanzas a second. Writing in the current *Yale Alumni Magazine*, Poet Borroff reports that the computer wrought "startling and at times strikingly effective imagery. . ."[3]

Time posited that "poetasters may now join the technologically unemployed," and said that the poems were filled with what it called "freaky fragments." Borroff mused dryly,

one gets the impression that the computer is obsessed with earthworms and caterpillars and that it has a penchant for making gratuitous references to locomotives and Vaseline.[4]

Indeed, the stanza contained the silly line, "Wail like a happy earthworm"; but it ended:

> The river
> Winks
> And I am ravished.

The issue raised by the computer poetry is not mechanical, but human; that is, it addresses not the competency of computer construction and programming, but the suitability of such artistic adventures.

Her conclusion: "There are no foreseeable limits to the complexity of electronic intelligence. Eventually, the key question will be not whether the computer can simulate the independent activity of a poet, but whether we want it to."[5]

Music and the Computer

The first computer sound synthesis took place at the Bell Telephone Laboratories, in New Jersey, in 1961. This was digital-to-analog conversion, and gave rise to the recognition that "the computer can perform any function that can be described as a computable procedure, or algorithm."[6] The composer creates the algorithm (via punched cards, magnetic tape, or magnetic disks) and loads it into the computer to realize the music. The composer may then write out a score that specifies the sound events. And of course, a synthesizer unit is needed if the music is actually to be produced as audible. And if the work is to be performed in public, a sound system of amplification is necessary, with loud speakers placed in the hall—perhaps four or five of them—to achieve the sound and spatial effects that the composer intended.

Many music algorithms have been created around the world in the past twenty-five years. One often-used model is the Music V, created in 1968 at the Bell Telephone Laboratories; another is the Frequency Modulation (FM) Synthesis unit, developed in 1973 at Stanford University in California. In all cases, the goal is to produce individual modules of sound and then devise a system to facilitate interaction among the modules.

The problem of the synthesizer is very much like that of Borroff's poetry: not the competence of the machinery, but the desirability of the procedure, however competent. In the past few decades, this has translated in music to the question of who should have control of music performance. The old apprenticeship view had been that the notation of music was rather like the writing down of a play script: it directed the actors, but by no means stamped them with creative necessity—Laurence Olivier's Hamlet was very different from John Gielgud's, and neither was under the direction of Shakespeare in the matter of physical appearance, sound of the voice, or even in interpretation of the character (which, in fact, could change according to the physical characteristics of the actor and even the year—or century—in which the interpretation was taking place). Apprenticeship composers felt in partnership with actors and directors, and the differences among performers' interpretations were among the glories of their art: the fact that several interpretations were possible was a wonder and a pleasure. The notation of music was a communication from composer to performer, a communication that would tell the performer what to do so that the audience would hear the effect that the composer intended. The performer, then, was a means of reaching the audience, a vital link; no work was complete until the performer bodied it forth.

But in the university tradition music was viewed as a finished product, an aural entity to whose details performers owed primary obeisance. The performer was obligated to duplicate this sound, to be like the projector of a film: not to make it, but to allow it to come through of itself. The notation of music was a blueprint of exactly what the audience was to hear; performers were at best servants of this process, and at worst deemed unnecessary. The use of the computer/synthesizer could obviate the performers and make them obsolescent.

It was not clear how this argument would come out; composers felt themselves to be the arbiters and the authorities, but performers felt that they too were important. The public, they knew, seldom attended concerts to hear the composer. It was the star name that drew them.

The domination of the composer was true only in concert music, however: the music of the popular sector still reveled in performance as not only a live but a lively, exciting aspect of music. In that sector performers and composers responded by becoming one; groups began writing their own materials. By the 1980s, it was difficult to tell whether the public was responding to the music, to the performer as a star, or to the performance itself. This coincided with the development of the VCR and italicized the dramatic presentation of music groups.

That question remains open. What is definite is that the computers have developed greatly in the last fifty years, becoming smaller, more powerful, and cheaper. Programs for the notation of music made personal computers useful to traditional (acoustical) composers as well as experimental (synthesizer) composers; computer programs for notation were used by publishers as well, perhaps giving new energy to an industry that had become tired in recent years, fighting a public resistance to new concert music on the one hand and takeovers by big corporations on the other hand—corporations that understood the financial, but not the musical, aspects of the business.

These problems are all soluble, left for the end of the century for decision. The beginning of the 1990s saw the digital-computer music systems surpassing tape-studio techniques and analog synthesizers established as the electronic medium of the future.

Synthesizing Instruments

Related to computer/synthesizer use was the development of synthesizing instruments, used for the most part in the popular field. In 1976, the Synclavier series, by New England Digital Corporation, led the way, followed by the Yamaha DX-7 (FM Synthesizer), with its choice of sounds and effects. More than a hundred thousand of these were sold, in many sizes and types, from small keyboard to large.

In 1983, the Musical Instrument Digital Interface (MIDI) was brought out. With it the performer could make significant decisions: what notes, what *timbres* (sound qualities), what dynamics, what nuances. It is not surprising that this soon became, and remains, the bestseller of such systems. The importance of MIDI lay to a large extent in its ability to

MIDI: Musical Instrument Digital Interface

timbre: the quality or color of sound

**Rhythm synthesizer—an
advanced drum machine.**
(Yamaha Corporation of America.)

pull together instruments by different manufacturers and to make them compatible with one another.

In 1984, the Casio CZ-101 was issued, similar to the DX-7, but battery-powered and cheaper. In that same year, the Kurzweil 250 keyboard surpassed its predecessors: it was digitally encoded, and could sound like a piano, or organ, or strings, or wind instruments. Both could be joined in MIDI groups.

So the hardware is here, raw material, ready to be used with art and imagination.

NOTES

1. *Encyclopedia Britannica*, 15th ed., 24:546.
2. Ibid, 24:702.
3. *Time*, 22 February 1971, p. 77.
4. Ibid.
5. Ibid.
6. *Encyclopedia Britannica*, 15th ed., 24:704.

BIBLIOGRAPHY

Encyclopedia Britannica, 1992 ed., miscellaneous articles.

Slonimsky, Nicolas. "Programmed Poetry." *Time*, 22 February 1971.

10

Reaching into the Future
(1961 to 1993)

T he recent past is always more difficult to assess than the years for which a perspective of time has been developed. But it is clear that the period 1961–93 was similar to the years 1840–80 in one way and to the years 1880–1923 in another. It was like the years 1840–80 in having two clear, parallel paths, one of them unifying and the other disunifying (as the ideals of western expansion had been unifying and the problem of slavery had been disunifying). The two paths in recent years have been the unifying exploration of space and the very modern disunifying issue of creating equality: equality among people in the United States and among people (and countries) in the world.

The problems were greatly sharpened by rising population: in 1900 the country had a population of 75,994,575; in 1950, it was 151,325,798, and in 1990, it was 249,632,692.[1] There were, of course, important demographic shifts, chiefly from rural to urban majority, and increasing numbers in the midwestern, then West Coast cities. New York remained the city with the greatest number of citizens from the 1790 census on (before that it was Boston), more than doubling from 3,437,202 in 1900 to 7,891,957 in 1950, then dropping to 7,322,564 in 1990; Chicago grew from 1,698,575 in 1900 to 3,620,962 in 1950 (the second largest in both years), but dropped to 2,783,726 (and to third place) in 1990; but Los Angeles came from outside the top ten in 1900 to 1,970,358 (and fourth place) in 1950, and then leapt to 3,485,398 (and second place) in 1990. In fact, New York, Chicago, and Philadelphia (third in 1900, fifth in 1950) were the only cities in the top ten in both the 1900 and 1990 census counts. San Francisco, ninth in 1900, was then the only city west of St. Louis to make the top ten, while the ten largest cities in 1990 included Houston, San Diego, Dallas, Phoenix, San Antonio, and Los Angeles, strongly reflecting the westward movement of the country's population. This trend was more than substantiated by state totals: California was first in 1990, with 29,839,250, New York came in a poor second, with 18,044,505, and Texas was a strong third, with 17,059,805.

The population shifted its character as well: the huge crop of baby boomers after the Second World War brought that population in like a wave, in their teens and early twenties in the late 1960s, and in their fifties by 1992.

The 1960s began with the inauguration of John F. Kennedy (1961–63). The two extremes of idealism and pragmatism were apparent at once, with Kennedy announcing the formation of the Peace Corps from the steps of the University of Michigan Union in Ann Arbor in 1961, and, in the same year, pursuing the Bay of Pigs

America's problems have been greatly sharpened by rising population.
(Josh Siegel.)

fiasco, while also intensifying the problem in Vietnam, expanding
the number of United States military advisors there from 700 to
16,000 during his short presidency. While in an automobile parade
in Dallas on November 22, 1963, Kennedy was assassinated, bringing to an end a surge of youth and hope that admirers had likened
to a political Camelot.

Lyndon B. Johnson, Kennedy's vice president, took the oath of
office on the plane en route from Dallas back to Washington, and
was president for six years (1963–69). Johnson turned to an expansion of Roosevelt's New Deal, an expansion he called the Great
Society; it included Medicare and Medicaid and the creation of the
National Endowment for the Arts and Humanities. But Johnson's
presidency also saw three more assassinations: Malcolm X, in 1965;
Martin Luther King, Jr., in 1968; and Robert F. Kennedy, also in
1968. And, in addition, direct military intervention in Vietnam was
begun in 1964 after Johnson's election to a second term. After hope
that that conflict was drawing to a close, the Tet Offensive of January 30, 1968, escalated the military involvement; there would be
over a half million troops engaged. Although Johnson began peace

The eternal flame at the grave of John F. Kennedy. (Josh Siegel.)

talks and limited the bombing, the end would not come during his presidency. These were dark years indeed.

Richard M. Nixon (1969–74) saw even darker years. The Woodstock Festival in 1969 and the Kent State and Jackson State incidents in 1970 italicized a disheartened and turned-off generation's discontentment. His first vice president, Spiro Agnew, resigned under duress, accused of malfeasance. But worse was still in store: the Watergate scandal and ensuing cover-up would cause the fall of the presidency. And in Vietnam, already the longest fighting period in United States history, there would be the sacrifice of fifty-eight thousand lives (and the spending of $140 billion) before it was over. Nixon expanded the fighting to Cambodia and Laos, while also pursuing peace. In 1972, peace talks were begun in Paris, and in January of 1973, the Paris Peace Agreement was signed. But the Watergate hearings had begun, and, fearing impeachment, Nixon resigned in 1974.

His successor would be, along with his appointed vice president, the only presidential team in the nation's history of which neither president nor vice president had been elected. Gerald Ford (1974–77) had been appointed vice president when that office fell vacant in 1973, according to protocol established by the Twenty-fifth Amendment, from his position as Speaker of the House. Then Ford had to appoint a vice president. Ford's presidency was in

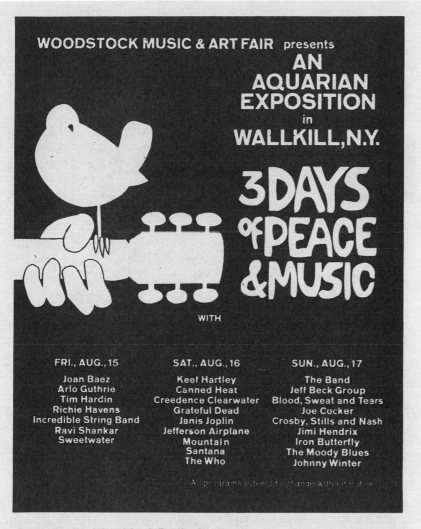

Poster for the Woodstock Festival. (The Hugh Jones Collection.)

large part an interim of recovery from the agonies of his predecessor. Hoping to calm the national nerves and restore inner as well as international peace, he pardoned Nixon a month after taking office, presided over the evacuation of Vietnam, and worked to achieve at least a standoff with the Soviet Union through the Helsinki Accord.

Jimmy Carter (1977–81), who had achieved a record of aggressive attack on racial prejudice while governor of Georgia (1971–75), continued to fight for racial equality during his presidency. Desegregation issues were examined in the North as well as in the South, and progress was made, if slowly. But Carter called for sacrifice of American individual interests for the good of the whole, and was not charismatic enough to make this policy the will of the people. He was a man of peace, who in 1978 achieved first the Panama Canal Treaty and then, in meetings at Camp David, the Israeli-Egyptian peace accord. But an energy crisis triggered rampant inflation, and hostages were seized in Iran following the Soviet Union's invasion of Afghanistan; Carter could not bring an end to the hostage crisis, and he was not reelected.

Ronald Reagan (1981–89) almost didn't have his eight years in office: in 1981, he was shot in an attempted assassination, but he pulled through and served two terms. He styled himself a hands-off President, shattering Johnson's Great Society programs and lowering the taxes of the rich; during his term the difference between rich and poor was pulled to a greater distance, and homelessness became a national scandal. But Reagan worked to establish a detente with the Soviet Union, while at the same time overseeing the largest military buildup in the history of the country. He was seen as not only hands-off, but as willing to let his staff run the government and to let issues of race and gender ride. He was also deeply influenced by his wife, Nancy Reagan; "indeed, she was said by White House watchers to have exerted greater influence on government operations than any previous First Lady."[2]

George Bush (1989–93) had been Reagan's vice president, and he was seen as continuing Reagan's policies. But Bush held that consensus was the vital factor in government, and he tried to follow national sentiment, while still holding to the hands-off governmental policies enunciated by his predecessor. The final dissolution of the Union of Soviet Socialist Republics, though a joyful consummation for the American spirit, could not offset the escalating national debt and involvement in Iraq (culminating in the military operation Desert Storm, sanctioned by the United Nations), with its fearful threat of greater sorrow. Bush lost the election in 1992, and the nation would enter the last years of the twentieth century hoping for resolution of the problems brought to a head in the last decades; the newly elected Bill Clinton was the first President born after World War II.

The frontier of these years was space. In 1961, Russia launched the first manned flight, followed a month later by a 15-minute suborbital flight by the United States. In 1961, President Kennedy committed the United States to putting a man on the Moon by the end of the decade. Six manned Mercury missions followed. In February of 1962, John Glenn became the first man to orbit the

Earth; and on July 20, 1969, Neil Armstrong and Edwin Aldrin, on *Apollo 11*, were the first humans on the Moon, landing the module *Eagle* there and then returning to the orbiting *Columbia* and fellow-astronaut Michael Collins. Other lunar landings continued until 1972, with longer walks and even the deployment of a lunar roving vehicle, but most of the 1970s and all of the '80s were devoted to other missions. In 1973, *Skylab* established a space station; in 1975, the American *Apollo* docked with the Soviet *Soyuz* in orbit; a space shuttle was under development in the late 1970s, and *Columbia* was launched in 1981. In 1986, the explosion of *Challenger*, with the loss of all aboard, put a damper on flights, but in 1988, *Discovery* flights resumed. The goals, announced by the National Aeronautics and Space Administration (NASA), now thirty years old, were the construction of the space station *Freedom*, the landing of an astronaut on the planet Mars, and the building of a permanent lunar base. These ambitions remain to be achieved.

Probably more important were the satellites sent into space for observation and research: *Explorer, Ranger, Surveyor, Lunar Orbiter, Mariner, Voyager. Voyager 2* photographed the planets Jupiter, Saturn, Uranus, and Neptune in 1977, and the Hubble Telescope, launched in 1990 and repaired in 1993 while continuing in orbit, sent back to Earth photographs of phenomena never before caught by any human eye or any lens.

THE UNIVERSITY TRADITION

Postwar Arts

The arts enjoyed a new energy in the years after World War II; at least they flourished in terms of the energy and imagination invested in them. Money was another matter, but President Johnson's establishment of the National Endowment for the Arts and Humanities helped in that regard, as did numerous grants from foundations and other organizations. These groups, such as the Ford and Rockefeller Foundations, however founded and funded, were administered by university men, sometimes graduates in the arts, but just as often graduates in other studies, such as history, and, increasingly, in the study of management. The arts in general were entering the university system; certainly this was true in music. In music, the university composers came into their own, since it was the university tradition that was best known to the foundation administrators.

radical serialism: the serialization of several elements of music in addition to pitch

pandiatonicism: diatonic music not in a key

primitivism: the introduction of pseudo-primitive elements into orchestral music

musical pointillism: a texture made of single notes rather than sustained melodies

universalism: the ideal of using musical elements of many cultures

chance music: music with elements selected randomly, rather than by an aesthetic choice

But all the arts were flourishing. Painters such as Robert Rauschenberg and Jasper Johns had, after World War II, led the country into a unique kind of modernism, the pop movement, which was evidenced in the 1960s by such painters as Roy Lichtenstein, Claes Oldenburg, and Andy Warhol. These painters turned everyday objects, such as soup cans and comic strips, into abstract artistic statements. But after the 1960s, art opened up into a number of "isms," none of which dominated the art scene. Abstract impressionism, color-field abstractionism, minimalism, neoexpressionism, and, finally, a new realism all vied for attention. "What had been permanently altered, too," wrote critic Hilton Kramer, "was the notion of the modernist artist as an isolated and rejected figure in American cultural life."[3] Painting and sculpture entered the mainstream consciousness of the nation.

So did literature. The Beatnik writers of the 1960s were followed by the wringing of hands, by such authors as William Styron and Stephen King, and the ringing of bells, by such authors as Arthur Haley and Toni Morrison. These last two authors, by bringing black history to the bookshelf of every American, set the stage for genuine integration. In 1988, the year of Morrison's Pulitzer Prize novel *Beloved*, Rev. Jesse Jackson spoke of the "Rainbow Coalition," the turning of everyone to mutual purpose. In 1993, Morrison received the Nobel Prize.

Poets too followed the path of postwar malaise (as with Sylvia Plath's *The Bell Jar*); and reached from John Berryman to Elizabeth Bishop—her complete poems were published in 1984 (five years after her death at 68).

And dance enjoyed a burgeoning popularity, with Russian immigrants and refugees, such as André Eglevsky, Rudolph Nureyev, and Mikhail Baryshnikov, but also American originals, from Martha Graham and Doris Humphreys to Twyla Tharp, all known for choreography as well as dance, and Arthur Mitchell, who founded the Dance Theatre of Harlem.

Postwar Music

Music fared as well, stepping not only into the mainstream but also, in the late 1980s, beginning a marvelous rapprochement of left and right, radical and conservative, American and foreign. In the post-war years, concert music was divided into camps and "isms," each with something to offer, but largely not speaking to each other. *Radical serialism, pandiatonicism, primitivism, musical pointillism, universalism, chance music*—each had its proponents and each had its day. Concerts were more and more dominated by university composers, particularly in chamber-music recitals. Those groups which had represented the Big Three mediums of European romanticism—the orchestra, the piano, and grand opera at the "big" houses on the East and West Coasts (where American works were still not welcome)—remained steadfastly with European romantic music. The foreign training of composers remained strong after World War II but gradually gave way to an American leadership, so that by 1985, foreign students were coming to the United States to study at universities across the land, and the country began to expand its base into a stunning lineup of small music centers, rather than two or three large ones.

Ross Lee Finney

Ross Lee Finney (born in Minnesota in 1906) was brought up in the shadow of university life (his father was a Professor of Sociology at the University of Minnesota), but was trained in the apprenticeship system. He received a BA degree from the University of Minnesota in 1927, and later studied in Paris, Vienna, as well as in Italy, receiving Guggenheim and Pulitzer traveling fellowships. During World War II, he served in the European Theater with the Office of Strategic Services, earning both the Purple Heart and the Certificate of Merit.

Ross Lee Finney. (Drawing by David Zuckerman.)

▶◯ Recommended Recordings and Video Cassettes

Ross Lee Finney's apprenticeship background has contributed to a paucity of recordings. Only one is listed in the Spring 1993 Schwann Catalogue, but college libraries may have others.

CRI CD-560. Piano music of Ross Lee Finney played by Martha Braden. Includes work spanning a half-century, form the *Piano Sonata #3 in E* (1942) and the *Sonata quasi una Fantasia* (1961) to *Narrative in Retrospect* (1984). This time span creates an opportunity to see how Finney's music has changed over time.

CRI 447. Finney's *Piano Trio No. 2*, along with William Bolcom's *Piano Quartet*. (LP).

CRI 116. Finney's *String Quartet No. 6* (1950), an exciting work. (LP).

Finney's *Variations of a Memory* is included in Edith Borroff, Anthology of Musical Examples (accompanying) *Music in Europe and the United States: A History* (New York: Ardsley House, 1990).

Finney taught at Smith College and later became Composer in Residence and Professor of Composition at the University of Michigan, where he virtually defined what university composition programs should be and established adjunct performance forums so that young composers could hear their own works—and also those of their fellow students.

As a composer, his output has been tremendous, ranging through vocal and instrumental forms and through a wide scope of styles. Among his works are eight string quartets; a baker's dozen of orchestral works, including four symphonies; seven concertos, including works for piano, violin, and alto saxophone; fourteen large choral works, including the trilogy *Earthrise*, *The Martyr's Elegy*, and *Still Are New Worlds*. His influence, both from his own work and through his students, has been incalculable.

Elliott Carter

Elliott Carter (born in New York in 1908) was also trained as a child; he went to Harvard as a literature student, and entered into study with Piston only in 1930. He went to Paris, taught mathematics, physics, and Greek; and then turned more completely to music, at the Peabody Conservatory, Columbia University, and, finally, Yale University. He received Guggenheim Awards in 1945 and 1950, spent 1963 in Rome, and then went to West Berlin in 1964. He won two Pulitzer Prizes, for his second and third String Quartets, in 1960 and 1973, and in 1985, he was awarded the National Medal of the Arts by President Reagan. His works are intellectually stimulating and cover a wide swath of media: early works include a Flute Sonata (1934); the *ballet Pocahontas* (1939); the

Elliot Carter. (Drawing by David Zuckerman.)

Symphony #1 (1944); later works include a Sonata for Flute, Oboe, Cello, and Harpsichord (1953); a Double Concerto for Harpsichord and Piano (1961—Stravinsky called it the "first true American masterpiece"); a Concerto for Orchestra (1970); a cantata, *Syringa* (1978); *A Celebration of Some 100 X 150 Notes* for orchestra (1987); and a Violin Concerto (1990).

ballet: an intricate dance form, presented by professionals, employing formalized steps and gestures to create expression through movement

Recommended Recordings and Video Cassettes

Elliott Carter is Finney's contemporary; he can be treated separately or in comparison.

CRI CD-610. Elliott Carter, *Syringa*, for Mezzo-Soprano, Bass-Baritone & Chamber Ensemble (1978). Includes also the *Suite from Pocahontas* (1939).

Elektra/Nonesuch 79248-2-ZK. Elliott Carter, *Sonata for Piano* (1946, revised 1982).

New World NW-347-2. Elliott Carter, *Concert for Piano and Orchestra* (1965).

▶️ Recommended Recordings and Video Cassettes

Milton Babbitt's music is best presented by itself, unique in its ambience.

New World NW-346-2. *The Head of the Bed*, for soprano, flute, clarinet, violin, and cello (1981).

CRI CD-421. *Groupwise* (chamber concerto) for flutes, piccolo, string trio, and piano (1983).

Music & Arts CD 606. String quartets by Babbitt (1970s?) and Mel Powell (1982).

Milton Babbitt

radical serialism: the serialization of rhythmic, dynamic, and instrumental, in addition to pitch elements; also called *total serialism*

combinatoriality: the theory of having not only twelve tones used serially, but also twelve dynamic levels, twelve time intervals, and twelve instrumental timbres

Milton Babbitt (born in Philadelphia in 1916) has been both a mathematician and a composer; he studied at New York and Princeton Universities, taught mathematics at Princeton from 1942 to 1945, then began to concentrate on music. He became interested both in synthesized music and in *radical* (or *total*) *serialism*: in connection with the former he introduced (along with Manchurian-born Vladimir Ussachevsky and Milwaukee-born Otto Luening) the Columbia-Princeton Electronic Studio; in connection with the latter he introduced *combinatoriality*, the theory of having not only twelve tones used serially but also twelve dynamic levels, twelve time intervals, and twelve instrumental timbres. He attempted to control music absolutely, whether it be synthesized or not; and was known for mathematical/musical pronouncements. Nicolas Slonimsky wrote of him that

> Babbitt's scientific-sounding theories have profoundly influenced the musical thinking of young American composers; a considerable literature, both intelligible and unintelligible, arose in special publications to penetrate and, if at all possible, to illuminate Babbitt's mind-boggling speculations.[4]

George Crumb

George Crumb (born in West Virginia in 1929) was one of the first modern composers to begin to explore the middle ground between theory and performance. Carter and Babbitt felt that audiences were beside the point; Crumb, like the apprenticeship composers of the preceding generations, felt that audiences were very much part of the musical act of communication. In fact, his father was a musician in the apprenticeship tradition, and, brought up in a musical household, Crumb was destined for the career of a musician, and particularly of a composer, from the beginning. He attended Mason College in Charleston, West Virginia, and the Charleston Symphony played a work of his when he was eighteen. He went to the University of Illinois for the Master of Music degree and to the University of Michigan, with a year of study in Berlin, earning the Doctor of Musical Arts in 1959. He taught five years at the University of Colorado, and then, from 1964 (after a year in Buffalo), accepted a professorship at the University of Pennsylvania, making his home in Philadelphia from that time.

Because Crumb sought to reach audiences, his work, for all that it was esoteric and experimental, was well received; his string quartet *Black Angels* (1970) was premiered in Ann Arbor by the University of Michigan's Stanley Quartet, and was praised in a review I wrote as a work of "authentic beauty and power." In that same year, his greatest success occurred; this was the vocal work *Ancient Voices of Children*, for soprano and chamber ensemble, to texts by Federico Garcia Lorca. It was premiered at the Library of Congress, called "powerful and moving" by one critic,[5] and soon after that, given performances in Philadelphia and Paris. It also won the UNESCO International Rostrum of Composers Award in 1971, along with a Koussevitzky International Recording Award for the Nonesuch LP (of 1970), in a stunning performance by Jan DeGaetani, which is still available. Crumb is not prolific, but he has created steadily, chiefly works for chamber groups (with and without voice), piano (*acoustic* and *amplified*), and orchestra (*Echoes of Time and the River: Four Processionals for Orchestra* won a Pulitzer Prize in 1967). He also produced *An Idyll for the Misbegotten*, for amplified flute and three percussionists, which premiered in Toronto in 1986; and *Zeitgeist*, for two amplified pianos, which premiered in Duisberg, Germany, in 1988. Perhaps his biggest work is *Star-Child: A Parable for Soprano, Antiphonal Children's Voices, Male Speaking Choir with Handbells, and Large Orchestra* (texts freely adapted from medieval sources), which premiered at Carnegie Hall in New York in 1977. Crumb uses exotic and folk instruments and materials.

acoustic: deriving sound from an instrument alone, without amplification

celesta: a keyed glockenspiel used in orchestras

◗○ Recommended Recordings and Video Cassettes

George Crumb's music is also best presented by itself.

Elektra/Nonesuch 79149-2. *Ancient Voices of Children* (the DeGaetani performance of the 1970 LP). Together with *Music For A Summer Evening (Makrosmos III)*, for two amplified violins and percussion (1974).

CRI ACS-6008 (cassette). *Black Angels*, for string quartet and electronic sounds (1970). Together with *Eleven Echoes of Autumn* (1966—a chamber work) and *Night Music I* for soprano, celesta, piano and percussion. An excellent trio.

New World NW-357-2. *Vox Balaenae ("Voice of the Whale")* for electric flute, electric cello, and electric piano (1971); *An Idyll for The Misbegotten* for amplified piano and three percussionists (1985); and *Madrigals* for soprano and instrumental ensemble (1965–1969).

Ellen Taafe Zwilich. (Drawing by David Zuckerman.)

Ellen Taaffe Zwilich

Ellen Taaffe Zwilich (born in Miami, Florida, in 1939) studied at Florida State University (BMus, 1956; MM, 1962), then in New York City. At the Juilliard School of Music she studied with Elliott Carter. She became the first woman to earn the DMA in composition, in 1975. Her works include two symphonies, the first of which won a Pulitzer Prize in 1983; *Trumpeten* (Trumpets) for soprano and piano (1974); *Emlekezet*, also for soprano and piano (1978); *Chamber Concerto for Trumpet and 5 Players* (1984); *Images* for two pianos (1987); and *Clarinet Quintet* (1990). Nicolas Slonimsky wrote of her that "there are not many composers in the modern world who possess the lucky combination of writing music of substance and at the same time exercising an immediate appeal to mixed

▶ Recommended Recordings and Video Cassettes

> *Recording of women's music is still on the slow side, but Ellen Taafe Zwilich's Pulitzer prize has assured her place.*
>
> New World NW-372-2. A representative grouping of works by Zwilich: *Concerto for Trumpet and Five Players, Concerto Grosso* (1985), and *Symbolon* (1988) for orchestra.

audiences."[6] She manages to support herself as a composer, without teaching.

Tania Leon

Tania Leon (born in Havana, Cuba, in 1943) came to the United States on the last "freedom flight" in 1967, having earned both the BA and MA in her native city. She attended New York University and earned an MS in 1973. Within a year of her arrival in New York, she became the rehearsal pianist for the Dance Theatre of Harlem, then its music director until 1980, when she decided to try to "make it on her own." She has become well known as a conductor, both in the United States and abroad, has conducted on Broadway (*The Wiz*, which opened in 1978), and, from 1985, was a resident composer at the Lincoln Center Institute. Her works concentrate upon the orchestral, the choral, and the solo vocal, and they include *Kabiosile* for piano and orchestra (1988), which combines Afro-Cuban, Hispanic, and Latin jazz elements within the traditional European concept of the concerto; the ballet *Dougla*, featured in the tour of Russia by the Dance Theatre of Harlem in 1988; and *Journey* for soprano, flute, and harp. In September 1992, the Dance Theatre of Harlem toured South Africa, and Leon went with them, conducting her own ballet, which was featured on the tour.

Avant-Garde Thinking

John Cage had said, "my purpose is to eliminate purpose."[7] This view summed up the avant-garde musical thinking of the 1950s and 1960s. But after 1970, composers were striving again for coherence, for beauty, and for communication. By the end of the 1980s, audiences were again being taken into consideration, and more and more new music became

▶ Recommended Recordings and Video Cassettes

> Avant 02. Works for guitar, including Tania Leon's *Ajiaco*, for guitar and piano.

New Music: a name for the modernism of post-World War II composers who aimed at a new ideal

positive, defined by what was put into it rather than by what was left out. Negativism in the arts is generally short-lived; it is a practical maneuver, like erasing the blackboard, after a long and powerful musical *modus vivendi* (such as romanticism) has captured creators and listeners alike in such a strong grip that it is difficult to break away. In fact, the composers who led the way toward a projection of a new musical ideal called themselves the proponents of the *New Music*.

THE NEW MUSIC

The New Music began when protest, political and musical, was the name of the game. The protest in music was basically against the theories and processes of romanticism. Romanticism had begun as a fresh, exciting, marvelous art, but was now tired beyond redemption—and romanticism, though evidenced in all of the arts, was primarily a musical movement. When musicians initiate a new principle of expression, works are short and to the point; but as the principle takes hold they become longer. And when the principle becomes old and tired, works become longer still! Symphonies, for example, had begun in the eighteenth century as ten-minute works, but by the beginning of the twentieth century an hour and ten minutes was not long enough. But experimentation is not likely to take place in a musical medium such as the orchestra, which involves so many players and so large a financial outlay; experimentation is much more likely to occur in chamber groups, which maintain just a few players and often hold performances in a small place (not always even in a concert hall, but in a lecture hall or living room).

After a period of negativism, a period of positivism ensues; first, however, there must be an interim of experimentation, a working with various ingredients to see what will succeed and what will not.

Music of Other Cultures and of the Past

Music of other cultures was a prime source, particularly after the war, when so many men and women in the armed services had heard music from far-off places. Pitch systems, instruments, and techniques of composition all provided potential materials. Characteristically, proponents of the New Music were interested in exact techniques rather than in general impressions, in accurately assessed materials used objectively rather than in exotic "flavor" or "color" used subjectively. More important, the esthetic of music was opened to the philosophies of other cultures. The idea of the essential superiority of Western Europe was dismissed as part of the romantic harness and was replaced by interest

A banquet scene from a fifteenth-century manuscript, *Le Miroir de l'Humaine Salvation* (Mirror of Human Salvation). (Newberry Library.)

in a wide scope of music and by genuine musical potential rather than by theoretical ideals.

Music of the past was reassessed in the same way, for the music of hundreds of years ago, even in our own European tradition, is for us today the music of another culture. In medieval days, for example, the use of physical space was a vital element of music, with groups spread to right and left of the audience, in front and behind, in stereo and quadraphonic effects, in huge castle halls and cathedrals, or in market squares. Taking space into the art of composition gave music a pithiness and spatial focus vital even in the shaping of musical form. In Renaissance days, small groups sitting as closely as possible and playing or singing as one, brought a delicacy and single focus to music. And then the baroque returned to a medieval concept of space.

The Cathedral of Notre Dame, Coutances, France. The Gothic style, with its upward thrust and high windows, furnished an early fulfillment of spatial elements in music. (Martin Hurlimann.)

Popular Music of the Past

madrigal: a popular part song

Popular music was reconsidered as well. Many a high school auditorium resonated with *madrigals*, which were regarded as popular music centuries ago; folk song and jazz were acknowledged as strong creative arts in their own right, different rather than inferior. Many colleges began offering courses in jazz. In addition, the ideal of making music for other people (not just for other musicians) gained a new respect. And cross-fertilization entered the picture: music and ideas, music and the other arts, music and the new humanism were paired in fruitful combinations.

Composition Techniques

The new techniques of music composition were beginning to bear fruit by the end of the 1960s. A performance of Finney's *Still Are New Worlds* was reviewed in 1966:

> A complex work based on texts that range from Kepler and Donne to Akenside and Camus, it concerns man and space, finite and infinite, the circle and the stretching to break out of the circle. It is an idiomatic work, not in the old sense of producing sounds comfortable for the instruments and voices, but by drawing from them new sounds which are so right that they do not so much surprise us as educate us to an increased sense of what they are meant to do.[8]

Concepts of Time, Space, and Sound

Perhaps music made the most riveting change from the old system in concepts of time. The old had been metrical, and the modern European tradition mixed meters with such abandon that no meter could be perceived by the listener. Composers of the New Music were concerned with the flow of time rather than with its regulation. The designation of time factors was increasingly drawn from theatrical concepts, where timing is vital but meter is irrelevant. The idea that time should be divided into measures was reversed: time should be defined by the events that create it. Rhythms of speech, motion, and natural and mechanical noises were examined. Proportional structures, exotic rhythms (particularly from India and Africa), and random rhythm (statistically random or indeterminate) were all considered viable. Regular pulse and meter were not excluded; they were now a matter of choice, and could, in fact, achieve a powerful effect by contrast.

Composers worked with *life rhythms*: a woman might be sweeping in regular two-fold strokes, a man might walk by in a separate steady pulse, a dog might rush in a sudden irregular trajectory to the window and bark at the man in a series of related, but unmeasured, accents, and the woman might talk (in speech rhythms) to a child playing in random rhythms in the yard. Such patterns, each with its own integrity, were synchronized rather than regulated. This brought to life concepts of *clock time* and *synchrony*, which specified beginnings (unanimous, staggered, or canonic), durations, and endings.

Basic to the New Music was a new idea of sound itself, particularly its tone color. If elements were to be heard as independent, they must also be heard as distinct qualities. Sound sources in the New Music were various, from traditional instruments used in both traditional and radical techniques, new and exotic instruments, and everyday sounds recorded and then manipulated through tapes. Some composers thought that instruments were no longer of significance, others elicited new sounds

maracas: a gourd rattle

tam-tams: small gongs

musical saw: a carpenter's saw played with a bow

damper pedal: the piano pedal that sustains sound

from them, and some went back to earlier concepts and reactivated them in new ways.

Musical space was redefined. In traditional theory, music was concerned with *high* and *low* sounds, pitting high soprano voices against tenors and basses, for example. But the new techniques are concerned with planes or layers, conceived as *foreground, background,* and *middle ground.* The new concept is one of distance, of depth. The composer conceives of shifting planes of sound and uses independence of dynamic strength, tone color, and rhythm to project them. Feedback echo recedes or approaches in space in an aural counterpart to visual perception of size. Principal elements are given to more vivid tone colors and assume the foreground; secondary elements are couched in duller, less provocative sounds. And layers of sound maintain integrity by moving at independent rates and in independent designs; they can be diaphanous or opaque, dense or clear.

In addition, the placement of elements in space underlines these elements. Differentiation is italicized by distance and by direction of the source of sound in performance. The placement of performers becomes important; percussion units are divided and space between players increased as the desire for unanimity is replaced by the desire for individuality. Scores often include stage charts, specifying the placement of the performers. Electronic compositions are also centered in the placement of sound sources: specification of the number of speakers and their deployment in the hall becomes significant as well. The separation of participating elements creates a strong interaction.

A New Consolidation

After a chance-ridden, wildly free stance had been defined in the 1960s, an inevitable tightening followed, a period of self-examination, and a consolidation; then in the 1980s, another expansion purposefully incorporated a wide vocabulary of effects, while tightening forms. In 1970, George Crumb exemplified this purposeful expansion in two works: *Black Angels: Thirteen Images from the Dark Land* (for electrified string quartet) and *Ancient Voices of Children* (for soprano, boy soprano, oboe, mandolin, harp, electric piano, and three percussionists—with twenty-eight instruments to be managed by the three). The sounds of these works were astonishing: the string players in *Black Angels* not only used electrified instruments, but bowed at the top of the finger board and across glasses of water, played *maracas* and *tam-tams,* and called out numbers (from one to thirteen) in seven languages. *Ancient Voices of Children* called for *musical saw,* the mandolin to be played in "bottle-neck" style, sleigh bells, and Tibetan prayer stones (among other unusual items); the soprano was directed to whisper into a speaking tube and to sing into the piano with the *damper pedal* down, the boy soprano to sing from off-stage. Crumb juxtaposed American folk idioms and ethnic *esoterica*, down-home techniques, and ethereal effects. And he sought aural beauty, which had been neglected in the music of his predecessors.

sitar: a long-necked lute from northern India

OPERA

American opera had been, from the beginning, a marvelous body of work. After World War II, it became a primary focus of the composers developing new styles, and production really took off. Growth was rapid, and by the end of the 1980s, 1285 opera companies were functioning in the United States.[9] The change in a little over a generation was astonishing, not only in the number of companies but in the number of American works produced. In the 1954–55 season, 210 operas were produced in the United States, all of them European; in the 1988–89 season, 731 operas were produced, 331 of them European and 400, American.[10] A few works previously produced as Broadway shows were moving into opera houses; perhaps the chief of these was Kern's *Show Boat* (1927), which was produced in 1989 by the Houston Grand Opera, the Portland Opera, Opera Pacific, the Minnesota Opera, and the Cleveland Opera. And Gerswin's *Porgy and Bess* (1935) was also getting performed in the full grand-opera style that the composer had specified and which had been denied him in his lifetime. In 1993, the work was produced and filmed in London, then telecast in the United States.

But most of the productions were of new operas. Such works as *The Celebrated Jumping Frog* (1950) by Lukas Foss and *Summer and Smoke* (1976) by Lee Hoiby were in the tradition of the American subject, which had been popular between the wars. In the 1960s, the multimedia concept found its way into opera, along with theories of the New Music. The new theory was strongly related to temporal definitions from India, studied by American musicians (as indeed by the rock group The Beatles) in the work of *sitar* player Ravi Shankar. But many composers also continued the traditions already strong in American opera.

Robert Ward

Robert Ward (born in Cleveland in 1917) studied at Eastman and Juilliard, taught at Juilliard, worked as an executive of the publishing firm Galaxy Music Corporation from 1956 to 1967, served as president of the North Carolina School of the Arts at Winston-Salem from 1967 to 1974, and taught at Duke University from 1979. His operas span almost forty years, from 1955 to 1994, and include *The Crucible* (1960), one of the most successful of operas by American composers. It was produced by the New York Opera in 1961, with performances on tour; and it won both the New York Critics Circle award and the Pulitzer Prize. It has recently been added to the repertoire of both the Pennsylvania Opera

Carlisle Floyd. (Drawing by David Zuckerman.)

Theater (1988) and the Des Moines Opera (1989). In 1993, Ward's opera *Roman Fever*, on a story by Edith Wharton, was performed in Durham, North Carolina. It confirmed the composer's sensitive lyrical gift and subtle skill in the delineation of character.

Carlisle Floyd

Carlisle Floyd (born in South Carolina in 1926) has composed eleven operas, mostly on American subjects. He drew attention with his early production of *Susannah*, which he called a "music drama," produced over the years in Tallahassee, Florida (1955), at the New York City Opera (1956), at the Metropolitan Opera (1965), and in Tulsa, Cincinnati, and Chautauqua, New York (all in 1989). More recent works were *Of Mice and Men* (1969), *Flower and Hawk* (a *monodrama*—that is, an opera sung by one person, in this case, Eleanor of Aquitaine, 1972), *Bilby's Doll* (1976),

T. J. Anderson.

◗◯ Recommended Recordings and Video Cassettes

Few American operas have been recorded, though some, such as Carlisle Floyd's Susannah *may be in college collections.*

Albany Records TROY 025/26-2. Robert Ward, *The Crucible*, opera in four acts (1961). Ward has a considerable list of recordings, including four of his eight symphonies.

and *Willie Stark* (1981, revised in 1992). Floyd taught at Florida State University and at the University of Houston; many of his works have been produced by companies in Tallahassee and Houston.

T. J. Anderson

T. J. Anderson (born in Pennsylvania in 1928) has taught at several universities, most recently at Tufts, from 1972 to 1991; he was previously Composer in Residence with the Atlanta Symphony Orchestra from 1968 to 1971. He orchestrated Joplin's opera *Treemonisha* in 1972. Anderson's operas include *The Shell Fairy* (1977), *Soldier Boy, Soldier* (1982), and *Walker* (about abolitionist David Walker, 1993), to a libretto by Nobel Prize winner Derek Walcott. His multimedia opera, *Thomas Jefferson's Orbiting Minstrels and Contraband* (1984, produced at Northern Illinois University in 1986),[11] contains an array of musical types from jazz to electronic music.

The multi-media work *Thomas Jefferson's Orbiting Minstrels and Contraband*, by T. J. Anderson, as presented by the College of Visual and Performing Arts of Northern Illinois University, DeKalb, in 1986. The work combines dance, visuals, speech, and music (string quartet, woodwind quartet, jazz sextet, and keyboard synthesizer, as well as singers.) (Northern Illinois University, Photgraphic Services.)

Terry Riley

minimalism: a kind of
music using very few basic
elements

Terry Riley (born in California in 1935), after earning an MA in composition at the University of California at Berkeley (1961), began working with dancers, in 1964, producing a work he called *In C*, based on shifting iterations and interacting patterns. He went to India to study, and his later works defined extremes of simplicity and complexity that were tightly controlled but which sounded very much like chance music. Since the music was spun out from basic elements used sparingly, he called his new technique *minimalism*.

Philip Glass

Philip Glass (born in Baltimore in 1937) continued the development of minimalism, with fifteen operas from 1976 to 1993. He studied at Peabody (he was a flutist) and the University of Chicago, 1951–56; then at Juilliard, earning an MS in 1962. He studied with Ravi Shankar, and visited Morocco as well, infusing that nation's music into his style. His operas were probably the most widely performed American operas of the 1980s. *Einstein on the Beach*, a five-hour work of 1976, made him famous through performances in Avignon, Venice, Belgrade, Brussels, Paris, Hamburg, Rotterdam, Amsterdam, and, finally, New York (all in 1976); *Satyagraha*, to a libretto in Sanskrit, followed, with performances in Rotterdam (1980), New York (1981), Chicago (1988), Seattle (1989), and

Philip Glass. (Photofest.)

San Francisco (1990). The trilogy was completed with *Akhnaten*, performed in Stuttgart, at the Guggenheim Museum in New York, and in Houston (all in 1984); the entire trilogy was produced in Stuttgart in 1990.

John Adams

At the end of the 1980s, a modified style was evidenced by such composers as John Adams (born in Massachusetts in 1947). Adams studied at Harvard after a childhood of private music lessons; he was a clarinetist who played with the Boston Symphony and the Boston Opera Company orchestras, and he conducted the Bach Society Orchestra of Boston as well. He taught at the San Francisco Conservatory from 1971 to 1981, and from 1982 to 1985, he was Composer in Residence of the San Francisco Symphony Orchestra. He won a Guggenheim Award in 1982. In 1987, his opera *Nixon in China* was produced in Houston, at the Brooklyn Academy, at the Kennedy Center, and at the Netherlands Opera. It was on television and it was recorded, receiving a great deal of attention. It was produced again in 1986 at the Guggenheim Museum in New York (excerpts only) and in San Francisco and Houston again (both in full) in 1987. His opera *The Death of Klinghoffer* (on the hijacking of the cruise ship *Achille Lauro* in 1985) was produced in Brussels and in Brooklyn in 1991. Thus, opera was becoming a salient part of the world of recent political events.

▶◯ Recommended Recordings and Video Cassettes

T. J. Anderson's operas are unrecorded, but a recording of his Intermezzi *for clarinet, saxophone, and piano (1983) is available in the following:*

New World NW 80423-2. **Videmus,** works by T. J. Anderson, David Baker, Donal Fox, and Olly Wilson.

Section I and part of Section VI of Anderson's opera Thomas Jefferson's Orbiting Minstrels and Contraband *is included in Borroff,* Compact Discs.

Terry Riley is more diversely represented.

Kuckuck 12047-2. *Songs for the Ten Voices of the Two Prophets* for voices and synthesizers (1982).

Philip Glass is the most often recorded of this group.

CBS 3 CDs-M3K-39672. *Satyagraha.* Opera in three acts, recorded by Glass's ensemble.

CBS 4 CDs-M4K-38875. *Einstein on the Beach.* Recorded by Glass's ensemble.

John Adams is also well represented on the record lists.

Elektra/Nonesuch 3 CDs 79177-2. *Nixon in China.*

Elektra/Nonesuch 79193-2. Excerpts from the preceding.

◗○ Recommended Recordings and Video Cassettes

| Borroff, Compact Discs contains Miriam Gideon's song cycle *Steeds of Darkness*.

Virgil Thomson

American opera was vital and various. In 1987, speaking of its production in Santa Fe in 1976, scholar Gilbert Chase called *The Mother of Us All* (1947) by Virgil Thomson (1896–1989) "the most American of all operas."[12] The libretto by Gertrude Stein was doubtless significant in that choice, but it is nonetheless revealing relative to both time and place: time, in pinpointing the beginning of the modern crescendo of interest in opera by Americans, which continues into the 1990s; and place, in making the point that this interest was kindled not in New York but in the American heartland.

Women Composers

The number of American operas since World War II is very great, and this art form has become of special importance in recent years. And of the over two thousand opera composers active in the United States from its founding to 1993, women are a significant percentage (about 13%). From Miriam Gideon's *Fortunato* (1958) to Dorothy Rudd Moore's *Frederick Douglass* (1985), women have provided a vital component of a thriving national art, equally the art of the theater and of music.

INTO THE NINETIES

American concert music moved with confidence and excitement into the 1990s. The old media were far from dead: the country was dotted with orchestras, string quartets, and bands (over thirty thousand by 1980); many churches still maintained pipe organs, but the surge of organ construction and new works was over. The piano remained popular, but the classical guitar and a variety of new chamber music combinations (frequently *ad hoc*) were gaining on it. Old instruments like the harpsichord, and old music like the American singing-school hymns, as well as later hymns such as "Amazing Grace," were increasingly popular.

But it was not only in juxtapositions of old and new that musicians felt a keen awareness at the end of the 1980s. A threefold mandate to musicians and their educators was clear: to acknowledge the many styles of music in our history (including the contemporary) as equally valid and equally interesting; to recognize the music of other cultures and of different musical realities within our own culture as worthy, not only of our minds, but also of our hearts; and to develop new teaching resources, methods, and attitudes that would prove yeasty in a new equality of respect toward all music.

The 1980s saw the coming of age of these views. African-American music was given long-merited attention; so was the music of women. Music of eighteenth- and nineteenth-century American composers was yet to be given its due; the scope of American music, from jazz and folk to concert music and opera, was yet to be viewed in all its splendor. But all of these entities were gaining strength. The radicals were beginning to value beauty again and to seek the enthusiasm of audiences; the works of conservatives, such as William Grant Still and Irwin Fischer, were newly valued and studied.

There was, it was discovered, not so much difference between radicals and conservatives as had been thought. Fischer's *String Quartet* (1972), for example, was a serial work, and like Crumb's *Black Angels* (1970), it was about death. Fischer's work was less "modern" perhaps in its pitch organization, yet in its statement about racial equality, it was more "modern" than *Black Angels*. Fischer's work was a statement for racial equality and tolerance, with the spiritual "Swing Low, Sweet Chariot" and the German chorale "Jesu, Joy of Man's Desiring," as set by J. S. Bach, used with equal respect and imagination in a layered technique of counterpoint with the serial elements. It became clear that the theoretical "modernity" of the Fischer quartet was not as important an issue as the fact that it said something new in a kind of music that had not been heard before. Originality, in other words, was once again becoming a matter not of musical theory but of musical idea.

And in world terms, the United States was in a position of musical leadership in the early 1990s. In a remarkable turnaround, a Festival of American Music, named in honor of Charles Ives, was held in Germany, with 109 events from September 1987 to July 1988, including 73 concerts featuring the music of over 60 American composers, of whom Ives, Aaron Copland, George Gershwin, and Samuel Barber were highlighted.

As Americans had gone abroad to study after the Second World War, Europeans and Asians are now coming to the United States to steep themselves in American music. What they find is a rich panoply of musical activities and types, an almost kaleidoscopic extravagance of venues and styles.

Yet within that extravagance and centrifugal abundance a growing consensus is being felt, the beginnings of a mutual tolerance and interchange that may well prefigure the unfolding of a new style of concert music, a new international consensus unfolding in America. One may not predict, but one may hope that a new style is indeed beginning to take shape; hope that the best of each type of music in this kaleidoscope will be honored, savored, and brought freely into the new style; and hope that the musically troubled twentieth century, coming out at last from the penumbra of romantic dominance, will yield to a musically resplendent twenty-first.

NOTES

1. Eric Forner and John A. Garraty, eds., *The Reader's Companion to American History* (Boston: Houghton-Mifflin Company, 1991), p. 855. The 1990 figure is preliminary.
2. Leo P. Ribuffo, *Ronald Reagan*, in Foner and Garraty, *American History*, p. 915.
3. Foner and Garraty, *American History*, p. 822.
4. Nicholas Slonimsky, *Baker's Biographical Dictionary of Musicians*, 8th ed. (New York: Schirmer Books, 1990).
5. Alan Rich in *New York* magazine; quoted by Donal Henahan in "Crumb, the Tone Poet," The *New York Times Magazine*, 11 May, 1975, p. 16.
6. Ibid.
7. David Hamilton, "A Synoptic View of the New Music," *High Fidelity*, September, 1968, p. 56.
8. Edith Borroff, *Ann Arbor News*, 3 November 1966, p. 39.
9. Edith Borroff, *American Operas: A Checklist* (Warren, MI: Harmonie Park Press, 1992), p. x.
10. Ibid.
11. *Thomas Jefferson's Orbiting Minstrels and Contraband* is included in Edith Borroff, *Compact Discs to Accompany Music in Europe and the United States: A History.*
12. Gilbert Chase, *America's Music*, rev. 3rd ed. (Urbana: University of Illinois Press, 1987), p. 551.

BIBLIOGRAPHY

Borroff, Edith. *American Operas: A Checklist*. Detroit Studies in Music Bibliography, no. 69. Warren, MI: Harmonie Park Press, 1992.

———. *Music in Europe and the United States: A History*, 2nd ed. New York: Ardsley House, Publishers, 1990.

———. *Three American Composers*. Lanham, MD: University Press of America, 1986.

Chase, Gilbert. *America's Music: From the Pilgrims to the Present*, rev. ed. Urbana: University of Illinois Press, 1992.

Forner, Eric, and John A. Garraty, eds. *The Reader's Companion to American History*. Boston: Houghton Mifflin Company, 1991.

Hamilton, David. "A Synoptic View of the New Music." *High Fidelity*, September, 1968.

Hitchcock, H. Wiley. *Music in the United States: A Historical Introduction*. Englewood Cliffs, NJ: Prentice-Hall, 1969.

Pendle, Karen, ed. *Women and Music: A History*. Bloomington: Indiana University Press, 1991.

Slonimsky, Nicolas. *Baker's Biographical Dictionary of Musicians*, 8th ed. New York: Schirmer Books, 1990.

11

Other Venues
(1961 to 1993)

oncert music was beginning to find itself as it entered the 1990s. Other venues entered the 1960s strongly, in some cases defined themselves strongly, and peaked in the '80s. It is a rule of thumb that nothing remains strong, but every art is pulled through contrasting phases of development, balancing its many vectors in the historical record, but generally out of balance at any one time. And of course, within each vector, a variety of styles and types vie for prominence. Thus, in the three decades from 1961 to 1992, the predominant venues were not those most prominent in the thirty preceding years; in fact, swing gave way to *rock*, radio gave way to television, and the Broadway score gave way to the movie score. National focus determines this to some extent; inventions (such as television) influence taste; and composers respond to inventions by tailoring music to suit demand.

DEVELOPMENTS IN JAZZ

The LP recording influenced jazz artists, injecting their art with a new power. The LP allowed its proponents to think in larger terms. *Free Jazz*, a 1960 album by Ornette Coleman (born 1930), had pointed to a breaking out of the three-minute imperative dictated by 78 RPM recordings. John Coltrane (1927–67) achieved a positive expansion that paralleled minimalist experiments: a four-piece suite called *A Love Supreme* (1964). His final album, *Expression*, assured that Coltrane's influence would not die with him.

Ellington, Armstrong, and Gillespie

Duke Ellington was honored with a seventieth birthday bash at the White House, April 30, 1969 (a day late!), and he was presented with a medal by President Nixon. In the late 1960s and early '70s (he died in 1974), Ellington continued to nudge the divisions between popular and concert music; he produced, at the end, concerts that used choirs and dancers along with the traditional small orchestra and solo vocalists. An archive of his work has been established at the Smithsonian Institution.

Louis Armstrong (1900–71) and Dizzy Gillespie (1917–93) continued to delight audiences throughout their lives; Gillespie went on to *bebop*, called "a revolution in two syllables."[1] Their styles were compared:

Duke Ellington and orchestra in *Cabin in the Sky*. (Photofest.)

Satch [Armstrong] played a sweet, raucous sound that kept its roots strong in the gumbo of hometown New Orleans. Dizzy knew how to nurse a tune too, but his armor-piercing solos tore those roots right up and replanted them farther north, in the new welter of urban angst. But his music, always intrepid, remained fleet. It was spontaneous reinvention in rhythm, a kind of fun that tweaked the far edges but never crossed them. . . . he initiated, almost singlehandedly, what's now called Afro-Cuban jazz, and as late as last year was still on the road, chops intact, wringing every note he could out of life.

He claimed he seldom listened to his records "because after you've played it, it's all gone anyway." When Dizzy laid it down, though, it changed tomorrow, and it will last forever.[2]

Wynton Marsalis. (Photofest.)

The Marsalis Brothers

The new generation of jazz specialists were just that. The Marsalis brothers, for example, have crossed the dividing line set up between jazz and concert music. Wynton Marsalis, a trumpet player, not only produces jazz albums such as *Citi Movement* (1993), likened to Ellington in its skill, style, and grace, but also teaches master classes at universities around the country. Branford Marsalis, a saxophonist, took his band into prominence in becoming music director of the *Tonight Show* in 1992. They exemplify the search within jazz for deeper meaning. Wynton says of his teaching:

> I always tell my students what my daddy told me: People who play for applause, that's all they hear. Music has a deeply spiritual component, and it doesn't reveal itself to you unless you prove that you really want to have that level of dialogue with it. Miss that opportunity, you have to pay some dues before it comes around again.[3]

Branford Marsalis. (Photofest.)

ROCK

But the important musical development after World War II was *rock 'n' roll*, soon known as *rock*. It had begun in the 1950s, an almost immediate American response to wartime pressures; the postwar generation was restive, with more energy than the culture would let them expend: the important element in rock was the expenditure of energy, along with the expression of the ideas of the postwar generation—ideas personal, cultural, and political.

rock 'n' roll: an early name for rock

Chuck Berry

The 1950s had seen two charismatic figures begin the musical statements and personal/political stance that would characterize rock. They were Chuck Berry (born 1926) and Elvis Presley (1935–77). Berry was a disad-

Chuck Berry. (Drawing by David Zuckerman.)

vantaged young black from St. Louis, who, by the time he "made it" with his first blues group (of three) in 1953 and his first hit, "Maybelline," in 1955, had already done time in reform school (for robbery) and worked on an assembly line (in an automobile factory) and as a cosmetologist. His works centered in teen-age views of life and rebellion against it, and they became immensely popular. His recording of his 1958 hit, "Johnny B. Goode," was part of the *Voyager I* package that was launched that year in hopes of encountering intelligent life in outer space.

Elvis Presley

But Presley became the byword of rock in its early stages. He was born in Tupelo, Mississippi, in 1935, but his family moved to Memphis in 1948, when he was thirteen. At nineteen he cut his first record, and only two years later astounded the world with "Heartbreak Hotel," "Don't Be Cruel," and "Hound Dog." Presley was a guitarist/singer who came up with a hybrid art, incorporating elements of *hillbilly, western, blues, gospel,* and *jazz;* it was driven by beat and was kinetic, loud, and metered in four, with heavy *triplets.* It was harmonically simple, as basic as the unadorned and uncompromising beat. It could be decorated, generally with idioms from the blues, and the form of the songs tended to be that of the blues as well. An important element of rock was a play of rhythmic forces: the accompaniment in fast triplets, the voice in a slower steady beat, and a visual beat that differed from both, delivered in a pelvic body-English that made the visual elements as important as the aural ones. The Presley music hit the nation in the right way at the right time; he sold fifty-five million records in his lifetime (and another eight million in the five days following his death).

hillbilly: a kind of country music

western: a popular song influenced by western folk music

triplet: three notes played in one beat

Elvis Presley. (Photofest.)

twist: a dance popular in the 1960s and '70s, featuring strong rhythmic turns and twists of the body

discothèque: a hall where greatly amplified recorded music is played for dancing

ensemble: a group performing together

Rock was accompanied by new dance types, as its visual beat would suggest. The first rock dance craze was the *twist* (1960), which was taken up by virtually all levels of nightclub and dancing social groups. The rhythmic layers of early rock paralleled African concepts, and so did the twist and its succeeding dance forms: they were single-position dances done individually with a repeated motion, rather than a series of contrasting steps. Thus, the effects of the music and the dance were cumulative, rather than organic.

Presley's phenomenal success (he has been called "the most revolutionary figure in the history of pop music"[4]) was probably more than any young man could manage; he served in the army from 1958 to 1960, centered his career in the movies, making thirty films from 1960 to 1968, returned to performance, but couldn't sustain his high standards, dying of a drug overdose at 42 (in 1977).

Discothèques

The dance craze led to a new type of dance hall, the *discothèque*, a flamboyantly decorated room, often lined with mirrors and enlivened by kaleidoscopic light shows made possible by new technology—as the surrounding of the dancers with sound by means of high-fidelity speakers (to which the light shows were parallel) had been made possible by new technology. Rock records were played in discothèques at high volume, and customers became intoxicated with sound, light, and cumulative musical and choreographic elements. Rock groups began to replace swing bands, and the combo of three or four became standard.

Early Rock Groups

Perhaps more important, the rock group became a very different *ensemble* from the bands and singing groups of the swing era. Those groups had been unified, known by a single name that sounds prim in retrospect: The Ames Brothers, The Lennon Sisters. The old groups had presented musical and spatial unity, and they had sung songs written by other people. Rock groups took names—like "Public Enemy," "The Clash," and "KISS"—that suggested (or even played with the words suggesting) musical or political or emotional elements; and they wrote their own songs. Probably the most important of these early groups was The Beatles, a British group (many rock groups have been British) from Liverpool, who made a sensation by their appearance in the United States, on the Ed Sullivan TV show in 1964. They incorporated the fully developed ideal of rock; a critic called them "innovating, experimenting, and consummating the musical concepts of pop. . . . Their appeal still lies in their vitality, the utter joy they communicate, their consistent, esthetic effervescence."[5]

▶ Recommended Recordings and Video Cassettes

Early rock is probably best served by the Elvis Presley records. Some of his movies are available on video cassette, and of these, the earlier the better. These films include Love Me Tender *(1956) and* Jailhouse Rock *(1957).* Blue Hawaii *was also good and serves to illustrate the Hawaiian musical tradition in certain ways But the essential artist is in his recordings, which been brought together:*

RCA 66050-2. *Elvis: The King of Rock and Roll.*

And others are, of course, excellent too.

Warner Brothers 2764. *The Grateful Dead: Skeletons from the Closet.*

Warner Brothers 3113. *James Taylor's Greatest Hits .*

Asylum 106. *Linda Ronstadt's Greatest Hits.*

Motown 5201. *The Jackson 5—Greatest Hits.*

Motown 937. *Motown's 20 #1 Hits from 25 Years.*

Beatlemania was powerful indeed, but by the 1970s, an amazing number of rock groups had sprung up in the United States: in 1968, there were about two thousand professional groups, and by 1970 an estimated three hundred thousand.[6] By the early '90s a university city such as Durham, North Carolina, with about 135,000 inhabitants, might sustain over one hundred groups.[7]

Beatlemania: a craze for the Beatles

new-wave jazz: a development in jazz of the late 1950s and '60s

country-and-western: country music of western (cowboy) type

soul: expressiveness in blues and jazz solos

Synthesis

The end of the 1960s was an important, culminating time; such separate genres as *rock, new-wave jazz, cool jazz, country-and-western, gospel,* and *soul,* kept apart by their separate social contexts, began to pull toward synthesis. The Memphis Birthday Blues Festival in 1969 included a variety of types whose tendency toward synthesis was epitomized by a group called The Insect Trust, which was billed as "the world's first country-jazz-folk-blues-rock-swing band."

Bob Dylan

Another strain of pop music was brought to the fore by the work of Woody Guthrie (1912–67), a folk singer and songwriter from Oklahoma who had sung in the 1930s of the Depression, of cowboys, of American patriotism, then later of the war and of personal tribulations and victories; from the early 1950s, he was incapacitated (by Huntington's disease) and was befriended by the young Bob Dylan (born in Minnesota in 1941), who visited him in the hospital and became his apprentice. Dylan became the quintessential folk-rock singer, a force in the civil

Woody Guthrie. (Photofest.)

rights movement of the early 1960s, of which his song "Blowin' in the Wind" became the unifying statement. After such highly effective songs as "Highway 61 Revisited" (1965), he was injured severely in a motorcycle accident (1966) and turned to more introspective songs. But in 1975 he issued an album, *Blood on the Tracks*, and in 1976 another, *Desire*,

Bob Dylan. (Photofest.)

Michael Jackson. (Photofest.)

which brought him back. Like Paul Simon (also born in 1941), Dylan entered the 1990s ready for new statements, hoping for a refreshed career. In 1992, a Bob Dylan Thirtieth Anniversary Concert was held in New York City's Madison Square Garden, featuring tributes from Stevie Wonder and Johnny Cash.

Michael Jackson

Perhaps Michael Jackson (born in 1958) sums up the rock movement at the end of the 1980s. He started as lead singer in a family group, The Jackson 5, at the age of nine, and broke away in the late 1970s to go on his own. His album *Thriller* (1982) sold over 21 million copies, and was followed by *Bad* and *Dangerous*, which launched him into the 1990s, along with an appearance in a TV interview with Oprah Winfrey, in early 1993, which was the fourth most-watched show in TV history (an estimated 36.5 million households). His performances are heavily theatrical, with lighting, costumes, and motion/dance portions carefully calibrated, and the lyrics geared to his own generation. His work is in the tradition of Elvis Presley, for whom motion on stage was a rhythmic layer of the musical work.

The 1990s

Motown: a popularized form of rhythm-and-blues originating in Detroit in the 1950s

rhythm-and-blues: a mid-twentieth-century popular music form that developed from blues and jazz

punk: a development in rock music in the mid 1970s that relied on sheer volume and rhythmic energy

After many varieties of rock (*Motown, rhythm-and-blues, punk,* etc.), the 1990s rock seems on the verge of another shift, to a more musically centered artistic integrity than the art has ever demonstrated. Social consciousness has changed from a litany of complaints to a prayer for strength and understanding in the healing of social ills. Music has always been part of the healing process of civilization, and by 1990, it had seemed ready to explore that role another time. In the mid-'90s, rock performers are reaching out to other venues, hoping to become less isolated, and were drawing closer to both concert and theater music.

For one thing, the rock album from the late 1980s might be a compact disc or a video as well as a cassette tape. Television, the medium of the 1980s, was making the visual elements of rock more and more important. From tapings of performance, videos developed quickly into dramatic commentaries on the songs, evocations of much more than the words and music could suggest. It is a testimony to modern technology that the video can reach so far beyond the auditory experience; the question, parallel to poet Marie Borroff's question about the computer as poet, is whether or not this is really music, whether or not we want it to be.

TELEVISION

Radio had had all too short a golden age. At first, it had been very much itself, becoming the entertainment of choice in the 1920s for the nation as a whole, then yielding place to movies when sound joined sight in "the talkies." It gradually became a venue for newscasters and, in response to the rock era, disc jockeys, then finally for the talk show.

The medium of choice that supplanted radio was television. It is impossible to date the maturity of this medium; for one thing, technical maturity is not programming maturity, and for another thing, we are still too close to it.

Theme Music

Music was used in television in several ways. First of all, every show, of whatever type, had theme music, that is, a brief, characteristic bit as short as a fanfare or as long as a song. Whether it was a news show, a soap opera, a dramatic series, or a variety show, every entity was introduced with its own music that remained a characterizing sound throughout the life of the show. Whether it was the series "Peter Gunn" (from 1958), whose theme music was composed by Henry Mancini, or "M*A*S*H" (from 1972), with music supervised by Lionel Newman and composed by a number of musicians, shows were given a specific personality by the music played for them. "Perry Mason" (from 1957) had theme music by Fred Steiner. That show can serve to illustrate the music for TV very well, for it played for several years (until 1965) and used a number of composers, such as William Grant Still, for the weekly background music. Still underlined action and dramatic tension with original material as well as variations on the theme music.

melodrama: a play or film consisting of action with spoken words, synchronized with music

Melodramas and Variety Shows

A dramatic television show, like a movie, is, in fact, a *melodrama*, a nineteenth-century theater form which used spoken words, but which had music synchronized with the dialogue and action; such a production was halfway to an opera. Sensitive, perceptive music made a tremendous difference; the music could make or break a television drama.

There were, in addition, variety shows. These were of several types. First there was the show that "starred" a master of ceremonies, like the Ed Sullivan and Garry Moore shows of the 1950s and '60s. This was, like vaudeville, based on the second half (the olio) of the minstrel show, and it featured a number of contrasting acts, generally in an hour format. Then stars themselves began hosting variety shows. The Bob Hope radio show had been typical of that venue in being like the first half of the minstrel show rather than the second, but as a television vehicle it became more and more like the second half of the minstrel show.

Liberace and Lawrence Welk

One musical star who had his own television show was the pianist Liberace (Wladziu Valentino Liberace, 1919–87). This was a musical show early in television's history; it played from 1951 to 1955 and again in 1958 and 1959, but was followed by tours and occasional broadcasts that kept Liberace in the public eye until his death. It featured the pianist (a very good one) as a flamboyant show-business personality, with a good deal of stage business antithetical to the concert ambiance, but it brought a great deal of music into a great many homes. The musical range of the star was considerable, from Broadway show tunes to concert music of composers such as Chopin and Rachmaninoff, often mixed together in a format that went from one style to the other in the course of an evening.

Another television musician was Lawrence Welk (1903–91), a North Dakota accordion player who formed his own band and became an important television figure very early, first in Los Angeles, from 1951, and then nationally syndicated, from 1955 to 1971, with reruns through the early '90s. Welk featured classical pieces, folk music (often danced) of many nations, including the United States, and liked to build a show around a theme (such as an annual Christmas show). Whereas Liberace's

Lawrence Welk. (Drawing by David Zuckerman.)

show was limited to one artist on one instrument, Welk featured many artists on many instruments, maintaining a company of instrumentalists, singers, and dancers.

Carol Burnett

"The Carol Burnett Show," a mainstay of the 1970s (with occasional revivals up to the '90s), developed from the "Garry Moore Show," on which Burnett had often been featured. Her show combined a troupe of regulars, who presented sketches from week to week, often in character parts, with guest artists, most often musicians. The sketches could be parodies (such as her spoof of *Gone with the Wind*); or a series (such as the family that eventually branched off with its own show); or a special, one-time event, perhaps with a guest star put to use in parody of the guest's usual persona, or displaying some special, but little-known, talent, or perhaps simply cast in a role ridiculously different from the star's usual material. In other words, the content of the show was tailored to the personality and the skills of both stars and guests, giving it the advantage (shared by the radio shows) of having some material the same from week to week, along with other material that changed from week to week as guest followed guest.

The shows could be remarkably inventive, not only in verbal content, but also musically. Sometimes a star would come on as a guest to do a bit from a Broadway show or movie—Robert Preston, in 1961, came on to do the *talk-song* from *The Music Man*, a Broadway musical that had just been made as a movie (Preston starred in both). But the shows could introduce new material as well, material that could not be provided in any other format. In 1978, for example, Burnett featured singer Eydie Gormé and sang with her in a wonderful modern *quodlibet*, a Renaissance form of popular music in which bits from many different numbers were put together, successively, but also at times one against the other simultaneously. The *quodlibet* that Burnett and Gormé mounted together could not have been done by either of them separately, and since they were two very different types of performers, it is doubtful that they ever would have appeared together in a movie or a Broadway production (Burnett also appeared with Julie Andrews). The *quodlibet* included snatches of "Goody-Goody," "Tangerine," "A-Tisket A-Tasket," "Don't Sit under the Apple Tree" (the last two combined), "I Had the Craziest Dream," "A Sunday Kind of Love," "I've Got It Bad and That Ain't Good," "Happiness Is Just a Thing Called Joe," "It's Been a Long, Long Time" (the last two combined), "Ol' Rocking Chair's Got Me," and ended with "And the Angels Sing"—a musical adventure of no mean proportions.

The End of Variety Shows

But as production costs mounted and taste veered to more down-to-earth sitcoms (such as "Cheers"), fewer variety shows were made, and by 1990, there were none left, except for occasional one-shot affairs. The place of the variety show was taken by the talk show, featuring such hosts as Phil Donahue, Larry King, and Oprah Winfrey.

Television occasionally produced an exciting large-scale drama, perhaps ten or twelve hours done as a miniseries, and music was an important part of these productions. The most famous, without doubt, was *Roots*, a dramatization of the Alex Haley novel, made in 1977 and the most successful production of its kind in television history. Quincy Jones (born in 1935) composed the score, which added immeasurably to the

talk song: a song recited by a performer to a musical accompaniment

quodlibet: a vocal piece made up of allusions to several well-known songs

success of the project. Jones had worked on the "Perry Mason" series, and had done the music for such movies as *Bob and Carol and Ted and Alice* (1970) and *Cactus Flower* (1971). He would also compose the highly lauded all-star black version of *The Wizard of Oz*, produced as the Broadway musical, *The Wiz*, in 1972. His use of African and nineteenth-century elements in the score for *Roots*, as well as his sensitivity to the shifting emotional demands of the story, brought stunning focus to the series.

TV movies, like miniseries, used musical scores; Mason Daring's score for *Stolen Babies* (1993) followed the visual effects, suggesting villainy and tension by rhythmic and isolated tonal effects, as the costuming and outré makeup of Mary Tyler Moore (along with her excellent acting), turned her into a formidable villain. The music was used sparingly, too, which highlighted dialogue with silence.

And finally, television became the medium for such groups as the Boston Pops, featuring Arthur Fiedler until his death in 1979, then giving the directorship to John Williams in 1980. The pops concert, with its background of the lovely park and such holiday visual extras as fireworks at the Fourth of July concert, made excellent TV fare.

And telecasts of orchestral evenings, recitals, operas, and other offerings of the concert tradition made a vital contribution to the cultural life of the country.

MUSICAL THEATER

Broadway contributed less and less to the music of the United States after the Second World War. For one thing, costs mounted precipitously in New York, making it prohibitive to take a chance on a new composer; this put a damper on New York's innovative production and encouraged the spreading out into the country that was already going on in operatic productions. Native composers had never had much of a chance in the big opera houses, such as the Metropolitan Opera in New York, which continued to feature nineteenth-century foreign works almost exclusively; so, the strong American operatic tradition had grown up outside of the big cities, in which European operas were the norm.

Operatic Traditions

But the operatic tradition was strong enough to influence the postwar generation of Broadway musicals. Movies first paved the way for operatic expansion, movies such as *Seven Brides for Seven Brothers* (music by Gene de Paul, 1954), which had pulled basic plot development through the film musically; movies such as *Gigi* (music by Frederick Loewe,

1957), which had characterized Paris, the life there at the turn of the century, and the people who lived there, through music.

While *A Chorus Line* (1975), with music by Marvin Hamlisch (born in 1945), followed the old tradition of the revue in the format of a musical, with a series of characters presenting themselves in a series of musical and dance numbers, other composers were leading the musical in operatic directions.

Stephen Sondheim

Chief of these was Stephen Sondheim (born in New York in 1930), who composed a school musical at fifteen (and enjoyed an apprenticeship with Oscar Hammerstein II), but went to Williams College and Princeton, where he studied with Babbitt (and was exposed to the university tradition). He began his Broadway career as the lyricist of *West Side Story*, with music by Leonard Bernstein, who had combined the concert and Broadway venues in his long career. Sondheim was soon composing his own scores to his own librettos and developing his own style. His first work as composer of a Broadway show was *A Funny Thing Happened on the Way to the Forum* (1962), and his style flowered quickly in a remarkable series of works: *Company* (1970), *Follies* (1971), and *A Little Night Music* (1972), for which he won three consecutive Tony Awards as Best Composer and Best Lyricist; in addition, all three shows won the New York Drama Critics' Circle Awards. *A Little Night Music* had already reached fairly far toward opera, and, secure in his art, Sondheim moved even further with *Pacific Overtures* (another New York Drama Critics' Circle Award, 1976) and *Sweeney Todd: The Demon Barber of Fleet Street* (1979). *Pacific Overtures* was ahead of its time; it dealt with the visit of Admiral Matthew Perry to Japan in 1853. The plot line made it easy to add the ethnic elements that were so vital in the concert tradition. Hal Prince (born in 1924), producer/director, was the originator of the work in its stage form (it had been brought to him as a play by its author, John Weidman). In an interview Prince spoke of his enthusiasm: "I thought what would it be like if we told this story from the point of view of a Japanese playwright using the Kabuki, Noh and Bunraki theatre techniques."[8] The work had a short life on Broadway, but it opened the 1987–88 season at the English National Opera.

Sondheim's *Sweeney Todd* was equally operatic, but because the subject was more accessible and the action more rambunctious, it proved more popular and led the public to an acceptance of the operatic. In fact, it was produced at the New York City Opera in 1986. Sondheim continued his operatic trend in later shows: *Sunday in the Park with George* (which won a Pulitzer Prize, 1982); *Into the Woods* (1987); and *Assassins* (1990), about people who have killed American presidents.

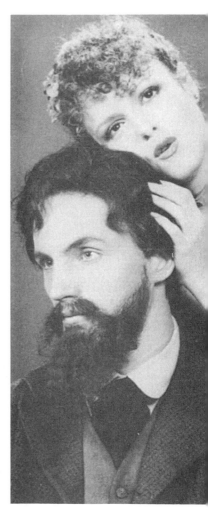

Stephen Sondheim's, *Sunday in the Park With George*, 1982, with Bernadette Peters and Robert Westenberg.
(Picture Collection, The Branch Libraries, The New York Public Library.)

The British Invasion

But Broadway had seen better days. In fact, American composers were drawn more and more into opera houses and less often into Broadway theaters. The British arrived on Broadway, and the most successful show at the end of the 1980s and beginning of the '90s was the British musical *The Phantom of the Opera*, by Andrew Lloyd Webber (born in London in 1949). This was a dark psychological work of spectacular staging. It was produced in London in 1986, in New York in 1988, and in Los Angeles in 1989. By 1991, six other versions of the play were on the boards, including *Drury Lane's Phantom of the Opera* with music adapted from Russian composer Peter Ilyitch Tchaikowsky's works.

Americans were after another kind of musical theater.

THE MOVIES

Through the 1960s and, to a lesser extent through the '70s, Americans were still finding a central unifying medium in the movies; this was being overtaken by television quite rapidly—one can speculate that the movies provided a temporary unifying medium between radio and television. Movies created a strange medium for a country: radio could follow events of national importance as they unfolded, once the technology of broadcasting had been developed and once the corporate networking was in place. Television could do the same, but had the same battles to win in the technical and business vectors.

For movies, the 1960s and early 1970s were a time of change from the era of the studio star system to the age of the independent filmmakers. In a way it was also a change from the moguls who viewed the making of films as a megabusiness to younger entrepreneurs who were more willing to see filmmaking as an art. The irony of this was that the old studio setup took for granted the necessity of grooming stars, of selecting promising young actors and actresses through screen testing, and then subjecting their choices to years of training. One critic lamented the passing of this system, which, he said, was the chief problem of moviemaking today and the reason that filmmakers "lack skill":

> The big studios of old no longer provide a training ground in which the apprentice can spend his first working years observing the masters.[9]

Films both reflected the national mood and gave form to national concerns. The double role was evinced in such movies as *It's a Mad Mad Mad Mad World* (1963), *Guess Who's Coming to Dinner* (1967), *Midnight Cowboy* (1969), *The Candidate* (1972), and *Grease* (1978), and continued into the 1980s on the more personal note struck by such films as *Kramer vs. Kramer* (an Academy Award winner for Best Picture, 1979), and *Sophie's*

Grease, 1978, with John Travolta. (Picture Collection, The Branch Libraries, The New York Public Library.)

Choice (1982). By then, the movies were expanding into separate artistic statements with an impressively wide range of scope both culturally and historically. The Best Picture Awards reveal this scope: *The Last Emperor* (1987), *Rainman* (1988), *Driving Miss Daisy* (1989), *Dances with Wolves* (1990), *Silence of the Lambs* (1991), and *The Unforgiven* (1992). These include a movie with an exotic setting (China at the end of the monarchy —with authentic music by Ryuichi Sakamoto), a film about an *idiot-savant*, one about a feisty southern lady and her chauffeur, one about Native Americans, one about a madman, and a new-age Western. None was a musical. The only movie that can be called a musical which won as best picture since 1970 was *Amadeus*, in 1984; this was a fictionalized story, based on the British play, about the Austrian composer Wolfgang Amadeus Mozart (1756–91) and a contemporary composer, the Italian, Antonio Salieri (1750-1825), portrayed as seeing Mozart as a rival and threat—it used music by Mozart, authentically performed in the eighteenth-century manner, but had no basis in his actual life story.

Walt Disney's *Mary Poppins*, 1964, with Julie Andrews in the title role. (Picture Collection, The Branch Libraries, The New York Public Library.)

Musicals

Movie musicals reached their zenith early in this period, beginning with *Mary Poppins* in 1964, followed by such films as *The Sound of Music* (1965), *Thoroughly Modern Millie* (1967), *Finian's Rainbow* (1968), *Funny Girl* (also 1968), *Fiddler on the Roof* (1971); and ending with movies such as *The Wiz* (1978), *Grease* (1978), and *Yentl* (1979). Several of these had been Broadway musicals. The last of these was already an artistic statement by a single person rather than a studio—Barbra Streisand not only starred in the picture but was co-writer, co-producer, and director.

The musical did not thrive in the 1980s, becoming so rare that it was a surprise when the animated Disney film *Beauty and the Beast* (1991) became a box-office hit, and its score, by Howard Ashman and Alan Menken, won an Academy Award.

FILM SCORES

Musically, however, musicals were not the most important products of the movie industry. From early post-World War II days, film scores had been in a position of leadership in modern music. Because film music

▶ Recommended Recordings and Video Cassettes

MGM/UA Home Video M^00041. *Forbidden Plant* (1956), score by Louis and Bebe Barron. The first electronic score by Americans.

was always tied to ideas and images (both verbal and visual), composers in that venue could experiment with particular freedom and have their music heard by the public with an understanding and enthusiasm that concert music, with its basic abstractness, could not muster. The first totally synthesized work in the United States, for example, was the score for the movie *Forbidden Planet*, in 1956, by Louis and Bebe Barron, though David Raksin had used synthesized elements in his score for *Laura* as early as 1944. The use of layering in music, though hardly new in 1976, was given depth and power by Leonard Rosenman in his score for *Sybil*. Rosenman's music was associated with stress and uneasiness; he had composed the scores for *East of Eden* and *Rebel without a Cause*, both in 1955 (and in 1975, he won the Academy Award for his score to *Barry Lyndon*); in *Sybil* he dealt with multiple personality and child abuse through the layering of elements at odds with each other, including

Barry Lyndon, 1975, with Marisa Berenson, film score by Leonard Rosenman. (Picture Collection, The Branch Libraries, The New York Public Library.)

standard popular material, children's songs, and classical music. The musical abrasions bespeak the psychological abrasions.

The period between 1960 and 1990 turned around the prewar practice of putting already-famous concert composers to work in the movies: now work in movies was allowed to educate and sharpen the skills of young composers. In other words, the movies began to provide the apprenticeship training to young musicians that it was denying to young actors and directors. And native-born composers replaced the European-born. The new style of movie composers included several composers of stature as film composers.

Alex North

Alex North (born in Pennsylvania in 1900) was trained early in the apprenticeship system, then went to Juilliard (but earned no degree there), went to Russia as a technician, studied in Moscow from 1933 to 1935, then returned to the United States, studied for two years (1936–38) with Copland, and then worked with psychiatrist Karl Menninger on the development of the psychodrama. He came to the movie industry late, writing two dozen scores for documentary films during the war. In 1951, he composed the score for *A Streetcar Named Desire*, and from that time was in great demand. His scores include *Spartacus* (1960—unusual in having an overture), *Cleopatra* (1963), *Who's Afraid of Virginia Woolf?* (1966), *Bite the Bullet* (1975), *The Dragonslayer* (1981), *Prizzi's Honor* (1985), and *Good Morning, Vietnam* (1988). In 1986 he was honored with a Lifetime Achievement Award by the American Academy of Motion Picture Arts and Sciences.

The Dragonslayer, 1981, with Peter MacNicol, film score by Alex North. (Picture Collection, The Branch Libraries, The New York Public Library.)

Elmer Bernstein

Elmer Bernstein (born in 1922) is responsible for many scores of very different types; *The Man with the Golden Arm* (1955) was a high-tension film in which Frank Sinatra played a junkie; the musical tension was built largely of jazz elements. *The World of Henry Orient* (1964) was, in contrast, a romp, the story of a concert pianist (played by Peter Sellers) pursued by two teenage-girl fans; the music is insouciantly rhythmic, using happy *hemiola* rhythms of a childlike energy and innocence. Bernstein also composed scores for *The Magnificent Seven* (1960) and *To Kill a Mockingbird* (1962), two very different types; he won his Academy Award for the movie musical *Thoroughly Modern Millie* (1967) and was nominated for another for *The Age of Innocence* (1993).

hemiola: three beats in the place of two

Henry Mancini

Henry Mancini (born in Cleveland in 1924) has been trained in both the apprenticeship and concert venues, with childhood musical study and

Henry Mancini. (Drawing by David Zuckerman.)

Days of Wine and Roses, starring Jack Lemmon and Lee Remick, film score by Henry Mancini. (Picture Collection, The Branch Libraries, The New York Public Library.)

then schooling, ending with graduate work at Juilliard in 1942; he continued his concert studies in Los Angeles. He worked as an arranger for swing bands, then in 1958 turned to television, for which he wrote the well known theme music for *Peter Gunn*. One of his first film scores brought him both Grammy and Academy Awards: *Breakfast at Tiffany's* (1961), which included the song "Moon River"; his 1982 score for *Victor/Victoria* brought him those two awards as well. And between them he composed scores for such films as *Days of Wine and Roses* (1962), *The Pink Panther* (1963), *Two for the Road* (1967), and *Once Is Not Enough* (1975).

Burt Bacharach

Burt Bacharach (born in 1929) has brought life to films of very different essences, such as *Lizzie* (1957), *What's New, Pussycat?* (1965), *Butch Cassidy and the Sundance Kid* (1969), for which he won Academy Awards for both song and score, and *Lost Horizon* (1973).

John Williams

John Williams (born in 1932) is still another composer with a two-track training: he had early apprenticeship work with his father, a film-orchestra musician, but the son studied at Juilliard. His movie career began in 1961 with the score for *The Secret Ways*, and he progressed to more ambitious films, such as *None but the Brave* (1965), *Valley of the Dolls* (1967), *The Poseidon Adventure* (1972), *The Towering Inferno* (1974), and *Jaws* (1975), for which he won an Academy Award. His broadly sweeping style then became associated with the space epic in a list of highly successful films, to which he contributed music that enhanced, even expanded their vision of other worlds: *Star Wars* (1977—Academy Award), *Close Encounters of the Third Kind* (1977), *The Empire Strikes Back* (1980), *Raiders of the Lost Ark* (1981), *E. T.* (1982), *Return of the Jedi* (1983), *Jurrasic Park* (1993), and *Schindler's List* (1993—Academy Award). Several suites were made from these scores for use by the Boston Pops Orchestra: Williams held that podium from 1980 to 1993.

***Raiders of the Lost Ark*, 1981, starring Harrison Ford, film score by John Williams.** (Picture Collection, The Branch Libraries, The New York Public Library.)

Dark Victory, **1939, starring Bette Davis and featuring Humphrey Bogart.** (Picture Collection, The Branch Liibraries, The New York Public Library.)

The Maturing of Film Scores

In the late 1980s, movie and television scores moved closer together, with many movies made for showing on television. The same high stand-ard applied to both. Filmmakers now hired music consultants as well as composers to be sure that authenticity would be maintained, histor-ically or culturally—sometimes both. In 1990, for example, musicologist Kate Van Winkle Keller was employed by 20th Century-Fox during the filming of *The Last of the Mohicans*, to supervise the historical and cul-tural accuracy of a scene in which a dance was held the night before Fort William Henry capitulated.[10]

Maturity in the writing of film scores was to be found in many films and by many composers, including a large contingent of younger people, men and (at last!) women, who characterized, supported, and italicized the action and the significance of the work. Silence was coming into its own as well. In the style of the 1930s, the music was most often continuous, often in surging strings for optimum dramatic effect. It is said that when Bette Davis heard the score for *Dark Victory*, she demanded that the huge orchestral sound be moderated: "Who is going up that stairway?" she asked, "I or the composer?"

By the late 1980s, scores were fully able to have dramatic purpose in addition to providing aural accompaniment. John Williams added a sense of the heroic to the story of an English boy caught in Shanghai in World War II, *Empire of the Sun* (1988).

And scores could also reflect the thoughtful, introvert aspects to films, often using foreign elements with authenticity and respect. Spanish guitar juxtaposed with polite Strauss waltz music italicized a cultural standoff in David Mansfield's score for *Heaven's Gate* (1980); Irish folk music was used in poignant understatement by Alex North in his score for John Huston's last film, *The Dead* (1987), after a Dublin story by James Joyce. North trimmed down the musical matrix into which the tunes were projected, varied them, and produced a movingly spare score that managed to enter the drama.

A MIXTURE OF TRADITIONS

American music in the apprenticeship tradition moved with mixed emotions into the 1990s. Some, who felt that the music of the past was still the same and would remain so, entered the 1990s with aplomb; others who felt that the music of the past was no longer enough were working to expand its concepts and to formulate expressions of a new and exciting kind—they entered the 1990s with elation.

What seemed so exciting was that a mixture of traditions, long talked about, was in fact beginning to happen. Jazz and concert music, for example, had come together in mixes of performing groups, as in the opera *Thomas Jefferson's Orbiting Minstrels and Contraband* by T. J. Anderson; but the ensembles tended to alternate, rather than to combine. Jazz and rock musicians (performers and composers—often the same person) used idioms from the concert tradition and composers from the concert tradition used idioms from jazz and rock. Probably more significant is that some composers worked in more than one tradition, even combining apprenticeship and concert venues. William Grant Still saw himself as primarily a symphonic composer, but he also worked as an arranger for swing bands and as a composer of film and TV scores; Duke Ellington was the first jazz master to compose a movie score—to *Anatomy of a Murder* (1959); John Williams worked on the West Coast as

The Glenn Miller Story, **1953, starring Jimmy Stewart and June Allison.** (Picture Collection, The Branch Libraries, The New York Public Library.)

a film composer and on the East Coast as conductor of the Boston Symphony Orchestra Pops Concerts.

In 1955, a movie was made, *The Benny Goodman Story*, for which Goodman himself provided the sound track of his groups. Glenn Miller appeared in several films, but *The Glenn Miller Story* (1953) was made after his death. Jazz musicians, from Count Basie to Duke Ellington, were often featured in films. Gershwin, a generation earlier, had expanded his activities to enter both the popular- and concert-music venues, and Ellington did the same. Wynton Marsalis gives workshops that cover the gamut of trumpet music from seventeenth-century concertos to twentieth-century bebop.

Conlon Nancarrow

Conlon Nancarrow (born in Texas in 1912) played jazz trumpet and then studied at the Cincinnati College Conservatory of Music, a school in the concert tradition, from 1929 to 1932. In 1956, he became a citizen of Mexico. His music combines intense mathematical formulas with virtuoso materials of musical density and complexity. He was awarded a MacArthur Foundation Grant in 1982. His works include several Studies for Player Piano (some of which were published in *Soundings 4* magazine in 1977), and these transcend what a human player can attain. His third String Quartet was premiered in Cologne, Germany, in 1988; a critic said that the Arditti Quartet, who had played it, was "perhaps the only ensemble in the world capable of realizing Nancarrow's exceedingly complex score."[11]

sacred chant: music for worship

Leonard Bernstein

Leonard Bernstein (1918–90) was born in Massachusetts and attended Harvard University, studying with Walter Piston, and then the Curtis Institute of Music in Philadelphia. He became assistant conductor of the Boston Symphony Orchestra in 1942; his early orchestral works, such as the *Jeremiah Symphony* (1944) and *The Age of Anxiety* (1949) established his reputation as a composer, and his versatility kept him in the public eye as conductor, pianist, and lecturer. Having established himself in the concert tradition, he turned to Broadway, succeeding with *On the Town* (1944), *Wonderful Town* (1953), and *West Side Story* (1957). His *Mass* of 1971 combined *sacred chant* (Christian and Jewish), traditional music, jazz, and rock.

▶○ Recommended Recordings and Video Cassettes

The studies for Player Piano by Conlon Nancarrow are not available on recording.
Gramavision R 21S-79440. String Quartet #3 by Nancarrow.

The music of Leonard Bernstein is in part covered on other listings in other chapters.
Deutsche Grammophon 437328-2 GH. Bernstein's *Candide*. The final 1989 version complete with songs.

RCA Gold Seal (Papillon Collection) 6806-2-RG. Bernstein's ballet *Fancy Free* (1944), along with music by Richard Rodgers, Ferde Grofé, and Morton Gould.

CBS 2-M2K. Bernstein's *Mass* (1971).

Deutsche Grammophon 415965-2 GH. Bernstein's vocal music: *Songfest* (1977) and *Chichester Psalms* (1965).

The film version of Leonard Bernstein's *West Side Story*, **1961, with Natalie Wood and Richard Beymer.** (Picture Collection, The Branch Libraries, The New York Public Library.)

Dave Brubeck

octet: a group of eight performers

Dave Brubeck (born in California in 1920) was trained in the apprenticeship system (studying piano from the age of four and cello from the age of nine), was pianist in a jazz group at thirteen, but then studied in the concert tradition at the College of the Pacific, Fresno, in 1941 and 1942, with Darius Milhaud at Mills College, Oakland, and, after service in World War II, with Schönberg. He formed an *octet* in 1946, a trio in 1949, and a quartet in 1951, working with the quartet until 1967. Brubeck and John Lewis (also born in 1920) were vital in bringing the concert tradition into their work. Lewis's Modern Jazz Quartet used numerous forms and styles from the concert tradition, from Renaissance and baroque to traditional folk music.

Gunther Schuller

Gunther Schuller (born in New York City in 1925) was also trained in apprenticeship (his father was a symphony conductor), and he became a horn player, working in the Cincinnati Symphony and the Metropolitan Opera orchestras. In 1955, he composed a *Symphonic Tribute to Duke Ellington*; he also performed with the Modern Jazz Quartet. In 1959, he composed two works that juxtaposed the Modern Jazz Quartet with ensembles of the concert tradition: *Conversations*, using a traditional string quartet, and *Concertino*, using a symphony orchestra. He coined the term *third-stream* to describe music containing such interchanges. In 1970, his children's opera *The Fisherman and His Wife* (story by the brothers Grimm, libretto by John Updike) was produced in Boston. And in 1982, his sur-

modern jazz: bebop and its derivatives in the 1950s, including cool jazz

third-stream: music that combines jazz and concert music

Dave Brubeck. (Photofest.)

▶○ Recommended Recordings and Video Cassettes

See listings for Gunther Schuller in both concert music and ragtime.

GM Recordings 2009 CD. *Eine kleine Posaunenmusik, for Trombone and Wind Ensemble* (1980). This is paired with twentieth-century European music.

realist multimedia work, *Der gelbe Klang* (The Yellow Sound), on a libretto by artist Vassily Kandinsky and using piano sketches by Russian composer Thomas de Hartmann, was performed in New York. Schuller also composed ballet music, creating the score for the 1961 work *Variants*, choreographed by George Balanchine. He also served as president of the New England Conservatory.

Wendy Carlos

Wendy Carlos (born in Rhode Island in 1939 as Walter Carlos and becoming Wendy in 1979) worked both with synthesizers and with the combining of traditions. In the 1950s and '60s, Carlos brought out several albums of baroque music in synthesized versions; the first of these, *Switched-On Bach,* matched, in the synthesizer, an album by the Swingle Singers, who produced baroque music in scat singing. Carlos also produced the opera *Noah* in 1954 and *Timesteps* for synthesizer in 1970. In addition to straddling these traditions, Carlos composed the film scores for Stanley Kubrick's *A Clockwork Orange* (1971) and *The Shining* (1980).

As the United States entered the 1990s, the adventuring in diverse venues was approached with enthusiasm and imagination. The true combining of styles is yet to come, however, and will inevitably be a surprise, different from anything anyone has imagined.

▶○ Recommended Recordings and Video Cassettes

The Switched-On Bach of Wendy Carlos is still worth hearing; it is, in fact, Americanized Bach. Her own music is worth hearing too.

Telarc CD-80323. *Switched-On Bach.*

CBS: MK-42333. *Digital Moonscapes.*

Also, some other electronic transcriptions might be in order.

Newport Classic NC-60042. *Rhapsody in Electric Blue.* Works by Gershwin (including *An American in Paris*) in electronic sound.

A Clockwork Orange, **1971, starring Malcolm McDowell, film score by Wendy Carlos.** (Picture Collection, The Branch Libraries, The New York Public Library.)

NOTES

1. Jay Cocks, "Dizzy Gillespie," *Time*, 18 January 1993, p. 57.
2. Ibid.
3. Eric Levin, "Talking with Wynton Marsalis," *People*, 8 February 1993, p. 17.
4. Jon Wiener, "Elvis Presley," in Eric Forner and John A. Garraty, eds., *The Reader's Companion to American History* (Boston: Houghton Mifflin Company, 1991), p. 866.
5. Ellen Sander, "Pop in Perspective: A Profile," *The Saturday Review*, 26 October 1968, p. 80.
6. "Start Up a Combo," *Better Homes and Gardens*, May 1970, p. L-6.

7. "Preview," *The Herald-Sun*, Durham, NC, 19 March 1993, p. 5, listed 110 groups to be heard the following week.

8. Bernard Carragher, "Change of Venue," *Playbill*, Winter Garden Theater, February 1976, p. 4.

9. *Halliwell's Filmgoer's Companion*, 8th ed. (New York: Charles Scribner's Sons, 1984), p. viii.

10. Kate Van Winkle Keller, "There are No Waltzes in 'The Last of the Mohicans,'" *The Sonneck Society Bulletin*, vol. 18, no. 3 (Fall 1992), p. 97f.

11. Nicolas Slonimsky, *Baker's Biographical Dictionary of Musicians*, 8th ed., p. 275.

BIBLIOGRAPHY

Cocks, Jay. "Dizzy Gillespie," *Time*, 18 January 1993.

Foner, Eric, and John A. Garraty, eds. *The Reader's Companion to American History*. Boston: Houghton Mifflin Company, 1991.

Hardy, Phil, and Dave Laing. *Encyclopedia of Rock*. New York: Schirmer Books, 1988.

Keller, Kate Van Winkle. "There are No Waltzes in 'The Last of the Mohicans.'" *The Sonneck Society Bulletin*, vol. 18, no. 3 (Fall 1992).

Levin, Eric. "Talking with Wynton Marsalis," *People*, 8 February 1993.

"Preview." *Herald-Sun, The*. Durham, NC. 19 March 1993.

Sander, Ellen. "Pop in Perspective: A Profile," *The Saturday Review*, 26 October 1968.

Slonimsky, Nicolas. *Baker's Biographical Dictionary of Musicians*. New York: Schirmer Books, 1990.

"Start Up a Combo." *Better Homes and Gardens*. May 1970.

12

A Musical Nation

rom the beginning, the Native American had an attitude toward the arts that Europeans could not understand. First of all, the arts were part of daily life, part of a harmony of the universe in which people felt that they must become part of the entire picture of the world and that art would help them in this endeavor. A Navaho song speaks eloquently of this.

> My great corn plants
> Among them I walk
> I speak to them
> They hold out their hands to me.[1]

Above all, this text speaks to a respect for the place of every living thing in the world; it speaks of the unity of living things. It speaks also to the unity of the arts; the touching of the corn plants is part poetry, part music, part daily round, part religious acknowledgment of one's place in the world, part drama, and part dance—motion, gesture, recognition: the very act of being.

Europeans, with their view of the arts as separate from the daily round, as additions to life (rather than as salient elements of life) rejected this view of the arts in general and of music in particular. The rural settlers had more in common with Native American views than the city folk. A barn dance or a hoedown, after all, came close to a connection of life's elements: it was at least an association of music and dancing with the very basis of life—with building and eating and interaction with other people. Many amateurs partook of lively musical offerings from early childhood also: there were children in that barn, children helping their elders prepare the dinner while the planting was going on, children watching when the planters returned, put down their hoes, and washed at the outdoor tub to prepare for eating and dancing.

City people tended to draw lines around music, by having special places and special times for the making of music as parenthetical to life. But they too enjoyed amateur musical activities: they maintained music in their living rooms, in their churches, and in such amateur groups as civic choruses and town bands. Music in the European tradition was a basis of life only for the professional musician, who, in the apprenticeship system, lived and breathed music from early childhood.

In fact, the bringing of music into daily life has always been a strength of American music.

William Sydney Mount, *Dance of the Haymakers, or Music is Contagious*, 1845. (The Museums at Stony Brook.)

THE NINETEENTH CENTURY

In the nineteenth century, music continued to interact with the important aspects of American life; songs about everything that interested people, parodies that sharpened perception of Americana, living room productions that reflected current events. In the eighteenth century, battle pieces, such as *The Battle of Trenton*, were immensely popular; these were often for band, but also published in piano versions. In 1874, a composer whose name was given simply as "F. Hyde" (which may have been a punning pseudonym) created a parody of these pieces, called *Battle of the Sewing Machines*. Elias Howe had patented his sewing machine mechanism in 1846, and by 1870, it had become a common household machine. The piece, typically, calls for piano and narrator, who begins, after a flamboyant introduction, by announcing a section (with rolls and "drums"), "'Howe' the battle began"; then describing the "Advent of all the 'best machines' and the irrepressible sewing machine man," a highly dramatic, somewhat military section. Finally, after several more sections, comes "Triumph of the 'Remington' Sewing Machine And everybody happy in 'Home Sweet Home,'" a presentation of that well-loved song, and a rousing finale of military fanfares.

Life on the frontier, of course, was far from over. Morris Treadwell (born in 1847) kept a diary as a teenager, concerning his upbringing on a farm near Binghamton, New York (178 miles northwest of New York City). He remained a farmer, and was never anything like a professional musician, so his musical and social entries are particularly valuable.

> February 16, 1863. . . . Ellen and I went down to Mr. Tomkins in the evening. Jim fiddled for us & we had an excellent time.
>
> September 28, 1863. . . . Ellen and I went with the young folks over to Mr. McDougalls new house to a Surprise Party in the evening. We had a jolly good time, playing games &C. Got home at 2 o'clock. 25 persons present. A beautiful moonlight night.
>
> October 14, 1863. . . . Ellen and I went over to Mr. McD's to a husking bee & Party in the evening. Had fiddling, dancing, games & a good time altogether.
>
> November 30, 1863. . . . We gathered at the school house for Singing School in the evening but it was stormy & the man did not come.

A farm near Binghamton, New York in the 1870s.

July 4, 1865. . . . The Declaration [of Independence] was read, band music was played, and there were speeches.
March 10, 1866. . . . I played on Maggie's Melodian.[2]

Treadwell, with the Singing School, the dancing to fiddle music, the mixing of corn husking with a social event such as a party, and the playing of a band on a civic occasion had summed up much of the American music scene in the nineteenth century.

The nineteenth century also included native-born composers trained in Europe, who could have competed well enough on equal terms with their European contemporaries, but were never given a chance to do that. The First Symphony of John Knowles Paine, for example, has been dismissed by twentieth-century scholars for a resemblance (real or imagined) to the Second Symphony of Johannes Brahms, when the Paine work was composed in 1875 and the Brahms in 1877. The fact that it preceded Brahms's work was ignored, as was the more important fact that Paine, having studied in Europe, was responding to the same influences to which Brahms was responding. In any case, the Paine symphony is a fine one (and so, of course, are others of his works, both symphonies and choral works with orchestra), and we ignore such American symphonic (and choral/symphonic) works at our peril.

THE TWENTIETH CENTURY

The twentieth century began as a continuation of the nineteenth, with the romantic movement in Europe at its height of acceptance by critic and public, even as composers were beginning to seek ways to transcend it. By midcentury, popular music was outdistancing concert music because American music was disparaged by critics and because foreign stars were imported to displace American talent. "All the indigenous forms in America have always been despised," said choreographer Agnes De Mille.[3] But at the same time, wrote a critic, "there is an exuberance of chamber music in America today—about two hundred and fifty professional string quartets (and more forming), as opposed to a dozen or so twenty-five years ago."[4] This reflected not so much a sudden love of Americans for chamber music, but a sudden recognition that music in the living room was a thing of the past, and chamber music, which had, in fact, been living room music in the United States, must, of necessity, find a public voice if it was to be heard at all. There were, of course, many more than a dozen-or-so string quartets in the United States in the early 1950s; but they played in homes, not on stages.

Interest in music of the past was more than nostalgic: as the twentieth century grew more knowledgeable musicologically, movies began to present music of many times and many places. The film scores of Alfred

Newman (1901–70) illustrate this: he composed over 250 of them, including the Academy Award winning scores for the all-American *Alexander's Ragtime Band* (1938) and the exotic *Love Is a Many Splendored Thing* (1955). Typical (if any one score can represent such a panorama of styles) is his score for *The Gunfighter* (1950), of marvelous energy and directness, modern in its long silences, and authentic in its presentations of nineteenth-century music: Stephen Foster's "Beautiful Dreamer" on the player piano in a bar, and the old hymn "Rock of Ages," a tune by Thomas Hastings, first published by Lowell Mason in 1831, sung to the leadership of a musician at the harmonium by an enthusiastic (though not musically gifted) congregation in a frontier church.

Religious Music

Religious music suffered in the twentieth century—in large part it was, in fact, suffering from the tremendous success of religious music in the nineteenth century, which, like music for band, came to a climax in the beginning of the twentieth century, and then languished into repetition of the tremendous nineteenth-century successes. There can be no twentieth-century Lowell Mason and there can be no twentieth-century Sousa: those composers were *forming* a tradition, and their successors can only *follow* a tradition. Churches were putting on concerts, or allowing other agencies to mount concerts in the sanctuary, and the concerts were for the most part European works in American performances. The most often performed work at such concerts was Handel's *Messiah* (1741), done so many times that many Americans know the famous "Hallelujah Chorus" by heart. But other works are done too, and so, now, are religious operas, often by American composers. Gian-Carlo Menotti (born in Italy in 1911 and living in the United States from 1918) composed *Amahl and the Night Visitors* for NBC television in 1951; its manageable length (50 minutes) and its Christmas association make it a surefire church work, which has rivaled *Messiah* of late in its number of performances, but there are many others. Barbara Harbach (born 1947), for example, has composed four church operas, all short, all practical: *The Littlest Angel* (1987), *Daniel and the Beastly Night* (1988), *A Page from the Christmas Story* (1989), and *The Loneliest Angel* (1990).

Churches also turned to the recorded orchestra (often synthesized) to use in performances, as audiences became tired of piano accompaniments, and good accompanists became increasingly difficult to find.

Most important of all, however, was the coming of gospel into popular music. In 1965, over one million copies were sold of "How Great

🔊 Recommended Recordings and Video Cassettes

Library of Congress LCCN 92-764097. *The Gospel Tradition: The Roots and the Branches*, Volume 1.

Thou Art," and the October 23 issue of *Billboard* was devoted completely to "The World of Religious Music."

Instrument Sales

Instrument making reflected an increased interest in music in general and the guitar in particular. A report in *U S News and World Report* in 1988 detailed instrument sales from 1940 to 1987:

Sales of bowed string instruments doubled from about 50,000 a year to over 100,000.

Sales of woodwind instruments rose from just over 100,000 a year to 347,000 in 1987.

Sales of brass instruments rose from about 70,000 a year, peaked at over 200,000 in 1970, and dropped to 146,000 in 1987.

Sales of pianos rose from about 115,000 a year to over 210,000 in 1980, then fell to about 175,000 in 1987.

And sales of fretted stringed instruments (almost all of them banjos or guitars) rose from under 200,000 a year to a peak of about 2,500,000 in 1970, fell to a little more than 1,000,000 in 1980, and rose again to 1,247,000 in 1987.[5]

The tremendous sale of guitars represents the importance of the popular-music traditions in the United States since the Second World War.

⌒ ⌒ ⌒ ⌒ ⌒ ⌒

Gershwin had said that "Jazz resulted from the energy stored up in America; . . . I like to think of [music] as an emotional science."[6] What was so compelling about jazz and rock was their sense of reality, their genuineness as musical expressions. People who played jazz were creating it, not recreating it; they toyed with a tune, taking simple music, common property, and making it individually splendid. One author described a performance:

A young man in shirt sleeves was playing bop piano. His fingers shadowed the tune, ran circles around it, played leapfrog with it, and managed never to hit it on the nose.[7]

That music of all kinds has always been a strong expression of the American personality is not in doubt. It was Emerson who had summed it up, in a way, most pointedly, in 1870: "'Tis wonderful," he said, "how soon a piano gets into a log-hut on the frontier."[8] Music has been valued and enjoyed in many venues throughout our history; it has maintained a secure, vital (and vitalizing) place in our culture from the beginning. Francis Hopkinson in the eighteenth century put into words the American delight in music:

Oh! I would die with music melting round
And float to bliss on a sea of sound![9]

NOTES

1. *Arizona Highways,* March 1977, p. 16.
2. *Morris Treadwell, Diaries of a Binghamton Boy in the 1860s.* (Endicott, NY: Union Press, 1985), pp. 56, 63, 65, 87, and 93.
3. "Dick Cavett Show," 25 August 1978.
4. Helen Drees Ruttencutter, "The Guarneri Quartet," *New Yorker,* 23 October 1978, p. 51.
5. *US News and World Report,* 14 November 1988, p. 131; data drawn from The American Music Conference, The National Association of Music Merchants.
6. Dan Morgenstern, *Composers on Music.,* in Ian Crofton and Donald Fraser, *A Dictionary of Musical Quotations* (New York: Schirmer Books, 1985), pp. 3 and 56.
7. Ross Macdonald, *The Name is Archer* (Bantam Books N5996, 1971), p. 44.
8. Crofton & Fraser, *A Dictionary of Musical Quotations,* p. 112.
9. Robert Stevenson, *Protestant Church Music in America.* (New York: W. W. Norton, 1966), p. v.

BIBLIOGRAPHY

Borroff, Edith. *Music in Europe and the United States: A History,* 2nd ed. New York: Ardsley House, Publishers, 1990.

Crofton, Ian, and Donald Fraser, eds. *A Dictionary of Musical Quotations.* New York: Schirmer Books, 1985.

Goossen, Frederic. "Ross Lee Finney." *Society for the Fine Arts Review.* University of Alabama, vol. 5, no. 1 (Spring 1983).

Hart, James D. *The Oxford Companion to American Literature,* new rev. ed. New York: Oxford University Press, 1956.

Macdonald, Ross. *The Name is Archer.* New York: Bantam, 1971.

Ruttencutter, Helen Drees. "The Guarneri Quartet." *The New Yorker.* 23 October 1978.

Simpson, Janice C. "A Few Good Women." *Time,* 5 April 1993.

Stone, Andrea, and Dee Ann Glamser. "Lawmakers and Laws Change." *USA Today,* 12 February 1992.

Tischler, Barbara L. *An American Music: The Search for an American Musical Identity.* New York: Oxford University Press, 1986.

Treadwell, Morris. *Morris Treadwell, Diaries of a Binghamton Boy in the 1860s.* Endicott, NY: Union Press, 1985.

U.S. News and World Report, 14 November, 1988. Report on instrument sales in the United States.

Walsh, Michael. "No More Business as Usual." *Time,* 2 April 1990.

Workman, Chuck. "Lasting Impressions." *Modern Maturity,* February-March 1993.

APPENDIX

Basic Musical Concepts

TIME

Music is energy shaped through sounds and silences and perceived in time.

Primary to music is its motion, which we (as children of Newton) call forward or ongoing, creating time, much as a painting creates its space. The basic unit of energy is an impulse, called a *beat*. But one beat cannot create a characteristic forward motion. The **beat** of a musical work refers to the continuing repetitions of the impetus; the beat is generally regular and steady, like a pulse, but it can also be irregular and free.

A continuing beat can provide a basis for musical performance, but, like a pulse, it is constant and theoretically endless—i.e., taking a pulse dips into your life-long continuity of pulses and begins and ends only when you start to take it and stop taking it. Most art requires more structure than that. Representing the continuing pulse as a series of x's is illuminating:

x x x x x x x x x x x x x x x x x x x x x x

Normally some of the beats are louder than others, most often in a regular grouping of two, three, or four.

2: X x X x X x X x X x X x X x X x X x X x X x
3: X x x X x x X x x X x x X x x X x x X x x X x x
4: X x x x X x x x X x x x X x x x X x x x X x x x

Because it is natural to give a secondary **accent** (or louder note, emphasis) on the third beat of four (making it **X** x X x **X** x X x), it is often difficult or even impossible to tell the difference between a beat organized in two and a beat organized in four. Sometimes this is due to the sloppiness of performers who do not make the distinction, but very often it is simply a technical matter of how the music is **notated** (written down), which is immaterial and of no concern to the listener.

Other groupings are of course possible. Most of the others are **compound meters**, such as six beats, which can be made up either as three groups of two (X x X x X x) or as two groups of three (X x x X x x). But five beats are also possible, made up either from three plus two (X x x X x) or two plus three (X x X x x). Five-beat groupings are common in many cultures of the world, but have been found in the United States only in the last half-century.

In "Happy Talk" (from *South Pacific*, 1949) Richard Rodgers called for a meter of eight beats that was built

$$3 + 3 + 2 \ (X \ x \ x \ X \ x \ x \ X \ x)$$

rather than 4 + 4. A meter of seven is built from two twos and one three, in any order:

$$X \ x \ x \ X \ x \ X \ x, — X \ x \ X \ x \ x \ X \ x, — \text{or} \ X \ x \ X \ x \ X \ x \ x$$

The makeup of eight can be as Rodgers did it in "Happy Talk," but it can also be 3 + 2 + 3 (X x x X x X x x), or 2 + 3 + 3 (X x X x x X x x). Above eight, such groups become very complicated indeed. And they are rare.

The regular groupings are called **meter** or **measure**. Measure refers more commonly to a single grouping (twelve measures of two appear on page 345, for example; eight measures of three; and six measures of four).

The beat has important characterizing traits. Of these, the most important is **tempo**, or speed. The same piece may be played at a number of tempos, from very slow to very fast, but it is most effective at one particular tempo.

In dance music tempo is at its most crucial, since physical activity is coordinated with it, and motion must be matched with the beat.

Also, the beat may be very loud, very soft, or inconsistent. A march *must* be consistent. And, generally, marches (which may be in either two or four) reinforce the meter by having the X x X x played "loud-soft-loud-soft." Such accents, which duplicate the nature of the meter, are called **metric accents**. Accents which go against the meter are called **syncopation**; if a march were syncopated, nobody could march to it.

If the beats are played with short disconnected notes, they are more highly energized; such notes are called **staccato**. If the notes are played more smoothly and connectedly than usual, they are said to be **legato**— bound together. A highly energized musical fabric can be created by having one layer of music playing (or singing) metric accents, while another layer plays (or sings) the opposite (x X x X = soft-loud-soft-loud); these off-accents are called **backbeats**.

In these terms the most highly energized beat would be fast, loud, staccato, and with backbeats; the quietest beat would be slow, soft, legato, and without backbeats. With four variables in creating a basic beat, the types of effects are virtually infinite and, in practice, are capable of the utmost subtlety.

SOUND

Of equal importance to the creation of music is *sound* itself, without which the energy of forward motion is merely theoretical and disembodied.

In addition to the existence in time (without which it could not be perceived), musical **sound** has a number of characteristics—chiefly, *tone color*, *pitch*, and *intensity*. **Tone color** or **timbre** is the quality of sound and is associated with the physical means of creating it, since our language is poverty-stricken in describing what we hear (relative to what we see). Nonetheless, every adult hearing person is able to tell the difference between a soprano and a bass singer or between a singer and a violinist or trumpet player, eyes closed and depending entirely upon information derived from the ears. We can call a voice "sweet," a violin "narrow," and a trumpet "rousing" or "pungent," but these are impressions, and however valuable for insight, have no technical standing. Tone color is subtle as well as large and categorical: as you can tell the difference between a soprano and a drum, you may also recognize the voice of a particular soprano among other sopranos, since no two have exactly the same quality, and one singer may be able to shade her voice in a number of qualities in an impressive range of subtleties.

A single note of music may well have *pitch* as well as quality. It *must* have quality (if it is audible), but some instruments are *unpitched*—generally percussion instruments such as *drums*, *cymbals*, *tambourines*, *wood blocks*, and *gongs*. **Pitch** is created by regularity of *vibration*, which means staying with a rate of vibration long enough for the regularity to be perceived. Speech has constantly varying pitches, and normally we can hear them only in sustained or monotonous speech—people calling out, train conductors, or auctioneers. If a second note has the same pitch as the first, it is called a **repeated note**; if it has a different pitch, it is perceived as either **higher** (more intensely produced) or **lower** (less intensely produced). Singing the highest note you can sing requires very tight muscles, whereas singing the lowest note means loosening your throat to the greatest possible extent.

Singing a meaningful succession of notes of different pitches creates a **melody,** which is not so much a series of notes as a shape in time. Musicians speak of the line of a melody (**melodic line** is a musical term) as being shaped by higher and lower pitches in **musical space**. Not all melodies are sung, of course: many are sounded by instruments. But most melodies are conceived as though they are intended to be sung, and all melody is perceived relative to the human voice. Most people can sing twelve to sixteen notes from the bottom to the top of their vocal capacity. That span is called the **range** of the voice. A professional singer has a wider range, most often from sixteen to twenty notes, but certain kinds of voices have more than that; the professional singer can also sing more rapidly, negotiate more complicated patterns of pitch, and sing longer on one breath.

The amount of melody sung in one breath is called a **phrase**, which is thus more or less comparable to a sentence in speech. A group of phrases (perhaps only two, perhaps several), conceived as a unit, is called a **section**. The average pop song has four sections, of which the first, second, and fourth are the same musically; the third is different and is called a **release**. The form of a pop song can thus be represented as *AABA*, repeated sections mirrored by repeated letters. (Blues form is *AAB*, three phrases—or one-phrase sections—of which the first two are the same and the third presents a contrast.)

Intensity is the third quality of musical sound; like tone quality it is characteristic of all sound, and therefore no musical sound can exist without it. Basically, **intensity** is degree of loudness, in a continuum from so soft that you can hardly hear it to so loud that you can hardly stand it. The degree of intensity in music is called the **dynamic level**.

In fact, the three components of musical sound are not separable, and they overlap technically as well as subjectively. A trumpet is a louder instrument than a flute, though a skilled trumpeter can produce a sound much softer than a loud—or even a medium—flute tone. But no trumpeter could produce a high trumpet note less intense than a low flute note, for most instruments become more intense in their upper range. The range of a voice or instrument has sections, higher and lower, generally two for a voice and two or three for an instrument—sometimes these are named and form a vital element of *technique* or mastery of the physical instrument. Being able to negotiate musical patterns in the highest register is very much associated with heroic skill (**virtuosity**) in performance.

Energy levels of musical sound are similar to those of the beat: high is more energized than low; instruments that produce mild sounds have less energy than those that produce shrill sounds, and, of course, loud sounds are more highly energized than soft ones. And these energy forces interact in countless ways together and with the energy and forces of the beat.

FABRIC

Time and sound elements are the basic components of the **musical fabric** or characteristic overall sound. Added to these are the complications of the number of different things going on at once, the manner of producing the sounds, and the relative steadiness or change of effect.

A singer rarely sings alone, though it is possible and is done occasionally. A single voice presents one line; if a violin adds a second line, drums a third, and a group of clarinets and saxophones play groups of notes all at once, the fabric is more and more complicated. A unanimous group of tones is called a **chord**; a chord is considered to be one thing. A succession of chords is called **harmony**. A number of melodies going on at once is called **polyphony** ("many sounds"). This element of musical fabric is called **structural texture**, rather like the structure of cloth fabric, and it varies from the simple to the complex.

The manner of producing the sounds creates a variety of effects, from the smoothest to the jerkiest and most disconnected. The musician calls the approach to a tone the **attack**, and this concept includes *legato*, *staccato*, *accents*, and *times of silence* (**rests**). This characteristic of musical fabric—the style of playing, rather than the delineation of what is played, is called **surface texture**.

Relative steadiness or change in the musical fabric creates an effect of consistency or restlessness in musical design or form. Most short works of music, including most elements in pop music, are consistent throughout; contrast in a musical show is much more likely to lie in an array of different and contrasting numbers than within individual songs or dances. Because of the norm of consistency, internal contrasts are often emphasized by a cessation of forward motion, or a substantial pause, rather like a stop sign most probably encountered by motorists when they change routes or direction; in music this stop is called a **fermata**.

Complexity has more energy than simplicity (though of course three simultaneous quiet elements can produce a more relaxed effect than one frenzied one), a high surface texture produces more energy than a low surface texture, and a changeable fabric creates more energy than a consistent one, especially when the changes are erratic or unexpected. These energy forces interact with those of time and sound to create a rich variety of virtually infinite wonder.

GLOSSARY

a cappella: choral music without instruments.

accordion: a hand-held reed organ in which the melody is presented by a keyboard held vertically at the player's chest while the player opens and closes the wind chest with sideways pumping motions.

acoustic: deriving sound from an instrument alone, without amplification.

adagio: slow.

Aeolian harp: strings placed in a box and activated by the wind.

afterpiece: a short section added to the end of a stage presentation.

alto: a low voice of a female singer, or an instrument of that range.

amplification system: a mechanism for making music louder electrically.

amplified instrument: an instrument made louder electrically.

analog synthesizer: a machine that creates sounds directly, rather than recording them.

anthem: a choral setting of a religious text for use in a church service.

antiphony: the sounding of music by two groups set apart in space.

Appalachian dulcimer: a dulcimer modified in the Appalachian region.

aria: a song, particularly in an opera.

arranger: the musician who adapts a composition for a medium other than the one for which it was originally intended.

autoharp: a zither with keys for playing chords.

back beats: accents on the notes not generally accented.

background music: music behind dramatic action.

ballad: a story song.

ballad opera: (in the United States) a play with songs interspersed.

ballet: an intricate dance form, presented by professionals, employing formalized steps and gestures to create expression through movement.

band: a performing group made of wind and percussion instruments.

banjar: *see* banjo

banjo: a plucked string instrument with circular frame.

bar: a unit of beats; a measure.

barbershop quartet: four men of varying voices singing a capella.

baritone: a middle voice of a male singer, or an instrument of that range.

barn dance: a dance featuring country music, originally held in a barn.

bass: a low voice of a male singer, or an instrument of that range.

basse dance: a Renaissance dance for couples, performed with gliding steps.

bassoon: the bass member of the woodwind instruments.

beat: the basic rhythmic unit; pulse.

Beatlemania: a craze for the Beatles.

bebop: a jazz type developed in the late 1940s and '50s, featuring highly complex solos, dissonant chords, and extreme tempos; also called *bop*.

bells: hollow cup-shaped units struck in the inside by a clapper.

big apple: a social dance in the 1920s and '30s.

big band: a swing band that used more than one player on some of the parts.

black bottom: a popular dance characterized by emphatic, sinuous hip movements.

"blue" notes: the inflection of notes, generally a lowering, for expressive purposes.

blues: a vocal type featuring "blue" notes.

bones: two animal ribs held in one hand and clacked together.

bongo drums: small drums of Afro-Cuban origin, played in pairs.

boogie-woogie: a pre-World War II jazz-piano type of music with a strong bass.

book: *see* libretto

bowed string instrument: an instrument with strings, played with a bow.

brass band: a band made entirely of brass instruments (no woodwinds and usually no percussions).

brass instrument: an instrument made of brass, using a mouthpiece instead of a reed.

break: a contrasting section.

bridge: *see* release

broadside: a song, lyrics, or an ad for a song, printed on a single sheet of paper, generally hawked on the street.

bugle: a brass instrument like a trumpet but without valves.

burlesque: a kind of musical show based in parody.

busker: a street musician.

cacophonic: sounding unpleasant or ugly.

cakewalk: a dance by plantation slaves in which the owners were mocked.

cantata: a piece in several movements for voice(s) and instruments.

cantico: an Algonquin dance contest.

cantor: the chief singer and prayer leader of a synagogue.

çarabanda: an Aztec dance.

carillon: a set of bells or chimes.

celesta: a keyed glockenspiel used in orchestras.

cello: the bass member of the violin family.

chamber instrument: an instrument suited for chamber music.

chamber music: music designed to be played in a room or hall.

chance music: music with elements selected randomly, rather than by an aesthetic choice.

Charleston: a vigorous, rhythmic dance that was the most popular one of the 1920s.

chimes: tubular bells.

choir: a group of singers.

choral: pertaining to a choir.

Choralcelo: an early electronic instrument.

chord: a group of notes sounding together as an entity.

chorus: a large group of singers performing together; also, music for such a group.

chromatic: using notes close together in pitch.

clarinet: a reed instrument with finger holes and keys.

classical music: music of the late eighteenth century.

clavichord: a keyboard instrument in which the strings are touched by the key mechanism.

clog dance: a tap dance.

Collegium Musicum: a group devoted to performing early music.

combinatoriality: the theory of having not only twelve tones used serially, but also twelve dynamic levels, twelve time intervals, and twelve instrumental timbres.

combo: a small group of varied instruments.

comic opera: an opera with spoken sections. Also called *light opera, operetta.*

compact disk: a recording device of the 1980s and '90s in which music is digitally encoded on one side of a 5-inch disk.

concert: a musical performance.

concert grand: the largest piano, eight or nine feet long.

concertina: a small accordion.

concerto: a work combining a soloist with an orchestra.

conductor: the musical director of a performing group.

conga: a Cuban dance performed in a single line, consisting of three steps forward, followed by a kick.

conservatory: a school for the training of musicians.

console: the organ keyboards and control at which the organist sits.

consort: a small group of singers or instrumentalists.

contrafactum: a process in which new words for a tune have been substituted for the original ones.

cool jazz: a lighter jazz style of the 1940s and '50s.

cornet: a brass instrument similar to a trumpet.

corps de ballet: the dancers of a ballet company performing together.

cotillion: a town dance featuring many different types of steps.

counterpoint: the study of combined melodies.

country and western: country music of western (cowboy) type.

country-western guitar: a traditional six-string acoustic guitar.

Coupleux-Givelet: an early synthesizer, exhibited at the Paris Exposition of 1929.

damper pedal: the piano pedal that sustains sound.

dance: aesthetic body movement.

dance hall: a hall where dances are held.

dialogue song: a duet song based in exchanges between singers.

diatonic: the normal ("do-re-mi") scale type.

digital synthesizer: a computer system for combining, modifying, and reproducing sounds.

discothèque: a hall where greatly amplified recorded music is played for dancing.

double: the repetition of a song in a different meter.

dramatic song: a song that is acted as much as sung.

drum: a hollow instrument played by percussive means.

drumhead: the top of a drum, often of hide; the part of the drum that is struck.

duet: a piece of music for two performers.

dulcimer: a shallow box with strings to be plucked or struck with small hammers.

dynamic level: degree of loudness.

eight-to-the-bar: eight beats to the measure.

electric instrument: an instrument played normally but amplified electrically.

English opera: British ballad opera, a stage work in which speech and song, action and dance, were mixed.

ensemble: a group performing together.

essential music: music presented for itself alone.

Ethiopian song: a song in the African tradition.

ethnomusicology: the study of the music of other cultures.

expressionism: a post-romantic development featuring musical objectivity.

fiddle: another name for the violin, especially in folk music.

fife: a small, high-pitched flute.

fife-and-drum corps: a small group, most often military, limited to fifers and drummers.

film score: the music of a film.

finger cymbals: a pair of small disks attached to the fingers and played by clicking them together.

first part: the first half of a minstrel show, featuring single acts and dialogues.

Flamenco guitar: a Spanish Gypsy folk guitar.

flute: the highest woodwind instrument.

folk ballad: a story song in the folk tradition.

folk instrument: an instrument used by nonprofessionals.

folk music: music, usually simple in nature, often of anonymous authorship, handed down by oral tradition.

fox-trot: a social dance with various combinations of slow and fast steps that was popular in the first half of the twentieth century.

free jazz: a free-form jazz style that disregards traditional structures.

French horn: a middle-range brass instrument.

frug: a dance derived from the twist, popular in the 1960s.

funeral music: music to be played at a funeral or memorial service.

gamelan: a Javanese instrumental group.

gavotte: a dance popular in the seventeenth and eighteenth centuries.

general ruckus: the grand finale of the minstrel show, including the dance for the whole company. Also called *walk-around*.

glass harmonica: an instrument, invented by Benjamin Franklin, in which sound is produced by rubbing the fingers on the rims of discs, revolving on a spindle.

glockenspiel: orchestral bells.

gospel song: a popular, rhythmic song whose text is based on a religious theme.

grand finale: the big final part of a show.

Grand Harmonicons: mounted musical glasses.

grand opera: an opera in which everything is sung and nothing is spoken.

group concert: a concert given by a group of singers, rather than one soloist.

guitar: a plucked string instrument.

hammered dulcimer: a dulcimer

hand bells: small-handled bells held in the hand.

harmonica: *see* mouth organ

harmonium: a reed organ.

harmony: the vertical element in music—that is, the relationship of tones sounded simultaneously.

harp: an open frame strung with strings to be plucked.

harpsichord: a keyboard instrument with strings plucked by the key mechanism.

Heldensinger: "hero-singer," one able to sing in the lush romantic style.

hemiola: three beats in the place of two.

heterophony: the simultaneous performance of a melody with variation.

hillbilly: a kind of country music.

hoedown: a musical celebration at the end of a day's farm work.

holler: a popular song style, originating outdoors (the field holler).

horn: the French horn; also, a jazz term for any instrument.

hot: having strong rhythm and inspired improvisation.

hymn: a religious poem.

hymnal: a book of hymns.

impressionism: a late-romantic development featuring responses to places and people.

improvise: to make up, extemporize.

incidental music: the music to a play.

indeterminacy: music that makes deliberate use of chance or random elements.

inflection: the subtle raising or lowering of pitch.

interlocutor: the master of ceremonies of a minstrel show.

jam session: improvisation by jazz players, characteristically in informal meetings.

jass: early spelling of *jazz.*

jaw's harp: another name for *Jew's harp.*

jazz: a twentieth-century popular development from ragtime, combining African, American, and western European influences.

jazz combo: a performing group (combination), generally small.

Jew's harp: a simple iron frame with one vibrating strip; the instrument is held between the teeth.

jig: an old sailor's dance, known for its speed.

jitterbug: a popular strenuous dance of the 1930s.

juice harp: another name for *Jew's harp.*

kazoo: a mirliton instrument.

Kent bugle: a bugle with keys.

key: a flap, generally metal, for playing brass and woodwind instruments.

keyboard: a row of keys.

keyed bugle: *see* Kent bugle

kithara: a large harp of ancient Greece.

Krummhorn: an obsolete instrument with an encased reed.

libretto: the text of an opera.

Lieder: songs (German), commonly referring to German "art songs."

light opera: *see* comic opera

lyrics: the words of a song.

madrigal: a popular part song.

mandolin: a small lute.

maracas: gourd rattles played in pairs.

march: a piece of music designed to be marched to.

marimba: a large xylophone.

maxixe: a rapid, syncopated Latin American dance adopted from the polka.

measure: the regular grouping of beats.

melodic embellishment: variations on a melody.

melodrama: a play or film consisting of action with spoken words, synchronized with music.

melody: the horizontal element in music—a meaningful succession of pitches.

meter: the regular grouping of rhythmic beats.

microtone: a musical interval smaller than a half step.

MIDI: Musical Instrument Digital Interface.

minimalism: a kind of music using very few basic elements.

minstrel show: a musical show based on plantation entertainment.

minuet: a stately popular dance of the seventeenth and eighteenth centuries.

mirliton: a buzzing device added to a musical instrument.

modern jazz: bebop and its derivatives in the 1950s, including cool jazz.

monodrama: an opera with only one singer.

Motown: a popularized form of rhythm-and-blues originating in Detroit in the 1950s.

mouth organ: a small reed instrument sounded by blowing and sucking.

multimedia: using other arts and effects in addition to music.

multiple bow: a pluriarc.

musical: a popular twentieth-century form of musical theater; also, a film in which the action stops occasionally for formal musical numbers.

musical bow: a hunting bow played by tapping the string with a stick.

musical comedy: a play or movie whose story is developed with song.

musicale: a private musical performance at a party or social gathering.

musical glasses: drinking glasses filled with differing amounts of water and played by rubbing the rims with wet fingers.

musical interlude: music in radio used to connect sections of dialogue or to announce changes of scene.

musical melodrama: a play or film with music coordinated with the action.

musical pointillism: a texture made of single notes rather than sustained melodies.

musical saw: a carpenter's saw played with a bow.

musical theater: plays produced with music.

music box: a box containing a cylinder with metal teeth that sound musical pitches when the cylinder is rotated.

musicology: the study of music from a technical point of view.

music system: a computer program for music.

musique concrète: music created by combining recorded elements.

mute: a device to soften the sound.

ncabagome: a Congolese drum-music type played at the announcement of a guilty verdict by a court.

ndamutsu: a Congolese drum-music type played at the appearance of the king.

neoclassicism: the use of classical elements in postromantic music.

New Music: a name for the modernism of post-World War II composers who aimed at a new ideal.

new-wave jazz: a development in jazz of the late 1950s and '60s.

note: a single musical sound.

oboe: a soprano reed instrument using two reeds vibrating together.

octave: an interval encompassing eight tones on a musical scale.

octet: a group of eight performers.

off-accent: the accenting of unexpected beats, particularly beats two and four of four.

olio: the second part of a minstrel show, featuring variety acts.

Ondes Martenot: a French electronic instrument.

one-step: an early twentieth-century dance performed to ragtime.

opera: a play performed in music.

operetta: *see* comic opera

oratorio: a large work telling a story, for soloists, choir, and orchestra.

orchestra: a large ensemble of varied instruments.

orchestra bells: small bells on a stand, played with hammers.

orchestral harp: a large harp used in a symphony orchestra.

orchestrion: an automatic instrument using a player piano and other instruments to produce the sounds of an orchestra.

organ: a wind instrument whose sounding elements are controlled from a console.

ostinato: a single phrase used over and over.

overture: a short orchestral piece played at the beginning of a musical show or opera.

pandiatonicism: diatonic music not in a key.

panpipes: a South American instrument made of small tubes of different sizes, played by blowing across the tops.

patting juba: clapping complex rhythms.

pedal: a foot mechanism on pianos and organs.

pedalboard: the low keyboard of the organ console, played with the feet.

percussion: instruments, often unpitched, generally struck.

phrase: a unit of melody comparable to a short sentence.

piano: a large instrument whose strings are struck by hammers controlled from a keyboard.

piano four hands: a piano played by two people.

piccolo: a flute higher than the soprano.

pipe organ: an organ whose sounding elements are pipes controlled by a player at a console.

pitch: the particular melodic tone achieved in a musical sound; intonation.

pit orchestra: a small orchestra playing in the theater pit during stage performances.

player piano: a piano activated mechanically rather than by a pianist.

pluriarc: a multiple musical bow.

polka: a fast dance originating in Bohemia, popular in nineteenth-century Europe and America.

polyphony: an interplay of elements—in particular, the simultaneous combination of melodies.

pops concert: an informal concert for large audiences, often outdoors.

popular music: music loved by many people rather than by a few—so, often commercialized.

primitivism: the introduction of pseudo-primitive elements into orchestral music.

producer: the person in charge of the finances and practical arrangements for a musical event.

program music: music that expresses nonmusical ideas or images.

progressive jazz: modern jazz in the 1950s.

psalmody: the singing of hymns or psalms.

punk: a development in rock music in the mid 1970s that relied on sheer volume and rhythmic energy.

quadraphonic sound: recording equipment providing four speakers.

quadrille: a nineteenth-century dance for four or more couples.

quartet: four people playing or singing together.

quintet: five people playing or singing together.

quodlibet: a vocal piece made up of allusions to several well-known songs.

radical serialism: the serialization of rhythmic, dynamic, and instrumental, in addition to pitch elements; also called *total serialism*.

raga: in India, a melodic entity subject to variation and elaboration.

ragtime: an African-American musical style characterized by high energy and off-rhythms.

range: the extent of a melody in low and high pitches.

rattle: a hollow percussion instrument with seeds or stones inside, played by shaking it.

recitativo: vocal music more spoken (recited) than sung.

recorder: a wooden flute with a whistle head, blown from the top rather than across.

reed instrument: an instrument sounded by the use of reeds.

reed organ: an organ with a reed mechanism, rather than pipes.

reel: a fast dance in which partners face each other in two lines.

release: the contrasting section of a popular song.

reproducing piano: an early player piano.

response: the final line of a three-line poetic stanza that contrasts with the opening line and its repetition.

revue: a musical production made of various segments or acts, usually without a unifying dramatic element.

rhapsody: a romantic instrumenal piece.

rhumba: a Cuban dance with complex rhythms.

rhythm: the impetus that makes music move forward in time.

rhythm-and-blues: a mid-twentieth-century popular music form that developed from blues and jazz.

rhythmic embellishment: the enhancement of a melodic line through spontaneous variation.

riff: a repeated harmonic unit.

rock: an outgrowth of rhythm-and-blues that developed in the 1950s and '60s, named for its style of beat.

rock 'n' roll: an early name for rock.

romanticism: a nineteenth-century development featuring strong musical emotion.

rubato: the pushing and relaxing of the beat for expressive purposes.

sacred chant: music sung during worship services.

sacred harp singing: a style of nineteenth-century hymn singing.

sansa: a box fitted with reeds activated by the thumbs of the player.

saraband: a slow dance, derived from the Aztec çarabanda.

saxophone: a reed instrument invented by Adolph Sax about 1840 for use in military bands; a "woodwind" made of metal.

scale: an orderly listing of musical pitches.

scat: singing to sounds rather than to texts.

semiclassical music: a concept including both formal and informal music.

serialism: a composition technique developed early in the twentieth century.

sheet music: short pieces or songs in separate publications.

shimmy: a dance step popular in the 1910s and '20s characterized by rapid movement of the two shoulders in opposite directions.

shout: an energetic singing of spirituals.

show: a theatrical production.

shuffle: a dance in which the feet are shuffled along the floor.

sidemen: jazz players who accompany a soloist.

sinfonietta: a small orchestra often used for the performance of semi-classical music.

singing school: late eighteenth- and early nineteenth-century courses in singing and music fundamentals.

sitar: a long-necked lute from northern India.

sleigh bells: small bells affixed to a sleigh or to the halters of horses pulling a sleigh.

snare drum: a small drum with mirlitons.

soft-shoe dancing: tap-style dancing without taps on the shoes.

solo: the performance of any piece or part by one person.

sonata: a multimovement work for one or two players.

song: a melody sung to words.

song cycle: a group of songs constituting a musical entity.

song plugger: a singer or pianist who sang or played songs in a store as a stimulus for sales.

soprano: a high voice of a female singer, or an instrument of that range.

soul: expressiveness in blues and jazz solos.

sound mix: the mixture of sound elements in radio.

sousaphone: a circular tuba played upright; named for John Philip Sousa.

spinet: a small harpsichord; later, a small piano.

spiritual: a folk or popular song with a religious text.

Sprechstimme: speech accompanied by instruments, with rhythm specified, but not pitch.

square dance: a folk dance for four couples forming a square.

stereophonic sound: sound from two or more speakers placed apart to obtain a richer effect.

stinger: a sudden accented chord, especially on an organ.

stomp tune: a melody intended to be danced to.

straight: as written, without variation.

string bass: the very low bass string instrument of the orchestra.

string quartet: two violins, a viola, and a cello as a group.

suite: a set of pieces to be played as a group.

swing: a slower, popular, dance-oriented, big-band jazz style that used more than one player on many of the parts.

symphonic poem: a one-movement orchestral work.

symphony: a long orchestral work, generally of four movements.

syncopated: on the off-accents.

synthesizer: a mechanism that manufactures sound waves directly, without a musical instrument.

tabla: a drum of India.

tala: a repeated rhythmic figure in India.

talking drum: a drum with such a variety of tones that it could imitate speech.

talk song: a song recited by a performer to a musical accompaniment.

tambourine: a small open drum with mirlitons of circular metal disks.

tam-tams: small gongs.

tap dancing: dancing with metal tabs (taps) on the shoes to emphasize rhythms.

tearjerker: a popular song of the 1890s, generally with several stanzas, with a sad, melodramatic text.

tempo: speed.

tenor: a high voice of a male singer, or an instrument of that range.

texture: the elements of musical fabric combined.

theme song: a song associated with a particular show or performer.

third-stream: music that combines jazz and concert music.

thumb piano: a sansa

timbre: the quality or color of sound.

Tin Pan Alley: a nickname for the song business, centered on lower Broadway, at the beginning of the twentieth century.

tone: a musical sound.

tone color: *see* timbre

total serialism: *see* radical serialism

transcription: the adaptation of a composition to a medium other than its original one.

trap drum set: a group of drums plus cymbals.

trimmings: spontaneous decoration in music.

trio: a group of three performers.

triplet: three notes, instead of two, played evenly in one beat.

trombone: a bass brass instrument.

trumpet: a soprano brass instrument.

tuba: the lowest-pitched brass instrument.

tune: melody.

turkey trot: an early twentieth-century round dance to ragtime for couples, consisting of a springy walk accompanied by swinging body motions.

twelve-bar blues: a blues song of three four-bar sections.

twist: a dance, popular in the 1960s and '70s, featuring strong rhythmic turns and twists of the body.

two-step: an early twentieth-century dance featuring sliding steps.

ukulele: a small guitar popular in Hawaii.

uli uli: Hawaiian rattles.

universalism: the ideal of using musical elements of many cultures.

upright piano: a piano with its mechanism in a vertical position.

variations: *see* trimmings

variety show: a show of various acts.

vaudeville: a show of various acts in a theater.

venue: the location and special musical profile of a particular kind of music.

vibraharp: a vibraphone.

vibraphone (vibes): an instrument of metal bars played with soft mallets.

vibrato: a tremulous, quick, continuous, subtle variation of pitch.

viol: a delicate, six-string predecessor of the violin.

viola: the standard alto string instrument.

violin: the standard soprano string instrument.

vocal music: music of the human voice.

voice: the human voice used as a musical instrument.

volta: a leaping dance from Provence, popular in Europe around 1600.

walkaround: *see* general ruckus

waltz: the most popular dance of the nineteenth century, in which the dancing couples revolve in perpetual circles.

waltz-ballad: a song with a waltz-like rhythm.

wa-wa: a mute for a brass instrument.

western: a popular song influenced by western folk music.

wind chimes: pieces of glass, metal or other substances strung up so as to hit each other and sound in the wind.

woodwind: an orchestral instrument (originally of wood) played by the breath.

work song: a song used to coordinate or energize work.

xylophone: an instrument made of wooden bars, played with soft mallets.

yodeling: alternating regular and falsetto notes.

zither: a set of strings in a shallow box, played by plucking.

zydeco: a style of black Cajun music.

INDEX

INDEX OF TITLES

THE COUNTRY	THE ARTS	MUSIC
Ellis Island opens, 1892	Mary Cassatt, *The Letter*, painting, 1891	Edward MacDowell made professor at Columbia, 1895
Pullman Strike, 1894	Stephen Crane, *The Red Badge of Courage*, novel, 1895	Cincinnati Symphony founded, 1895
William Jennings Bryan's "Cross of gold" speech, 1896	First movie for paying audience, New York, 1895	First player piano manufactured, 1897
First Stanley Steamer automobile, 1897	First comic strip ("The Katzen-jammer Kids"), 1897	Ben R. Harney, *Rag Time Instructor*, 1897
Spanish-American War, 1898	Elbert Hubbard, *A Message to Garcia*, essay, 1899	John Philip Sousa, "Stars and Stripes Forever," 1897
First motor-driven vacuum cleaner patented, 1899	Frank Baum, *The Wonderful Wizard of Oz*, novel, 1900	Scott Joplin, "Maple Leaf Rag," 1899
Hawaii granted territorial status, 1900		Amy Beach, *Piano Concerto*, 1899
First vacuum tube, 1900		

1901 TO 1950

THE COUNTRY	THE ARTS	MUSIC
Carrie Nation attacks saloons, Kansas, 1901	Edwin S. Porter, director, *The Great Train Robbery*, first film with a plot, 1903	George M. Cohan, *Little Johnny Jones*, 1904
Wright Brothers build first airplane, 1903	Kate Douglas Wiggin, *Rebecca of Sunnybrook Farm*, novel, 1903	Ferdinand "Jelly Roll" Morton, "Jelly Roll Blues," 1904
First World Series, 1903	O'Henry, short stories, 1906–10	Charles Ives, *The Unanswered Question*, 1908
Earthquake, San Francisco, 1906	Ashcan School of painting formed, New York, 1908	"When the Saints Go Marching In," anonymous, 1908
Model T Ford, 1908	Armory Show, New York, 1913	Irving Berlin, "Alexander's Ragtime Band," 1911
NAACP founded by W. E. B. DuBois, 1909	Robert Frost, "Mending Wall," poem, 1914	Marie Bergersen, *Three Silhouettes*, 1911
Number of newspapers peaks at 2600, 1910	D. W. Griffith, director, *Birth of a Nation*, film, 1915	R. Nathaniel Dett, *In the Bottoms*, 1913
U.S. intervention in Nicaragua, 1911	Edith Wharton, *The Age of Innocence*, novel, 1920	Victor Herbert, first film score, *The Fall of a Nation*, 1916
Jim Thorpe wins two Olympic gold medals, 1912	Sinclair Lewis, *Main Street*, novel, 1920	First jazz band, 1917
Income tax imposed by Sixteenth Amendment, 1913	George Wesley Bellows, *Dempsey and Firpo*, painting, 1924	Charles Ives, *Concord Sonata*, 1919
First assembly line (Ford Motor Company), 1913	F. Scott Fitzgerald, *The Great Gatsby*, novel, 1925	Eubie Blake, *Shuffle Along*, 1921
Panama Canal opens, 1914	Charlie Chaplin, director, *The Gold Rush*, film, 1925	George Gershwin, *Rhapsody in Blue*, 1924
U.S. involvement in World War I, 1917–18	Theodore Dreiser, *An American Tragedy*, novel, 1925	Clarence Loomis, *Yolanda of Cypress*, 1926
Black Sox scandal, 1918	Ernest Hemingway, *The Sun Also Rises*, novel, 1926	Jerome Kern, *Show Boat*, 1927
Women receive right to vote, 1919	Willa Cather, *Death Comes for the Archbishop*, novel, 1927	Roger Sessions, *The Black Maskers*, 1928
Prohibition, 1920–33	First Mickey Mouse cartoon (Walt Disney), 1928	Abram Chasins, *Three Chinese Pieces*, 1928
Lincoln Memorial opens, 1922	Thomas Wolfe, *Look Homeward, Angel*, novel, 1929	Edward Kennedy "Duke" Ellington, "Mood Indigo," 1930
Technicolor process developed, 1922	Edward Hopper, *Early Sunday Morning*, painting, 1930	"Star Spangled Banner" made national anthem, 1931
Native Americans declared citizens, 1924		William Grant Still, *Afro-American Symphony*, 1931
Teapot Dome scandal, 1924		Ruth Seeger, *String Quartet*, 1931
Scopes Trial, 1925		
Admiral Byrd flies over South Pole, 1926		
Nicola Sacco and Bartolomeo Vanzetti executed, 1927		

THE COUNTRY	THE ARTS	MUSIC
First nonstop transatlantic flight, by Charles Lindbergh, 1927	Grant Wood, *American Gothic*, painting, 1930	George Gershwin, *Porgy and Bess*, 1935
Electric shaver patented, 1928	Empire State Building, New York, 1931	Radie Britain, *Lights*, 1935
St. Valentine's Day Massacre, Chicago, 1929	William Faulkner, *Sanctuary*, novel, 1931	David Guion, *Cavalcade of America*, 1936
Stock market crash, 1929	Georgia O'Keefe, *Cow's Skull*, painting, 1931	Harold Rome, *Pins and Needles*, 1937
Lindbergh baby kidnapped, 1932	Frank Lloyd Wright, Fallingwater, residence, 1936	Frank Churchill, film score, *Snow White and the Seven Dwarfs*, 1937
New Deal legislation introduced, 1933	Sara Teasdale, *Collected Poems*, 1937	Walter Piston, *The Incredible Flutist*, 1938
Roosevelt's Good Neighbor Policy, 1933	Thomas Hart Benton, *Cradling Wheat*, painting, 1938	Marian Anderson sings at the Lincoln Memorial, 1939
Tennessee Valley Authority established, 1933	Thornton Wilder, *Our Town*, play, 1938	Richard Rodgers, *Oklahoma!*, 1943
150,000 Jewish refugees from Germany, 1935–41	Alexander Calder, *Lobster Trap and Fish Tail*, mobile, 1939	Aaron Copland, *Appalachian Spring*, 1944
Life magazine published, 1936	Victor Fleming, director, *Gone with the Wind*, film, 1939	William Schuman made president of Julliard, 1945
Golden Gate Bridge opens, 1937	John Steinbeck, *The Grapes of Wrath*, novel, 1939	Gian-Carlo Menotti, *The Medium*, 1947
World's Fair, New York 1939–40	Richard Wright, *Native Son*, novel, 1940	Virgil Thomson, *The Mother of Us All*, 1947
U.S. involvement in World War II, 1941–45	Orson Welles, director, *Citizen Kane*, film, 1941	Samuel Barber, *Knoxville: Summer of 1915*, 1948
G. I. Bill of Rights, 1944	Eugene O'Neill, *The Iceman Cometh*, play, 1946	Long-playing record marketed, 1948
Atom bomb dropped by U.S. on Japan, 1945	Tennessee Williams, *A Streetcar Named Desire*, play, 1948	Leonard Bernstein, *The Age of Anxiety*, 1949
United Nations founded, 1945		Elvis Presley, "Hound Dog," 1950
U.S. plane breaks sound barrier, 1947		Frank Loesser, *Guys and Dolls*, 1950
McCarthy Senate hearings, 1950		
Korean War, 1950–53		

1951 TO 1994

THE COUNTRY	THE ARTS	MUSIC
Kefauver Senate investigation of organized crime, 1951	J. D. Salinger, *The Catcher in the Rye*, novel, 1951	Richard Rodgers, *The King and I*, 1951
First transcontinental telecast, 1951	Marianne Moore, *Poems*, 1951	John Cage, 4'33", 1954
Hydrogen bomb invented, 1952	Jackson Pollock, *Convergence*, painting, 1952	Douglas Moore, *The Ballad of Baby Doe*, 1956
Execution of Julius and Ethel Rosenberg, 1953	E. B. White, *Charlotte's Web*, novel, 1952	First electronic film score, Louis and Bebe Barron, *Forbidden Planet*, 1956
Brown vs. Board of Education, 1954	James Baldwin, *Go Tell It on the Mountain*, novel, 1953	Meredith Willson, *The Music Man*, 1957
Ralph Bunche at United Nations, 1954–71	Saul Bellow, *The Adventures of Augie March*, novel, 1953	Chuck Berry, "Johnny B. Goode," 1958
Montgomery bus boycott, 1955	Eudora Welty, *The Ponder Heart*, novel, 1954	Stereo disks marketed, 1958
First civil rights bill since Reconstruction, 1957	Allen Ginsburg, *Howl*, poem, 1956	Columbia-Princeton Electronic Music Center founded, 1959
First U.S. satellite in orbit, 1958	Jack Kerouac, *On the Road*, novel, 1957	Irving Berlin, *Call Me Madam*, 1959
NASA established, 1958	Louise Nevelson show, *MoonGarden + One*, 1958	Robert Ward, *The Crucible*, 1961
Walter R. Rostow, *The Stages of Economic Growth*, 1959	Archibald MacLeish, *J. B.*, play, 1958	The Beatles on "The Ed Sullivan Show," 1964
Bay of Pigs invasion, 1961		
U.S. involvement in Vietnam War, 1961–75		